Additional Praise for

OVERBOOKED

"[A] meticulously reported and often disturbing exposé of the travel industry."

—*The New York Times Book Review*

"Elizabeth Becker has found a giant gap in journalistic coverage and stepped squarely into the middle of it. Even though it's under our noses, beneath our feet, even in our happier dreams, rarely has the investigative story she recounts in her new book previously received the coverage it deserves: the rampant growth of travel and tourism."

—*National Geographic*

"Required reading for anyone interested in the future of travel."

—Arthur Frommer

"The definitive account of the rise of the modern tourism industry, from its beginnings as a small, fanciful pastime among elites, to its explosive growth after World War II, to its present as an economic engine valued at $7 trillion."

—*Bloomberg Businessweek*

"Ms. Becker is a skilled, critical writer delivering illuminating information, telling engaging stories, and advancing her own personal observations. *Overbooked* appeals to a wide audience: those who make the billion trips annually; those who have a stake in the places impacted, sometimes for better, but all too often for worse, by those travelers' visits; and all who have a stake in the global economy."

—*New York Journal of Books*

"In the tourism industry, image is definitely everything, but Becker shows readers the flip side of all this luxury and play, exposing the seedy underbelly of a business gone haywire from Cambodia to the United States."

—*Kirkus Reviews* (Starred Review)

"Travel is a huge global industry, rivaling oil and finance in economic value. Now, a terrific reporter gives us a full picture of its dimensions and its future. Elizabeth Becker does so, not by loading us down with statistics but by taking us around the world to match up the daunting numbers with places, adventures, and even pitfalls that will keep you reading."

—Steven Brill, author of *Class Warfare*

"[A] comprehensive, often alarming, and sometimes puzzling examination of an oft-invisible powerhouse . . . *Overbooked* succeeds in demonstrating the growing heft of the travel industry and the numerous problems that are associated with it."

—*The Weekly Standard*

"Journalist Becker travels widely, experiencing and analyzing 'the stealth industry of the twenty-first century.' . . . [I]mpressively wide-ranging . . . [i]ntriguing and eye-opening, this book will leave few in doubt that tourism deserves more consideration than it has hitherto received in larger discussions of globalization and public policy."

—*Publishers Weekly*

"Tourism is one of the world's largest—and unexamined—industries. Elizabeth Becker takes us on a compelling journey across continents to show us just how essential tourism is to global prosperity. You will never book a room, ascend the Eiffel Tower, or see the sites in quite the same way again."

—Zachary Karabell, author of *The Leading Indicators*

"Follow Elizabeth Becker on this trip around the world and become a more mindful traveler. She is not only an intrepid globetrotter, but a terrific reporter who asks all the right questions!"

—Sylvia Nasar, author of *Grand Pursuit* and *A Beautiful Mind*

"Will tourism in America go the way of Venice and Cambodia, or France and Costa Rica? Elizabeth Becker's thoughtful, informed book should move that discussion along."

—*Seattle Times*

ALSO BY ELIZABETH BECKER

America's Vietnam War:
A Narrative History

When the War Was Over:
Cambodia and the Khmer Rouge Revolution

THE

EXPLODING BUSINESS

of

TRAVEL

and

TOURISM

OVERBOOKED

Elizabeth Becker

SIMON & SCHUSTER PAPERBACKS

NEW YORK   LONDON   TORONTO   SYDNEY   NEW DELHI

Simon & Schuster Paperbacks
An Imprint of Simon & Schuster, Inc.
1230 Avenue of the Americas
New York, NY 10020

First Simon & Schuster paperback edition February 2016

SIMON & SCHUSTER PAPERBACKS and colophon are registered
trademarks of Simon & Schuster, Inc.

For information about special discounts for bulk purchases,
please contact Simon & Schuster Special Sales at
1-866-506-1949 or business@simonandschuster.com.

The Simon & Schuster Speakers Bureau can bring authors
to your live event. For more information or to book an event,
contact the Simon & Schuster Speakers Bureau at
1-866-248-3049 or visit our website at www.simonspeakers.com.

Designed by Ruth Lee-Mui

Manufactured in the United States of America

10 9 8 7 6 5 4 3 2 1

The Library of Congress has cataloged the hardcover as follows:

Becker, Elizabeth.
    Overbooked : the exploding business of travel and tourism / Elizabeth Becker.
        pages   cm
1. Tourism.   2. Tourism—Cross cultural studies.   3. Tourism—Political aspects.
4. Tourism—Moral and ethical aspects.   I. Title.
    G155.A1B382 2013
    338.4'791—dc23   2012032848

ISBN 978-1-4391-6099-2
ISBN 978-1-4391-6100-5 (pbk)
ISBN 978-1-4391-6750-2 (ebook)

For Bill, my husband and traveling partner

Contents

OVERBOOKED

OVERBOOKED

Introduction

In the early 1980s, my mother, Mavis Becker, was a widow living quietly in West Seattle on the money she earned from part time work and Social Security checks. She had raised six children. And, not counting Canada, she had traveled outside of the country only once in her life, to Ireland with our father just before he died. Mom was ready for a change. She moved into an apartment near Holy Rosary church, sold our family home and with the profits declared that she was going to see the world. With other widows in her parish, Mom set off and visited every continent except Antarctica. She went on an African safari. In India she saw a Bengal tiger and was awed by the Taj Mahal. She attended the Passion Play in Oberammergau, Germany, and danced the tango in Argentina.

Her albums from those adventures were piled high on her coffee table, replacing a jumble of magazines. When her doctor told her that her cancer had returned, Mom took one last trip—to newly opened China.

That is the power of travel, the reason why people go dreamy-eyed when they speak of that first taste of other worlds and the liberating freedom of taking a break from their own lives. They don't think of travel as one of the world's biggest businesses, an often cutthroat, high-risk and high-profit industry. But it is, and here is one reason: when Mavis Becker made her first voyages of discovery, she was one of some 250 million travelers crossing international borders. Today that figure is one billion and growing.

This book is a rare attempt to examine what the modern travel and tourism industry means for countries, cultures, the environment and the way we live. There are countless tourism books about where to go and what to do once you are there but very few that treat tourism itself as something that matters, as arguably the biggest industry in the world. Few foreign policy experts, economists or international policy gurus discuss the subject, much less ask whether tourism is enhancing or undermining a distinct regional culture, a fragile environment, an impoverished country. Like any industry, tourism has winners and losers, and keeping it out of critical discussions about the direction of the economy or international debates about the environment is short-sighted. For Americans, this is especially true because the U.S. government has been the least likely to acknowledge the role of tourism.

While not encyclopedic, *Overbooked* tackles the major issues. Each chapter is generally devoted to a single country or destination and the handful of issues associated with the country. The chapters are assembled into sections: the first is grouped around the reasons people travel: to see the world's cultures; to shop, eat and party; and for nature and the outdoors. The last sections look at the giants in the field: China and the United States.

To examine the industry, I traveled extensively and in my acknowledgments thank the people who assisted me. Everywhere I was reminded of the wonders of travel. But I was also taken aback by the sheer numbers of people flooding the planet in search of those pleasures and the mixed record of the industry. My investigations into the policy and politics of tourism led me in multiple directions. Tourism is octopuslike, its tentacles reaching out to aspects of life that are as diverse as coastal development, child prostitution, the treatment of religious monuments and the survival of a threatened bird species or native dancing.

The best and the worst of tourism have governments at the center. The best examples include the creation and protection of national parks in the United States and the restoring of the French city of Bordeaux. In some of the worst, the Cambodian government oversaw the expulsion of farmers from their homes to make way for beach resorts and casinos, and officials of Venice are allowing tourism to push out local residents and hollowing out their society. Governments sell their countries—think of those advertisements telling us to sun ourselves on Greek islands or ski Austria during our winter holidays. Governments decide how to regulate businesses, who can visit their countries, who benefits from tourism and who loses. As tourism becomes the top money earner for more and more countries, those government decisions are critical.

During my five years of research and writing, I often thought of my mother's last decade of adventures and wondered how future travelers will discover the world.

PART ONE

THE BUSINESS

WILLIAM NASH

Sunday at the Louvre Museum, Paris

1

TOURISM BECOMES AN INDUSTRY

For aficionados of travel magazines filled with breathtaking photographs of boutique hotels on sugar-white beaches or yachts cruising turquoise-colored seas, the United Nations World Tourism Organization is a letdown. This agency dedicated to one of life's great pleasures is housed in a nondescript ten-story building on Madrid's Calle Capitán Haya, hidden in a leafy neighborhood with far more impressive government ministries and foreign embassies. It looks like what it is: one of the more obscure organizations in the enormous United Nations, a backwater near the bottom of the international pecking order. Moreover, it is dedicated to the business of travel and tourism, not its romance.

Most of the writers of those glamorous travel articles have never heard of the UNWTO, and of those that have, few have visited the office. "I get their emails, but I rarely read them," said Stuart Emmrich, then editor of the influential Travel section of the *New York Times*.

This disconnect is a testament to travel and tourism's reputation as a worry-free break from the real world, not a serious business. The UNWTO is one of the few institutions that recognizes travel as one of the largest industries in the world and studies its extraordinary dimensions to understand how it is changing the world.

The very idea of describing travel and tourism as a serious industry or business is an oxymoron to many people. The oil industry is serious. Finance is serious. Trade is serious. Manufacturing is serious. Foreign policy and economic policy are serious. Tourism is a frivolous pursuit: fun, sometimes educational in the lightest sense, often romantic, even exotic.

Tourism's low reputation is a big reason why the agency is in Spain. When it came into being after World War II, the United Nations ostracized Spain because it was led by Francisco Franco, Europe's last fascist ruler. Spain remained something of a pariah on the world scene in the 1950s. (Adolf Hitler had been a supporter of General Franco; Nazi armed forces helped Franco come to power.) The U.N. slowly accepted Spain back into the normal world of diplomacy as Franco loosened up and Spain became more democratic. Finally, when Franco was on his deathbed, the U.N. agreed to set up a small tourism policy office in Madrid in 1974. The sufficiently inconsequential tourism body wouldn't raise too many questions, and Spain could be selected over two rivals that were not considered top-caliber at the time.

"There were three finalists—Zagreb, Mexico City, and Madrid," Patrice Tedjini, the UNWTO's historian, told me in his office at the Madrid headquarters. "We wanted to show that democracy was moving in Spain."

Back then, the tourism office was a lowly subsidiary of another U.N. body. It would take another thirty years for the World Tourism Organization to win status as a full-fledged independent United Nations agency, a reward for the work it had done to define the industry and fitfully raise its profile.

The drab UNWTO office in Madrid was my logical first stop in a five-year-long study of the tourism industry. The UNWTO is the repository of rare data on how tourism works, how it drives economies and how governments direct it, so its headquarters was the logical place to begin my research into how all of the industry's disparate pieces fit together and determine what it means to be a tourist. Snorkeling in the pure waters off Costa Rica, studying documents in Paris, tracking down the "anonymous" benefactor of a Zambian wildlife preserve, interviewing Chinese tour guides who promote the Communist Party while reciting the virtues of pandas, I inevitably saw the world through an entirely new prism. If war and revolution marked the last century, the competition for prosperity and the marketing of ways to enjoy that new wealth is molding the early years of the twenty-first century. The travel and tourism industry, with its romantic promises and serious perils, is central to that constant commerce. This book is about that journey as well as its findings.

Tourism has a history of confounding countries and societies. The first time the world powers tried to regularize tourism was in 1925, between the world wars, when it was considered a traffic issue. Several European countries created the International Congress of Official Tourist Traffic Associations to minimize border formalities for tourists. That small office was the origins of the World Tourism Organization.

Nine years later, tourism was recalibrated as a propaganda, or public relations, issue focused on spreading the word about where and how to travel. In that incarnation the office was named the International Union of Tourist Propaganda Organizations. Finally, after World War II, it was decided that tourism had risen to the level of government relations requiring the coordination of tourism agencies of various countries like the French Office National du Tourisme and the Italian Ente Nazionale per le Industrie Turistiche. Practical questions were rising along with the increased tourist traffic: Should tourists pay duties on their cameras and automobiles when traveling into a foreign country? Aren't they imports, and what if they tried to sell them?

By the 1960s the jet age of mass tourism was taking off. In 1958 a Pan American 707 flew from New York to Brussels, the first commercial jet flight across the Atlantic without stopping for refueling. A decade later a TWA 707 flew around the world beginning in Los Angeles and flying west after the plane was blessed by three Buddhist monks. Lower fares and bargain flights followed. European countries relaxed passport restrictions and began to see tourism as an important economic engine. "Tourism — Passport to Peace" became the organization's motto in 1967, capturing its higher purpose to open borders in the promotion of better relations as well as the practical motive of making money.

As the U.N. shifted its notion about tourism, the U.N.'s tourism office was moved from The Hague to Geneva, where it was dwarfed among the cluster of U.N. offices and the International Red Cross. The move to Madrid was a step up the bureaucratic ladder even though it meant exile from Geneva, one of the power centers of the U.N.

In Madrid the tourism organization confronted the dilemma that faced the industry: how to prove that tourism was an industry. There was no question that travel and tourism were growing. In 1950, shortly after World War II, there had been only 25 million trips recorded by foreign tourists. By 1975 that figure had exploded to 222 million trips. But there was no agreement about what that meant for any national economy. Tourism wasn't considered a single, unified economic activity. It was viewed as a constellation of industries—airlines, hotel chains, railway systems and tour agencies to name just a few. Separately those industries were taken seriously but not grouped together as the single economic activity of tourism.

Most conspicuously, tourism was not listed as a separate industry on national indexes. For example, when the United States created its gross domestic product index in 1937, tourism was not included as a distinct industry. It was impossible for most countries to measure what tourism added to their economies.

Then there was the question of motivation. Are business trips and tourist trips part of the same industry; can you easily distinguish between the two and should you? The answer was to define the industry as travel and tourism since the infrastructure was the same. Another issue was trade. On national balance-of-trade ledgers, tourism showed up as a service that is "exported" to the foreigners who come to visit the country. Finally, there were few educational institutions that studied tourism and could help measure the industry; another example of tourism's irrelevance. (Switzerland was the rare nation that fostered top-flight "hospitality" schools; to this day, their graduates fill management spots in hotels, restaurants and resorts around the world.)

What countries could count were the numbers of visiting foreign tourists, a figure that was crude at best. Without a place on national budget sheets, tourism could be ignored by the economists. Yet every day there was growing evidence that tourism was becoming a staple of modern life; an essential part of the family calendar. The middle classes were luxuriating in newly affordable travel and most of the newest tourists were Americans. Their newspaper travel sections were plump with advertisements. By the 1970s, industries in the travel and tourism complex were the single largest source of advertising for American newspapers. Americans were mostly traveling in one direction—across the Atlantic and discovering Europe. And they were spending a lot of money.

Many were carrying a thin red book called *Europe on $5 a Day*. The author was Arthur Frommer, an American G.I. turned lawyer turned publisher. His success exemplified the potential of tourism that the fledgling U.N. organization was trying to capture.

Frommer's book offered Americans the possibility of traveling through Europe in a few weeks rather than the months required in another era and at the same time of enjoying three-course French meals without breaking their budgets. Frommer told me he figured out "how to travel cheaply" when he was stationed in Berlin after World War II. "Before, only the elite could afford to go to Europe, make the grand tour. No one cared about the poor slob who had never traveled before," said Mr. Frommer in his sun-filled Manhattan apartment, where books and curios cover every surface.

Now a legend—the Walter Cronkite of tourist guidebooks—Frommer consciously began writing as the champion of people who thought they couldn't afford to travel. He was drafted into the U.S. Army straight out of Yale Law School and trained as an infantryman to fight in the Korean War, but his orders were amended and he was sent to Europe to work in intelligence. Stationed in war-scarred Berlin, Frommer used his fluent Russian and French at work, and then on the weekends as he mastered the skill of catching free rides on military planes to travel the continent. "I was a poor boy from the United States and here I was flying all over Europe," he said. He still remembers his first freshly baked croissant and Spanish paella. After watching Frommer hitching rides to London, Stockholm, Barcelona, Venice and Paris, all on the pay of a lowly G.I., a few of his friends in the barracks asked Frommer to explain how he got to travel so much while they were stuck in Germany. His answer was *The G.I.'s Guide to Travelling in Europe*, written in stilted military jargon. The initial run of 10,000 copies of *The G.I.'s Guide* sold out in one afternoon.

Frommer had discovered what was critical to modern travel writing and decided to write a guidebook for civilians, as he put it, once he was out of the service. Above all, most people wanted help mastering the logistics of travel—airplanes, ships, hotels, restaurants, visas, traveler's checks. What they saw once they arrived in the country was almost secondary. In a sense, Frommer reversed the order of the travel books that had come before him. Or as he told me, "People weren't looking for a big travel book with a thorough explanation of a country's history and culture that would stay on their book shelves for years. They wanted a guide."

His ambitions were focused: he wanted to show the masses how to travel without breaking the bank. "I wanted everyone to be able to experience different cultures, to confront opposite views, to celebrate the world's diversities," he said, remembering the purity of his intentions. Frommer's timing was impeccable. The American middle classes had begun to enjoy two-week paid vacations, an idea first instituted by the French in 1936. And private airline companies were offering passage across the Atlantic at prices the middle class could afford, sort of. "But there weren't enough travel books back then to fill half a shelf in a standard bookstore," said Mr. Frommer.

To write his first book Frommer scouted Europe for bargain hotels, cafés, restaurants and boat trips and wrote it all up in clear, simple itineraries punctuated by lush descriptions of the glorious sights of medieval and Renaissance cities that sparked his uncritical love affair with travel. In one of his favorite passages, he describes Venice at night: "As you chug along, little clusters of candy-striped mooring poles emerge from the dark, a gondola approaches with a lighted lantern hung from its prow. The reflection of a slate-gray church, bathed in blue spotlight, shimmers in the water as you pass by. This is the sheerest beauty and a sight that no one should miss."

Europe on $5 a Day was published in 1960, and its modest first run of 5,000 copies also sold out in a single day. Frommer quit his day job at a prestigious Manhattan law firm to start his own publishing company and launch a movement. His style of providing the mundane details of where to stay and what to eat with an overlay of rhapsodic descriptions of the delights of travel became the hallmark of travel writing in the modern age. "I stumbled into this intense desire to travel," he said as explanation for his phenomenal success. His series grew to fifty-eight titles and *Europe on $5 a Day* became ubiquitous. Ten years after its debut Nora Ephron wrote a tongue-in-cheek essay called "Eating and Sleeping with Arthur Frommer." By then, one out of every five Americans traveling to Europe that summer was following his red travel guide like a bible, booking inexpensive hotels and eating at out-of-the-way cafés, literally eating and sleeping with him and sending fawning thank you notes like one from a woman in Massachusetts saying that "not a day passed that she did not bless the name Arthur Frommer."

What Frommer had discovered was that tourism was becoming an industry and needed to be reduced to its parts for consumers—book a plane, find a hotel, eat some meals, go on a sightseeing tour—and he was more than happy to act as that go-between with his guidebooks, making a small fortune in the process. The question for the U.N. World Tourism Organization was how to bottle that elixir, measure it and claim it officially as an industry. The answer came in two parts—first from geopolitics, then from the industry itself.

It took nothing less than the fall of the Berlin Wall and the end of the Soviet Empire to open up minds and horizons. The Berlin Wall was the most famous of the barbed-wire barriers erected by eastern and central European puppet governments to cut off their people from their continental neighbors during the Cold War that had pitted the Communist countries against those in the democratic market system of capitalism. Since the end of World War II, the two sides had fought hot wars through proxies in Asia and South America and aimed nuclear weapons at each other in the ultimate standoff for supremacy.

The Soviet side lost and the Berlin Wall came down in 1989, marking the beginning of the end of the Cold War. In 1991, the Soviet Union disintegrated. By then Communist China had begun to open its doors to the West, positioning itself against the Soviet Union. The stark divisions of the Cold War were obscured and then eliminated. Those physical and allegorical "walls" melted away from the northern Baltic Sea, from countries like Estonia and Latvia, through Eastern Europe—Poland, Czechoslovakia, Hungary, Yugoslavia—down to the Adriatic Sea and Albania. On the other side of the globe the Mekong Delta nations of Vietnam, Laos and Cambodia were no longer off-limits. For the first time in modern history the world opened to tourism.

The end of the Cold War had a profound effect throughout the world, reshaping countries and lives. The impact on tourism was obvious, since the industry is premised on the ability to cross borders and visit foreign countries. Before 1990, Western Europe was the overwhelming center of the tourist world, grabbing more than 60 percent of international tourists, visiting countries like France, Great Britain, Italy and Spain. Afterward the tourist map was redrawn, now including vast swaths of Africa and Asia and reinvigorating the western hemisphere, which until then accounted for less than one-fourth of tourism. The world was on the verge of a tourist explosion, for better and for worse, and largely unnoticed.

The geopolitical milestone ending the Cold War was matched by a technological revolution. Everything required for traveling had become modernized. Long-haul airplanes could transport travelers halfway across the globe within a day or two. Travel was becoming relatively inexpensive. Medical advances had made travel safe with vaccines and access to doctors and medicines. European and American comforts were to be found in far-off countries not known for modern luxury.

Tourism had hit a unique historic sweet spot. Now all it needed was recognition. Two separate groups stepped in to fill this vacuum: the United Nations and the World Travel & Tourism Council, an industry group that grew out of a decision by the U.S. government that travel and tourism were nonessential during the energy crisis of the late 1970s and therefore not at the top of the government's list for precious energy supplies. James Robinson III, then the CEO of the travel giant American Express, was furious. First he convinced Congress to reverse the finding; then he started examining the tourism industry.

Robinson did his homework. He ordered a review of American Express receipts to see who ranked as its biggest customers. Robinson wanted to know what the solid base of the company's business was. Even though American Express had been a travel company long before it became a giant credit-card firm, Robinson was surprised by the results of his inquiry. The answer was unequivocal: the top companies as measured by the amount of money billed through American Express credit cards made up the core of the tourism industry, from Disneyland to Hertz Rental cars to United Airlines. Armed with these results, Robinson hosted a 1988 gathering in Paris, inviting his fellow industry executives—the CEOs of Hertz and Avis, Regent and Accor, American, United and Singapore airlines, East Japan Railway, Disney and others, to gauge their interest in joining a new high-powered tourist council representing all the industries that make up the travel and tourism industry.

"By the time we left Paris, we agreed there was significant work to do and that we needed to enlist the Wharton School at the University of Pennsylvania to help us build a solid body of data about the industry," said Robinson.

With the opening up of borders in 1990, there was no question that travel was on a big upswing, with extraordinary opportunities to make money in the nascent global travel boom. Robinson wanted to erase long-held prejudices and band together all the strands of the tourism business from the airline companies that considered themselves too important to associate with car rental companies to the high-end hotel chains that wouldn't mix with low-end resorts. That was the only way to present a united front as the world's biggest industry and create new business strategies to multiply profits and create new markets. Remaining separate would mean losing a vision that might place tourism at the top of the global business hierarchy.

Robinson took the first step toward a modern definition of the tourism industry with other executives by inaugurating the World Travel & Tourism Council in 1991 in Washington, D.C. The new industry group was dedicated to using the full economic and social power of their companies to advance the business of tourism. Robinson was elected chair of the new board and set as its top priority the discovery of a formula for calculating the full economic power of tourism. That was the data that was missing. If the new council could measure how much money tourists spent, the industry would know how much it contributed to national economies as well as the global marketplace. From there they could begin flexing their muscles. The WTTC teamed with the Wharton School to produce a statistical model that a region or country could use to measure income from tourism. The statisticians defined the industry by categories: accommodation services; food and beverage services; passenger transport; travel agencies, tour operators and tourist guide services; cultural services; recreation and other entertainment services and a final miscellaneous category that included financial and insurance services. It was an expansive definition meant to capture every American dollar, German mark, French franc, British pound or Japanese yen spent on a trip. And it required years of research and consultations before it proved accurate.

At the same time, the United Nations tourism organization had embarked on a similar project to calculate tourism's full economic impact in order to influence public policy. In 1993 the U.N.'s statistical commission recommended a new reporting concept called Satellite accounts for tourism that would measure the "economic and employment impact of consumer expenditures, capital investment, government revenues and expenditure, foreign trade and business expenditure from tourism."

Working in parallel and eventually together, the WTO, the new WTTC and the Organisation for Economic Co-operation and Development came up with the Tourism Satellite Account system. Canada was the first country to try it out. The United Nations refined and adopted it in 2000, and it is used around the world today. "A movement has been started," said Francesco Frangialli, then secretary-general of the UNWTO, after its approval.

The new satellite formula defined the industry as the production, supply and consumption of tourism commodities: transport (airplanes, cars, railroads, boats); accommodation (hotels, resorts, home rentals, time shares, cruise ships); food; entertainment (anything from sports activities to gambling to theme parks, to dancing to movies to live theater); tour operators; tour agencies. This followed the U.N. tourism organization's definition of tourism itself as "the activities of persons traveling to and staying in places outside their usual environment for not more than one consecutive year for leisure, business and other purposes."

Seven years later, when an updated draft was issued, the methodological framework for the Tourism Satellite Account system was 135 pages long. Its calculations were nothing short of a revelation: the tourism industry contributed $7 trillion to the world economy in 2007 and was the biggest employer, with nearly 250 million associated jobs. (And those figures don't include people who vacation in their own countries.)

Even with this recognition, travel and tourism remains the stealth industry of the twenty-first century. Few politicians, government leaders, foreign affairs pundits or economic experts consider the industry an important subject. During the Great Recession of 2008, travel and tourism leaders were left out of the inner circle of decision-makers who outlined the road to recovery, even though tourism by most standards was among the largest world industries.

The dimensions of the industry are astonishing.

For the first time in history, the U.N. tourism organization celebrated reaching 1 billion international trips in a single year in 2012. The graph line for this travel phenomenon goes straight up: 25 million tourist trips to foreign countries in 1960; 250 million in 1970; 536 million in 1995; 922 million in 2008; 1 billion in 2012. Overall, that represents an annual increase of over 6 percent.

In gross economic power it is in the same company as oil, energy, finance and agriculture. At least one out of every ten people around the world is employed by the industry, according to Wolfgang Weinz of the International Labour Organization, who told me that the figure is probably greater, perhaps one in eight or nine, but it is hard to collect accurate numbers in many countries.

Tourism creates $3 billion in business every day.

If frequent-flyer miles were a currency, it would be one of the most valuable in the world. In 2005, frequent-flyer miles were worth more than all of the American dollars in circulation. (When that figure was released, several U.S. legislators wondered if frequent-flyer miles should be taxed as income.)

The tourism industry has expanded its scope to embrace everything one can do on a trip, beginning with religious pilgrimages, which is the oldest reason for traveling. The modern Hajj, the Islamic religious pilgrimage, is now a multibillion-dollar enterprise and the single biggest tourist event of the year. No longer a humble religious trek, many of the older, modest hotels and boardinghouses for devotees have been replaced with glitzy five-star hotels for the well heeled, to the consternation of preservationists and some religious groups. Families from poorer Muslim countries like Bangladesh pay a lifetime's savings to buy the required airplane and hotel package for an aging parent to fulfill a religious goal and make the Hajj. Itinerant pilgrims are no longer common at the Hajj.

At every point of every trip, the industry is figuring out how to make a profit on every experience, be it a made-for-tourist local dance ensemble, the purchase of a length of silk or taking a motorboat cruise up a jungle river. Serendipity and happenstance, once the main point of travel, are disappearing. What were once journeys of discovery, escapes from the daily dullness of life, or a plan for retirement are now packaged trips with nearly every aspect planned in advance. Senior travel by retirees is known as silver gold and has become a mainstay of the industry. Everything can be packaged into a tour, including cooking classes and bamboo-weaving demonstrations, and then finely tuned to avoid mishaps. Entire Austrian, Swiss and German villages rent themselves out for as little as $70,000 a week.

Family reunions, simple vacations to the beach (known as fly-and-flop in the industry), a tour of the old Silk Road in the steppes of Asia or a tour of old and new art galleries in Istanbul—all marketed by the industry. One of the biggest earners are conventions or meetings. Known as MICE, the industry acronym for Meetings, Incentives, Conferences and Exhibitions, this category covers a huge gamut of legitimate meetings, film festivals, academic gatherings and boondoggles that have multiplied in the last decade, filling airline seats and hotel rooms. Las Vegas, with its casinos, sports, conference centers, hotels and nightlife, is the undisputed capital of MICE; underlining its motto "What happens in Vegas stays in Vegas."

As in other businesses, the industry expands its profits by expanding the reasons for travel. One of the biggest new fields is medical tourism, which pairs foreign doctors and hospitals with the travel industry to make a package deal of an operation and a vacation for recuperation on a beach or by a swimming pool. The field has grown quickly in the United States as costs of health care and health insurance skyrocketed. Now when faced with surgery costing hundreds of thousands of dollars in the United States, a patient can opt for an attractive tour package with medical care in Argentina, India, South Africa or closer to home in Mexico or Costa Rica often at one-tenth the price of the same treatment in the United States, vacation included. That is thanks to cooperation in most of these foreign countries between the ministries of tourism and the ministries of health.

Travel has also become a default fund-raising technique. Every day letters or brochures are sent out by colleges and universities, bookstores, museums, magazines, public radio stations, arts and music institutions inviting people to go on a tour or a cruise to have fun and raise money for a good cause.

Tourism was born and nurtured in Europe, which still depends mightily on foreign visitors, increasingly from China. In 2011, when it was still in the grips of the Great Recession, Ireland turned to tourism to dig out of debt, earning 9.1 billion euros that year.

Today poor nations see tourism as their best bet out of poverty, second only to oil and energy as the major engine of development. Thailand is the world's biggest exporter of rice, yet tourism is its number-one money earner. With that comes political clout. When Thai protesters wanted to change their government in December 2008, they took over the airport to keep out tourists, which brought the economy to a halt and victory to the protesters. Costa Rica has turned its wilderness into a venue for highly profitable ecotourism. As soon as Sri Lanka, and now Burma, began seeing an end to conflict, they opened the door to a rush of tourists. After the Arab Spring uprising, Egypt sent out a plea to cruise companies and tour operators to return and kick-start the economy, where one in eight jobs depend on visitors. Winning status for a temple or old city neighborhood as a World Heritage Site from UNESCO, the United Nations Educational, Scientific and Cultural Organization, is a guaranteed tourist draw.

The U.N. tourism organization now places poverty reduction as one of its top objectives, along with the high-minded ideals of improving international understanding, peace and prosperity. Since the end of the Cold War and the opening of the world for travel, tourism has become an important source of foreign exchange for the world's poorest nations, often the only one. While tourism requires some infrastructure, from airfields to modern highways, it is less expensive than building factories. In theory, poor countries should be able to use the new revenue from the tourism industry to pay for the infrastructure while raising standards of living and improving the environment. One hundred of the world's poorest nations do earn up to 5 percent of their gross national product from foreign tourists who marvel at their exotic customs, buy suitcases of souvenirs and take innumerable photographs of stunning landscapes.

But just as tourism is capable of lifting a nation out of poverty, it is just as likely to pollute the environment, reduce standards of living for the poor because the profits go to international hotel chains and corrupt local elites (what is called leakage), and cater to the worst of tourism, including condemning children to the exploitation of sex tourism. Like any major industry, tourism has a serious downside, especially since tourism and travel is underestimated as a global powerhouse; its study and regulation is spotty at best. Tourism is one of those double-edged swords that may look like an easy way to earn desperately needed money but can ravage wilderness areas and undermine native cultures to fit into package tours: a fifteen-minute snippet of a ballet performed in Southern India; native handicrafts refashioned to fit oversize tourists. What is known is that tourism and travel is responsible for 5.3 percent of the world's carbon emissions and the degradation of nearly every tropical beach in the world. Without global enforcement of basic rules, cruise ships are a major polluter of the seas and pose serious risks. The dramatic capsizing of the *Costa Concordia* cruise ship off the Italian coast in 2012 killed at least 32 people and raised questions about the safety of these mammoth ships.

To make way for more resorts with spectacular views, developers destroy native habitats and ignore local concerns. Preservationists decry the growing propensity to bulldoze old hotels and buildings in favor of constructing new resorts, water holes and entertainment spots that look identical whether in Singapore, Dubai or Johannesburg; a world where diversity is replaced with homogeneity. Another catastrophe for countries betting on tourism has come from wealthy vacationers who fall in love with a country and buy so many second houses that locals can no longer afford to live in their own towns and villages.

Among the more thoughtful questions is how mass tourism has changed cultures. African children told anthropologists that they want to grow up to be tourists so they could spend the day doing nothing but eating. The tourists who do not speak the local language and rely on guides to tell them what they are seeing and what to think marvel at countries like China with its new wealth and appearance of democracy. Environmentalists wonder how long the globe can continue to support 1 billion people racing around the world for a long weekend on a beach or a ten-day tour of an African game park.

In reaction, concerned industry leaders—large and small—and environmentalists have created the idea of ecotourism, a form of travel to promote the protection of natural habitats and eventually the preservation of local landscapes, cultures and people. The idea has become so popular it has entered the lexicon of political correctness. Philanthropists are underwriting ecolodges in Central America and wild game parks in sub-Saharan Africa. Tourists opt for vacations on organic European farms, while some add volunteer days at the end of their vacations in Asia to build homes for the poor. Few nations have shown more caution about the tourism industry and its downside than Bhutan. The Himalayan nation that measures progress through its happiness index has purposefully kept the number of tourists low to insure that the country's culture, environment, faith and economy aren't perverted by huge influxes of foreign tourists. The government says it limits tourists by regulating how many hotel rooms are available and limiting other tourist "infrastructure" as well as imposing a high tourist tariff. Bhutan calls this "low volume and high value" tourism.

At the opposite end of the spectrum are countries like Cambodia and cities like Venice. Cambodia encourages so many tourists to visit its great eleventh-century temple complex at Angkor that the rare temples are sinking because the surrounding water table is being drained by hundreds of new tourist hotels. In Venice, with a native population of less than 60,000, over 20 million tourists descend on the city every year, an onslaught that is pushing the locals out of their homes and emptying the city of essentials like neighborhood greengrocers and bakeries.

In the globalized economy—with cheap transportation, the Internet and open borders—travel has become the ultimate twenty-first-century industry, which means these problems are not going away.

• • •

It is difficult to find issues of travel and tourism debated in public. Historians, political scientists and economists routinely omit tourism from studies about how the world works. Foreign policy journals and experts rarely touch the subject.

Normally the media would ask routine questions about whether the right to travel also included the responsibility to respect a country, its environment, people and culture. But my profession often gives travel and tourism a pass. Unlike the oil industry, which is scrutinized at all levels, travel writing has become an extension of the industry. With few exceptions, travel writing and travel sections share the singular goal of helping consumers spend their money pursuing the dream of a perfect trip. They seldom write critical reviews; only articles about what to do and what to buy and how to experience a destination. This "feel-good" approach is rare even in lifestyle journalism, which is where to find the travel sections. Other lifestyle or back-of-the-book journalists thrive on critical reviews, explaining how and why they judge movies as great or miserable; whether the food at a restaurant is mediocre or exquisite; and describing music concerts as electric or boring. Imagine if movie reviewers only discussed their favorite films, if restaurant critics only wrote about their preferred haunts and music critics never wrote a scathing review of a badly performed opera. That is what travel writing has become.

As unsettling, many travel writers accept free transportation, lodging, food and entertainment from the very destinations they write about. That is forbidden in nearly every other form of journalism. This adds up to a largely pliant media that has become an extension of the industry it is supposedly covering, blocking the public from seeing both the larger picture and the problems inherent in any industry, and preventing travel and tourism from being taken seriously.

It wasn't always this way. Modern travel writing took root in the late nineteenth century—the age of ocean liners and trains—when writers took it for granted that travel meant adventure, not comfort, and that anyone making a month-long trip overseas wanted to dive into foreign lands and cultures. In those days writers rarely specialized in travel alone. They saw themselves as the gatekeepers to the world, noting all that was miserable as well as glorious about foreign cultures. Their touchstone was Marco Polo, the grandfather of all travel writing. When his *Description of the World* was published around 1300 the Italian public thought Polo's description of China under Kublai Khan was utter fantasy. The tales of the Khan's lavish court, his palaces of marble, gold and silver, his benevolence toward his subjects, his bizarre invention of paper money and the precise details of the enormous bridges and roads he built across his empire were ridiculed as impossible.

Two hundred years later, Christopher Columbus carried his well-worn copy of Polo's masterpiece on his voyage across the Atlantic Ocean in search of China. That spirit of adventure jumps off of the pages of the earliest guides. Admittedly, travel in the nineteenth and early twentieth centuries was for the elite or the professional diplomats and colonial bureaucrats who could spend weeks admiring the ancient wonders like the pyramids. Travel was considered such a privilege that people spent months in preparation, relying on their guidebooks to find hidden paths and a bed for the night. The German-based Baedeker travel guides published a handbook in 1876 for *Jerusalem and Its Surroundings* that captures the day-by-day account of how to travel by horseback to the Holy City. "At a fig-tree our path is joined by another from the left, and reaches the village of Biddu, surrounded by heaps of stones and destitute of trees. This scene is a foretaste of the stony wilderness of the ancient Judah."

Once in Jerusalem, the writer warns with an honesty missing from today's travel writing that it is "only by patiently penetrating beneath the modern crust of rubbish and rottenness which shrouds the sacred places from view that the traveler will at length realize to himself a picture of the Jerusalem of antiquity."

For the next eighty pages, the Baedeker describes the holy city's history and sights in vivid commentary, detailing the scholarly basis for its descriptions of the buildings and monuments. Practical information on hotels, restaurants, banks, consulates, pharmacies and tailors takes up less than two pages. For the handbook for Egypt and the Sudan published two years later, Baedeker hired nearly a dozen scholars—historians, archeologists, linguists—to write about Egypt's art, history, religion and hieroglyphics. He included a nineteen-page dictionary of "essential" Arabic words and expected the traveler to spend at least four weeks in the country to fully appreciate what they were seeing. Nothing should be missed: "The Sphinx, the guardian of the sacred enclosure of the Second Pyramid is a colossal recumbent lion with the head of a king wearing the royal head-dress. . . . The head is now deplorably mutilated; the neck has become too thin, the nose and beard have been broken off and the reddish tint has almost disappeared. But in spite of all injuries it preserves even now an impressive expression of strength and majesty."

By today's standards, the writing in these books is more stuffy than lyrical, but the guides were complete. In those days, if you made only one trip to Peking or Rome, you wanted to inhale as much history and culture as possible and be prepared for every possible mishap.

In the United States, the *National Geographic* magazine offered something different: armchair travel. Arriving on the scene about the same time as the Baedekers, the *National Geographic* was a magazine with scientific intentions to explore unmapped wilderness and publish articles about the geography of the planet. The first editions featured stories about the river systems of Pennsylvania and the digging of the Panama Canal, which describes the author's overland trek surveying the jungle, including nightly suppers of wild pig, monkey or iguana. Explorations were as common as articles about "The Hermit Nation of Korea" or "Peking: the City of the Unexpected."

By the time of World War I, travelogues were taking on the air of anthropology. Traveling by camel caravan across the Sahara to Tunisia's prize date gardens, Thomas H. Kearney began his article with an Arab proverb that the palm tree thrives with "its feet in the water and its head in the fire" in the Sahara oases. By the 1920s, the *National Geographic* had declared itself "pre-eminently a magazine of travel," reducing its emphasis on scientific explorations. Showing a new inclination to savor travel, the *Geographic* published articles like a winter's "ramble" through Concord, Massachusetts, to honor Henry David Thoreau by retracing the poet's steps to photograph "ice that looks like a loose web of small white feathers."

The world still needed explorers—Admiral Richard E. Byrd received the *Geographic*'s Special Gold Medal of Honor in 1930 for his Arctic voyage—but more of the globe was now pleasant enough for tourists. Authors like Rudyard Kipling and Evelyn Waugh wrote sophisticated essays for the *Geographic* that resembled articles by foreign correspondents, weaving current events into portraits of foreign cultures and countries.

A master of the genre was Rebecca West. In her *Black Lamb and Grey Falcon, A Journey Through Yugoslavia*, Ms. West produced a travelogue that any tourist could follow, bringing the country and culture to life and plotting out the routes she took across the region, painting unforgettable portraits: "Under red and white umbrellas in the market place of Zagreb the peasants stood sturdy and square on their feet. The women wore two broad aprons, one covering the front part of the body and one the back, overlapping at the sides, and underneath showed very brave red woolen stockings. They gave the sense of the very opposite of what we mean by the word 'peasant' when we use it in a derogatory sense, thinking of women made doltish by repeated pregnancies and a lifetime spent in the service of oafs in villages that swim in mud to the thresholds every winter. This costume was evolved by women who could stride along if they were eight months gone with child, and who would dance in the mud if they felt like it, no matter what any oaf said."

She also explored why this region was the source of such trouble for Europe. Written as World War II was about to break out, she presumed the traveler wanted to understand the complicated history that had turned this corner of Europe into a tinderbox. Her goal, she said, was to write about "the past side by side with the present it created. . . . Bosnia and Herzegovina had driven out the Turks and had been cheated out of the freedom they had fairly won by the Treaty of Berlin, which had given the Austro-Hungarian Empire the right to occupy and administer them. This had enraged the Slavs and given Serbia a grievance."

Fifty years later, when the Bosnian War broke out and Yugoslavia was torn apart forever, *Black Lamb and Grey Falcon* was the favorite book used by journalists trying to understand the spirit of the country as well as its history. The rich and long tradition of literary travel exemplified by Rebecca West remains alive and well. Some date it back to Homer and his epic poem of the travels of Odysseus. The nineteenth-century writers and explorers Richard Burton and Freya Stark are part of the pantheon that added many more literary travel writers in the twentieth century: Bruce

Chatwin, Paul Theroux, Jan Morris, Bill Bryson, Pico Iyer and others who have kept up the standards and expanded the genre.

The earliest publishers of travel brochures were wary of advertisements for hotels or luggage that might expect special recommendations in their books and newspapers. Karl Baedeker handled that problem by promising his readers in Victorian language that "the Editor begs to intimate that a character for fair dealing towards travelers is the sole passport to his commendation, and that no advertisements of any kind are admitted to his handbooks."

Most publications couldn't afford such high-minded scruples. After World War II the travel industry became the single largest source of advertising for newspapers; at its high point in the 1960s the industry accounted for one-fourth of all the ad revenue.

Normally there is a firewall between advertisers and journalists; advertisers do not receive special treatment from reporters. But the travel industry wanted more than the privilege of buying ad space. They hired public relations firms to work hand-in-glove with journalists, giving them free trips, meals, hotels and nights on the town and then expecting them to write rave reviews.

Stuart Newman was in on the ground floor of this eventually corrupt relationship. Newman is very much in the mold of Arthur Frommer. A veteran of World War II, he, too, jumped into the world of travel after he was discharged from the army, but he landed on the public relations side. He opened his own firm in Miami, and saw manipulating travel writers to the benefit of his clients as the purpose of his business. It seemed straightforward to Newman: convince newspaper reporters to write about a new travel destination, give away free trips to the destination and, when necessary, help write the articles.

Newman told me that in those days the relationship between public relations and the press "were considerably more relaxed." By "relaxed" Newman said he meant that when he wanted a story that promoted one of his clients' restaurants or hotels or nightclubs "I would frequently go to the city rooms of the *Miami Herald* and *Miami News*, sit at a manual typewriter, use their copy paper and knock out stories."

Soon the standard form of influencing travel writers was with the free trip, known in the trade as a "fam" trip or a trip to "familiarize" the writer with the destination being promoted. Newman said he gave away more airplane tickets, hotel vouchers, drinks at nightclubs and meal vouchers than he can remember. "The biggest challenge in generating major coverage for our travel industry clients remains the policies of media which prohibit press trips and complimentary resort and cruise accommodations. This was not the case in earlier years," he said. "In the 1950s and early 1960s the *Miami Herald's* travel editor had no problem with complimentary travel," he said. The exceptions were the *New York Times* and Time Life magazines, which refused to take anything for free.

The practice was so prevalent that some journalists took the free trips but never wrote about them in their newspapers or magazines. It got so bad that companies like the now-defunct Pan American Airways would only give away free tickets to journalists who signed a letter of intent to write up the trip.

The media made this habit even more questionable by hiding the fact that its reporters had accepted freebies. To this day, American travel writers are not required to admit in their stories that their travel was paid for by the hotel, restaurant and airline that are the subjects of their articles. It is the equivalent of allowing the Republican and Democratic parties to pay the expenses of the journalists covering their political conventions and then never publishing the fact. That would be declared corrupt and the antithesis of ethical journalism. Yet it is the engrained way of writing about travel in the United States, much of Europe and Asia. From the beginning, publications didn't question the idea of getting free trips. The editors told themselves it was the only way they could afford to cover the travel world. And the public relations professionals were thrilled, knowing that a handsome write-up or recommendation in a magazine was far more credible than an advertisement or brochure.

The *New York Times* Travel section stands out for its refusal to take any free travel and for its breadth of coverage. (I was a *New York Times* correspondent but never wrote for the Travel pages.) The 1980s were a golden age for the paper's Travel section, which grew to an enormous size, filling 38 to 46 pages each Sunday. Reporters routinely wrote 3,000-word articles that read like literary essays.

Michael Leahy was the *Times* travel editor from 1982 to 1986, and he credits Arthur Gelb, the newspaper's managing editor, with the decision to make travel writing "livelier and more ambitious." Comfortable travel was no longer confined to Europe but extended to parts of Africa, South America, Asia and the Middle East, and Australia. If the Soviet Union and other Communist bastions were closed off, it mattered little to tourists. With his new mandate, Mr. Leahy published articles by the newspaper's foreign staff, including R. W. Apple, Jr., the London bureau chief whose well-researched and witty articles on Europe became the standard for travel writing; Drew Middleton, the military correspondent who wrote vivid set pieces like one walking through Churchill's command post; and Joseph Lelyveld, whose travel articles from South Africa never erased the cruel reality of apartheid from the dazzling landscape of the continent. These were not travel writers discussing thread counts of bed linen at fancy hotels but foreign correspondents who knew these countries intimately.

Mr. Leahy went far afield when commissioning stories from luminaries in other fields. Muriel Spark, the novelist, wrote about Tuscany; V. S. Pritchett, critic and essayist, wrote on Seville; Patricia Wells, the food critic, on Paris restaurants; Sari Nuseibeh, a Palestinian academic, wrote on Jerusalem as an Islamic city; and Elie Wiesel, the Holocaust survivor and author, wrote about Jerusalem as the Jewish City of David. It didn't hurt that these were the years that advertising from the tourism industry often accounted for one-fourth of newspaper advertising revenue. "The sections were very, very fat but you had this Chinese wall between the advertising side and the editorial side. All I knew is that I had great big sections and the luxury of space," said Mr. Leahy.

It meant that he could publish essays like Apple's article comparing British to continental European cuisine. "Eating in Britain, like most things there, has a good deal to do with class," he wrote. "French families of modest means save for months to eat a superb meal on a birthday or a holiday. . . . They were accustomed, they told me, to eating in restaurants about once a week, and they went to the best bistros they could afford except for their twice or thrice-yearly splurge. When they ate at home, I am sure, they also ate well, if simply. There are just not very many people like that in Britain, and without people like that, there is no way that good restaurants will ever be the norm, as they are in France and Italy and Belgium."

Those are strong conclusions in a nuanced and reasonable piece about Britain and its place in European cuisine in the 1980s. It was not an exercise in self-indulgence that was more about Apple than England. However, all of that was about to change.

Nancy Newhouse was in charge of the Travel section when the Cold War ended. "We covered a great deal more of geography," said Newhouse, who went to Eastern Europe to see for herself the attraction of these newly open nations. Prague, she told me, "was definitely a sleeping beauty. It was like opening a door and seeing this magical city." Dresden in the former East Germany was "sad, deeply sad and yet they saved all the art, an astonishing collection."

An elegant woman who had been the editor of the newspaper's influential Style section, Newhouse was a veteran of the "lifestyle" genre of reporting. With so many more nations to cover and technological changes in the travel industry, she refined her writers' mission to concentrate on describing the experience of traveling to a certain destination and to write consumer stories to help tourists make the most of those trips. "It was an evolution from travel writing to up-to-the-minute consumer travel reporting," she said in a long interview at her brownstone in Manhattan. "We still had literary pieces but on the other end of the spectrum we ran consumer pieces."

These new consumer pieces were shorter and reported on lower fares and bargain flights, and they were decidedly subjective, emphasizing the personal point of view. "If you lose the vision of an individual, how they interpret a country, you've lost the heart of travel," Newhouse said. Travel writing was becoming reporting an "experience" where the reporter didn't need to know that much about Burma as show a talent for telling a good story about the experience of visiting Burma and well-researched recommendations for where to spend the night.

This produced the major emphasis on "good news only" consumer travel writing. Travel sections told the reader where to go and what to do, but not what to avoid. Newhouse believes this is appropriate journalism and says that her reporters will check out ten hotels in a city in order to recommend the four best. They won't mention the six that didn't make the cut. "We didn't give out the bad report cards."

"We never did the ten worst, only the ten best," she said for emphasis.

There were hints of problems—overcrowding at historic sites like the Taj Mahal, pollution by cruise ships—but the larger picture of the enormous changes in the travel and tourism industry, and the dark side of those changes, went unmentioned. "At our staff meetings we constantly brought up changes in travel and we used changes in the industry as a jumping-off point to discuss changes in the way we travel," said Newhouse. "It was the whole newspaper's failing not to cover the tourism industry—the sex trade in tourism, environmental and cultural degradation; that's legitimate news but not for us, for the travel pages," she said.

That is the standard for travel journalism at its best, according to more than one dozen travel editors I interviewed. The critical judgment, they all said, came in their recommendations for best value or exotic new destination. And they rejected any suggestion that this kind of writing looked more like an extension of the industry—telling readers how to spend money traveling.

The rise of the Internet confirmed this direction. With its websites rating hotels, airlines, restaurants, and tours, travel writing became singularly focused on practical consumer information. Catharine Hamm, the travel editor of the *Los Angeles Times*, told me she has made news and consumer information her chief mission to lure back readers. Her reporters write about the fluctuating dollar, the change in passport requirements, effects of the price of gasoline, the best luggage and travel clothes or, more recently, which hotels have serious environment standards.

"Our competition is everybody and everything. Travel news and information is so big out there—guidebooks, websites, magazines, that we compete with anything that takes time or eyeballs away from us," she said, explaining she needs those eyeballs to hold on to advertisers. Despite their mission statements and the hard work it takes to put out their sections, travel editors know their pages are meant to attract advertisements.

Travel sections are not and never have been an essential part of the core journalist mission of a newspaper, said Stuart Emmrich, the successor of Newhouse at the *New York Times*. Instead, he said, "travel is designed to bring readers to the newspaper." To that end, Emmrich has enlivened the section with off-beat angles on travel and a "frugal traveler" feature that has erased the paper's image as one for wealthy readers only.

Few newspapers or websites have the budgets of the *New York Times* or the *Washington Post* and magazines like *Condé Nast Traveler* and the *National Geographic* that pay all the expenses of their reporters and forbid accepting gifts. The transformation of travel writing into an extension of the tourism industry was cemented by the financial difficulties in the media business. In every other form of journalism free travel is a gift and considered a serious conflict of interest. "If you take ethics seriously, the same policies that cover news gathering have to apply to travel coverage," said Kelly McBride, an ethics specialist at the Poynter Institute. "Free travel is not acceptable."

Without free travel, most self-described travel writers would be out of business. And those free trips don't come easy. Writers have to compete for them. Laura Daily, a freelance travel reporter, was the 2008 president of the Society of American Travel Writers, a professional networking organization with over 1,000 members that helps arrange the junkets. Daily defends the free trips and routinely accepts them from the destinations she covers. "There is no way in this day and age that you can go to Antarctica and sell the story to newspapers without some sort of subsidy," she told me. "If you're lucky, a newspaper will pay you $350 for a lead story."

She said she never questioned why a cruise ship pays for her trip rather than buys an advertisement. But she said that the subsidies did not affect her judgment. "No quid pro quo is allowed. That is a no-no. No coming on a media trip in exchange for a positive story," she said.

She did say that her articles are generally positive—she could not give a single example of writing a negative review.

Her description of how those free trips are doled out suggests considerable influence by the industry. At conferences of the Society of American Travel Writers, journalists meet with travel industry publicists like Stuart Newman. There the journalists pitch stories to the publicists to convince them to pay for their trips. Daily described the event as "sort of like speed dating," where journalists hop from table to table to discuss new tourism venues, new trends and get approval for new trips paid for by the industry.

Virginia Sheridan is the president of M. Silvers Associates, a public relations firm that specializes in the travel industry. She is a member of the travel society and attends those conferences because, she told me, her relationship with journalists largely consists of pitching stories for her clients in the same way that political operatives pitch stories that help their candidates. And with today's tighter deadlines and fierce competition among freelance reporters, she said, "our relationship with the lifestyle and travel and tourism journalists has gotten closer."

There are exceptions to this close relationship. The *New Yorker* magazine publishes an annual travel issue that often includes in-depth articles on the industry. Writers Rick Steves, Anthony Bourdain and Rudy Maxa are not only travel gurus for consumers but can be critical of the industry. Among daily newspapers, the *Miami Herald* has a beat in the Business section dedicated to the industry, thanks in part to Tom Fiedler, one of the few newspaper editors who routinely covered tourism as a major industry, not simply as a pastime or lifestyle. First as a reporter and then as executive editor of the *Herald*, Fiedler watched the tourism industry transform Florida, and not always for the better. When he became the newspaper's executive editor, Fiedler created the tourism beat and assigned Douglas Hanks III to cover Florida's $50 billion industry.

As the *Miami Herald* tourism reporter, Hanks routinely wrote about the extraordinary power of the Florida tourism industry, including its successful lobbying to prevent Florida schools from lengthening the school year by shortening summer vacation—a change that would have prevented high school students from working the entire summer tourist season. Hanks wrote about the tourism board's iron-clad influence over development, taxes and other issues that the industry fears might cut into tourism to the "Sunshine State." He interviewed British travel writers eating lobster bisque at an upscale South Beach restaurant on a free vacation organized by the Greater Miami tourism board, which gives away three hundred trips a year that include free meals at Miami restaurants and free hotel rooms. The publicist for one of these restaurants told Hanks that giving travel writers free meals was the only marketing she did. It was much more effective and much cheaper than old-fashioned advertising.

However, Jane Wooldridge, the former *Miami Herald* travel editor and now the newspaper's business editor, said she often ignored the newspaper's strict prohibition against accepting freelance journalist articles if those pieces were based on travels subsidized by the industry. She said she had to fill her section and didn't want to depend solely on wealthy writers who paid their own way. "It's a pile of crap that we're all pure," she said.

Fiedler, now the dean of the College of Communications at Boston University, said the line between a tourist pamphlet and a travel piece is far too fuzzy. He blamed the extraordinary amount of advertising revenue newspapers earn from the tourism industry. "I don't know if it's a cultural mindset that takes hold so you only write good news stories," he told me. "If you were looking at it cynically, it is a conspiracy of silence."

Travel writing and its refusal to treat the industry seriously can take some of the blame for tourism's frivolous reputation.

The final anomaly is the central role of government. Tourism is that rare industry whose "product" is a country. Travelers first decide what countries to visit, and then what city, region, beach resort or historic site. And all travelers to foreign lands must pass through borders that are controlled by a government that issues visas, stamps passports or turns people away.

That is only the beginning. Governments are like the head of the octopus, controlling in obvious and subtle ways just about everything that affects travel and tourism. Governments can preserve cultural sites or allow them to be destroyed; they can set aside wilderness areas or issue permits to build resorts along a deserted beach; they can require sewage and water installations for any new construction or they can build super airports that flood rural areas with tens of thousands of tourists. Some preservationists see proper tourism as a salvation for remote areas; others see tourism as slow death. Governments—local, regional and national levels—decide whether an international company can build a new hotel, whether to give a new route to an airline, whether to build a conference center, whether to bid for an international event like the Olympics. The list is endless and is critical to the industry.

Finally, governments are the main sales force for tourism. Offices and ministries of tourism spend millions of dollars promoting their country to tourists, with brands and slogans like "New Zealand—100% Pure";

"Incredible India"; "Austria. You've arrived!"; "South Africa: Inspiring new ways" or "Smile, you're in Spain." National tourism websites are the starting point for many travelers; some websites are translated into up to ten languages. Embassies in foreign countries provide tourism information as well as visas. The best wildlife resort in Zambia depends on the government promoting Zambia to lure tourists to the game parks.

The United States is the exception. The Republican members of Congress sponsored and passed legislation to remove government from the tourism business in 1996. The Clinton administration dismantled most of the government tourism agency and the United States resigned from the U.N. World Tourism Organization. Patrice Tedjini, the historian of the UNWTO, said the U.S. resignation created a crisis for the organization. The tourism industry is built around countries. Cooperation, innovation, improved policies, require government participation. When the United States pulled out of UNWTO, it was the most popular tourist destination in the world. Since then, the U.S. growth has flattened and countries like China are becoming big forces in the industry.

"Now we are in a new period," said Tedjini. "We believe we are in a great period."

I interviewed Tedjini and six other UNWTO experts during several days at the Madrid headquarters near the Cuzco subway stop. The city sparkled; now it is anything but a punishment to be posted in Madrid, with its noble museums and restaurants that stay open late, serving tapas long after midnight. Marcelo Risi, spokesman at the UNWTO, organized my visit and guided me through the cramped office complex. In several decades covering international organizations, I have probably seen only one underfunded U.N. agency—this one. As the smallest full-fledged U.N. agency as well as the newest—winning that status in 2003—the tourism organization is strapped for cash and operates with a staff of 100 people. The members include 150 countries, and hundreds of member affiliates, including universities, industry groups and nongovernmental organizations. Yet at times it can barely afford to translate its works. A 2008 study of the cruise industry, with its growing popularity as well as its spotty record of polluting the seas, was only available in Spanish during my visit; no English was available due to budget cuts.

Its mission is to keep statistics on the tourism phenomenon and help governments and organizations figure out how tourism can be more of a help than a hindrance to the planet. A representative of the UNWTO attends climate control talks, environmental conclaves and endless tourism conventions, providing expert reports and advice.

Little of that is interesting to travel writers; you rarely see journalists from upscale glossy magazines at the UNWTO office. Most visitors to the headquarters when I visited in June were foreign tourism officials or academics who happily bought specialty volumes on subjects like how tourism can protect local handicrafts or the interplay of tourism, religions and culture. The visitor ledger that first day listed three professors from the University of Surrey and one from the University of Hawaii. Risi and other experts took pains to describe how the industry is slowly moving toward accepting rules and guidelines that would put "sustainability" or intelligent growth at the center of their policies. "The issue of numbers of tourists, what they do, that is the key to sustainability," said Luigi Cabrini, the UNWTO's expert on the subject. "We have to get away from the idea that sustainability is just ecotourism with five people alone walking in a forest. We need models of good practices."

"The reputation of tourism is often poor, and rightly so," said Cabrini. "It is an extremely sensitive sector. We need ethics codes, guidelines, statistics and data that help the industry, and to work with business, education, governments. That means also looking at pollution; environmental degradation; corporate cultural monotony of tourist establishments; international tourism that undermines local economies and dealing with the sheer number of tourists. In the end, tourism plays an important role alleviating poverty, widening appreciation of different cultures, as informal diplomacy and exchanging wealth from the rich to the poor nations."

The hot June sun lit the medieval square where I was waiting near the crowded Rialto Bridge of Venice. I was early for an appointment with Claudio Paggiarin, who is active in a community group trying to control tourism in their city. Paggiarin and I had traded emails, and he had agreed to meet me with two of his friends for a Saturday morning coffee. I had forgotten to ask how I would recognize them. There was no shade at the central fountain, our meeting spot. My husband Bill and I were both sweating. Would the Italians show up? Then on cue, the men arrived from different directions, laughing at each other's tardiness and introducing themselves to me. I had forgotten the basic rule that locals know their town, know who normally mingles in that square and would pick out foreigners like me in a heartbeat.

That scene was repeated countless times during my travels for this book. Strangers opened up their lives and guided me through their role in the industry. This book is a narrative of those journeys; of the people who graciously explained how they fit into the industry, demonstrating why it is known as the hospitality industry; of the countries with their special history and culture that determined how tourism worked whether in Europe or the Middle East; of the tourists and their experiences on trips that cost them a nice chunk of their income. All with the goal of trying to grasp the extraordinary dimensions of the industry. There seemed no better way to describe the "product" and the industry than actually taking those trips and telling the story from every possible perspective.

In Sri Lanka, a senior diplomat who had been transferred to the Tourism Ministry explained to me how, just months after Sri Lanka's long civil war finally ended, the country was betting its future on tourism. Bill and I tested that assertion, touring the tropical southern coast to meet hoteliers and investors, and traveling up the hills around Kandy on bumpy roads with monkeys swinging in the trees and the proverbial paradise waiting to be exploited.

On a typical Caribbean cruise from Miami to Belize and back, fellow tourists told me in the cavernous, elegant dining room that they rarely got off the ship to visit a foreign port and then attended ship lectures on how to buy diamonds mined in Africa and sold in shops at the Caribbean ports expressly designed for cruise passengers. A few months later I flew back to Miami, where the head of the cruise line explained why his company refuses to register as an American company and be subject to many American laws.

In Brazil I went from a lavish banquet with international tourist executives at an Atlantic coast resort to the vast, seemingly empty Amazon forest, where some of those same travel leaders were trying to save a corner of the wilderness. History was everywhere, especially in nature. During an African safari in Zambia, the normal road to our base camp was flooded, forcing our Land Cruiser to take a circuitous route through the hills and allowing me a rare glimpse, at twilight, of one of Africa's majestic sable antelopes. They could disappear, I was told repeatedly, since those wildlife parks are still viewed suspiciously as a legacy of white colonial rule rather than as an essential part of Africa's culture.

The most familiar countries offered surprises. During my first research trip to Cambodia I asked the minister of tourism a basic question: what is the most popular tourist spot in Phnom Penh, the capital? His answer was "Tuol Sleng." I nearly dropped my pen. Tuol Sleng is the former torture and execution center of the Khmer Rouge. Like other researchers, I have spent countless hours studying its files, doubling over with horror at the story they tell of sadism and pain: the antithesis of "tourism." Yet Tuol Sleng's cells and instruments of torture preserved as a cautionary museum are now part of a new phenomenon known as "dark tourism."

One morning I took the five-minute ferry across Bangkok's Chao Phraya River to the Oriental Thai Cooking School of the Mandarin Oriental Hotel. My fellow students included a professional chef from Australia working on a yacht, a Portuguese financier visiting from Hong Kong and a newly-wed bride from Brazil. They were expert with knives and Asian spices, and able to take advantage of an expensive course: roughly $100 for a three-hour, hands-on lesson that became our three-course lunch. Chef Narain Kiattiyotcharoen's menu that day included pad thai, the spaghetti of Southeast Asian cuisine. For me it was an introduction into the world of "gastronomic or culinary tourism," which brings in as much as 5 billion euros to Italy alone. Ultimately, I decided to spotlight wine tourism in a trip through Bordeaux. Likewise, my interviews with young Spanish hotel owners trying to cobble together a gay-friendly tour circuit had to be put aside. The gay and lesbian tourism market is considered potentially among the most lucrative, as is the retired-seniors market, but this book is not meant to be encyclopedic.

I crossed the two continent-size countries central to the travel industry; in China, traveling roughly north to south from Beijing to Shanghai and then Xian and Chengdu, and in the United States going east to west from the Shenandoah National Park in Virginia to the beach on Waikiki in Hawaii, readjusting my interview schedules as I examined the connections between the two behemoths. Gambling in Macau undercut gambling in Las Vegas. Generations of dreams of Disneyland translated into theme parks in Shanghai.

Everywhere, I ran across wilderness areas modeled after America's national park system: a favorite was an island off Costa Rica that was a former penal colony left to return to nature along with its surrounding seas, where we swam in crystal-clear water.

In the sands around Dubai and Abu Dhabi, I watched the stream of airplanes taking off and landing that have turned this once-deserted corner of the globe into a massive tourist hub, rivaling Singapore and Britain. Europeans have become so concerned about the pollution caused by the constantly growing air traffic that they have included airplanes in their carbon emissions trading system and as of 2013 are imposing a small carbon allowance on every airplane ticket for travel to, within and from the continent—roughly $3 per ticket.

Pollution and environmental degradation are the serious downside of those crowds of tourists and travelers who are making 1 billion discrete foreign trips every year and possibly three times that many trips within their own countries. With over 7 billion people now on Earth, there is little doubt that the number of trips will rise, raising urgent questions about responsibilities. Travel is an extraordinary pleasure and was once a privilege. Now it is considered a basic right without limits or a sense of responsibility for how all this travel is affecting the places we love.

A tour of the Louvre in Paris is a case in point, a rare example of smart crowd control that has worked, so far. President François Mitterrand commissioned I. M. Pei to create a new entryway to help guide the growing number of visitors, which became the glass pyramid built in 1989 in the central courtyard. The redesign transformed the museum.

On a recent summer morning I joined an English-speaking group guided by Julian, a tall French graduate student with long hair, a beard, scarf and not-quite-scruffy jeans. He said he was completing his doctorate in art history. Besides English, he gives tours in his native French as well as in Spanish. Wearing his headset with microphone, he led our group of twenty tourists to the bowels of the old palace and an exhibit of Egyptian art, through the Greeks, then the Romans, then Renaissance Italians and then the *Mona Lisa* by Leonardo da Vinci, the star of the museum.

"Be careful," he said, "follow me and we'll see how close we can get."

She is now housed in the enormous, gilded Salle des États, redesigned in 2005 to reduce the traffic jams of the painting's admirers and to better showcase the most famous painting on the planet. With our headsets pressed to our ears, we could barely hear Julian above the loud babble of the crowd. The *Mona Lisa* with her mysterious smile is now sheltered behind a massive clear glass shield and hangs by itself on one wall. The painting is lit so subtly that visitors can admire it from great distances in the room. The renovations cost $6.2 million and were paid for by Nippon Television of Japan, a testament to the painting's popularity.

"It is not only famous, it is important in art history," said Julian, expertly opening a path for us.

When the *Mona Lisa* was relocated in this gallery, the Louvre counted 6.6 million visitors a year, more than three-fourths of whom said they had come to see that one painting. Seven years later the number of visitors has jumped to 8.8 million. The Louvre has kept up with the demand and remained the most visited museum in the world because it invested $16 million to build the pyramid and the Japanese refurbished the Mona Lisa gallery. What expensive adjustments will be required when the number of visitors double?

France, as the number-one tourist destination in the world, is a country with a government that thinks deeply about such questions.

PART TWO

CULTURAL TOURISM

France, Venice and Cambodia

A gondola in Venice

2

LES VACANCES

On a drizzling Sunday morning, a crowd gathered early at the base of the Eiffel Tower waiting to ride up the lattice legs of the world's most famous national symbol. African vendors had staked out their territory on the wet sidewalks, selling glittering Eiffel miniatures displayed on uniform four-foot-square cotton scarves. It was the tail-end of summer—children had returned to school—and the crew of thirty-eight gardeners had weeded and pruned to perfection what remained of the flower beds. Signs in six languages warned tourists to beware of pickpockets. The bust of Gustave Eiffel, the engineer who built the tower for the 1889 Universal Exposition, was stationed modestly near the north pillar.

Standing on the second-level viewing platform was an Australian couple—Liz and Shane—who were celebrating their retirement with a month-long trip through the capitals of Europe. "You can't come to Paris and not go up the Eiffel Tower," Liz said, asking me to photograph the two of them standing bravely against the rain with Paris as a backdrop. The picture that would say they had done the tour.

Every day tourists climb the Eiffel Tower or catch their first awestruck view of its elegant silhouette from taxis or trains bringing them into the city that has become the symbol of foreign travel, the reason why people empty their savings accounts or load up their credit cards to squeeze into an airplane and fly off for a glimpse of another world. It is no accident that the Eiffel Tower is the ubiquitous icon of travel and romance and epitomizes why Paris is the first choice of travelers looking for that new experience.

In the twenty-first century France has become the most visited country in the world, beating out the United States, the former champ. France is the reigning diva of all things travel; the favorite cover for travel magazines—the newest wrinkle in Paris nightlife or a hidden corner of the French countryside—and the favorite destination.

This is no small achievement for a country smaller than the state of Texas. It has no tropical beaches like Hawaii, no Alaskan glaciers, no Grand Canyon or Yellowstone national parks. Yet France outdraws the United States and every other country, welcoming some 78 million visitors every year who happily spend over $48 billion to live like the French for a week or so.

This is infuriating to Americans in the tourism business who have watched France edge out the United States. "More Chinese visited Paris (in 2009) than all of the United States," said J. W. Marriott, Jr., who heads the American hotel giant founded by his father.

That, too, is no accident. The French understood before most other countries that tourism is a serious business, integrating it into major government policy decisions and nursing it as a parallel business that multiplies the economic benefits of all things that are French. Tourist spending boosts the profits of perfume-makers, vintners, art dealers and the corner boulangerie. Now tourism is the premier economic sector in France, the number-one source of employment and the number-one export. (Tourism counts as an export, not import, on the trade balance books.)

France is a master of this seemingly invisible trade that is everywhere and nowhere. Its component parts are spread around the country— airports, train stations, wilderness parks, restaurants, hotels and beaches— essentials of a normal life, not just tourism. The French have figured out the paradox that since tourists are drawn to a country, not a particular resort, it follows that the more France remained France, the better for tourism. So the French national tourist strategy evolved to guard the national lifestyle. That means coordinating with urban and rural planning, cultural majordomos and environmental regulators. They figured the French could remain arrogant forever, but they had to speak English—and now Chinese.

Many governments woke up to the power of this illusive giant when the World Travel and Tourism Council created an accounting system to measure the economic effect of tourism on a city, state or country. With the help of the United Nations, this system of Satellite Accounts has been set up by nations around the world to count the dollars, or euros or pounds or pesos, spent by tourists in their economies. Tourism turns out to be the top single revenue source in countries as diverse as France and Thailand.

With that economic power tourism also became a huge, if unacknowledged, cultural phenomenon. Early on, anthropologists were measuring the consequences on poor and often isolated societies when legions of wealthier, foreign tourists visited. Among the emblematic stories is one told by the British researcher Dianne Stadhams, who asked a young girl in Gambia what she wanted to be when she grew up: "When I grow up I want to be a tourist," she answered, "because tourists don't have to work and can spend their days sitting in the sun, eating and drinking."

Tourism has had just as powerful an effect on the richer countries. In bookstores and many personal libraries, travel guides have replaced history books as the way to understand the world. Walk into your favorite bookstore and the section devoted to travel books will be double or triple the size of those devoted to history.

Tourists are the consumer engine of the world, turning airports into a system of shopping malls and "duty-free" into a way of life. Activists harness the power of tourism to accomplish what would otherwise be a long-shot goal: saving a threatened African wilderness park by turning it into a new tourist destination, or buying up miles of beaches in Central America for a green tourist resort, or even declaring the homely bogs of Ireland a national treasure and putting it on the tourist trail.

No country better exemplifies the power and unstoppable force of tourism than France. No other country has tried harder to harness the tourism beast and avoid its downsides. And no other country has climbed to the top of the heap doing as well as France has.

Yet publicly the French government underplays the role of tourism in its economy, preferring to leave it invisible. Depending on tourism makes the French slightly uneasy or ambivalent, as if they are selling themselves. You rarely hear the French president or prime minister praising tourism as the country's single biggest economic engine; on the contrary, they are more likely to use the word in a pejorative sense, and while the French government has thousands of bureaucrats working in tourism, there is no senior-level minister of tourism. But there is a secretary of state for tourism, a second-tier cabinet position and an expanding national tourism agency, ATOUT France.

This is an expression of the uncomfortable fact that tourism is seen in France and much of the world as lightweight, a business that makes serious money but on its face doesn't seem as important as, say, making airplanes or running international banks. It is a question of face, or pride. Travel and tourism may be the world's biggest industry, it may be everyone's favorite pastime, a sign of how wealthy we all have become, but it doesn't fit the self-image of a country like France.

France is the nation of Napoleon, a former empire with colonies that stretched around the globe. For the last fifty years the French government has worked fanatically to remain a major player on the world scene: to insure French remains a universal language of diplomacy; to hold on to one of the five permanent seats at the United Nations Security Council and, as a nuclear power with the world's fifth-largest economy, to remain a member of the most elite gatherings, attending the political and economic forums. The French are willing to pay the price for that status, turning out some of the world's best-trained and -educated people and maintaining their top industries and building modern transportation systems.

Yet the multibillion-euro travel and tourism industry in France brings in more money than any other single sector, whether luxury goods, fashion, agriculture, weapons or airplanes—even if it doesn't fit the high-powered profile of France.

"At a minimum, tourism accounts for seven percent of the national product—it is the premier source for our balance of payments, but despite all of this economic power it is always viewed poorly by the public," said Philippe Maud'hui, the senior planning official at ATOUT France.

He tried to explain the paradox of the government which, behind the scenes, understands the critical importance of tourism to the economy and the popular French culture that considers tourism a less-than-noble profession. You could say they are snobs about it.

"In business it's not considered the route to an elite career. No one wants their son to go into tourism. Everyone takes vacations. Everyone is an expert on taking a vacation. Voilà—tourism isn't serious."

There is an important economic aspect to this ambivalence. In this era of hyperglobalization, success at drawing tourists could be France's downfall. The more France depends on tourism, the more the government has to guard against the runaway mass tourism that is destroying life in Venice and the beaches of southern Spain. And tourists can be fickle, looking for the next great destination.

There is no bureaucratic answer to those puzzles. The attraction of France comes from centuries of civilization, not a series of ad campaigns. The country's tourism business routinely survives the annual spate of protests and labor stoppages. No official edict is responsible for the alchemy of French wine and food, for the geniuses of French art, literature, music, theater, ballet and the movies.

French officials have even debated whether the government has any power to keep alight the modern world's obsessive love of all things French, in particular Impressionist art. "We can't explain any of that, really, why even the Chinese are so crazy about these painters and we can't take credit for it. All around the world they love Cézanne, Picasso," said Marco Marchetti, of the Ministry of Culture's department of patrimony, in an interview in his office around the corner from the Louvre.

What the Ministry of Culture and the government can do, he said, is mount blockbuster exhibits that fans love and which draw millions of tourists to France. Pablo Picasso and Paul Cézanne have been the rock stars. Claude Monet joined the pantheon with a 2010 exhibit of his paintings at the Grand Palais in Paris. But the government rarely acknowledged that among its motives behind these exhibits is to promote the tourism trade.

These shows are for higher purposes. When he opened the Monet exhibit, then President Nicolas Sarkozy said it reflects the "unmistakable emblem of the international influence of French culture."

Underneath this public posturing, the government understands that tourism will be a driver of the French economy for years to come and that tourism is too powerful and too important to be left to its own devices; either you control tourism or it controls you. The French government stands apart for its early intuition about the importance of tourism and the world's itch to travel. Now France is at the center of that explosion: over half of travel is to Europe, nearly 20 percent to Asia, 17 percent to the Americas— North and South—and less than 5 percent to Africa.

To keep its position the French government has become tourism's most important partner, improving or building new transportation systems, national parks, or museums that can make or break a tourist season. Tourism is regulated, promoted and subsidized by the government at all levels. Planning begins in town halls or rural regional boards and moves upward to bureaucrats in Paris who then help transform the world's love of all things French into more money for a new ski resort in the Massif Central or a camping ground in the Lubéron.

The French dominate on the international scene as well. The United Nations' World Tourism Organization grew into an independent U.N. body under Francesco Frangialli, the Frenchman who was secretary-general for eleven years. He steered the tourism organization to global prominence, promoting those satellite accounts to prove tourism's economic heft and pushing the organization into international conferences on development and environmental issues.

Ultimately, the French are gambling that tourism will bring in the money that allows French society to remain French while blocking the relentless drive of the industry from reducing the culture to the single-dimension fluff it appears to be in those countless travel pieces. Put in the most common terms—will officials prevent tourism from turning France into a Disneyland for adults?

In some ways that is an old question. France has been a magnet for foreigners for more than 150 years, long enough to have suffered and recovered from disasters and the sort of hit-or-miss decisions that deform many other countries today.

The first tourists were the intrepid and often-eccentric English. The educated elite of the nineteenth-century British Isles were easily the most adventuresome people of the era. They routinely decamped to the far corners of their empire, from Kenya to the Raj in India, and returned decades later with baubles and hair-raising stories. Members of the English upper classes with the time and money to travel abroad invented the grand tour of the European continent and called it tourism. Their itinerary included long stays in Paris, Florence, Venice, Rome and Naples. Italy was the destination, the seat of European culture, while Paris was a delightful stop along the way.

These English were self-consciously modern, traveling to see the world described in history books, absorb culture, tramp in nature and collect beautiful objects or "souvenirs." Hippolyte Taine, the French historian and critic, described the typical English tourist he encountered in Paris as a strange creature with "long legs, thin body, head bent forward, broad feet, strong hands, excellently suited to snatching and gripping."

The British further whetted this new appetite for travel by hosting the first true world's fair in 1851. The Great Exposition in London's Crystal Palace celebrated scientific advances from around the world and was a huge success, overcoming initial ridicule and drawing large crowds from the British Isles and overseas. The passion for travel spread to the United States where Americans, calling themselves excursionists, not tourists, adopted the grand tour as a sophisticated rite of passage.

Mark Twain memorialized these excursionists in his book *Innocents Abroad*, a journal of his 1867 voyage across the Atlantic through the Mediterranean to the Holy Lands. For most of the journey Twain is his humorous, acerbic self—that is, until he arrives in France and becomes just one more tourist to fall head over heels in love with the country. He disembarked with several passengers at the port of Marseilles to catch a train for a side trip up to Paris.

"At last, and beyond all question, we were in beautiful France and absorbing its nature to the forgetfulness of everything else, and coming to feel the happy romance of the thing in all of its enchanting delightfulness," he writes. "What a bewitching land it is! What a garden!"

He was besotted with Paris, its cafés, the Nôtre-Dame Cathedral and the Père Lachaise Cemetery. Twain returned to his ocean liner wrestling with his admiration for France. Americans "are measurably superior to the French in some things, but they are immeasurably our betters in others," he wrote, and one of those was the city of Paris. "We shall travel many thousands of miles after we leave here and visit many great cities, but we shall find none so enchanting as this."

Twenty years after Twain's visit, Paris hosted its greatest fair—the 1889 Universal Exposition celebrating the centennial of the establishment of the French Republic. This required a centerpiece that would reflect France's forward-looking democracy. A contest was held and Mr. Eiffel won. His proposed 10,000-ton tower, with its latticelike construction for the entry to the fairgrounds, was an imposing engineering challenge that met the requirement to demonstrate a scientific advancement.

After much official grumbling about the cost and the aesthetics of the candle-shaped tower—several of the establishment's leading artists and intellectuals described it as an "odious column built up of riveted iron plates"—the people of Paris fell in love with Eiffel's folly. At the inauguration Gustave Eiffel said with slight exaggeration that "the tower is now known to the whole world; it has struck the imagination of every nation, and inspired the most remote with the desire of visiting the Exhibition."

Foreigners did visit, over 1 million from the Americas, Europe, Africa and Asia, spending over $324 million—huge numbers in 1889. When the tower was slated to be torn down at the end of its twenty-year contract, the city of Paris granted an extension in the face of its international renown. In the century since the tower was built, after the powers-that-be got used to its leggy beauty, the French government has used it shamelessly to evoke romance, longing, sophistication and an intense desire to visit France.

Before long, the growing legion of English tourists wanted to "discover" parts of France beyond Paris. Fond of the seaside in their own country, the English took ferries across the Channel to French coastal towns that the French had never found particularly interesting. Towns like Deauville and Dieppe on the Normandy coast were turned into fashionable resorts, the first example of what would later become mass tourism. Locals did not fare very well. Developers expropriated their land with the connivance of officialdom and made a small fortune off this new craze for beachside resorts. Migrant workers arrived and found work in the new resort jobs of waitress, cook, beach attendant and fishing guide. Prostitutes followed, long before the term "sex tourism" was invented. The pattern was repeated on a vastly larger scale over the next century as tropical beaches from the Caribbean to Thailand became resorts for mass tourism.

But as small as it may seem in retrospect, that first example of a modern tourist resort overwhelmed the northern coast of France. As the historian Graham Robb wrote: "Nothing of this magnitude had happened to the coast of Normandy since the Viking invasions and the Hundred Years War."

The French government noticed all the money passing hands in these tourist resorts and in 1911 created a Tourism Board devoted to the new industry. This office was assigned the job of producing "propaganda" to entice more foreigners to visit. Before this experiment got traction, World War I broke out and France became a bloody battleground. In the immediate, heady days of peace, France revived its Tourism Board and opened bureaus in Barcelona, Luxembourg, London and Geneva to sell France as a holiday destination. To that end, the Tourism Board commissioned modern Art Deco posters to promote rail travel like the Le Train Bleu to the Riviera or wintering on the sands of Juan-les-Pins at Antibes, posters that have since been endlessly reproduced to evoke those early stylish days of luxury travel.

Since tourism involved international commerce, the French government helped form the International Congress of Official Tourist Traffic Associations in 1925 to regulate the tourist traffic between neighboring European countries, focusing on classic issues of border security, tariffs and tax collection. The biggest problem at the time was how to keep track of automobiles crossing international borders. In 1934 the Europeans added the International Union of Official Organizations for Touristic Propaganda in Brussels that became a forerunner for the current UNWTO.

The biggest contribution of the French government to the tourism industry was inadvertent.

In 1936, France elected Léon Blum as its first socialist prime minister. In that era of strikes and industrial clashes, Mr. Blum ran on a platform appealing to the workers, promising to ease their burden, shore up the fledgling unions and help farmers and the new middle class share in the wealth of industrialized France. He made good on his word and passed a number of sweeping reforms, including a 1936 law that required two weeks of paid vacation for every French citizen.

It is impossible to exaggerate the effect of this law and its mandate of the unheard-of luxury of a paid vacation. It was easily the most popular of Blum's reforms and spread across Europe. Under Blum, the government arranged low-cost trips for French families to the Alps and various camping grounds. "Les Vacances" (French for "vacation") created a minor revolution. In one stroke, travel and leisure became a right of the masses, not just the privileged or the elite.

"Before 1936, there wasn't a real tourism industry," said Mr. Maud'hui of the ATOUT France agency. "That is when we leaped into another era. Now travel was for everyone, for everyone."

Three years later World War II broke out. France was occupied by Germany, and when the war ended in 1945, the devastation to French society and its economy was enormous; the immediate postwar situation desperate. The French turned to the Americans for help. At that stage the United States was the only wealthy nation still standing; its economy accounted for half of the manufactured goods in the world.

Washington responded, generously, with the Marshall Plan, spending billions for the economic recovery of the countries of what was then known as Western Europe. It was motivated in part by humanitarianism and partly by politics to insure that none of the countries became a part of the Soviet bloc in the beginning years of the Cold War.

When the United States extended aid to France through the Marshall Plan, officials from both countries decided that tourism would be the best avenue for reviving the French economy. Back then, the logic of turning to tourism seemed obvious. France was broke. It was incapable of quickly rebuilding its manufacturing sector in order to sell goods overseas and earn the hard currency it needed. What made sense was to bring the money to France, to have American tourists with dollars fill the tables at cafés and restaurants, buy souvenirs, take train rides and patronize hotels and country inns. The one thing that had survived the war was the French way of life, the siren song for Americans since the days of Mark Twain. During the years between the world wars, American writers like Ernest Hemingway memorialized the free-spirited glamour of Paris in books and composers like George Gershwin in song. Americans already knew they were enthralled with the idea of Paris.

The economics of the program were sound. The goal was to more than double prewar tourism to at least 3 million visitors by 1952. That required a complete overhaul of much of the industry, starting from the ground up. Top French hoteliers and restaurateurs were sent to the United States for training in modern business aimed at pleasing American tastes. Most hotels in Paris were as tired and tattered as the country. In the United States, the French hoteliers learned new basics like supplying plump pillows, placing a lamp by the bedside for reading and making sure windows could open easily. They were taught the grander requirements that could help them earn handsome profits, such as installing expensive gift shops in their hotels where tourists could buy souvenirs easily and adding large meeting rooms to the hotel so it could host conventions.

The French were excellent students; they wanted to make money. Once they understood what makes a hotel modern and comfortable, they convinced officials at the Marshall Plan to help underwrite a miniboom in hotel room construction. By the end of the plan France boasted 452,471 rooms, more than any other country in Europe. They also latched on to the idea of making Paris a popular city for conventions. From those American-inspired beginnings, Paris grew to become the world's most popular city for meetings.

Getting American tourists into those hotel rooms was the next step. Airfares were out of reach for middle-class America, so Marshall Plan officials fought hard to convince the airlines to add a lower "tourist fare" for flights across the Atlantic. They won but only by promising to subsidize the lower fares for the airlines. Then they set up propaganda or promotional committees made up of French and American government officials as well as private companies like Pan American Airways, American Express and the European edition of the *New York Herald Tribune*, the precursor to the *International Herald Tribune* in Paris. The committee spent millions on advertisements to convince Americans to travel to France; advertisements to promote the 2,000th birthday of Paris in 1951 cost the then-huge sum of $100,000.

U.S. officials also hoped that American tourists would play a role in diplomacy. In one of the first modern instances of tourism purposefully used as public diplomacy, both governments decided that American tourism would strengthen the ties between the two people and win the French over to the American side of the burgeoning Cold War. At that moment the French Communist Party was one of the strongest political parties in the country. The French government sided with the United States against the Soviet Union but not because of those American visitors. On the contrary, this was the moment when the Americans and the French discovered how much they didn't like each other. The American tourists thought the French were "haughty," and the French thought the Americans were vulgar consumers. At one point the U.S. State Department had to print advisories to American travelers with "tips for your trip" for getting along with the French.

This was the first hint that simply letting tourists loose in a foreign country would not necessarily lead to better understanding. Mass tourism by people who couldn't speak the native language often had the opposite effect. (The French eventually solved that problem by learning English, now the international language.)

The plan did fulfill the American goal of getting France back on its feet and firmly within the western camp, as well as establishing a new pattern of trade with the United States. The biggest impact, though, was on France, which exceeded its goal of wooing 3 million tourists to the country in 1952. American government aid had kick-started the modern tourism industry in France with those hotel rooms, tourist airfares and inculcation of the idea of Paris as the ideal city for glamour. From then on, the French government kept its hand in all aspects of tourism.

This American-subsidized tourism fit in nicely with the new order being established by some of France's most conservative politicians. They wanted to erase any possibility of European nations fighting each other in yet another world war. So they initiated the idea of a new European community with Germany and other European powers that would eventually become the European Union. This new Europe began with the notion of shared authority over coal and steel and the shared belief that the state should spend its money on social benefits such as health, housing, education, pensions and public infrastructure—not armies and weapons.

This time tourism had the desired social effect and helped bring together these European neighbors. During what the French call "the golden years" of the 1960s, two- and three-week paid vacations became the norm in Europe. People from the north—English, French, Swiss and Germans—headed south, to the warm Mediterranean climates. They took the railways or drove in their newly affordable cars to the seashore. The coast of Spain became the Miami of Europe, with inexpensive pensions and new package vacations. New, inexpensive charter flights took tourists farther afield to places like the Greek islands.

Again presaging modern mass tourism, the Europeans traveled in packs—the English with the English, the French with the French, the Germans with the Germans—so that the exotic would be familiar. It was an extension, of sorts, of the Marshall Plan. The wealthier Europeans of the north traveled south to the poorer areas of their continent, spending their money where it was needed. What economists strive for—redistribution without taxation.

About this time, France took a step that inadvertently elevated the standard of tourism by creating the world's first Ministry of Culture in 1959. The newly elected President Charles de Gaulle wanted to revive and enhance French culture. He appointed the writer André Malraux the first minister of culture, with a mandate to give the public free access to the culture of France.

The hyperactive Malraux jumped into the job. With equal doses of imagination and egalitarianism, Malraux assembled a bureaucracy to register, repair and recover all that was considered France's patrimony or national heritage. Malraux built on the work begun a hundred years earlier by Prosper Mérimée, also an author, who as France's inspector-general of monuments spent over eighteen years listing and protecting France's historic masterpieces. He blocked locals from destroying masterpieces, saving 4,000 buildings by classifying them as historical monuments, including the bridge at Avignon and the basilica at Vézelay. Malraux institutionalized this preservation and went further by getting laws passed requiring the centuries-old buildings to be cleaned. And he declared that, if at all possible, these gorgeous buildings and monuments had to be open to the public—French and foreign alike.

Under Malraux, the French museum system became one of the most expansive in the world. Paris alone seems to add a new major museum every decade: the then-audacious Centre Georges Pompidou, which included the National Museum of Modern Art, opened in 1977; the Musée d'Orsay was a masterful 1986 conversion of a Beaux-Arts railroad station into the permanent home of the country's collection of Impressionist paintings, and most recently the Quai Branly Museum of indigenous art was inaugurated in 2006.

That is just a portion of the cultural world opened up by the new ministry. From the beginning, Malraux was keen on establishing and supporting arts festivals around the country: music in Aix-en-Provence, photography in Perpignan, film in Cannes. The aim was to raise the profile of French culture; the result fifty years later was a multimillion-dollar cultural tourism business.

And so it went for several decades. Decisions and innovations of the French government, somehow, eventually provided the undergirding of the classic tourism industry of today. Tourism officials told me repeatedly, "This was done without regard to tourism," while relating how critical some innovation had been for tourism.

Trains and transportation came next. The French were among the first nations to bet their future on a system of fast trains. Called Train à Grande Vitesse (train of great speed), or TGV, the government began laying the first tracks for the system in 1974. Soon the whole country was tied into this expanded rail network of fast and common trains, allowing the French to travel without using their cars and freeing up the clogged highways. Eventually, the trains were connected to the airports. Paris's Charles de

Gaulle Airport became a model hub, with its connections by commuter train, bus and the TGV copied by countries around the world.

Another turning point came at the dawn of industrialized agriculture. At risk were those gentle green fields and quaint villages so admired by Mark Twain. As the agricultural powerhouse of Western Europe, France saw farming as its destiny, and by the 1980s the Ministry of Agriculture was pushing back against pressure to promote huge farms found in countries like the United States. Instead, the government promoted a mix of farm subsidies to preserve local small farmers and the French way of life. Through national and European laws, the government paid a premium to farmers who followed old-fashioned conservation practices like planting grass and tree buffers along river banks to keep the waters pure and prevent soil erosion. Farmers who grew hedge rows or repaired their scenic barns were rewarded by the government. And so were the farmers whose vineyards, fields and orchards supply the chefs in Paris with the fresh, high-quality produce they need, whether Roquefort cheese or baby spinach. A complicated system that uses subsidies and specialty labels eventually insured that French cuisine and small French farmers could survive modernization.

By 1990, when the world tourism industry cracked open with the end of the Cold War, the French innovations of the previous forty years were a boon rather than a drag on high-quality tourism. Instead of being passed over for countries newly open, France became the top attraction with its museums, easy transportation and special regional flavors.

So France started pulling together the disparate strands of government policy that affected tourism, however indirectly, to make a unified policy and to work with private industry to organize tourism so it didn't distort society, pollute the country or turn livelihoods upside down. They created a planning process that is painstakingly tedious. Bureaucrats, committees, reviews, studies, analyses, more reviews, studies and analyses, then new policies to be implemented, reviewed and studied. But they are happy with this singular approach.

"It is much better to do tourism with the same eye, one supporting the other," said Philippe Maud'hui. That is the price of aiming for the high end of tourism, not necessarily the rich but those who will leave France better than they found it. Since every country is looking for the same mix,

France is attracting attention from other ministries of tourism asking if the French have found the answer for good tourism or a momentary sweet spot.

Bordeaux is wine—the grand, expensive red wine of connoisseurs. The prized vineyards begin inside the city limits of Bordeaux and spread in all directions—south, east, north and west—through suburbs and villages, flat plains, soft ridges and knots of pine trees, hugging both banks of the Gironde River, which flows into the nearby Atlantic Ocean. Nothing is too good for these fields of stubby, carefully pruned vines that have enriched the famously tight-fisted and conservative Catholic elite of Bordeaux for centuries. They once traded barrels of their red wine for wool, cotton, spice and sugar at the river port in the heart of Bordeaux City, in front of the customs house when trade with the new world and Africa made it one of the busiest European ports on the Atlantic. Today the wine is bottled and labeled and then shipped in cases to nations around the globe; a single bottle of the best premier cru can sell for hundreds, even thousands, of dollars. While French fashion, films, art and architecture have their ups and downs, French wine has remained the standard against which all other wines are measured. And Bordeaux is at the top of the heap.

Until recently Bordeaux was the antithesis of tourism. Yet I had come to Bordeaux with my husband at the strong suggestion of officials in Paris and New York. I had asked them to name the best example of the future direction of tourism in France—a region that has put in place all the elements they talked about at length during my interviews with them. I was surprised at the answer:

"Bordeaux—thanks to Alain Juppé, that is where you can see the future of tourism."

"Juppé has given us a work of art in Bordeaux."

"Bordeaux. Alain Juppé is bringing it up to the level of a major destination, like Florence, Italy."

This sounded as unlikely as saying Savannah, Georgia, was the future of the American tourist market. When I had lived in France in the late 1980s, raising two young children there, Bordeaux had the reputation of a boring, faded beauty, its former glory hidden behind grimy buildings and abandoned warehouses. My French friends warned me against traveling there for anything but the wine. The city was a wreck.

Then Alain Juppé became mayor of Bordeaux in 1995 and he transformed the city. It was by-the-book planning, all bottom-up, with local officials deciding what to save, what to raze, what the city could support, what was beyond its means or desires. Then the city coordinated the plans with the regional, national and European authorities, who approved them and then paid a good share of the costs. It took more than ten long years.

Mayor Juppé's plan was simple, which made it all the more difficult. Return the town to its breathtaking eighteenth-century beauty by ordering the owners of historic buildings to follow the law passed by Malraux and clean off the dirt that had caked the façades since the industrial era. Scrubbing off the grime revealed an almost golden sheen to this rare urban masterpiece. Then he attacked the industrial wasteland of abandoned warehouses that lined the river port and cut the city off from the beautiful Gironde. The warehouses were pulled down and replaced by a riverside park designed by Claire and Michel Corajoud, top French landscape architects. The quai became a promenade with gardens, paths and in the center a long shallow reflecting pool or "water mirror" to catch the light from the sky and reflect the old eighteenth-century bourse, or stock exchange.

Finally, Juppé built a modern tramway system that eliminates unnecessary driving and opens up the old city to pedestrians again with public squares, green spaces and car-free walkways.

For Bordeaux, this was the equivalent of the Boston Big Dig. For French tourism officials, it was the Big Payoff. From the beginning, they had watched and fostered the renaissance of Bordeaux, promoting this "sleeping beauty" as returned to the living and figuring out how Bordeaux could add new glamour to the French tourist agenda.

During our trip to France, Bill and I caught a rapid train from Paris and in less than three hours arrived at Bordeaux, in the southwest corner of France near the Atlantic Ocean, the Pyrenees Mountains and a little farther to the east, the Mediterranean.

Our first day in Bordeaux we were bowled over; once again it was the city Victor Hugo had described as a cross between commercial Antwerp and elegant Paris, but without the capital's crowds or high prices.

To avoid a full blast of propaganda from the city's tourist office, we went first to the vineyards, to ask the old families what they thought about this new transformation and the tourism that followed, whether they felt as if their city had sold out to the tourism gods.

Château Haut-Bailly is one of the region's finest wineries, producing Graves Crus Classés. The château sits on a high ridge just south of the city of Bordeaux, surrounded by vineyards that are four centuries old. Véronique Sanders is the manager, and she said the wine is in such demand these days that it takes her a mere twenty minutes to sell her entire annual production—about 160,000 bottles. England, which ruled the region for three hundred years, is still the top market, but the Japanese and Chinese are buying more and more.

"When I go to Asia, it's like I'm a rock star," she said. In Hong Kong she is asked to autograph bottles and in Japan she was made into a character in a *manga* comic strip. The château has always been part of her life. Her great-grandfather Daniel was a Belgian wine merchant who bought the vineyard in 1955. The family eventually sold the property to Robert Wilmers, an American banker, and his French wife Elisabeth. The Wilmers completely restored the eighteenth-century villa and asked Véronique to stay on, making her the fourth-generation Sanders behind the exclusive label and the rare woman leader in the stuffy wine hierarchy of Bordeaux.

She said one of her first changes as manager was to open the doors of the château to tourism, albeit tourists at the high end.

In 2003, as Bordeaux city was beginning to draw tourists, she had a long conversation with Mr. Wilmers about getting ahead of the trend and using tourism to boost the reputation of Château Haut-Bailly. She said she told him: "Let's consider tourism a new métier, a new profession, in addition to what we do. We need to have a dedicated team for tourism—get organized. If we open up to high-quality tourism, we will be better known as a top-quality wine."

Wilmers agreed despite a high cost that Sanders politely refused to disclose. Sanders showed us how she built the tourism around the heart of the operation. We circled the edge of those formidable old vines raised without chemicals, their heavy fruit about to be harvested by hand and piled in small baskets. Sanders bent down over a squat vine and cradled a bunch of grapes. "This is where all the work is done—90 percent of wine is made here, outside, in the fields."

Next we went to the outbuildings where the alchemy takes place: the vats and cellars. They have been updated but not airbrushed. "My grandfather insisted that cellars be humble; he said they are cellars, not cathedrals."

Then we headed to the small boutique, the first part of the new "métier." The shop sells books, goblets, decanters, aprons, tee-shirts, but very little wine. Château Haut-Bailly is not aiming for the large tour bus crowd that generally buys inexpensive "souvenir" wine. "We want them to buy our wine when they return home," she said.

The true focus of the tourism trade was two new large reception and conference rooms built for meetings, seminars, meals and tastings. Lunches are served at $154 per person and dinners at $196 a person, always accompanied by a variety of the château's wines. To insure the food matched the wine, Sanders hired a young chef from a three-star restaurant to supervise the kitchen.

At first, her boss wondered why he was shelling out so much money for these "indirect benefits," said Sanders, but now he is a convert. She has no trouble filling up her bookings with Frenchmen and foreigners who don't flinch at paying these prices for the chance to dine at one of Bordeaux's majestic wineries.

Afterward, we tasted that wine in the château's airy salon and over lunch in the classic high-ceilinged dining room. The menu was haute cuisine: small plates of foie gras with quail and grape, then lamb and gnocchi, Dutch cheese and candied peach, ending with figs and red fruit.

We were now six: Véronique, her husband Alexander Van Beek, who is the director of two nearby châteaux, and another couple who own a glossy French magazine, *Vins & Spiritueux*. Finally, I asked about Juppé and tourism. There was uniform enthusiasm. No Gallic shrugs, no mouths turned down at the corner, no acid asides.

"He is an excellent mayor. It helps a lot that Bordeaux has had a face-lift and is pulling in so many new tourists," said Van Beek, who added that his wineries are making a handsome profit in this new era.

For all of these changes, we felt we were back in the late nineteenth century while driving through wine country on our way back to the city. The landscape and the mood, the dominance of those vineyards, still have the feel of the novels of François Mauriac, the Bordeaux native who won the Nobel Prize in Literature in 1952.

"There we stood together," he wrote in *The Knot of Vipers.* "The future harvest of the grapes was fermenting under the blue-tinted leaves, drowsing in the sun."

Many of the old Bordeaux families from the Mauriac novels still live in the region and have proved less hidebound than their reputation. Olivier Cuvelier, a wine trader and member of one of those families, said the change in Bordeaux, and the influx of tourism, has been "huge, huge, and very strong. Before, we were important here, in the region. Now we sell around the world."

The transformation coincided with the explosion of wine drinking in countries that had never indulged before—especially in Asia. Now Bordeaux hosts regular wine expositions and the only problem is the lack of enough good hotel rooms. "Our city breathes again, we welcome visitors, and our wine is selling."

More people travel, more people drink wine, more people come to newly revived Bordeaux. Tourism, once a negligible part of the economy, now brings in 1 billion euros, or $1.4 billion, a year to the region, second only to wine in economic importance. And receipts for wine are growing; they are now up to 3 billion euros, or $4.1 billion, a year. Each nurtures the other.

I spent five days trying to find a tourism skeptic in Bordeaux and I failed. Typical was Yves Harté, the associate director of the *Sud Ouest*, the top newspaper of the Bordeaux region. He moved to Bordeaux when it was at its worst. "I wrote the story of the last cargo ship to make a delivery to Bordeaux. It was around 1980 and the ship was named the Yo *Pugon* and was carrying trunks of wood from Africa," he said. "I used the event to write a portrait of the city. Then it was closed, hidden, very dark, its charm disappearing."

We were having coffee in the city's spacious central plaza, which is flanked on one side by the restored opera house, at one time the largest in Europe, and on the other by a mansion that is now the city's only five-star hotel. I told Harté that I was naturally suspicious of the Cinderella story about a politician resurrecting the city. Juppé is a brilliant former prime minister from a conservative political party who was on the path toward even higher office when he was convicted in 2004 of misusing public funds for his political party, in effect taking the fall for his party's corruption. While he was prime minister, Juppé was also mayor of Bordeaux. (In France officials can hold several offices at the same time.)

Harté laughed. "I am sure, without a doubt, that none of this transformation of Bordeaux would have happened without Juppé," he said. "He changed the whole look of the city, and rapidly. Before, we used cars for everything, now we walk and we have the tramway. . . . We are all rediscovering our city."

So are tourists. Walking around Bordeaux, across the clean modern tramway tracks, past the golden stone façades of the Old Town's eighteenth-century architecture and over to the glorious promenades along the river, it was clear the town's rejuvenation was contemplated with tourism in mind. There was evidence everywhere. L'Intendant, the city's famous wine shop with an interior shaped like the Guggenheim Museum, has a full-time Chinese sales clerk. The tables at the two-star St. James restaurant are filled with foreign tourists like my husband and me.

Charlie Matthews, a thirty-six-year-old Englishman fluent in French, agreed. He left his job as a wine salesman in London and moved to Bordeaux a few years ago to join the tourism gold rush. As Bordeaux beautified, he saw a niche for himself. No one was doing wine tourism. Through his contacts selling the wine of various châteaux in the region, he put together a tour agency to bring Brits to Bordeaux to visit those châteaux and drink their wine. "I knew the English market very well and the French market. I wanted to be in France," he said.

Like everyone else in Bordeaux, he aimed for the top. Matthews's tour agency is called Bordeaux Uncorked, which for $1,600 a person, offers a visit of four nights and three days through the city and top vineyards. Each tour is tailor-made "to avoid château fatigue." Within one year Matthews was making a good profit with a staff of two—himself and his wife. His core clients, he said, are the exclusive clubs of London: "The Carlton Club, the St. James Club—the traditional market where red wine, or claret, always means a glass of Bordeaux."

When the tour is made up of men from an elite London club, it includes meals in the best châteaux. "These clubs buy lots of wine and that will open doors."

It all seemed of a piece, this renovation and the tourism boom. I asked Stephan Delaux, the president of the Bordeaux Tourism Bureau and the deputy mayor of the city, how it had happened, the chicken-and-egg question about which came first. Delaux had been at Juppé's side as the plan for the city took form.

He gave me a surprising answer. On the one hand, Juppé's plan was to rejuvenate the city, he said, not bring in tourism, and that was why it succeeded. The key to good tourism is to do your planning for the people who live there, for the citizens, and if that is done well, then the visitor will be happy. At the same time, Delaux said he and the mayor knew from the first days that "very clearly the project will be the foundation for creating Bordeaux as a tourist destination."

"I was born here, I've lived here all my life and I know the beauty of Bordeaux, it is part of me," he said. "We had been a city of millionaires fascinated by the river and trade since the eighteenth century, a golden age . . . then Bordeaux lost its role, no trade, no industry, and we treated our city's patrimony badly . . . our wines are absolutely magical, so why wasn't Bordeaux seductive, too?"

Delaux said the tourism campaigns were planned in parallel with Juppé's urban renewal. "Before, Bordeaux was absolutely not touristic—no, not at all. Tourists were condescending towards Bordeaux. They were only interested in the vineyards."

The public works proceeded apace, cleaning the city, uncovering buildings that had been shrouded in two centuries of filth. "We were shocked by its beauty."

The tourism policy was built around the city and the wine—"le vin et la ville"—and coordinated between the city, region, and national governments and tourism agencies. Delaux said it would take days to describe the system.

In 2002, while the city was still torn apart by construction of the tramways and landscaping the river front, Delaux tested the waters and invited travel writers to Bordeaux. Success. From the *New York Times*: "With layers of grime stripped away, the true, tawny splendor of elegant neo-Classical cornices, pediments and porticoes has re-emerged. The effect is spectacular."

Five years later the renovation was complete. In 2008, after serious lobbying, greatly aided by Juppé's connections, Bordeaux was named a World Heritage Site by UNESCO, the United Nations' cultural organization. Half of the old city was declared to be of universal significance worth preserving. Within the tourism industry, recognition as a World Heritage Site is the equivalent of winning four stars for a restaurant or an Olympic gold medal for an athlete. Bordeaux's profile as a top tourist destination soared.

"Now everything has changed. Tourists came from around the world. Starred chefs came to open restaurants.... Families came.... Deluxe tourists came. *Tout le monde*," said Delaux.

And tourism to Bordeaux and the region went from a negligible industry to the second-biggest source of income.

Mr. Juppé was out of the country when I visited Bordeaux; I later met him in Washington, where he was on an official visit to the Pentagon. After his official talks he had a short time to talk about Bordeaux.

"I was not surprised by the success of our project," he said. "I was reassured. Bordeaux is extremely attractive now."

On the role of tourism, Juppé was just as strong. "Surely, I thought, it will be attractive to tourists. And that was very, very important that it attract tourists. That would be our financial foundation. Those fifteen years of work of rejuvenation led to Bordeaux becoming a World Heritage city."

When I asked how much it helped that he was a mayor with national and international experience and connections, he smiled again. "Ah, that is a specialty of France. That we work at all levels. Above all, yes, it helps very much that I had been a minister and a mayor. It works together."

One of the most perceptive comments came from Robert Parker, the

American wine expert who is careful with his praise. Parker has visited Bordeaux as often as three times a year for decades to taste and give scores to the wine. His ratings are revered and feared the world over.

After the renovation Parker gave the city of Bordeaux a personal rating: "I remember the old days and the rotten, abandoned buildings on the waterfront; now it is a ravishing destination."

"Tourism cannot be outsourced." Philippe Maud'hui of ATOUT France made that declaration in his crowded office on the Place de Catalogne, surrounded by stacks of documents and data showing how much tourism contributes to the economy and how. It is so obvious it was startling. But the fact that tourism is the rare industry that will never be replaced by factories in Vietnam or by I.T. centers in India is often forgotten, he said, and another reason why the French government is investing time and energy in it.

ATOUT France alone has 480 employees, more than half of whom are posted overseas to thirty-five countries to sell the merits of a vacation in France as tourism diplomats. The newest offices were opened in Brazil, China and India. The agency's budget is $106 million, with only $46 million paid by the national government. (The rest comes from private businesses and local public partners.) While Maud'hui says this isn't enough to keep up with the competition, it is enough to underwrite the extensive research done to help shape government policy, describe tourism's economic contributions, pinpoint who comes to France and why, and then plot the future.

In a series of interviews in Paris, Maud'hui and other French officials gave me thick books with a full profile of tourists and tourism in France: which nationality prefers to come to Paris for luxury shopping, who goes hiking in the mountains, who goes to casinos and who rents homes in the countryside. They know that Disneyland outside of Paris is the most visited site and that the Louvre remains the most popular museum in France, and the world. Germans and the British are the most numerous by far. Americans rank eighth but are falling behind.

"By 2020 more Chinese will visit France than Americans," said Christian Delom, also of ATOUT. "That means we have to make many changes

. . . more Chinese-French restaurants, Chinese speakers in luxury-goods stores, and monitoring Chinese tour agencies."

These tourists are spending money throughout the economy. Marco Marchetti, of the Ministry of Culture, gave me a 2009 study showing that heritage tourism, by the French and foreigners, contributed $20 billion to the French economy. It was important data to have as the government began slashing budgets during the Great Recession and culture looked vulnerable. The study showed a solid return on the government investment and that rather than costing money, "protected heritage is an important source of jobs and revenue."

When the global recession hit in 2008, all European governments re-examined their budgets, cutting back across the board. In France, though, the Culture Ministry's budget was spared the worst. In 2010, France actually increased its culture budget by 2.7 percent, while most European countries were slashing theirs. Frédéric Mitterrand, the minister of culture, said this showed that "the cultural offering is a determining element in our attractiveness as a country and its economic development."

Adding to the culture budget reflects the overall design of French tourism. In the age of global homogeneity, when a luxury shopping mall in Dubai looks an awful lot like the new malls in Shanghai, French tourism is definitely and obsessively moving in the opposite direction. It is concentrating on what is unique, digging down, not flattening out, and betting on what can never be outsourced.

All the other tourism policies flow from this: avoiding mass tourism, tying the country together with efficient public transportation, taking advantage of often impossibly rigorous environmental regulations, and leaving it up to the locals to decide what's best for them.

"We rejected the models found in Spain and Morocco of resorts with everything included, especially beach resorts. It goes against who we are. Our accent is on cultural tourism, on local tourism. We make great efforts to oblige tourists to meet French people. Sure we have the Riviera and Deauville, but they are the exception," said Delom, director of strategy for the French tourism agency.

I stumbled across an unexpected example of this a few years earlier when I interviewed the deputy secretary of planning at the French Ministry of Agriculture about a completely different trade issue. Behind his desk I noticed three large colored maps; two seemed out of place. One traced the passenger train lines spread across France like overlapping spider webs. The second was sprinkled with symbols representing the annual cultural events. The third was a typical topographical map showing arable lands.

Alain Moulinier, then the deputy minister, explained that the maps showed how agriculture and tourism need each other. "Tourism brings in three times more money than agriculture," he said, and the appeal of France to tourists is rooted in its landscape and cuisine, in its countryside or "*la France profonde.*" The trains take the tourists around the country. The festivals are spread out to attract visitors to every corner of France and spread the wealth. And the farmers raise the food that will fill their plates at remote one-star restaurants.

To keep that countryside beautiful, France slowly developed layers of rules and regulations that many farmers and developers find odious. All of the coasts are public preserves—from the sandy strands of the Mediterranean to the cliffs along the English Channel stormed on D-Day. "We can't fill our beaches with hotels like Spain; they are all protected," said Delom.

"It's not perfect, but what we try to do is have national laws for protecting nature. Then with development codes and work rules we have created the qualifications we need to reject industrial tourism."

The attention to detail spans the ministries, including farm subsidies, either from the French government or the European Union. I met Christian Vachier, the last sheep farmer in his small commune in the mountains of the Lubéron in the northern regions of Provence, not far from Bordeaux. During most of the year Vachier raised his flock on thirty-six acres of pasture. In the summer he sent them off to wild mountain meadows where they grazed a wide swath that acted as a firebreak in the hot, dry forests. This traditional, land-intensive and expensive form of animal husbandry was underwritten by checks from the E.U. and the French government and done with the full approval of the tourism side of government since Vachier and his lambs preserve the landscape. And once slaughtered, the lamb is featured in smart restaurants in nearby Aix-en-Provence, which in turn brings in more tourists.

"Those beautiful landscapes—hills, pretty forest, vineyards—are largely maintained by man. In France we don't forget this is why many tourists come here," said Patrick Falcone of the Ministry of Agriculture. "Now each region has to decide what is acceptable before it opens up. Tourism has to improve the economy, for as many as can benefit, and improve the local quality of life—perhaps create more public spaces, improve cultural life, build a new railway station . . . maybe bring better train or bus service."

When all of that has been accomplished, the marketing campaign kicks in. These campaigns with catchy slogans receive the lion's share of attention. National tour agencies spend millions on the ads that pop up on the computer screen, the lush color enticements on television and the full-page advertisements in the newspapers and magazines. Behind these schemes is the data collected that tell the French how to sell their country overseas: outdoor adventure and camping to the Dutch, city and urban vacations to Americans, cultural events to Brazilians. Their marketing force is divided into three groups: Europe and Africa; the Americas; Asia and the Middle East. And it is divided by specialties: urban and rural with river, forest, camping and mountain specialties; families, senior citizens, youth, gays and the handicapped; sports, service and study; culture, wine and cuisine; and special events. The list is endless.

Jean-Philippe Pérol heads the American division from his office in New York. He told me that France has evolved into a brand that appeals to what is known as the "global village" tourists. "They have a higher education, with the kind of lifestyle that means they travel a lot, expect luxury and look for the trendy hotel, the trendy exhibit. That is what we do well."

These marketing campaigns are done as if France were a commodity, a product. Officials said they have to protect their brand, or label, that tourists have to feel they receive high quality at a reasonable price—a goal more than a few might question when faced with the high prices in Paris. And every year, like good corporate executives, the government tourist officials put out an annual Report on Activity that runs over 120 pages and reads like a corporate report to shareholders.

For all of their successes, and their role as a world leader, French tourism is still plagued with problems. Some are predictable, such as underinvestment in lodging in many areas, with an insufficient number of hotel rooms in new markets (like Bordeaux) and not enough vacation homes to rent (Provence). Crowds are also growing unmanageable in the summer in Paris. The Left Bank is colonized by visitors during July and August, and popular spots like Giverny, the former home of Claude Monet, become mob scenes on many weekends.

At Giverny you feel the familiar twinge of regret at the sight of the intimate home of a revered artist forever fossilized for visiting crowds. It is the price for preserving the stunning flower beds that Monet planted in splashes of bright colors just as he painted his landscapes. Tourists who take photographs on the bridge over the famous lily pond later buy coffee mugs, straw hats like the one worn by Monet and posters at the cavernous gift shop in a former studio. In 2010 those visitors included Brazilians in large numbers, Americans visiting from a cruise ship, Danes, Swedes, Italians and a large number of Japanese. This is a museum after all, and generous benefactors, led by Americans, saved Giverny. "We don't understand why so many tourists like to visit the homes where artists painted their works," said Marchetti. "But it enriches our patrimony."

The question more than a few French are asking is whether in this age of tourism their country has gotten so used to being admired by the throngs peering at their "patrimony" that a subtle shift is taking place and France is failing to produce more artistic wunderkinds like Monet.

That question feeds into the French feeling that there is something unhealthy about this tourism, that it desecrates their lives, and reduces their country to that product sold by the marketers. This uncertainty only deepens as tourism penetrates into more pockets of life in France.

Many are reluctant to acknowledge how pervasive tourism has become. Nina Sutton, a lifelong Parisian and a close friend of mine, is a prime example. She is a first-class journalist and writer who rose in the ranks when women were still rare, living through the ups and downs of raising two daughters while maintaining a career. Now that her children are grown, she rents out one of her two adjoining apartments to tourists. Her apartment in Montmartre is the epitome of late-nineteenth-century Victorian Paris, with her family's paintings and furnishings evoking that luxurious era. She has no problem renting her flat; the income is a boon. Yet no one is more eloquent about the downside of tourism than Nina.

"I worry that we will become commodities in tourism. Motor coaches pollute the air to stop for five minutes in front of Notre Dame, five minutes at the Tour Eiffel. Herds of tourists who do not respect or appreciate what they're seeing," she said.

When I asked her how she squared that with her small tourism operation, she sounded like the tourism officials I had just interviewed in her city. "My visitors aren't like that at all. They are precisely the kind of people you want to meet. That is the key to productive tourism, to respect each other. The British are the best," she said.

Alain Minc, an economist and close advisor to former President Sarkozy, confirmed this ambivalence at the highest level. Minc said that he was never able to engage Sarkozy on the subject of tourism—diplomacy, war and peace, yes, but not tourism even in the depths of the world crisis of 2009.

"There was never any discussion by the president about the importance of tourism to the economy, not even during the recession," said Minc. "I'm convinced with the right policy we could have even more tourism, but it was not easy to convince him to do more. He told me, 'We are the number-one tourism place in the world. Why do we need to change?' "

Minc said tourism is of sufficient economic importance that French ambassadors around the globe should consider encouraging tourism part of their portfolios. "Tourism should be a business of diplomacy. There is nothing more cosmopolitan than tourism," he said in his high-ceilinged office with its outsize Richard Avedon portrait of Samuel Beckett. "We have such a competitive advantage."

But the biggest problem brought on by tourism is the same one threatening many countries in Europe. What keeps officials awake at night is the fear that too many tourists are buying second homes in France, a phenomenon that is snowballing and pushing locals out of their homes. Cities aren't immune. In some neighborhoods of Paris, such as the popular sixth arrondissement on the Left Bank where I once lived, foreigners are colonizing apartment buildings and the local café is giving way to brand-name luxury stores like Ralph Lauren. "There are *quartiers* where most Parisians can't afford to live anymore," said Maud'hui.

In the French countryside some villages are nearly ghost towns in the winter when the second homes are boarded up and their wealthy owners return to their lives in another country. Local shopkeepers disappear and the village is without the *boulangerie*, the café or the grocery store.

"In France, too, tourism can be an illness, a malady," said Falcone, of the Agriculture Ministry. "You have the big problem of second homes that raises the prices for all homes. It becomes more and more difficult for locals to buy, and they move. This undermines your village life and soon your rural life."

The trade-offs are difficult. In the seventies and into the nineties, foreigners played the opposite role, buying decrepit buildings for a song, restoring them and bringing life back to many isolated villages. Peter Mayle, a British writer, made a small fortune writing about his life in Provence beginning with his trials while redoing a two-hundred-year-old farmhouse in *A Year in Provence* and then living the dream of the French "vie en rose" in *Toujours Provence*. Those days are over, and now the French fear they might be reaching the point of no return.

France may suffer from too many fans. Despite its reputation as overpriced, France is consistently rated as one of the best countries for retirement, for "luxury on a budget." *Forbes* magazine called it especially friendly for American retirees because of its high-quality, low-cost health care system. Europeans have voted it one of their favorite retirement spots because, in the words of the *London Daily Mail*, France is "sheets ahead of its European counterparts for quality of life."

That indescribable charm and *joie de vivre* was uppermost in the mind of Ambassador Frances Cook when she bought a second home in France. Retired from the U.S. Foreign Service, she is now chair of an international consulting firm based in Washington and traveling often. Her roots in France are deep, beginning with a junior year abroad in Aix-en-Provence and continuing with official assignments in Paris. She wanted to live in the south, in Provence, in an apartment with character. When canvassing the region to look for such a gem, she had one stipulation. She would only buy in a village with a thriving primary school. "I didn't want to buy into a dying town or a town that was all foreigners, and the best gauge is the school," she said.

She found her ideal apartment in a restored convent in Bargemon, a village in the foothills not far from Saint-Tropez. When in Bargemon her days are spent with the French villagers and doing the rounds at the cafés, restaurants, greengrocers, hairdresser, *boulangerie* and *boucherie*. The village boasts two pharmacies, two medical clinics, ten art galleries and studios, a garage, a bank, a plumber, three electricians, a mason and several general contractors. The caliber of the musical concerts at the village church is astonishing and religious feasts are celebrated with the sincerity of earlier eras.

At the same time, Cook is part of a thriving foreign community dominated by Europeans who have moved to this Var region permanently and others, like Cook, with second-home hideaways. The British outnumber all others and publish a community newsletter called the *Var Village Voice*, which they began in 1995. (There are roughly 200,000 Brits living permanently in France—most clustered in the south or up north along the English Channel.)

It is idyllic in the Var and the *Var Village Voice* chronicles the rarefied expatriate lifestyle: news of wine tastings, a citrus fruit festival, art exhibits—often by foreign artists—new restaurants, choral ensembles, truffle festivals, operas, balls, and appreciative letters like this one from a man who identified himself only as Graham. He wrote: "We enjoyed as always the Christmas edition and put the Foies Gras article to good use, much to the amusement of the shop in Le Touquet as we read each label with care avoiding the tins which he was keen to move. . . ."

But some stories about the "ugly foreigner" seep into these otherwise light news items. Some of the expatriates are more famous than others: actor John Malkovich, Peter Mayle (of *Toujours Provence*) and Ridley Scott, the English film director. Scott made headlines for launching a "chicken war" against his French neighbors who raise poultry. Sir Ridley complained that the "chickens cackled offensively and the smell wafted into his property," according to the *Var Voice*, which noted that Christophe

Orset, the neighboring chicken farmer, has lived in the village for thirty years, while Sir Ridley visits only a few weeks a year. The courts threw out the case and the famous director lost his chicken war.

That battle between Scott and the chicken farmers is something of a metaphor for the French fear of foreigners upending their lifestyle. The French prefer foreign owners like Ambassador Cook, who consciously tries to support the French lifestyle in all of its quirkiness and not fight against it. But they are looking warily at what is happening to other European countries to see how to avoid matters getting out of hand.

Recently a British government report on rural living loudly warned that rich foreigners and British citizens, especially from London, were buying so many second or vacation homes that local residents couldn't afford to live in their villages. They had become "ghettos of the very rich and elderly" without the working people and families needed to keep villages alive. The language was more dire and vivid than the warning in France in part because much of the best regions of rural England have already been ceded to the second-home world. The report, called "Living Working Countryside," was published in 2008 and painted a picture of real estate prices out of reach of locals. The answer, said Matthew Taylor, the report's author, was not to build more houses willy-nilly, which would destroy the rural countryside and turn it into a "Costa Brava" of concrete. Instead, the report recommended methods to use zoning laws to restrict second-home buyers and to encourage the construction of "social homes" at low prices for locals. Cornwall, at the southwestern tip of England, has become an extreme case. It is the wealthiest county in England because of the predominance of rich second-home owners. Yet it has such deep pockets of poverty that it is the only county in England that qualifies for emergency poverty funding from the E.U. It is a grim picture of what happens when the balance tips in favor of wealthy second-home owners. Instead of reviving a dying town, these outsiders buy it out from under the locals. But British officials, many of whom own second homes, refused to take action to restrict them. Lord Taylor wrote to me in an email that he had been "made aware in advance that (second homes) was the one area that the government would not touch—either because they were unconvinced there was any need, or—in my view—because it was too much of a hot potato."

The French have more safeguards to allow locals to control their development through zoning and development rules. In extreme cases mayors can purchase a home or a *boulangerie* for the village and then rent it out to a French citizen to maintain the "equilibrium." Or the mayor can freeze new development.

"Tourism development must, must work for the local population," said Maud'hui of ATOUT. "There is a limit when foreigners owning a second home change the economy and the environment. Say 15 percent or 20 percent may be the limit. Eventually too many foreigners will narrow the future."

And that is when tourism becomes that nightmare the French most fear. "We are far, far from that, but we think about it," said Maud'hui.

France, the gold standard for tourism, with strong government support to protect local communities, still has to work overtime to avoid the pitfalls of mass tourism. In Venice, tourism has already undermined its way of life.

3

POSTCARD FROM VENICE

Matteo Gabbrielli was easy to spot in the early-morning rush of tourists at St. Mark's Square. Slender, dark hair peeking out from his 1920s cap, narrow brown eyes and that arresting Venetian nose—he had to be our local guide.

"You are Matteo?" I said as we sat down for a coffee and pastry on a cool June morning. Bill and I had arrived the day before on the overnight train from Paris. Even after several visits to Venice, the first sight of the city never fails to take my breath away. I was muttering about the city's insane beauty, the light on the water, the masterpieces in the churches, Matteo nodding his head. Then I asked why only Japanese were lining up outside the basilica. "They are always the first to come. They spend fifty-five minutes on culture, then one hour buying souvenirs—'Venetian' masks made in China—then back to their buses."

How could they come all the way to Venice and spend only one hour seeing the glories of one of the world's great cities? This former Mediterranean empire was home to merchants who traded in all corners of the known world, a naval power that conquered cities as mighty as Constantinople and a cultural mecca whose artists created a treasure-house of churches and paintings, sculptures and bells ringing over noble palazzos from the Renaissance and Gothic eras.

Matteo shook his head. "Venice is dying, slowly, slowly. But it is dying." He wasn't referring to the classic Venetian problem of rising water. A flood in 1966 nearly destroyed the foundations of this magical city of islands. That near disaster spawned countless "Save Venice" committees and convinced donors and governments to spend $4 billion constructing an underwater system of sluice gates between Venice and the sea that will limit the flooding of the city. The United Nations' UNESCO has an office in Venice to oversee this and the newer problem of global warming that has added to the issue of rising waters.

The disease that Matteo believes is killing Venice is tourism; the crowds of tourists gathering all around us, crowds descending from enormous cruise ships whose wakes often cause more damage to the city foundations than the famous "aqua alta" following heavy rains. Tourism is hollowing out the city. Venetians are being pushed out by businesses that cater to tourists with the blessing of the city fathers. Rents are astronomical. Real estate is prohibitively expensive. Zoning favors the hotel business and international chains rather than local businesses or local residents. The population of the historic city has dropped to 59,000 today from 164,000 at its peak. Every year 20-to-24 million visitors descend on Venice. That means that on any given day, there are always more tourists than Venetians. If and when the waters again flood Venice, only the tourists will be threatened, he said with black humor.

"It would be hypocrisy for me to complain about tourism but, yes, tourism is killing Venice," he said. Matteo pointed toward the square, rousing us to our feet with descriptions of the Byzantine and Renaissance roots of the masterworks around us. He holds a doctorate in archeology, with a specialty in Islamic architecture, and spent five years on excavation projects until most of that work disappeared as budgets were cut. Determined to stay in Venice, he sat for the tour guide examination, passed and became one of only 200 guides wearing the badge of an official guide. (In Rome, he said, the city gives out 3,000 tour guide badges.) We were the beneficiaries of his studies. Guidebooks alone don't begin to give you the sense of place and history that someone like Matteo provides. From plaza to plaza, he pointed out the Byzantine influence in archways, the Gothic traits in decorations. What booty came from the Venetians' endless naval victories; which paintings celebrated divine intervention in those battles. We stopped at a *fondaco*, a building that was once a state-owned storage and living space that traced its name to the Arabic word for "warehouse." The famous merchants of Venice bought and sold their goods from these *fondacos*: the warehouse was on the ground level, offices on the first floor, living quarters on the second floor and servants' quarters on the top. We passed through twisted, narrow alleys without seeing another tour group. "Most tourists don't go beyond St. Mark's or the Rialto Bridge, missing most of the city."

Matteo's parents are native Venetians who were forced out when the price of living rose beyond their means. He has gone to great lengths to become an official resident, refusing to relinquish the city to tourists, especially wealthy foreigners looking for a vacation home. "Mine is a mission of repopulation with Venetians—it is idealism."

I thought of those French tourism officials who said their greatest fear was too many foreigners buying up property until entire villages lost their souls. And I thought of the British lawmaker who tried to put a hold on more foreigners buying up properties in rural England. Venice most nearly reflects the real nightmare of those officials. The city has become so popular with foreigners buying up properties, hotels replacing homes, and poorly regulated tourism, that locals are being forced to abandon the city.

The three men arrived on time for a 10:30 morning coffee near the Rialto Bridge. Flavio Gregori, a professor of English at Università Ca' Foscari. Claudio Paggiarin, an architect. Marco Malafante, tourism professional. The last two are Venetian natives; the professor is a long-time resident. They agreed to give up a Saturday morning with their families to explain to me why they were active in 40xVenezia, an organization of mostly young professionals in their forties dedicated to reining in the runaway tourism in Venice.

The sun was scorching. We found a café on the canal with umbrellas and ordered drinks. The men started talking at once, laughing as they interrupted each other.

First, the problem as they saw it: "When our population reaches under

60,000, Venice stops existing as a living city. We are worried from several points of view. All the prices are boosted up by tourism. Whenever there is a palace for sale, it's very likely to be bought by a major hotel corporation. I used to work in a palazzo, now it's been sold by the university and it will become a hotel," said Flavio, the English professor.

When they saw their lives in Venice threatened, they created 40xVenezia in November 2007.

Claudio picked up the story. "We felt excluded from the government and the decisions of the city. Our coming-out was a demonstration '*Venezia non è un albergo*'—'Venice is not a hotel.'"

Since this is Venice, the demonstration they held the next spring was anything but ordinary. At the sound of the noon bells of San Marco nearly 1,000 protesters froze like statues. When the bells stopped, they all applauded and then rushed behind an enormous banner that said VENEZIA NON È UN ALBERGO. The police arrived on the scene.

"The children held the banner. The chief of police took it away from them and the children started crying. And the tourists took pictures," said Claudio.

The group was protesting a proposed law to further expand the dwellings in the city that can rent rooms to tourists. Already the city had allowed the number of properties offering tourist accommodations to rise by 450 percent since 2002. (The city leaders had also granted permission for double the number of cruise ships to visit Venice.) "*Basta*—enough" they said.

The protesters won; the law didn't pass, but the city still felt imperiled. The next year another group of protesters—younger and more daring—staged a mock funeral for the death of Venice. They placed a plywood coffin painted neon pink into a gondola and floated it down the Grand Canal, again at noon to the sound of the bells of San Marco. The citizens of Venice were finding their voice.

"We're not opposed to tourism," said Marco, the tourism professional. "We're opposed to losing our city to tourism."

Evidence of that loss is all around.

"Here's an example," said Flavio, the professor. "A few years ago, I had to dash to my butcher for meat for dinner and wasn't paying much attention to where I was going. I entered a shop and realized I had made a mistake. It was a souvenir store selling masks. I said I was sorry and was about to leave when they said, no, I wasn't mistaken. The butcher couldn't pay the higher rent and they had replaced him. The next year I lost my greengrocer and then my neighborhood bakery. Now I wait in long lines with the tourists at a new bakery. It's the same boarding a vaporetto (boat taxi). Sometimes you can't get in, waiting behind tourists. Try going around the streets with a baby stroller—it's about impossible with the crowds."

Real estate prices are astronomical because zoning laws have loosened up, favoring wealthy foreigners and international companies. Even the laws meant to protect locals are poorly enforced, these men said. People buy houses and pretend they are primary residences but then rent them out under the table to tourists. In sum, locals can no longer afford to live and own a business in Venice and are forced to leave for the mainland. As they disappear, so too do the clinics, schools and other services necessary for a city in a seemingly endless chain of cause and effect.

"Just apply the law. Everything has to compete with tourism for space: student housing for our universities versus hotels; workers' housing versus hotels; local shops versus souvenir shops and big-name designer boutiques. There is no space for locals. We always lose," said Claudio. "Our politicians have to consider the social consequences of giving in to the tourism lobby—it is so powerful with so much money. We want the Venetian leaders to acknowledge that this is our city; that we deserve to live within our own patrimony."

The 40xVenezia group has remedies. First, they want authorities to enforce all the laws against cheap foreign copies pretending to be fine Venetian crafts. Murano blown glass has been undercut by cheap foreign copies, leading to more local unemployment. Kempinski Hotels recently bought up one of those abandoned factories on the island of Murano. The press release announcing this new hotel said: "This veritable gem of a building offers dazzling vistas across the lagoon to Venice and is directly connected to Rio dei Vetrai Canal. Apart from its outstanding location, the hotel will feature approximately 150 rooms and suites, a sun terrace, bar with a terrace, café, spa area and fitness center, a ballroom as well as meeting and convention facilities."

With factories transformed to hotels, "Murano glass" as well as souvenir masks are more likely to be mass-produced in China than made in Italy.

To alter the city leaders' fixation on tourism, the group has asked that the city's books and audits be opened up to determine how much the city, and the city's inhabitants, actually gain from tourism and how much goes into deep pockets elsewhere. They want to regulate the number of tourists. They want to reroute the cruise ships out of the canal to sail directly to the mainland, eliminating the damage being done in their wakes. "Why not send them around so they drop off their tourists to take small boats and buses? The majority of Venetians don't like these cruise ships smashing into our city. Don't let them just dive into the city as if we were their theme park."

"You could organize tourism better and at the same time give other industries a chance to exist in this town," said Marco, the tourism expert, who listed a better Internet system, protection of traditional artisans, emphasis on education and high-end conferences.

Several groups even challenged whether Venice should continue to enjoy the status as a United Nations World Heritage Site if local and national leaders refuse to protect it. UNESCO, the U.N. agency that oversees those sites, paid for a full-page advertisement recently praising the "collective riches" of the city and warning that tourism "could help send the vulnerable Venice to a watery grave." UNESCO recommended a combination of putting a physical ceiling on the number of visitors, diffusing the flow of tourists, coordinating bookings and offering incentives "to make tourists more aware of the challenges."

There was more. We spent an hour going through the need for subsidized housing for the working class, new laws to preserve public spaces and services like health care, schools, sanitation and high-speed Internet. The city had to concentrate on reducing expenses for the inhabitants, to create "the political will to make things happen outside tourism. Otherwise, Venice becomes a golden cage."

We finally rose from the table. I was depressed by the litany of wrongs afflicting this city, described as the "greatest surviving work of art in the world" by Evelyn Waugh.

I took refuge in the Church of San Giorgio Maggiore, the Palladio masterpiece, to remind myself why Venice is known as "Serenissima," the Most Serene One. One hour at the church, whose exterior pillars open into the sunlit altar, paintings and sculpture, and I recovered from the dispiriting conversation with those Venetians who had to live with the worst of tourism. I met Bill back at our hotel, the Pensione La Calcina. It is informally known as the Ruskin house because the English art historian John Ruskin stayed there while researching his influential *Stones of Venice*, a multivolume examination of the art and architecture of Venice published in the 1850s. The city was already considered an open-air museum by then, thanks in part to Lord Byron's verses about the city of canals as a decadent former beauty. "Venice once was dear/ the pleasant place of all festivity/ the revel of the earth/ the masque of Italy." In his classic novel *Death in Venice*, published on the eve of World War I, Thomas Mann famously described the city as "half fairy tale and half tourist trap."

So while the current crisis was long in the making, it was now being pushed over the edge by twenty-first-century industrial mass tourism.

The next morning as we sipped coffee looking out across the Giudecca Canal, a cruise ship sailed right in front of us: then another and another. Bill counted five within the hour. Passengers were lined up against the deck railings, looking down on us while amplifiers blared out incomprehensible remarks about the city. This time we didn't look at the ships as a weird oddity but from the viewpoint of the Venetians we had met over the week—Marco, Flavio, Claudio and Matteo. They were worried about the flood of tourists and the pollution from the diesel engines that are kept running while the ships are docked (the engines act as their major power source). The air pollution from just one of the docked giant ships is the equivalent of 12,000 idling cars every day. In a city that bans automobiles, that is a major source of air pollution.

With our new vision, we headed toward St. Mark's, going by vaporetto, the efficient if crowded water bus system of the city. We caught a boat at the Accademia stop and crossed the Grand Canal in search of a true Venetian souvenir. Along the way we started counting the oversized advertisements hanging like banners from building scaffolding with photographs of famous actors selling designer clothes, champagne, watches, and perfumes. While Venetians may abhor these ads, the city says it has no choice but to accept them in order to pay for the necessary preservation work being done behind the scaffolding. This is Italy, after all, one of the worst-governed countries in Europe, with corruption and mismanagement at all levels. It is also the country with the most historical treasures; Venetians know that they can't rely on often-unscrupulous politicians in Rome to fully fund their budget for restoration and preservation. Since all of the advertising money goes directly to those projects, the mayor said there should be no complaints. Commercialize this city of art in order to save it. Some citizen groups believe a new tax on tourism to cover maintenance costs would be better.

At St. Mark's Square we ran into the real problem. We wanted to buy a beautiful piece of Murano glass and instead we ran into blocks of brand-name fashion stores that rivaled the Champs-Élysées of Paris. Familiar Italian names like Prada, Armani, Gucci and Ferragamo were joined by Dior and Burberry. The night before, we had dined at the fabled Osteria da Fiore, an extraordinary one-star restaurant that uses Murano glasses, which enchanted Bill. He asked for the name of the shop where we could buy a good piece of glass. There it was—the Venetian gallery called L'Isola—the one local artisan showroom buried in the midst of those high-end boutiques that you can find in any major shopping city of the world.

We walked in and were stunned. Bright oranges, purples, greens and yellows swirled in playful patterns on perfectly formed goblets, vases and water glasses. I spoke in my mangled French-Spanish hoping to hit upon a word that would sound Italian. The salesman switched to French and after a few minutes asked my nationality. I said American and he smiled, answering in perfect English. "We don't see many Americans anymore. Welcome to our shop."

His name was Brian Tottle. He was British, married to an Italian, and a twenty-six-year veteran of the Venetian glass industry. After we bought a wine carafe, I asked him what had happened to the glass business in Venice.

"Mass tourism," he said. "Cruises, bus tours, they take tourists in boats to the island to so-called glass factories where they are taken into showrooms. Real glass factories are closed to the public," he said.

High-pressure salesmen tell tourists they can buy the glass at a "50 percent discount," but still they pay more than twice what it's worth. It isn't Murano glass. It's shoddy glass mass-produced somewhere else: Taiwan, China, Russia, the Czech Republic—who knows.

"We've complained to the authorities that this is false merchandising. The Chamber of Commerce doesn't do anything to help honest tourism, either."

In the meantime, his company simply refuses to work within that corrupt system. No commissions from tours or taxi boat drivers or concierges to steer business their way. And you will never find phony, knockoff glassware in the store.

Then he walked out on the street with us and pointed out the stores that had been pushed out by the high-fashion stores on his street. "That first alley on the left—it used to have a butcher, a florist and a bread shop. All disappeared. It's only the international fashion people who can afford the rents."

With our package in hand we strolled to a taverna for lunch. Matteo had told us where it was but made us promise to never tell another tourist. And, sure enough, we were the only people in the intimate restaurant who did not speak Italian. The only other foreigner was a Norwegian woman who had lived in Venice for several years and was back visiting friends. The antipasto was a buffet the likes of which I had never seen. I filled my plate with voluptuous red peppers and eggplants dribbled with olive oil from heaven, saving a small space for delicate anchovies. Our entrée was fish, caught that morning and delivered to our table without a word; it glided on our forks. What a luxury to eat at a restaurant that offers one entrée that is the best the day can offer. The only decision we had to make was whether to drink the house red or white wine. Superb!

Back in the street we started noticing the other trend that worried our Venetian friends—the wave of Chinese tourism hitting their already overcrowded city. Matteo had pointed out the pizza parlors and cafés recently purchased by Chinese in order to cater to the rising number of Chinese tourists. I suggested there was something racist about worrying specifically about the Chinese and not, say, the Russians, who are just as likely to buy up property but are harder to distinguish by their looks. No, said Matteo, the Chinese are doing business specifically for Chinese tourists. I countered that this was what international hotel chains did as well. The French want to stay at a Sofitel; Americans at a Marriott. Matteo said it was worse. Some Chinese were caught setting up dress factories in Italy using illegal Chinese labor just to be able to put a "Made in Italy" label on the clothes. I guess it is China's turn to be the "ugly tourist" after we Americans and then the Japanese played the role so well. But then again, only the Chinese are expected to break all records and take 100 million trips every year beginning in 2020.

Donna Leon is the author of a mystery series set in Venice. Guido Brunetti, the series' fictional hero, is a police detective who knows the vaporetto schedule by heart as well as the best trattoria in any neighborhood. In the series, the waters lapping the canals are both welcoming and menacing as Brunetti solves crimes despite endemic corruption and modern intrusions, like tourism. In the novel *A Noble Radiance*, Brunetti says: "I remember when, for a few thousand lire, you could get a good meal at any trattoria or osteria in the city: risotto, fish, a salad and good wine. Nothing fancy, just the good food that the owners probably ate at their own table. But that was when Venice was a city that was alive, that had industry and artisans. Now all we have is tourists, and the rich ones are accustomed to fancy stuff like this. So to appeal to their tastes, we get food that's been made to look pretty."

A few months after our trip we attended a reading by Donna Leon from her latest book—the twentieth of the series. During the question period I asked her to expound a bit on why she writes about tourism as if it were a major problem for Venice.

"It's at the top of the list of problems of anyone who lives in Venice," she answered. "It has changed everyone's life."

Then she recited all of the environmental, social, cultural and financial problems tourism has caused, problems that were now familiar to Bill and me: the homes that are now hotels, the dwindling populations, lost industries, lost jobs and the damage from cruise ships, including the pollution from the engines left idling for power.

"Living in Venice now is like living in a parking lot," she said. "And the city says cruise ships cause no damage."

"So of course people who don't benefit from tourism are distressed at how the city bends over backwards every way it can for tourism," she said, pointing out that there are "perks" to be had by playing along with the industry while publicly claiming to do all that is necessary to limit tourism.

A member of the audience called out that Venice had no choice, that tourism was its only industry.

Leon shot back: "In a way that's like saying to a drug addict mainlining heroin that it's the only life he knows."

Like a drug addiction, she said, the Venetian addiction to tourism was gradual, over three decades, as bit by bit tourism was given special treatment by politicians that led to the disappearance of other businesses and a dramatic rise in costs so that Venice today is "virtually an unlivable city for the average person."

"Venetians who own tourist enterprises—they favor it," she said. She does not: "I think of tourism in terms of drug addiction. It's too late now. It's the only industry."

And as anyone who reads her books knows, Donna Leon has a special passion against those cruise ships.

4

GETTING IT WRONG

The Cambodian War introduced me to the seductive power of tourism. It was the early 1970s. Cambodia was the last country drawn into the larger Vietnam War, and it was being torn apart by massive bombings, indiscriminate shelling and horrifying atrocities. I was a young reporter learning my trade, thankful for any interruption in this progression of death. At the end of a nasty day, when a mortar attack had torn into an open-air marketplace and wounded dozens of women and children, I caught a ride back to the city with Dith Pran, a Cambodian colleague.

My horror subsided during the drive as Dith Pran and I talked about what we had seen and what it meant. To lighten the mood he switched to one of his favorite topics: the monumental temples at Angkor in northwest Cambodia.

"Becker," he said, "you have to see Angkor. I'll show you around, you'll be a tourist."

Dith Pran would later become famous as the hero in the movie *The Killing Fields*, but at that point he was simply a journalist who, like so many other Cambodian journalists, had worked around the temples of Angkor when his country was at peace. When war broke out in 1970, these former tour guides, hotel clerks and drivers were hired immediately by foreign journalists who needed help translating the language and the country. Tour guides knew their way around Cambodia and knew its history. Sok Nguon, who had been trained at the EFEO Center, the French archeology school that restored the Angkor temples and researched their history, was snapped up by Reuters as an interpreter and driver. For them, the temples at Angkor—one of the most elegant wonders of the world—symbolized their country at peace, at its best.

The Communists gained control of the temples in the first days of the war, and they were off-limits to those of us living on the government side. That made them even more beautiful in memory. On the hottest, most dispiriting days, Cambodian journalists would reminisce about driving tourists in a white Mercedes sedan to see the temples at dawn. The wartime markets of Phnom Penh still sold the remaining temple rubbings made of the bas-reliefs along the galleries and courtyards of the most famous temples of Angkor Wat and Angkor Thom, scenes of Hindu and Buddhist gods, demons and dancing angels, the battles with warriors on elephants, all capturing the history and people of the Angkor Empire—"the greatest in ancient Southeast Asia."

The zenith of their life as tour guides was the day in 1967 that Jacqueline Kennedy came to Angkor, "fulfilling a childhood dream." The guides followed *her* around as she climbed the worn stone temple stairs, and saffron-robed monks stole glimpses of her from the shadows. That day the world was reminded of the former glory of Cambodia, a point of pride later on during the war as they saw the country falling apart day by day.

"Becker, you have to see the sun set over Angkor."

The romance of tourism was imprinted on my twenty-five-year-old soul as we moved from one grisly scene to another, often driving in those same white Mercedes that had been used for tourism at Angkor.

Cambodians had to wait twenty more devastating years for peace to come, twenty years of unimaginable hell. The war ended in 1975 but the victorious Khmer Rouge immediately launched a revolution that killed off one-fourth of the people and purposely destroyed most of Cambodia's sophisticated, cultured society. That fatal madness was followed by another decade of decay and neglect as Cambodia was fought over as a dubious prize in the last decade of the Cold War.

The United Nations finally sent a peacekeeping mission to Cambodia in 1993, putting an end to foreign intervention and years of war. They supervised a democratic election, but the losers threatened a civil war if they weren't included in the government. The U.N. gave in to their demands and anointed a joint government that included some brilliant officials, some incompetent officials, many corrupt officials, all working in an atmosphere of mistrust. These were the people charged with reviving a poor, exhausted country with few resources.

They did agree on one matter—tourism would be essential to their recovery. There wasn't much left standing after war, revolution, genocide, famine and degradation: manufacturing had been depleted by 1975; farming was largely at a subsistence level thanks to too many radical experiments; and many of the surviving professionals and educated classes had fled Cambodia for life overseas. Tourism, centered on Angkor, that would attract wealthy middle and adventurous classes, was the only industry that could bring in desperately needed foreign exchange.

This was a somewhat radical idea for a poor country in the early 1990s. If it hadn't been for Angkor and its cultural cachet, Cambodia wouldn't have had a chance at that end of the market. But it made sense at the time, with tourists looking for "exotic" destinations and with modern air transportation hubs in nearby Bangkok and Singapore.

Among poorer countries, Cambodia became a pioneer in using tourism as a development strategy at the end of war. In theory, the country had everything: the exquisite ruins at Angkor, comparable in their majesty and cultural importance to those in Greece and Egypt; unspoiled beaches and islands on the southern coast along the Gulf of Thailand; and the sophisticated French colonial legacy that could be seen in the cities and towns with their blend of Cambodian and French colonial architecture that was as seductive to modern tastes as the overlay of the British Raj in India. The fact that the country had been forbidden to tourists for decades made it all the more attractive. Cambodia was "authentic," with its tragic history, delicate art, dance and cuisine, and its reputation for enchantment as well as cruelty.

Cambodia's timing couldn't have been better. Tourism was gaining the respect of economists and development experts. Over the last two decades it has become the second-largest source of foreign exchange, after oil, for half of the world's poorest nations. The United Nations World Tourism Organization describes tourism as "one of the few development opportunities for the poor" and publishes thick reports on how those poor nations can use the tourism industry to create modern infrastructure, higher standards of living and improvements in the environment. That rosy outcome is a rarity among the one hundred poorest countries that earn up to 5 percent of their gross national product selling themselves to foreign tourists who marvel at their exotic customs, buy suitcases of souvenirs and take innumerable photographs of stunning sites.

Cambodian tourism started out well. Roland Eng, a young politician and diplomat, was named the first minister of tourism in 1993. He was an inspired choice. Like many of his compatriots, Eng had suffered the anguish of losing his parents and all but one of his siblings during the Khmer Rouge regime. He had been stranded as a student in Paris during that time. In Europe he served as a private secretary for Prince Norodom Sihanouk and later became a functionary and diplomat for the Cambodian non-Communists in exile. Worldly, multilingual and intelligent, Eng was a welcome face to foreign visitors.

As the first minister of tourism, Eng saw his role as a mixture of diplomacy and business. Diplomacy because in the modern world people shape their opinions about foreign nations during visits as tourists as much as from reading newspapers or contemporary histories. Tourism could resurrect Cambodia's reputation from its low point as the site of the "killing fields" of the Khmer Rouge genocide. On the business side, tourism could set the tone for quality development and allow Cambodia to skip the early, shabby stage of tacky hotels that foul the cities and beaches of other nations while doing little to raise living standards.

Eng aimed high. At the start of Cambodia's questionable recovery, he pushed aside low-end proposals from foreign companies with "friends" in the Cambodian government and instead reached a deal with the luxury Raffles Hotel chain based in Singapore to invest $80 million to renovate Cambodia's most celebrated hotels: Le Royale in Phnom Penh and the Grand Hotel outside of Angkor. "It was daring of them, in 1993 and 1994," he told me. Those hotels are now ranked among the best in the country and Art Deco masterpieces of Asia.

To protect Angkor, the country's most prized asset, Eng threw his full support behind tentative proposals for an unusual agreement with sixteen foreign countries and the United Nations to restore and preserve the Angkor temples under the authority of Cambodia. The agreement was eventually reached. Eng's abilities were noticed and in 1995 he was named Cambodian ambassador to Thailand; four years later he presented his credentials in Washington as the Cambodian ambassador to the United States.

Cambodia's tourism industry then grew under several new ministers who lacked Eng's credentials or vision. In 1997, Hun Sen took over full power of the country following a coup d'état and much of the balance of power in the government was lost. In the tourism field that meant an increase in cronyism and corruption. Since then, Cambodia has broken nearly every tenet of good tourism management set out by organizations like the U.N. World Tourism Organization. Under the government of Hun Sen, most decisions are made at the very top with little or no community input. Regulations that exist on paper are rarely enforced; courts can be bought off with bribes; and corruption is so endemic that foreign investors list it as the major stumbling block to doing business in the country.

Tourism brings in $2 billion each year, but it enriches Cambodia's elite rather than helping the underprivileged. Poverty and unemployment is worse around tourist areas, especially Angkor. It is changing the face of Cambodia—not for the better. In two recent surveys the *National Geographic* evaluated how countries cared for their priceless cultural heritage sites and coastlines. Cambodia was the only country that ranked among the worst in both categories. Angkor still impressed but was criticized for the unrestricted flood of tourists under "atrocious" management, the overdevelopment of nearby hotel areas that was threatening the temples themselves, and the exclusion of local Cambodians from benefiting from "this resource."

Tourism has thrived on the practice of the government grabbing land from the farmers and peasants and then selling the property to firms tied to a few dozen elite officials. They are behind the country's new resorts, hotels, spas and prime beachfronts. Those beach resorts in the south were singled out by the *National Geographic* jury for shoddy development, with too many seedy bars and hotels, poor waste management and a strong whiff of corruption.

The most troubling side of tourism is Cambodia's new reputation as one of the globe's hot spots for sex tourism. Men can easily buy young boys and girls for the night despite laws against it. Even the national tragedy of the Khmer Rouge period has become a lucrative niche market of "dark tourism" for foreigners.

Little of this is evident from the vantage of tourists staying in air-conditioned four-star hotels, traveling in air-conditioned sedans and seeing the country in the care of polished tour guides. Cambodia's beauty can be breathtaking: Angkor gives many visitors a taste for the mystical. At the same time, tourists are often moved by this splendor in contrast to the country's tragic modern history and poverty.

And on the surface the tourism industry is a huge success. Tourism proceeds account for 20 percent of Cambodia's domestic product. Tourism is the second-largest employer in the country, providing 350,000 jobs, just behind the garment industry. Roland Eng, who is still a champion of his country's tourism industry, presciently warned a few years ago that while tourism can bring wealth, alleviate poverty and conserve natural and cultural heritages, it has to be regulated. "Left to itself, tourism development does not necessarily fulfill those roles," he wrote.

Now Cambodia is a model of tourism gone wrong. It is a far cry from the mythical golden era remembered by Cambodians like Dith Pran and Sok Nguon who in the middle of war found inspiration remembering the dignity and pleasure of showing foreigners the glories of their country.

Siem Reap is the modern town in northwestern Cambodia that grew up near the ancient city of Angkor. Once a sedate French colonial market center, it is now a loud tourist town of hotels, restaurants and karaoke bars, with nearly three million visitors every year augmenting a permanent population of 173,000 people.

The highway into Siem Reap is one long strip of hotels—the Royal Angkor, the Apsara Angkor, the Majestic Angkor, the Empress Angkor, etc. Few are top-flight. Many cater to Koreans or Chinese or Vietnamese. They come in all sizes and quality, often with giant faux-Angkor statues guarding the front doors. There are blocks of massage parlors and nightclubs like the Café Bar-Noir and the Zone One Club. At many of these nightspots the young girls and boys introduced as waiters or hostesses are prostitutes, and as they say on the blogs, they are "available." Nightlife in Siem Reap is fast-paced for the foreign tourists: live music, karaoke, massage parlors and bars and drugs everywhere set against a lush tropical town with colored lights strung overhead.

The single-minded pursuit of high-volume tourism has nearly destroyed the charm of the town. What remains can be found in the Old Quarter along the banks of the Siem Reap River that flows through the town center. The old Grand Hotel with its gardens is an axis for a neighborhood of classic wooden Cambodian homes and French colonial villas where cafés still offer dining al fresco under shade trees. Further downtown, the covered marketplace has been preserved with vendors and artists and a lively mix of locals.

The vast majority of tourists are Asian, with South Koreans and Vietnamese sharing the number-one spot. They fly in directly from Seoul, Hanoi, or Ho Chi Minh City. Almost daily flights from Bangkok; Singapore; Vientiane, Laos; and Kuala Lumpur, Malaysia, bring in more neighbors. Europeans and Americans are now the distinct minority even though they, too, arrive by the thousands, pushing tourism to Cambodia from 176,617 in 1994, the first full year of peace, to nearly 3 million in 2011. Cambodia's online visa service makes it one of the easiest countries to visit.

The reason for the influx is Angkor, which now has a permanent spot on the lists of one hundred places you must see before you die. The spires of Angkor have joined the rarefied company of the Pyramids of Egypt, the Taj Mahal in India and the Great Wall of China as ancient wonders on any traveler's list. Travel writers gush over the sheer number of temples. The sculpted faces of the Bayon are routinely described as otherworldly. In that sense, little has changed. Ancient poets tried to capture the magnificence of the Angkor era with its city of temples "enclosed in immense walls like the mountains that girdle the world . . . ponds dotted with lotus flowers in bloom that echoed with the scream of flamingoes and cranes . . . grand avenues, streets and squares with wide staircases, houses, assembly halls and the abodes of the gods."

Most of that is long gone, lost when the Angkor Empire fell and the capital moved to Phnom Penh. The intricate water system of ponds and irrigation ditches is a shadow of its old self. Now heat and dust await tourists arriving by taxi at the main entry gate to pay the $20 government fee and join the often-immense crowds. The splendid sacred spaces are lost in a scrum of foreigners with guides shouting in competing languages. There is no limit to the number of people allowed in the tourist complex.

The guides have a hard time. "It is not good. Most of the time we miss specific parts of a tour because there are too many people and we are pushed around, pushed away," said Yut, a guide. "We guides talk about this and many more things—there should be regulations about how many people are allowed in during the day, more areas should be roped off, more wooden walkways, and they should stop putting spikes in elephants' heads to control them—that makes the elephants cry."

The tourists have a difficult time, and the frustration can be intolerable until they catch a first glimpse of the spires, see the sensuous curve of an Apsara (angel) statue nestled in a temple, and find their way to Ta Prohm, the temple left as the early French archeologists found it with roots of the banyan and fig trees folded over the stones, the jungle encasing the sacred.

I saw all this through the eyes of my daughter Lily when we took a mother-daughter trip there for her twenty-fifth birthday. After three days she had fallen in love with Angkor, rising early to be the first at the entry gate and staying until the last minute before closing time at sunset. She was in no mood to hear me complain, often, about the irritating crowds that block your view and destroy the spirit of Angkor. She asked me to please stop being so annoying. On the last day she went off on her own.

It was true. I was guilty of nostalgia and unrealistic hopes that Angkor would recover its old grace. I apologized, and that afternoon we sat together watching the sun set over Angkor.

On a subsequent trip I learned that my complaints weren't so far off the mark. It turns out that those crowds are extremely bad for Angkor. It took five hundred years, beginning in the late twelfth century, to build this complex of temples and walkways, moats and causeways, which culminated in the reign of Jayavarman VII. Now, in less than a decade, the onslaught of tourists and tourist developments is threatening their very foundation.

The temples of Angkor were built for worship and contemplation. The rulers poured their wealth into them, gilding the spires in gold and silver, commissioning carvings that memorialized their conquests and statues of Hindu gods that were in fact carved to resemble the kings and queens of Angkor. Hundreds, not millions, walked the temples.

"For sure, these temples weren't made to welcome the world, only to pray to God. It is a place solely for God, not even like a western Cathedral where people were meant to assemble," said Dominique Soutif, head of the EFEO Center.

Soutif was sitting in his office in Siem Reap, at the storied Center, where the restoration and study of the temples was begun in 1907 by French archeologists and scholars who literally rediscovered the ancient history of Cambodia through their work. My last visit to that office had been in 1974, when war was advancing and Bernard-Philippe Groslier was shutting down the Center. Statues were crated, marked and ready for shipment; libraries carefully boxed. Through binoculars you could just see the spires of Angkor Wat five miles away. One could sense a fear of impending loss.

Groslier and his father George, both scholars, had dedicated their lives to Angkor. Now the son was forced to abandon it. I asked if he thought the Khmer Rouge would destroy the temples. He shook his head and said no. The temples were too important to both sides: to prove their nationalism, their patriotism, the superiority of the Cambodian culture. He said he believed the armies would be more protective of the stones at Angkor than the Cambodians who revered them. He was right. Through the six-year war and the Khmer Rouge revolution that ended in 1979, the temples were left largely untouched. Whatever damage they suffered was from decay.

Instead, since the war, the worst culprits have been bandits who stole the statuary, often cutting off the heads, and now it is tourism. Soutif outlined the immediate damage being done by the millions of tourists who march all over the temples, their fingers touching the intricate carvings, their arms brushing up against the stones.

"Wat Phnom Bakheng, the temple on the hill, the effect of the daily traffic has degraded the temple considerably," he began. "The steps of Angkor Wat are slippery from the damage by tourists. Inevitably with millions of guests the bas-reliefs have been touched by them and that's extremely detrimental. I've seen Korean guides hitting those bas-reliefs with sticks to demonstrate an historical fact. It's all just inevitable."

What can be done to reduce the sheer numbers of tourists and prevent this cumulative damage? His answer was revelatory, as if the other shoe had dropped.

"It is not as simple as you think," he told me. "Without the tourists, there would be no restoration, no research," he said.

That is the price the foreign preservationists and archeologists pay: they have become a very sophisticated clean-up crew, repairing damage caused by tourism as the quid pro quo for the privilege of working at Angkor. The arrangement goes something like this. Angkor draws in the millions of tourists who bring in billions of dollars to this poor country. That tourism volume, in turn, draws the attention of foreign investors who put more money into the country, much of which lands in the private bank accounts of officials. The system works brilliantly for some, but it rests on the splendor of those temples in Angkor. They have to be restored and maintained.

This is where the foreign archeologists and their governments enter the picture. In order to have the key role in Angkor, sixteen foreign governments offered to provide their expertise, their labor and their money to restore and research the site. The Cambodian government accepted this proposition on the express condition that this work cannot interfere with tourism at Angkor.

These countries, along with the United Nations, became part of the International Coordinating Committee for the Safeguarding and Development of the Historic Site of Angkor (ICC-Angkor). The Cambodian government created a complementary Apsara association that works with the foreigners while the Cambodian government retains authority over all decisions regarding Angkor as "an historic site, a natural site and a tourist site."

To streamline the effort, each country "adopts" a temple for restoration and posts signs showing that Hungary, Japan, India or the United States is financing the recovery and maintenance of that temple. Germany is the master for stone conservation. France trained a 300-member Cambodian heritage police force to prevent thieves from hacking off statues, bas-reliefs and lintels with hammers and saws. Now theft has largely ended in the official Angkor area. All of the countries praise the "very great openness of the Cambodian authorities to debate aspects of the country's economic, environmental and social policies that elsewhere would remain jealously guarded."

Soutif said that forgetting the tourism angle, this proposition works. "It's easy to raise money for Angkor—a *belle image!*" And Cambodia wins friends in the rarefied world of the arts for being wise enough to avail itself of foreign expertise and money to preserve what is a cultural heritage of the world.

"For years we've worked daily with these people, helping to form the Cambodian archeologists," said Soutif, who listed all of the scholarships and studies abroad for them. "It's a unique example for a developing country and a good example for UNESCO [the United Nations agency that created the system]."

One report by the association stated the limits of their influence: "We don't discuss what they should do, we don't have the right—that is a Cambodian question but we can have conversations about issues."

What the foreign governments can discuss are ideas—ideas about regulating the circulation of visitors in the temples; encouraging people to visit more than the "big three," which includes Angkor Wat, considered the *Mona Lisa* of Cambodia; preserving some bas-relief under glass; and building wooden stairs over the worn stone steps for over-sized foreign tourists.

Other organizations are less inhibited about describing the damage. The nonprofit Global Heritage Fund reported in 2010 that "hundreds of thousands of visitors climb over the ruins of Angkor every year causing heavy deterioration of original Khmer stonework." The report about safeguarding cultural sites said this was inevitable given that the number of visitors to Angkor Wat has increased by 188 percent since 2000.

A mounting problem is water. Siem Reap does not have the modern water and waste system to accommodate these tourists. The temple foundations are sinking as the surrounding water table is being drained by hotels that drill down as deep as 260 feet into ponds and underground aquifers, emptying them in order to have enough water to allow tourists to shower and flush toilets, to clean their clothes and to irrigate hotel landscapes and golf courses at an unsustainable rate. There is no adequate system to filter and dispose of the resulting sewage and the Siem Reap River has been polluted from the irresponsible dumping of waste.

The result is an ongoing threat to the foundation of the temples. At the Bayon, fifty-four towers have started sinking into the ground. Experts worry that the sandy soil is becoming so unstable it could threaten other temples.

Son Soubert, an archeologist and member of Cambodia's Constitutional Council, said he first raised the serious threat of sinking temples in 1995 but to little avail. "Obviously our authorities are mindless and see only the financial benefits, to the detriment of the monuments they are meant to preserve and restore," he told me.

The World Bank sounded a similar alarm in a 2006 report on tourism in Cambodia, stating that because of poorly regulated mass tourism in Siem Reap "energy, water, sewage and waste are all significant problems."

The same foreign governments that restore the temples have been given the additional responsibility of solving the water problem. In a report, the groups euphemistically said that water is "a complex issue wherein the survival of the temples must be reconciled with the sometimes effervescent get-up-and-go of Siem Reap town."

With the Cambodian government's approval, Japan drew up a master plan and is building a water supply system for the city of Siem Reap. Korea began building new drainage and sewage networks. France is cleaning up the Tonlé Sap River. The Asian Development Bank is loaning money for some of the projects, and a few hotels have promised to install recycling systems for their used water, all with the aim of repairing the damage done by draining the water table.

The government has made no attempt to finger the culprits who are pumping or drilling for water or measuring how much water is being sucked out of the ground. That might discourage investment in tourism.

South Korea is a major patron of the Cambodian tourism industry in Siem Reap. Overall, South Koreans account for billions of dollars of private investment in the Cambodian economy, with a strong accent on tourism. (Only China has invested more money in Cambodia.)

Korean visitors fly to Cambodia on one of Korean Airlines' nearly daily flights from Seoul. In Siem Reap, Koreans have invested in restaurants, hotels and karaoke bars. The largest project is a new $1.6 billion international airport for Siem Reap that, in theory, could bring up to 14 million tourists to the temples every year. Another South Korean developer is building a $400 million casino resort near Angkor with the avowed goal of drawing the high rollers from Macao and Singapore. The government not only promised the Korean company incentives like corporate tax holidays and low gaming levies; Prime Minister Hun Sen himself entertained the developer in Phnom Penh.

Koreans are so favored that one enterprise received rare government approval to stage variety shows in Angkor Wat itself. A Cambodian whistle-blower complained that the company had drilled holes in the temple to light the "Angkor Night Show." The show was canceled, although there was no punishment for the Korean company. Instead, the Cambodian whistle-blower was forced to leave the country under threat of arrest by the government.

The government is determined to turn Angkor into a tourism money machine. To which many may ask, what's wrong with bringing in millions of dollars to a poor country? The answer is that those tourist dollars do little to help most of the people in Cambodia.

Siem Reap is the prime example.

In the 1960s, before all the war and genocide, Siem Reap was the richest per capita province in the country, famous for its rice fields and fish. Today with its multibillion-dollar tourism business it is the poorest per capita. The promise of tourism to raise the livelihoods of the poor has failed miserably in Siem Reap. The "leakage" of money out of the province is among the highest in the world, according to Douglas Broderick, the United Nations resident coordinator in Phnom Penh.

"More tourism money stays with the locals in parts of Africa than it does in Siem Reap," he said.

Broderick pointed to a 2009 United Nations Development Program Report which said that the majority of tourist spending doesn't reach the poor. "The pro-poor benefit is very low in Siem Reap, an estimated seven percent (of tourist receipts)," a statistic that compares badly to neighboring Vietnam and Laos. This is not the result of lack of money: at least one-third of direct foreign investment goes to tourism in Cambodia. Instead, the report fingers government corruption, uncertain regulations, and poor management as the reason.

Cambodia's official Apsara preservation agency in Siem Reap confirms that the plight of the poor has worsened with the tourism boom there. "The province of Siem Reap is now one of the poorest in Cambodia," wrote Uk Someth, of the agency. "Villagers profit little from tourism, while (foreign) investors and suppliers have the advantage."

Hotels import 70 percent of their needs from companies outside of Cambodia. They purchase only 5 to 10 percent of their food from Cambodian farms. Well-trained foreigners are hired for the upper-level jobs, while Cambodians scramble for the lower-paying positions that offer long hours, little training and seasonal employment—a common problem for the low end of the tourism industry, according to studies by the U.N. International Labour Organization.

"In the middle of all this wealth, the average pay in Siem Reap is thirty dollars a month," said Soutif, of the EFEO Center. "Cambodians work two jobs, study at night, anything to improve their lives. They are courageous."

Yut, the Angkor guide, told me that corruption is another hurdle to finding a good job. To get anywhere you have to pay bribes. For instance, to become an official guide at Angkor, Cambodians must attend a government guide school where tuition is $130. But it is nearly impossible to be admitted without paying a bribe.

Yut avoided paying the bribe because he is a retired monk. The twenty-nine-year-old was born and raised in Siem Reap, and by the time he left the monastery three years ago, he had mastered the articles of faith and the intricacies of Khmer history well enough to pass the guide's test. Still, he had to attend the school to receive his license. A guide for a top tour agency is paid $15 to $30 a day; the tour agency charges the tourists $60 a day. "It is difficult even for guides to earn a good living," said Yut.

Prime Minister Hun Sen argues otherwise. In a recent speech he claimed that tourism was the "green gold" of Cambodia that "plays a vital role in improving the livelihood of locals, mainly local communities at the tourist sites."

Tourists aren't stupid. They see the gaping disparity between the comfort and luxury of their tourism bubble and the poverty around them. Some even wonder how the elite Cambodians can live so well while the average Cambodian appears so poor. The average income in Cambodia is $2,000 a year and some 30 percent of Cambodians fall below the national poverty line. For many tourists, this is the first time they've seen that degree of poverty, and they feel moved to give back, either with money or as volunteers.

This impulse has become institutionalized as travel philanthropy or "volun-tourism" and is very much in vogue. All over the globe, travel agencies and nonprofit groups are offering inventive and mostly painless ways to be a philanthropist on vacation. In parts of Africa, Central and South America, as well as Asia, some of this philanthropy has helped individual families and small communities. Other projects have done little beyond relieving the consciences of travelers as they struggle with the scale of inequities.

In Cambodia these well-meaning tourists have proved ripe for scams. A website called Scambodia posts examples of phony orphanages. One advertised for "Volunteers Abroad", asking each volunteer to pay $1,000 a week for room and board while working in an orphanage—which turned out to be filled with children from neighboring families. One of the young foreign volunteers turned them in.

Even real institutions raise questions. Many evenings a local orphanage sends a parade of children marching under its banner through the Bar Street area of Siem Reap, beating drums, dancing and inviting the tourists to "visit our orphanage." Tourists take the bait and drive over to a newly built mansion on the outskirts of town. There they are ushered to bleachers in a courtyard where the young children dance and put on puppet shows on a stage festooned with colorful streamers. They pass around a bucket that the foreigners fill with dollars. At the program's end the tourists are invited back on special days to visit and play with the children and "give them the love they are missing."

When the tourists do, they add to their donations and leave sincere notes saying how much they appreciated this opportunity to know the love of these children. One woman wrote, "I now know why Angelina Jolie has so many orphan children."

I went one day, unannounced, and found thirty-six children running around the mansion with no supervision. No one was in school. A foreign tourist named Christian, a man in his twenties from Toronto, was playing with a few of the older boys in the large salon. With no one to stop me I went upstairs to check out how the children benefited from these "donations." Their bedrooms were a mess: there were no beds or cupboards, only clothes and bedsheets tossed on dirty floors. The bathrooms were locked; the children said the toilets were broken and that they bathed outside. They showed me the pump in the backyard where several children were soaping down and splashing themselves off.

They said they had no expectations of being adopted. Sophan, an eighteen-year-old boy, said he had been living with his aunt when he was offered a place at the orphanage four years earlier. "We play with foreigners," he said. "No adoptions."

To be fair, the establishment never actually says the children can be adopted.

In 2012 the United Nations published a report about orphanages in Cambodia entitled *With the Best Intentions*. The study said that foreign tourists were major funders of a system that hurt children more often than helped them. The children in these orphanages usually had at least one living parent: 44 percent had both parents; 61 percent had one parent or close immediate family. Their impoverished families had placed them in the orphanages under the false promise that the orphanage would provide them with an education.

Instead, these pseudo-orphans spend their days raising money.

"Tourists play a major role in funding residential care," said the report, citing children staying in their orphanage to play with foreigners or being pulled out of school to dance for foreigners. Remarkably, with peace and stability for the first time in its modern history, there has been a 75 percent increase in children taken to orphanages since 2005.

"Sometimes I think people leave their brains at home when they go on vacation," said Daniela Ruby Papi, the American founder of PEPY, a nonprofit organization in Siem Reap that casts a questioning eye on westerners who are conned into thinking they can change lives in a few days or weeks. As anyone in the development world knows, that requires years of commitment.

Tourists who rarely volunteer at home are easy prey. Scams have been uncovered where tourists helped pay, and even build, schools that will never have teachers or students. They have paid for wells that were already drilled.

Papi has a check-off list for tourists who want to volunteer, but she believes the most you can do on vacation is to learn about Cambodia, to understand the joys and difficulties of the people. She gives tours on bicycles so foreigners can go into the countryside and meet her Cambodian partners who are working on education, health and the environment. The goal is getting the tourists out of their bubble and into the real world. "That's the one thing they can do," she said.

If you want to make a monetary contribution to the poor, she said, you should tip generously.

Dozens of shaven-head monks dressed in gray, orange and scarlet robes quietly filed into the modern Sofitel Angkor resort dining room. Chimes punctuated the silence as the monks filled their plates at the buffet. They had traveled to Siem Reap to celebrate Vesak Bochea, one of Buddhism's holiest days, at Angkor. Cambodia had won the honor of holding the world convocation and had organized the ritual prayers at the Angkor temples as well as multicolor light shows at night. Banquets were part of the celebration.

Thong Khon, the Cambodian minister of tourism, flew to Siem Reap to greet the monks as they arrived from other Asian nations, and that is where I caught up with him.

Charles-Henri Chevet, the French general manager of the hotel, showed us to our table and thanked the minister for all he was doing for tourism. The minister watched the procession of monks at the steam tables and was elated. "We can sell Cambodia to the world, Cambodia—Kingdom of Wonder," he said, "Buddhist Cambodia."

A medical doctor, Thong lost most of his family, including his blind father, during the murderous reign of the Khmer Rouge. After their overthrow he stayed in the country, refusing to emigrate to the West. He worked first in public health, then as mayor of Phnom Penh. When he was named deputy minister of tourism, Thong said he knew nothing about business or tourism. By 2007 he was the minister. Like other top government officials, Thong said he has earned his luxurious lifestyle after surviving twenty years of unimaginable deprivations through war, revolution and more war and occupation.

"We rebuilt with nothing, nothing," he said. "I learned by doing."

In his government's vision, questions about social justice and equality take a backseat to development and catching up in the material world. Because Cambodia has risen from the ashes, with an overall economic growth rate of 10 percent each year, Hun Sen and his cabinet believe they are the only ones capable of leading the country.

Thong spoke with me over lunch; none of my questions fazed him. He said problems of corruption, bribes, sex tourism or sinking temples had either been solved or were exaggerated.

"We will change—we want to change from mass tourism to quality tourism in the future," he said, qualifying his statement. "I don't say that we want fewer people to come, but our tourism has to be better managed . . . We're trying to enhance."

The question of the sinking temples and related water shortage and sewage pollution were being resolved, he said, thanks in large part to the work of the United Nations and in particular the governments of Japan, Korea and France. "The deterioration is over. Yes, before there were problems, but now it is recognized that this area is well managed."

He disposed of the question about the explosion of sex tourism with equal ease. "The government policy will not encourage sex tourism—we fight it, absolutely fight child trafficking and child prostitution."

He hesitated for a moment. "Tourism provides positive impacts and negative impacts," he said. "The positive is providing jobs and revenue. The negative is drugs, prostitution and sometimes crimes, but not much."

He was proud, he said, that Cambodia had passed laws to stop this "negativity." And he was crafting a new tourism master plan that would tackle all the hot-button issues: sustainability, climate control, ecotourism, biodiversity, protecting wildlife, even "contributions to the poor."

I told the minister that my research told a different story. Tourism was often spreading inequality, injustice and misery in the country. The laws may look good on the books, but they are enforced haphazardly to favor the rich and powerful. The poor are evicted from their land, which is then sold to the highest bidder regardless of property rights or regardless of the poor effect on protected wilderness or the environment.

Thong shook his head. Evictions, he said, made land available for new development that was necessary to lure tourists. Half of the foreign tourists visit Siem Reap, but only 3 percent make it to the southern beaches. The government had to broaden the base of tourism so those peasants had to lose their land, homes and livelihoods.

"We have to diversify to the beaches, to our coastal zone," he said. "Our new strategy is to make [the south] our new destination."

His other big idea to expand Cambodia's tourism appeal was to promote "dark tourism," or genocide tourism. The Ministry of Tourism wants to create an official tourism "genocide trail" of the sites where the Khmer Rouge once tortured, murdered or buried their victims. Tourists are already drawn to them, he said. "More foreigners go to Tuol Sleng (the torture center) than Cambodians. We want to promote that . . . train guides in London . . . bring in more tourists."

Instead of erasing Cambodia's reputation as a home of the dark side of human nature, the home of the killing fields, as Roland Eng once wanted to do, the Ministry of Tourism is turning it into a profit point for tourism.

Tuol Sleng was a high school that became the Auschwitz of Cambodia. The Khmer Rouge transformed the quiet tree-lined campus in Phnom

Penh into the regime's central interrogation and torture center after their victory in 1975. At least 14,000 people were murdered there after being whipped, raped, water-boarded, hung upside down and forced to watch the execution of their loved ones. All victims were photographed when they were booked, mothers often holding a child. I knew some of the Cambodians killed there.

When they invaded in 1979, the Vietnamese preserved Tuol Sleng as they found it, modifying a few details to turn it into a museum. They left the classrooms that had been divided by brick walls into cells as well as the instruments of torture that had replaced the school desks on the classic red-and-white-tiled floors. The Khmer Rouge had left extensive records of each victim and these were kept filed away in cabinets. The Vietnamese mounted photographs of the victims on the walls and opened the museum with the clear propaganda goal of justifying their occupation of Cambodia.

Today, Tuol Sleng is the single most popular destination of foreign tourists visiting Phnom Penh, averaging five hundred visits a day. It is the centerpiece of the dark tourism, or genocide, trail that the minister of tourism is promoting. Cambodia is now on the circuit of dark tourism that includes the Nazi death camps at Dachau, Germany, and Auschwitz, Poland; Sarajevo, Bosnia, and Kigali, Rwanda. Travel agents now specialize in those tours.

There is a thin line between memorialization and manipulation when creating museums to honor the victims of genocide or a mass attack. Questions were raised when a Pennsylvania farmer charged $65 a person to tour the site of the crash of United Airlines Flight 93 on September 11, 2001. Similar issues have been raised in Cambodia about making money from foreign tourists following a trail of genocide.

Other curators of genocide museums have wrestled with those questions. Holocaust museums and memorials routinely reject the idea of operating to make a profit and instead say they are dedicated to peace and understanding. One rule of thumb is to put the dignity of the victims first, identifying them by name and telling their stories as much as possible. At the U.S. Holocaust Memorial Museum, the surviving victims have had a major role in designing the displays, said Michael J. Abramowitz, director of the Committee on Conscience at the museum.

"Holocaust institutions do everything they can to avoid even the slightest appearance that they are exploiting the history of the Holocaust to raise funds or in any way profit from the murder and suffering of millions," said Abramowitz.

Cambodia opted for profits along with memorialization for its genocide tourism. After repairing and restoring Tuol Sleng the government encouraged tour buses to drop off foreign tourists. The price of admission is $2, with an additional cost of $3 for a guide.

Inside, the museum breaks the cardinal rule of respect for the victims. Haunting photographs are hung throughout Tuol Sleng, but most of the victims are left anonymous—no names and no stories about their lives and deaths even though the information has been available for decades. Instead, the accent is on the barbarity of the Khmer Rouge and how they tortured these people. Most visitors leave the museum stunned.

Nearby is Choeung Ek, the killing field south of Phnom Penh where the Khmer Rouge clubbed countless Cambodians to death and buried them in mass graves. It is the second site on the proposed genocide trail. The government erected a memorial using 8,985 skulls collected from the grounds. These skeletons were never given the religious rites and cremation required by the Buddhist faith; instead, they are on permanent display, some organized by age and gender but, again, without names. This does not feel like a sacred space but one of utter desecration.

In 2005 the government turned Choeung Ek into an official commercial enterprise by signing a thirty-year contract with a Japanese company to enhance its tourism possibilities. The Japanese added amenities and built a visitor's center, raising the price of admission from 50 cents to $2. Youk Chhang, the executive director of the Documentation Center of Cambodia that documents the crimes of the Khmer Rouge, tried to prevent that Japanese contract. He said that "the Japanese have commercialized the soul of the Khmer Rouge survivors and provided a superficial education to the foreign tourists.

"How can we learn from history so that it cannot be repeated if we continue to fail to understand that the memory of those who have died cannot be commercialized?" he said.

The government was surprised by Youk Chhang's anger and asked him for advice on the proper preservation of the genocide sites and training of tour guides. Chhang told me he agreed to work on the master plan to insure the sites were educational.

The third site is Anlong Veng in western Cambodia, the last holdout of Pol Pot, far from Phnom Penh. In 2001 the government issued a circular ordering the preservation of Anlong Veng for "historical tourism."

At the same time as it was promoting genocide tourism, the Hun Sen government was blocking an international trial of the former Khmer Rouge leaders who were living quietly in Cambodia and had never been arrested. After a decade of negotiations, an agreement was reached and in 2009 the first trial was held more than thirty years after the Khmer Rouge defeat. The first man convicted was Kaing Guek Eav, or Duch, who had headed Tuol Sleng. By then his old torture center had welcomed nearly 1 million foreign tourists.

The building that houses the Ministry of Tourism in Phnom Penh is a metaphor for how the government has robbed the people of their land, their heritage and their livelihoods to profit the tourism industry.

For the first decade of peace the ministry was housed in a grand French colonial villa on Phnom Penh's waterfront in the heart of the capital, where three rivers meet as they flow toward the sea. This is one of the most exclusive areas of the city. The fifteenth-century Wat Ounalom Buddhist temple is directly across the street, and the golden walls of the Royal Palace compound are a stone's throw away. The palace resembles an illustration from an Asian fairy tale, with a royal pavilion, throne hall, royal court, silver pagoda, Moonlight Pavilion for royal ballet performances and private residences laid out for a dream potentate. Behind the palace is the National Museum, built in traditional Khmer architecture that houses the world's finest collection of Khmer art. It was the perfect neighborhood for the Ministry of Tourism to make a visual statement about the history and treasures of Cambodia.

Then one morning in 2005 workers came, and in three days they had torn down the ministry's building. Local reporters rushed to the site thinking this was an illegal demolition of one of the city's historic villas. Not so. The destruction was legal. The reporters were told that the government had given the property to a new Cambodian development company in exchange for a nondescript new building on Street Number 73 in a non-descript neighborhood. No money was exchanged for the villa or the land that was worth millions. The company did pass out $100,000 to divide among the employees of the Ministry of Tourism to thank them for accepting the deal. The developer, in turn, built a hotel on that prime property.

This noncompetitive sale of public property for private gain was being duplicated around the country. The government has orchestrated the sale of state assets to new private business ventures that had close ties to top officials and their families. The government used the same dictatorial powers to declare privately held lands part of new "development zones" to sell those, in turn, to business ventures tied to the government. This was all done behind closed doors with no competitive bidding, public hearings or judicial review.

The Ministry of Tourism was unhappy with the building on Street Number 73 and set its eyes on land in the central district of Phnom Penh known as Borei Keila. It was home to some of the city's poorest residents, including a high concentration of people suffering from AIDS. The area was declared an "economic concession" and the families were evicted from there. The government then sold the land to private developers who promised to replace the hovels with clean modern apartments for the poor. That didn't happen. The dispossessed were never given market value in return for their land and only half received new apartments. A Cambodian nonprofit organization trying to help the evicted said it was difficult to find any proof that money made from the sale ended up in the national treasury.

The Ministry of Tourism was given a large parcel of the newly empty land in Borei Keila. In 2009 the ministry constructed a brand-new home — an imposing, pink-toned modern building on a large piece of property on Monivong Boulevard, the main artery in the capital. Forty-seven families were thrown out to clear the land for the new ministry building. Most of those families ended up under tarpaulins near their old homes or in camps far from the city center, not in the promised new apartments. When Prime Minister Hun Sen cut the ribbon for the ministry's grand inauguration, a video on the Internet showed how the evicted families were still living in green tin sheds with no electricity, no running water and garbage strewn in their narrow living space. A father begged Hun Sen: "We are Khmer residents. We have rights, please save us."

The video was filmed by LICADHO, a Cambodian human rights organization that represented the residents before the government and courts. Founded by Kek Galabru, a Cambodian doctor who played a critical role in bringing peace to her country, LICADHO is one of a handful of human rights groups whose research and advocacy has laid bare the enormity of the land-grabbing by the country's elite and its ties to tourism.

"This group had a very strong claim on their property based on the law of Cambodia. They were discriminated against. They were moved, 'relocated,' to animal stalls. That was their compensation for losing their homes," said Mathieu Pellerin at LICADHO.

This is a distortion of a government's right of eminent domain for the public good. Cambodia uses those powers to the opposite effect, creating the multimillion-dollar racket that grabs land from the nation's poor to enrich the elite.

There is nothing hidden about this epidemic. In 2009 the United Nations Office of the High Commissioner of Human Rights called for a moratorium on further evictions and said it was "gravely concerned over reports that since the year 2000, over 100,000 people were evicted in Phnom Penh alone; that at least 150,000 Cambodians continue to live under threat of forced eviction; and that authorities of the State party are actively involved in land-grabbing. . . ."

Global Witness, the nonprofit British advocacy group, has documented how 45 percent of the country's land has been deeded to private interests through these land grabs. (Land is also grabbed to sell to agribusinesses as plantations, to mining companies, to logging firms and, recently, to oil and gas companies.)

Land for the Cambodian tourism industry was opened up in 2005 when Prime Minister Hun Sen said he was resuming his land concession program despite earlier pledges to wait until those already evicted could be resettled.

"I have to make a decision for my country's development," he told a group at the Government Private Sector Forum in Phnom Penh, a government group that coordinates private investment, especially foreign investment. "I can't wait. So I have gone ahead to provide concession land to investors. This is a necessary way to attract investment."

The government then revoked the protected public status of the southern coast and its pristine islands, putting the property up for sale to private, largely foreign, investors. This breathtaking breach of the public trust put on the market the country's coastline along the Gulf of Thailand, which had been declared state public land by the coalition government of the 1990s. Reversing that designation was as shocking for Cambodians as it would be for Americans if the government in Washington suddenly put most of the U.S. national parks up for sale to foreign bidders.

Adding to the insult, the government sold the land at bargain prices and gave foreign investors extraordinary financial enticements, including nine-year tax holidays. The country already had a reputation for lax enforcement of money-laundering laws, and it allows holding companies in Cambodia to be 100 percent foreign-owned.

Within three years the entire coastline and most of the islands were privately owned, and resorts for tourism were under construction everywhere. Cambodia's natural heritage of coral reefs, endless stretches of empty, palm-fringed beaches, and sapphire-blue waters had been sold off.

The human cost was enormous. Whole communities were summarily evicted despite a 2001 law that requires due process and full compensation in these cases. Farmers and fishermen fought back as police and the army burned down their villages on government orders, bulldozing fields and orchards and tearing down docks.

Photographs of the evictions are heartbreaking. In one series, a khaki-clothed official orders everyone to lie on the ground facedown as police officers torch their thatched huts. Helmeted police with shields and batons beat back anyone who protests. Fires burn away everything but villagers' large earthen water jars. With their plastic bags and confused children, the newly homeless villagers are forcibly marched away.

Those villages and wild open spaces were replaced by a mix of seedy hotels, private luxury resorts, and rampant sex tourism. Coastal resorts from Sihanoukville, the largest and the least attractive, to Kep and Koh Kong, exploded with tension as the new private owners took control of the land.

Stories of evictions and clashes over ownership are commonplace. More than 100 families fought eviction from the homes overlooking Serendipity Beach and lost. Now that beach is famous among the *Lonely Planet* crowd as the Waikiki of Cambodia.

An army of bulldozers and trucks filled with armed men cleared one section of the Occheuteal Beach in 2006, tearing down 71 homes and 40 local restaurants. A resort project on Independence Beach in 2008 required the eviction of "scores" of other families. The litany is endless. It's safe to say that any tourist spending a day or two in Sihanoukville has partied on property stolen from the locals.

This is not to say that all foreign developers are evil. The Brocon Group, an Australian company, has retrained out-of-work Cambodian fishermen for new employment and has appointed a marine biologist to clean and preserve the area around their new resort on the island of Song Saa, opposite Sihanoukville.

And the southern beaches are still beautiful, the water a startling blue, and the wildlife is hanging on.

In Koh Kong, which borders Thailand, the evictions were part of a drive to bring casinos to Cambodia. There a judge divided a swath of land between two well-connected businessmen without consulting the forty-three families who lived on it. The families were thrown out by the police despite a request from Cambodian King Norodom Sihamoni for an official investigation to determine if the families' treatment was legal. Now Koh Kong has its casinos, half a dozen hotels and guesthouses, restaurants, spas, and fenced-off land for future tourist development—most of it built on land grabbed from its residents.

Cambodia has defied the common wisdom that a developing country should stay away from gambling, especially in Asia, where gambling is woven into the culture and the poor are especially vulnerable to betting their futures on Lady Luck.

To lure foreign tourists, Cambodia has opened flashy casinos on its borders with Thailand to the west and Vietnam to the east. Thailand has no legal casinos, while Vietnam has allowed only four casinos, which are open to foreigners only. (Vietnam requires a $4 billion investment for a gaming license.) Gamblers from both countries arrive by the busloads to

Cambodian border casinos with a decided Las Vegas look and with "massage parlors" attached to the gambling halls. To build just one of these larger casinos in Poipet, along the Thai border, the authorities evicted 218 families.

Today, Cambodia has at least 32 casinos, many underwritten by foreign investors attracted to the country because of low taxes, low fees for licenses and low wages and construction costs. For all of these concessions and the agony it cost Cambodians who were evicted, the taxes from casinos contribute only $17 million to the Cambodian treasury. This distinguishes Cambodia from other gambling capitals in Asia, especially Macao, which draws the high-rollers from China and Japan, where casinos are outlawed. One regional gambling expert calculated that if the Macao taxing regime were applied to Cambodia, the taxes from a single casino in Phnom Penh alone would be $43.6 million.

These loose rules and poorly enforced laws have made it relatively easy for money to be laundered through casinos, giving Cambodian casinos a taint that has put off some high-end investors, who have stayed away. Cambodia also has rivals.

Straitlaced Singapore recently gave up its laws against gambling and legalized the activity, joining the race for tourist dollars in Southeast Asia. After watching Cambodia and Macao attract planeloads of gambling tourists, Singapore approved the construction of two casinos that opened in 2010 and rival any palace in Macao. Resorts World Sentosa advertises itself as an "eco-resort and casino" and was designed by the famed American architect Michael Graves. Singapore officials said they expect Asia's gamblers to spend enough at the two casinos—Sentosa and the Marina Bay Sands—to boost Singapore's GDP by $2.5 billion, or nearly 1 percent.

While Cambodia's border regions are now studded with casinos, only one has been allowed in Phnom Penh. The government gave Chen Lip Keong, a Malaysian businessman and senior economic advisor to Hun Sen, the exclusive license for a casino in Phnom Penh through 2035. He built NagaWorld, a splashy casino resort on multiple lots along the city's waterfront district in 2003. The neon-lit façade of the NagaWorld now flashes across the boulevards and rivers and attracts Chinese gamblers as well as Vietnamese, Thais and Malaysians.

It is also a sore point for Cambodians, who are unhappy that Chen has the gambling monopoly in Phnom Penh. NagaWorld made $35 million in profits in 2010, according to its listing on the Hong Kong stock exchange. Local Cambodian newspapers have editorialized that NagaWorld openly violates the law against locals gambling and "is operating to extract money from people addicted to gambling in Cambodia, earning colossal profits."

Cambodia has become a new center for sex tourism. Bangkok in neighboring Thailand was a pioneer in tourism for sex beginning in the 1960s, when American soldiers took their rest and rehabilitation, or R & R, in the Thai capital along the infamous Patpong red-light district. The bars offered risqué sex shows and young girls waiting to be chosen for the night. The soldiers returned home to the United States with stories, and diseases, from that strip where everyone seeking flesh was welcome for a small price.

Sex tourism spread beyond Patpong, throughout Bangkok, and became part of package tours in Thailand. Advertisements began appearing in Europe and Asia like this one from Roise Reisen of Germany: "Thailand is a world full of extremes and the possibilities are unlimited . . . especially when it comes to girls. Still it appears to be a problem for visitors in Thailand to find the right places where they can indulge in unknown pleasures. It is frustrating to have to ask in broken English where you can pick up pretty girls. Roise has done something about this. For the first time in history, you can book a trip to Thailand with erotic pleasures included in the price."

Yoko Kusaka, a Japanese anthropologist, examining why Japanese men were attracted to sex tours to Bangkok found they were looking for easy sex without humiliation. Japanese tourists were met by Thai tour operators at the airport and taken to their hotels, where Thai girls with the job of "special services" accompanied each man to his room. Alternatively, the men could board a bus and visit massage parlors where Thai girls were waiting to give the same services.

Brothels returned to Cambodia when the United Nations peacekeepers arrived there to enforce the peace agreement in 1992. During their stay of less than two years the number of girls in brothels jumped from 6,000 to 20,000 and the average age of the girls entering the trade dropped from eighteen to twelve. This was the first post–Cold War peacekeeping mission where the peacekeepers faced charges of sexually abusing girls. Back then Yasushi Akashi, the special representative of the U.N. Secretary General, refused to take the issue seriously, saying "boys will be boys."

In subsequent years, as U.N. peacekeepers faced increasing allegations of sexual misconduct, the U.N. stepped in to forbid most abuses, including giving money or food to young girls for sex.

Cambodia became just one of the countries where sex tourism sprang up in the 1990s during the chaotic transformation of Communist nations to capitalist and the sudden opening of closed borders. Rogue gangs and organized crime got footholds in many industries, including tourism and prostitution, when governments were at their weakest. The money was eye-popping and bribes helped the trade dig deep roots. In Eastern Europe underground syndicates took over prostitution in the former Czechoslovakia along the "Highway of Shame" originally patronized by German truck drivers.

"Before the dust from the Berlin Wall had even settled, gangsters and chancers were laying the cables of a huge network of trafficking in women," wrote Misha Glenny in *McMafia: A Journey Through the Global Criminal Underworld.*

Estimates from individual countries suggest that these criminal syndicates earn in the hundreds of billions every year. Sex tourism provides anywhere between 2 and 14 percent of the gross domestic products of Thailand, Indonesia and the Philippines, according to the U.S. Department of Justice, which monitors the aspects of sex tourism that are criminal behavior.

And it is a crime to traffic in women and children and to have sex with underage girls and boys. Foreign male tourists convicted of any of these crimes can be punished with long prison terms in the home countries.

The tourism industry publicly opposes child sex tourism. Respectable hotel chains prohibit guests from bringing underage children to their rooms and forbid all solicitation on their premises. Many hotels cooperate with the police, contribute to campaigns to stamp out the scourge and pass out information leaflets to tourists about illegal prostitution of minors.

However, the industry is also quick to point out that they can't stop sex tourism or be held responsible for the brutal trafficking of women and children—that is the job of the local authorities. The industry may condemn tourists traveling to foreign lands to buy sex with an underage girl or boy or a young woman who is being held against her will, but it remains a cornerstone of its profit earnings, an extension of the idea that you can let your hair down on vacation and indulge in fantasies.

I saw this confirmed in the middle of an earnest discussion at an exclusive conference of tourist executives in Brazil. Brett Tollman, president of the Travel Corporation, interrupted comments about responding to tourists' desire for environmentally responsible travel by saying many young men travel just "to drink and get laid."

The crowd of mostly men broke out into knowing chuckles. Sex tourism makes billions of dollars from those fantasies, and that money is spread throughout the industry—agencies, operators, airlines, hotels, restaurants and, of course, brothels. The Czech Republic is famous in the business as a magnet. Cheap flights to Prague are routinely filled with young men looking for a sex vacation. Czech brothels are cheap and operate in a legal gray zone. During the recent 2008 Recession, when tourism dropped, the Czech hotel industry lobbied hard to legalize prostitution and boost business. (Tourists account for 60 percent of the $500 million sex trade in the Czech Republic.) The government said no, but in the economic rebound, sex tourism, along with hotel bookings, is up.

Cambodia is recognized as a hot spot for child sex tourism along with India, Thailand, Brazil and Mexico. At least 2 million children are prostituted in sex tourism around the world, according to the U.S. Department of Justice, and millions of lives ruined. In the global world system there are international rules and regulations to govern the trade of goods and services. But even though every minute of every day a child or a woman is coerced into sex as a prostitute, there are no rules covering sex tourism.

Marina Diotallevi of the World Tourism Organization is an expert on the sexual exploitation of children. "Sometimes a normal tourist goes to a poor country and sees this new opportunity and says, 'Why not—I'll try this and I'll do these poor children a favor and give them money.' That is the crime. Tourism is not the crime."

As she points out, the battle against sex tourism has been going on for more than thirty years, and some of the biggest victories have been won in Thailand, where much of it started. There are international campaigns to inform consumers, including an international code of conduct, increased prosecutions of sex offenders by their home nations, more reporting of crimes even without prosecution and greater cooperation between the industry and international organizations. Yet she can't say whether all this effort has reduced the risk for poor children.

"It is such a big world," she said. "Most of these countries don't want to admit they have such a big problem with child sex tourism."

There are few things more odious than walking along Phnom Penh's waterfront and running into a white-haired old man walking to an assignation with a girl young enough to be his granddaughter. That image of the old man is something of a misnomer. Young men buy sex from prostitutes on vacation at least as often as old men. One study found that twenty-seven years was the average age of the 80,000 Italian men who travel abroad for sex. Male tourists traveling to Cambodia for sex ranged in age from twenty-eight to sixty-eight, according to one study, and they come to Cambodia because law enforcement is lax and sex is cheap.

"Visitors taking a trip as part of a tour group inevitably ask their guide where to go for sex services," said one agent in a Phnom Penh study, adding that they delivered sex workers for the tourists. "The tour guides are there to help. . . . the customer is king."

That demand is met by girls, boys and young women who are mostly held against their will, drugged and beaten into submission. The sadism has been chronicled by human rights campaigners who have documented whippings, burnings, live burials and repeated rapes while the girl is handcuffed or tied to a bed. The most hair-raising and eloquent testimonies have been written by the women themselves.

Somaly Mam, a Cambodian woman, has told her story in a stark memoir, *The Road of Lost Innocence*. Somaly tells how she was forced into prostitution when she was twelve years old and became a sex slave. She was brutally tortured and raped almost daily and was suicidal until other girls inspired her to flee. She escaped and over time set up a nonprofit organization that frees underage children from brothels, with the cooperation of the police, and then rehabilitates them.

She says it is inspiring for her to help young girls. What is striking is that sex tourism is so prevalent in Cambodia today that Somaly Mam is one of Cambodia's most famous women, at home and abroad. In the first months of 2012 alone she spoke at the United Nations and met First Lady Michelle Obama at the White House.

Somaly Mam was not in Phnom Penh during my two research trips, so I visited her center to rehabilitate former prostitutes with her assistant Lin Sylor. The center charges a $100 visitors' fee. Even though I never pay for interviews, in this instance I paid $50 as a courtesy and since the center said the fees help cover the costs of caring for the young women.

The compound, on the outskirts of the city, is close to idyllic. When I arrived several dozen young women were in classrooms learning sewing, hairdressing and computer skills. Others were taking remedial reading and writing in the Khmer language. All were described as women liberated from sex slavery. They stayed about two years and no one was held against her will. But I was forbidden to verify this information.

Our first stop was the kitchen, where four young women were preparing lunch. I struck up a conversation with a woman who introduced herself as Sreya and said she was twenty-six years old. Then a large Cambodian woman came up to me and said our conversation had to end. "It is too traumatic for these girls to talk about their former lives," she said.

I turned to Lin Sylor, my escort, who said I would not be able to interview any of these young women about their past despite promises to the contrary. I could ask them about their dreams for the future and nothing else. I went elsewhere to find out more about sex tourism.

Today easy sex draws nearly as many tourists as the Angkor temples. In a survey, tour agents estimated that 21.7 percent of male tourists to Cambodia were looking for sex and 32.5 percent for culture. Another survey did a profile of these men's nationalities. In recent years Asian men are the most numerous—from Korea, Japan, China, Thailand and Malaysia. Chinese sex tourists stand out for being obsessed with buying the services of young virgins, willing to pay hundreds if not thousands of dollars for them in the belief this will enhance their masculinity and health. French and American men top the list of westerners.

You can find these male tourists seeking girls and boys in brothels and on the street. At dusk male tourists find young boys near the Royal Palace or the Central Market in Phnom Penh. They know where to look thanks to Internet chat rooms and local motorcycle and taxi drivers. Similar transactions take place just outside the main gate at Angkor. The most blatant trolling for sex is in the south, on the beaches of Sihanoukville. Since neighboring Thailand began cracking down on child sex tourism, hundreds of sex tourists have arrived in Cambodia with its lax law enforcement and beautiful beaches.

The Ministry of Tourism has joined with several private charities to stop child sex tourism, in part in response to growing pressure from Europe, the United States and the World Tourism Organization. "Don't Turn Away, Turn Them In!" is one of the campaign slogans. Cambodia has passed laws that are better than even those in Thailand, and some Cambodian police work with foreign nonprofits to capture foreign tourists caught having sex with minors. In 2009 three American men from California were arrested in Cambodia for having sex with young prostitutes and extradited to the United States. Among them was a forty-nine-year-old man charged with having sex with a ten-year-old girl and a forty-one-year-old man charged with having sex with young boys for $5 and $10.

The International Justice Mission or IJM, a human rights group with an office in Phnom Penh, played a central role in that arrest. Ron Dunne, the head of the IJM office, took me on a "brothel crawl" through Phnom Penh to show me how difficult his job is and how ineffective those anti-sex-tourism campaigns are.

Dunne is a retired Australian military officer whose last post was attaché at the Australian embassy in Phnom Penh. As we drove around Phnom Penh, he explained how sex tourism ruins lives and society. "Most of the young children are sold by families who are deeply in debt. They're farmers, coming from the rural areas where they can't make money. They'll wait to sell a virgin girl to the highest bidder—a foreign tourist who will pay from eight hundred to four thousand dollars," said Dunne.

"After she loses her virginity, the girl works in a brothel—often drugged and beaten—and by her mid-twenties she's finished. She's lucky to make $10 a night. You rarely meet girls over twenty-six years of age in a brothel. That is the life cycle for sex tourism."

We spotted some single foreign men nosing around a café that fronts for a brothel in the club district. The Soul Club was on the right. Dunne remembered a particularly difficult investigation in the area that included several well-paid informants spending lots of hours gathering evidence, presenting the evidence to the police, shepherding them through a raid and finally freeing the underage girls.

I asked why he didn't just buy the young prostitutes from the brothel. "First rule—*never* buy a girl. It only keeps the system going and encourages other families to sell their children," said Dunne.

Dunne had high praise for a Cambodian general recently appointed director of the government's juvenile section antitrafficking division. "He's good, but he can't prevent all the snitches from tipping off the brothel owners about a raid."

The rescue is only the beginning. The difficult task of rehabilitation of the children takes years. That is done by several charities at a cost of $800 a month for long-term care of as much as eight years or short-term care at $1,200 a month over two or three years.

"Often we can't send the girls back to their families because that would risk the family exploiting them all over again. They depended on the girls for their livelihoods. We have a program to train the families to find other methods of employment and to reintegrate their daughters. Sometimes they do return to their families."

Since 2005, Dunne's group has rescued 406 children from brothels and helped investigate 186 sex violators. As the sun set and the clubs began to open, Dunne pointed to the right. "Look—that corner with the children—they could easily be underage prostitutes. That would never be permitted in Thailand. Here, the police and courts are far more corrupt," he said.

We saw foreigners ducking into a doorway that Dunne said led to a brothel. "It costs a tourist twenty dollars for a night; it costs us at least twenty thousand dollars to rescue the girl and put her on the road to recovery."

The supply of those girls seems endless. As more families are thrown off their land, as rural Cambodia is left behind and the urban elite prospers, poor young girls have few options other than "tourism." The youngsters are sent to tourist spots to sell trinkets, where their families end up selling *them*.

PART THREE

CONSUMER TOURISM

Cruises and Dubai

Cruise ships docking in Cozumel, Mexico

5

CRUISING: DESTINATION NOWHERE

"Welcome to the vacation of a lifetime."

"Smile, you're taking the vacation of a lifetime."

We had flown from frigid Washington, D.C., to Miami in the middle of December, the high season for Caribbean cruises, and by the time we'd reached our cabin, five different waiters and staff members had congratulated us on embarking on this "vacation of a lifetime." We felt like we had won the lottery before we unpacked.

This was the first cruise for my husband Bill and me and we were both excited and wary. We'd heard such a mixed bag about cruises: from "The food is delicious, you'll gain weight no matter what you do" to "Watch out for the crowds at night when they've had too much to drink."

We had boarded at the pier marked Royal Caribbean in Miami, the mother node of a network of cruise ports that stretches up and down the east and west coasts and is invisible to those who have never taken a cruise vacation. Florida has three of the largest ports, all built with public money, like airports. Rising before us was our colossal ship *The Navigator of the Seas*. Weighing twice as much as the *Titanic* and measuring three times the length of a football field, it towered above us like a small sky-scraper.

By taking this five-day cruise down the eastern coast of Mexico to Belize, I hoped to understand why vacation cruises are among the fastest-growing and most profitable segments of the tourism business. The marketing genius of the cruise was evident at security, where a man took our photographs for our official "SeaPass." These identification cards were our room key, our credit card aboard ship and our identification card when we made port visits in foreign countries.

Tangy sea air hit us as we climbed the gangplank onto the deck. A calypso band played toned-down reggae in the afternoon sun; little children and their parents danced on the polished deck. Teens inspected the disco and video arcades. The twenty-somethings were already ensconced at the pool bar. The ship was near full capacity, only a few souls shy of its 3,200-passenger limit.

Our cabin was a pleasant surprise: a lounging area with a couch, the smallest of bathrooms with shower and toilet, and a sleeping area with a double bed. A sliding door opened onto our own private, very petite balcony. It was remarkably luxurious for the price: $1,200 for the two of us—that included the cabin, our meals and all the entertainment and activities we could squeeze into five days.

That works out to $240 a day, barely enough for a no-frills hotel room in Manhattan. The allure of these cruises was becoming obvious. At sunset, as the ship pulled away, Bill and I were leaning on the balcony railing, smiling.

It was time for entertainment. The boat was made to have *fun*. The gilded Casino Royale gambling hall opened for business three miles out from shore. Attractive young women hosted the gaming tables, offering special deals and running tabs for the habitués. Further down was the multistory atrium. This was the ship's center and social hub, anchored by "The Royal Promenade," a replication of a classic European city street with shops and arcades, pubs and wine bars.

We dressed for dinner and went to the ship's masterpiece, a huge banquet hall designed in shades of red and cream to resemble a turn-of-the-century opera house, with a glittering crystal chandelier and a dramatic winding staircase connecting three levels. Glasses and goblets sparkled on the white linen tablecloths. Waiters in handsome uniforms crisscrossed the room in constant motion, serving plates of food and pouring wine. This was the pampering and luxury that the passengers had come to expect. Afterward the evening's "Welcome Aboard Showtime" capped the first day. Simeon Baker, the wiry and indefatigable cruise director, sang and danced and clowned before a band in the five-story Metropolis Theater, welcoming everyone to "five days of fun and excitement." Dancers, comedians and music followed to sustained applause.

Back in our cabin we found a card left on our pillows: "Sweet Dreams. . . . of Happy Shopping" with an invitation to a shopping seminar the next day. Shopping proved to be a major activity.

We explored the ship the next day; Bill settled on a routine of early exercise followed by reading on the balcony with his feet propped on the railing. We arrived late for lunch. Two waiters—Ercan from Turkey and Hagar from India—served us. (All the waiters and housekeepers on the ship wear pins stating their names and nationalities.) Soon they told us they were both college graduates, one with a degree in tourism. Hagar still lives with her parents back in India, and said she sees her job on the ship as an adventure. "I get bored after a month back home," she said.

The food arrived and the conversation shifted. Ercan told us his seven-month work contract on the ship paid $50 a month with no days off. We thought we had misheard him.

"You mean fifty dollars a week," we said, exchanging glances that said "I can't believe this guy could make up such a story."

No, he said, he had meant $50 a *month*. Hagar backed him up. Their work days routinely lasted twelve hours. They rarely leave the ship during those months and then for a few hours at most. In essence, they relied on tips from passengers for their wages, which was the whole point of this conversation. Trying not to sound too appalled, I said that they had free room and board, didn't they? Yes, they said, they have free room and board, but they are required to pay their airfare to the ship and back home.

They explained they had to earn $1,500 in tips each month to cover expenses and earn a small living. We got the message. The passengers subsidized their salaries. Doubtful, I went to the information desk and asked the young Canadian woman on duty what the wait staff is paid by the month so I could tip proportionately. She answered: "Fifty dollars."

Shopping seminars were the only lectures offered on the cruise—nothing on Mexico or Belize, our two ports of call. At the seminar, Wesley and Victoria, the shopping gurus, told us there were world-class bargains in the ports and passed out a free map with lists of reliable stores that they said had qualified to insert paid advertisements in the brochure. Cozumel was especially strong on diamonds, Wesley said, even though diamonds are not mined, polished or set in Mexico. He recommended Diamonds International for the best bargains "to round out your diamond wardrobe"; it had won the cruise line's distinction as the best in diamonds. He asked who in the crowd wanted a diamond tennis bracelet and many yelled back "me, me."

"Stick to the stores on the map," said Wesley. "If you're silly enough to buy something from a store *not* on the map, then my hands are tied when something goes wrong."

Each cruise ship has a live production with dancers and singers. Ours began at five in the evening with an "Ice Dancing" performance starring Oleksander & Tettiana and an international ice skating cast on the ship's rink. The skating, costumes and music were captivating. After dinner Tettiana was back, starring in "Ballroom Fever," a musical production with the Royal Caribbean Singers and Dancers that tipped its hat to both Fred Astaire and John Travolta. Dancers switched from jazzy to period costumes, twirling, leaping and snaking across the stage.

Kathy Kaufmann, a professional dancer in New York and a friend, told me what it was like to be a member of a dance troupe aboard a cruise ship. She described it as something you do when you're young, "a little like backpacking through Europe." The work is demanding; the pay adequate. During a cruise on a Holland America ship, she danced in the two productions each night and then rehearsed from midnight to five in the morning, when the stages were empty. The artists slept through the day in cell-sized rooms well below sea level, "which is a little depressing but great for sleeping since there are no windows." After a year, she said, "I couldn't do that again."

I thought of Kaufmann watching the dancers on our ship.

The next morning we docked at the island of Cozumel. We were part of a mini-armada of eight cruise ships that arrived the same day, each adorned with trademark funnels—Mickey ears on the Disney liner, a splayed red tail for Carnival—and each carrying at least 2,000 people. That meant at least 16,000 people were all getting off at the same time for an afternoon of fun.

A Native Mayan in a feathered headdress, his face and body painted in beguiling swirls, greeted us at the gangplank. Bill pulled out his camera to snap a photo of me with the Mayan when a ship photographer blocked him.

"We paid for the Indian to be here, only we can take his picture," he said. "Ship rates at a hundred dollars for the first four copies; ten dollars a copy afterwards."

"But we're passengers on this ship," said Bill, wondering why we had been put in the camp of "us versus them."

At the cruise port of Puerto Maya Pier, there are no passport checks, thanks to a special arrangement with Mexico and other Caribbean countries. Instead, we walked into a special duty-free zone dominated by three Diamonds International shops.

Fifty years ago the French oceanographer Jacques Cousteau visited the then unknown and sparsely inhabited island of Cozumel and declared its clear waters among the best for scuba diving. Today, every year, 1 million cruise passengers visit the thirty-mile-long island with a population of 100,000 looking for a few hours of sightseeing and shopping in the now densely commercial strip of San Miguel, where, again, a Diamonds International store dominated.

We saw cruise passengers on excursions arranged by the ship, snorkeling near the shore, or swimming with dolphins. (Forty minutes for $122.) We walked past a thatched-roof al fresco bar where other passengers were clasping dripping cold beers. At the pier, buses were disgorging passengers who had taken tours of Mayan ruins. At 4:30 P.M. the "All aboard" signal rang. We had had five hours in Cozumel.

Walking back onto the ship, we went through a security check where the guards were largely concerned about hidden alcohol. No, Bill and I said, we did not buy any liquor. One of the most stringently applied policies of Royal Caribbean is the ban on bringing any beer, wine, or spirits on board. If passengers had purchased a bottle of tequila in Cozumel, they had to hand it over to security where it would be "sequestered" until the cruise was over and the ship docked in Miami.

The only alcohol passengers were allowed to drink had to be purchased at the ship's bars or restaurants. The penalty for disobeying this policy is severe. In our rules book Royal Caribbean states that guests concealing alcohol "may be disembarked or not allowed to board, at their own expense, in accordance with our Guest Conduct Policy."

Those drinks tabs added up. My husband and I were not reveling into the late hours, but our wine at dinner and occasional cocktails over five nights ran to several hundred dollars. When your key card is also your credit card, it is easy to lose track of what you're spending. Essentially everyone has a rolling tab. We passengers were the ultimate captive audience, spending our time and money on that one ship for five days, watching our bargain vacation quickly spiral into a more expensive getaway. Temptation was everywhere. The Portofino Italian Restaurant and the Chops Grille required a surcharge of $25 a person. Massages cost as much as $238.

Our next and last stop was Belize, due south of Cozumel on the Atlantic side of the Yucatan Peninsula. Belize is an English-speaking former British colony that once supplied London with logs and dyes and now relies on agriculture as well as nature tourism. The Belize Barrier Reef is the longest in the western hemisphere and among the country's protected wilderness areas of beaches, coastal regions and untouched expanses of tropical forests.

Landing in Belize, we had to walk through a Diamonds International store to enter the country. The ship again offered excursions: a helicopter tour of the coast for $259 a person, a two-hour walk through a rainforest for $89, scuba diving for $115 or a two-hour boat ride down tropical rivers for $82. Bill and I decided to walk around Belize City. We crossed the narrow Swing Bridge and stepped into a crowd of local Belize shoppers filling the sidewalks of this old colonial capital. Vintage Christmas decorations were strung over streets lined with concrete shops and wooden inns painted soft pastel colors. We stopped at the Medina & Medina jewelry shop in a half-empty department store. A handsome silver necklace made by local artisans cost $100. I asked Mr. Medina how many foreign tourists bought from his store during the year. Very few, he said. The tourists only buy at the duty-free shops on the pier. "And I can't get a permit to sell inside the Tourist Village," he said.

With five thousand tourists landing in Belize on that day, we had expected business to be booming all over the city. But the tourists were off on excursions or were shopping at the pier, following the warning that anything at local stores not approved by the ship would be sketchy.

After five hours we were back on the ship, attending the "Grand Finale Champagne Art Preview" at the Ixtapa Lounge, a warm-up for an auction offering pieces by Pablo Picasso, Salvador Dalí and Henri Matisse. Derek, the auctioneer, taught us how to bid with a paddle and quizzed us on our general art knowledge. He represented Park West Gallery, headquartered in Southfield, Michigan, which advertised itself as one of the biggest art galleries in the world. The next day, at the actual auction, the first art up for bid were serigraphs and hand-embellished graphic works by lesser-known artists. Those were followed by more pieces by artists we had never heard of. Puzzled by the selection, we left before it was over. Back in our cabin, Bill calculated tips for the waiters and housekeeper. Royal Caribbean made it clear that passengers were expected to pay tips or gratuities to "thank those who have made your cruise vacation better than you could have imagined" and had left envelopes in our room with forms listing the rates we were expected to pay: $5.75 a day per person to our housekeeper, $3.50 a day per person to our dining room waiter, $2.00 a day per person to the assistant waiter and $0.75 cents a day per person to the headwaiter, or maître d'hôtel.

We understood this was the basic wage for all of them. Bill wasn't pleased by this sleight of hand, having passengers pay salaries disguised as tips; his revenge was to pay nearly twice as much as suggested.

The Last Night; we could choose from the Final Jackpot Royal Bingo, the Farewell Variety Showtime, the Farewell Dance Party, the Farewell Pajama Party, the Finish That Lyric Game Show, or the final Holiday Street Parade. It was fun, but was this foreign travel?

Just before dozing off that night we got news of a snowstorm moving up the east coast, threatening Washington, D.C. By the time we got home, the Christmas blizzard had dropped more than 16 inches of snow. Once home, I realized the one thing I missed on our cruise was the touch of the ocean: perched so high above the water, you never felt the spray of a wave, could never jump into the water for a swim.

Now I had a sense of the appeal of cruises. It is effortless travel aboard these ships, taking all of the risk out of foreign travel. Once you buy that single ticket, you don't have to lift a finger again. No planning, no moving from one hotel to another, no navigating buses or taxis to find a café that proves to be a disappointment. The excursions on land are tightly programmed, requiring no understanding of foreign languages or cultures. You unpack your suitcase once, sleep in the same bed, and read an activities bulletin each morning to decide whether you want to enter the "Men's Sexy Legs Competition," attend a complimentary slot machine lesson or take a merengue dance lesson for "fun fitness," which were all offerings on our second day at sea. It is the ultimate package tour.

How the cruises made their profit was less obvious: onboard sales of everything from photographs to Internet service to yoga classes was the cash cow. But a lot didn't add up: these are American cruise line companies, but we didn't meet any American employees. And the wages paid were definitely below the American minimum.

Behind the carefree holiday of a cruise—the dancing waiters, the constant shows and events, the spreads of great food and the escape from daily drudgery—is a serious industry that has changed what people expect out of a vacation. It was built by several entrepreneurs who took advantage of changes in American lifestyles, married the design of a resort with the rhythm of a theme park, put it on a boat and won sweet deals through giant loopholes in American laws.

Understanding how these businessmen cobbled together the new industry—where they bent the rules, how they designed a ship to match social behavior—goes a long way toward explaining why the cruise industry is both admired and reviled today and why it is considered a harbinger of where mass tourism is headed.

The 2012 disaster of the *Costa Concordia*, an Italian cruise ship, brought some of these issues to light. The pilot ran the ship aground off

Italy's coast, capsizing it, killing 32 people and destroying the 54,000-ton vessel. The Italian line Costa Cruises is owned by the Carnival Corporation, headquartered in Miami, where multimillion-dollar lawsuits have been filed. The U.S. Congress held hearings questioning the overall safety of cruise ships and decided nothing more needed to be done. The most lasting impact was on the public. The photographs of the downed ship brought immediate comparisons to the *Titanic*, and sales for Carnival cruises immediately dropped.

The creation story of modern cruise companies begins with Ted Arison, the founder of Carnival Cruise Lines. His is an outsize personality, and he lived an astonishing life that contains all the incongruities of the cruise industry. His struggles have been diminished into a soothing legend: Arison built his empire with one dollar; his first big launch was a memorable disaster when the first Carnival Cruise ship went aground on Miami's beach in front of gawking tourists; and yet out of these confused beginnings Arison used his fierce determination to build a success that is "a classic tale of the American dream."

That last line is part of the official Carnival history and its up-from-ashes narrative. Like most sanitized stories, the Carnival rendition diverges dramatically from the real man. Arison was not born poor; his well-to-do family has a long history in maritime shipping. He invested millions in Carnival Cruise Lines over several years before turning a profit, leaning on wealthy friends to come up with the money. But he was bold and brash and imaginative as he redefined what it meant to take a cruise, filling ever-larger ships with thousands of fun-seeking passengers and giving them non-stop entertainment sailing the seas. He decided port visits should be almost incidental, offering a few hours on foreign soil before returning to the real pleasure of eating, drinking and playing on board.

As an industrialist, he did what all embryonic businesses require: cut costs in order to sell his ocean voyages at very low prices and bring in the customers. Under his watch, cruises went from an elite pleasure to a mass market rite of passage. And that is where the story becomes interesting. Arison saw the Wild West nature of late-twentieth-century globalization before the term was invented. He understood the moment. He figured out how to circumvent American laws and regulations—to become global—by claiming the ocean as his home and then selecting an exotic nationality that fit his purposes to make a healthy profit. It was the equivalent of outsourcing without borders. He made Miami the home base of Carnival Cruises, where it remains today, with full access to the American market and use of American infrastructure. His cruise line made the Port of Miami the cruise capital of the world. And yet he accomplished these seismic changes without having to follow American laws and regulations that govern everything from pollution to minimum wages.

As a business model, the cruise industry has been phenomenal, a $40 billion industry in the United States alone, and the fastest-growing segment of the global tourist industry. Cruises are the future.

But cutting corners and avoiding laws have had serious downsides. Cruise ships are not subject to the requirement for federal permits covering sewer and waste disposal systems that are de rigueur for the resorts and hotels on land. As a result, all of those millions of passengers and crew members dining and defecating and showering on the oceans have left filthy discharges in their wake. On land, the cruise crowds streaming into foreign ports by the thousands have disfigured beaches and plazas, building resentment among many locals. Cozumel isn't the only port that has taken on the life of a strip mall. St. Mark's Square in Venice is now a field of kiosks selling cheap imports and lines of tourists waiting to visit the basilica.

This business model was a smashing success for Arison; he died in 1999 one of the world's wealthiest men, with a fortune estimated at $5.6 billion. His heirs have stayed wealthy: his son Micky runs Carnival and is a power broker both in the business and in southern Florida. He is worth over $4 billion and is the owner of the Miami Heat professional basketball team. Arison's daughter Shari is the fourth-wealthiest person in Israel.

The various owners of Royal Caribbean have done just as well: Sammy Ofer was one of the wealthiest men in Israel with assets worth $4 billion before he died in 2011; members of the Pritzker family, who were billionaires before they bought into Royal Caribbean, are permanent fixtures on the Forbes list of wealthiest Americans. (Penny Pritzker, a high-profile member of the Chicago family, was a chief campaign fundraiser for President Barack Obama.)

Once realized, Arison's vision of the cruise industry ultimately supported some of the most handsome family fortunes in Florida and Israel.

Born in British-controlled Palestine in 1924, Arison was the son of a multimillionaire shipping magnate. Merchant shipping in the area was built on the proud legacy of the Phoenicians. The young Arison came of age in a time of war, of the unspeakable bloodshed of the Holocaust in Europe and unrest in Palestine. He rose to the occasion in both instances, showing physical courage and a maturity beyond his years. He volunteered in the Jewish brigade of the British army during World War II, an unsung unit that fought against the Fascists in Italy. After the Allied victory he returned to Palestine and within a few years was fighting again, this time against the British as a member of the Israeli army in that country's war for independence from Britain and against Arab neighbors.

With independence, Arison threw himself into building the new state of Israel, imbued as Israelis all were with patriotism for the new country and its people. But Arison was a merchant at heart, and he began to sour on Israel when the new government issued laws and drafted economic programs that he considered obstructions of free enterprise.

Unhappy, he liquidated the family business and immigrated to the United States, where he started a cargo shipping line in New York. When that business flopped, he bought an air transportation company. Still restless, he sold that company in 1966, saying he was retiring, and headed to Miami, where the holiday cruise story begins.

Southern Florida was beginning its explosive tourist boom. The region was the petri dish for developing mass tourism, just as Silicon Valley in northern California gave birth to Internet technology decades later. The Florida state government was bending over backward to support new business that would bring tourists to the state, especially ones that enticed America's newly thriving middle class to take winter vacations in the sun. Cruise ships appealed immediately to the retired folks in Miami who had moved south from the snowy north. They had time on their hands and money to spend, and they filled the first cruise ships, creating the impression that cruises were vacations for old fogies.

Arison first tried charter cruises, but they did poorly. He changed course and started a vacation cruise business with a new partner, using remodeled ferries sailing from Florida to Jamaica. The firm advertised their Caribbean cruises nationally, betting that they could fill their 3,000 berths every week by convincing Americans that a Caribbean cruise was a natural part of the American lifestyle. Things went well until Arison's partnership exploded in mutual incriminations and lawsuits.

Once again he was on his own, but this time he had salvaged 1 million dollars from that blow-up. He turned to Meshulam Riklis, an old friend from Israel who had become a successful and wealthy businessman. Together they created a very small business in 1972 and named it Carnival Cruise Lines. Arison then bought an old passenger liner that had been dry-docked after airlines took over the role of carrying passengers across the Atlantic. Arison, former owner of two shipping companies, saw the opportunity in these sidelined ocean liners. He refitted the old Canadian passenger liner and rechristened it the *Mardi Gras* to remain true to the carnival spirit.

This was the ship that ran aground on the tip of Miami Beach. It recovered, and sailed on that maiden voyage. After two years the fledgling Carnival company was $5 million in debt. Riklis bailed out. He sold his share of the company, and the debt, to Arison for one dollar—the second event in the legend.

From this rough beginning, Arison took the company from debt to profits in five years. He practiced tight cost controls and economy of scale, packing as many people as possible into a ship. He had two basic and radical concepts: redesign a cruise ship to become a vessel of entertainment, rather than a form of transportation; and achieve his high volume at low cost by operating inside the United States as a foreign company, thereby skirting many of the rules, laws and regulations that applied to his land-based competition. Arison played the game that Asians describe as "neither tiger nor horse." By shape-shifting, claiming in one instance to be a resort and in another a ship, the new floating hotels escaped paying billions of dollars in taxes and wages and implementing systems required under environmental regulations.

These ideas evolved slowly. Arison's Carnival Cruise and his chief competitor, Royal Caribbean, were retrofitting cruise ships for Caribbean cruises to include space for shows: live entertainment with comedians; live musical productions; movies; bands playing in the ballroom for late-night dancing; and game shows with audience participation. Food and drink were heavily promoted. The decks became adult playgrounds. Activity schedules promoted nonstop fun.

The *Mardi Gras* was not large enough to accommodate all this entertainment, so Arison bought its sister ship and named it *Carnivale*. This time Arison had his model ready and *Carnivale* turned a profit its first year. By then the company had discovered its theme.

In his book *Selling the Sea*, coauthored with Andy Vladimir, Bob Dickinson wrote that when he joined Carnival Cruise Lines in 1973 the firm fixed on the term "fun ship" to describe their cruises. "The ship itself became a destination and the ports of call became green stamps [extra bonus]. This was a total reversal of previous cruise marketing. Up to that time, cruise promotion had been destination driven," he wrote.

"By focusing on the ship rather than the ports of call, Carnival could communicate to the public what the experience of the ship and cruising on her was all about."

Popular culture caught on to the potential romantic appeal of cruises. Hollywood veteran Aaron Spelling created a television series that starred one of these new cruise ships as the locale of romance and glamour. *The Love Boat* went on air in 1977 and was a Saturday night staple for a decade. Shot aboard ships from the Princess line, now part of Carnival Cruise Lines, the show featured new passengers sorting out their love lives with the help of the sympathetic captain and crew and a bevy of ship dancers known as the "Love Boat Mermaids."

Each episode opened with the lush and pounding theme song: "Love—exciting and new—Come aboard, we're expecting you," followed by shots of the jazzy guest stars who romanced each other while sailing from California to Mexico and back. No public relations campaign could have done a better job of wiping away the old cruise image of the aged playing shuffleboard and comparing stock tips. These cruises were for the young, the dynamic and, yes, the middle class. It was a floating party.

Enter Kathie Lee Gifford, the entertainer hired by Carnival Cruise Lines to sing a company jingle that lodged permanently into American culture. While the camera followed her around a cruise ship, jumping down a water slide, having her nails done, lifting a glass at dinner and posing with show girls, Gifford sang a tweaked version of "Ain't We Got Fun," the paean to the poor from the golden age of the flapper and the very wealthy. The original lyrics were:

Every morning, every evening, ain't we got fun?
Not much money, Oh, but honey, ain't we got fun?
The rent's unpaid dear, we haven't a bus.
But smiles were made dear, for people like us.

For the Carnival commercial, the stanza was transformed from happy commiseration to a pitch for cruises for the spending classes.

Every morning, every evening, ain't we got fun?
Not much money, Oh, but honey, ain't we got fun?
The food is great here, there's never a bill.
We'll stay up late, dear, let's not miss a thrill.

But having fun on a ship sailing in the middle of the ocean requires prosaic essentials re-creating all of the systems hotels on land take for granted as well as the underpinnings of the ship: the navigation system, engines, power plant, water filtration and purification plants, sewage plants, photography plants, laundry and dry-cleaning facilities, kitchen galleys, a morgue, and storage lockers for the 100,000 pounds of food required to feed 3,000 people every day on a cruise. Also hidden from view are the below-sea-level accommodations for the 1,200 crew members.

These fun ships grew ever larger to incorporate all the services necessary to run a miniature town, becoming megaships with space for elaborate playthings like the skating rinks and climbing walls. And the passengers kept coming.

The jingle promising fun remains the basic appeal of a vacation cruise, along with that inexpensive ticket price. Those bargain prices are possible because of Arison's second innovation—avoiding American laws and regulations.

It is no anomaly that cruises singularly turned a profit in the recent

Great Recession of 2008. While Las Vegas and its casinos suffered and the airline industry went into the doldrums, the cruises were the financial rock star of the tourism industry, remaining the most profitable sector of tourism.

One key is the very cheap wages cruise ships pay.

In the nineteenth century, British fishermen rebelled against their government's restrictions on how many fish they could catch. They turned to an obscure maritime practice known as flying the flag of convenience. They pulled down their Union Jack flags and registered their boats in Norway and even in France, their perennial competitor, flying their flags, escaping the British limits and fishing as much as they wished.

After World War II, when the American shipping industry was hobbling back to life, American companies grabbed on to that same antiquated practice of flying foreign flags and registering in foreign lands. They saw it as a lifeline for becoming competitive again not by avoiding fishing limits but by circumventing American minimum wages, which meant paying their sailors far less money. Under strong pressure from the shipping industry and its friends, the U.S. Congress upheld the legality of foreign registration and flying flags of convenience.

Former Secretary of State Edward Stettinius helped put this new system into play by assisting the African nation of Liberia in setting up a ship registry program in 1948. The offices were in New York, not in Monrovia, the Liberian capital, to make it easy for American ships to register as Liberian. Another office was added later in the Washington suburbs. American shipping firms replaced the Stars and Stripes with the unfamiliar flags of Liberia and later the Bahamas and Panama.

This supposedly temporary fix to reduce labor costs and avoid expensive regulations became a fixture in the world of maritime transportation. Today the majority of shipowners are based in wealthy maritime nations like the United States, Great Britain, Norway, Greece and Japan, but their ships are registered and flagged in foreign countries with "open registries"—that essentially have no minimum wages, labor standards, corporate taxes or environmental regulations and only a flimsy authority over the ships flying their flags. All these countries require is that ship lines pay a handsome registration fee.

These fat maritime loopholes caught the eye of Arison and the other leaders of the leisure cruise industry. So what if these maritime rules were meant for ships transporting goods, not floating hotels. A ship is a ship. Even though Carnival was an American corporation headquartered in Miami with an American client base, Carnival decided to register and flag its ships in foreign countries that had nothing to do with their business. It didn't matter where the ships traveled or where they established home ports. Cruise companies could register and flag their ships wherever it was best for their bottom lines.

Dickinson wrote in his book that the reason cruise ships adopted this practice was simple: following the rules and laws of the United States meant paying minimum wages.

"Many countries, including the United States, Norway, and Britain, have strict regulations concerning unionized labor which severely constrain the ability of a ship to staff with an optimal crew mix, and almost invariably create a higher labor cost than a free-market environment. Other countries, so-called flag of convenience countries, do not have these constraints. . . ."

Carnival registered its fleet in Panama. Royal Caribbean registered its ships in Liberia. (During its two-decades-long civil war, Liberia earned at least $20 million every year by acting as the off-shore registry for foreign ships.)

Cruise lines gain another enormous advantage by registering as a foreign corporation. The Internal Revenue Code exempts any income from airlines or ships from taxation as long as the foreign nation gives the same benefit to American corporations. Neither Liberia nor Panama nor any other open-registry country levies a corporate income tax.

In a symbolic gesture to its original Norwegian owners, Royal Caribbean flew the Norwegian flag on a few of its ships, but in 2005 the firm announced that all of its ships would fly the flag of the Bahamas. Richard Fain, the chairman of Royal Caribbean, said this was necessary because "the competitive nature of the cruise industry is intense, and we must ensure our competitiveness throughout the business."

It was now free to follow the industry leader, Carnival Cruise Lines, and pay third-world wages with no paid vacations or overtime pay while charging first-world prices for the journeys. With some 44,600 crew members on its ships, that amounts to an annual savings of millions of dollars for Royal Caribbean. That's how their waiters could be paid $50 a month with no days off for up to seven months.

This business model is every corporation's dream. Indeed it has been so successful that Carnival and Royal Caribbean have been able to buy out their smaller competitors while expanding their fleets with new ships. Today the two firms account for 66 percent of the global market; Carnival at 45 percent and Royal Caribbean at 21 percent.

As the American lines expanded to the United Kingdom and the rest of Europe and then into Asia, annual passenger load tripled from 500,000 in 1970 to 1.5 million in 1980, and then grew exponentially to 4 million in 1990 to over 13 million in 2010. Passengers came from every economic class and every level of sophistication from people who had never seen the sea before to people who had seen everything and wanted an easy way to travel. They helped propel the cruise industry to reach the phenomenal growth rate of 1,000 percent in four decades.

After his company had made him a billionaire, Ted Arison returned to Israel, leaving behind his son Micky to take over Carnival Cruise and a solid record of promoting the arts through his own foundation and sports by bringing a top-flight professional basketball team to Miami. In Israel he set up Arison Investments and again spent millions on philanthropy. His prize project was the Arison School of Business, which he founded at the Interdisciplinary Center in Herzliya, a well-regarded institute with strong ties to the government and conservative parties. He died in 1999 a very wealthy and happy man. Yet it is hard to square Arison's strong attachment to the special land and people of Israel with his cruise line's business practices that have helped erase what is distinctive in so many other spots on the globe.

American unions fought back against cruise line practices in the 1960s and 1970s, but they were on the wrong side of history. The battle was joined just as globalization took off, opening up previously sheltered markets around the world, Communist and non-Communist. Manufacturing was moving out of Europe and the United States and into South America, Africa and Asia, where China became one great factory employing very

cheap labor. In this new atmosphere, trade agreements centered on opening new markets and protecting investments. Negotiators rarely discussed
labor protections or environmental regulations.

American unions and international labor organizations were blocked.
They opposed the use of flags of convenience and foreign registries; the
International Transport Workers' Federation launched its first campaign
against flags of convenience in Oslo, Norway, in 1948. But that and every
subsequent campaign has failed, in part because there is no enforceable
law in international waters and secondly because unions have fared so
badly in globalization.

Still, with a fleet of over three hundred ships, the cruise industry employed a lot of waiters, busboys, housekeepers and laundry workers. When
they weren't happy with the working conditions, crew members jumped
ship and told their stories at American ports.

Eventually, Congress held hearings on cruise ship labor issues.

Representative William Clay, Sr., then serving as a Democrat from
Missouri, introduced legislation in the early 1990s to require cruise ships
to pay minimum wages and provide other U.S. labor protections to workers
on cruise ships operating out of American ports.

Lawmakers heard testimony from cruise ship crew members that was
considered explosive at the time: crew members working ten-to-twelve-
hour days with no overtime pay and no days off for months; hourly wages
as low as 53 cents; waiters living on tips because their monthly salaries
were a token $50. During hearings Mr. Clay asked why cruise companies
headquartered in the United States and operating out of American ports
should be allowed to ignore labor laws that had been won at a heavy social
price.

The bill stalled in subcommittee and in 1993 Mr. Clay gave up. He
had been stymied by the classic alliance of power and money against the
measure and little public demonstration in its favor. This was no accident.
The cruise industry had courted politicians since its inception, creating
its own trade association, now known as Cruise Lines International Association or CLIA, in 1975. They made strategic campaign contributions
to important allies in Washington and the coastal states—in ten years the

industry gave away $16,953,807 in direct and indirect payments to national political campaigns and locally in Hawaii, Alaska, California, Oregon, Washington and Florida.

The industry won the war over labor handily. Congress even helped the industry's bottom line by reducing fees paid to the Immigration and Naturalization Service. The industry also blocked early bipartisan opposition to cruise companies avoiding corporate income taxes. Representative John Duncan, Republican from Tennessee, argued that "it is totally unfair to let Carnival Cruise Lines pay nothing on profits just because it was incorporated in Panama. . . . Foreign flag lines are, in effect, getting an indirect subsidy from the U.S. government."

The industry refuted those charges, saying it pumped billions of dollars into the American economy—upward of $40 billion in 2010—and created thousands of jobs in the United States.

The unions haven't given up, though. The International Transport Workers' Federation recently launched a campaign against what it called "sweat-ship" conditions on many cruise ships, raising the issue of Dickensian wages, months without days off, inadequate accommodations and routine exhaustion. But the cruise lines are more than happy to refute these charges.

Adam M. Goldstein is the president and CEO of Royal Caribbean International. He is a slight man with a quick, dry sense of humor and a résumé that includes a degree with honors from Princeton, a law degree from Harvard and a master's degree in business administration with distinction from a top European business school.

Three months after my cruise aboard the *Navigator of the Seas*, he agreed to a rare interview at his Miami headquarters, next to the pier where Royal Caribbean cruise ships are docked. We talked for more than an hour in his sunny, relaxed executive suite. It was March and the weather was ideal; he planned to go running once the interview was over.

He answered the industry's critics with ease, once accusing them of snobbery. His main defense was the popularity of cruises. "The single most important driver of our success is how happy we make our customer. So you can talk about other things, you can talk about legal or tax regimes and you can have that conversation, but if we didn't make our customers really happy on a regular basis at the highest level that we know of in travel and leisure, none of the rest of it would matter."

To accommodate everyone—families, teenagers, party-hearty couples and singles, retired people and the multigenerational groups—modern cruise ships are designed to create "zones." Like Disneyland, the layout of the ship considers moving traffic at meal times, or through high-volume shopping and gaming areas, theaters and sports areas.

Goldstein used the image of an accordion when describing how every taste and age is considered on the ship. For example, this is how a cruise works well for a family reunion.

"The family stretches out during the day, the grandparents doing what they like, the parents do what they like, the children doing what they like, and then they all get together at dinner," he said. "They talk about what they did today and what they are going to do tomorrow and they talk about whatever else they talk about, and then when the dinner is over, the accordion stretches out again and they go off to their respective pursuits again.... And that only works if each generation is constantly finding some programming that they like."

That level of service and entertainment at such low prices explains the success, and those low prices depend on paying very low wages to crew members.

Goldstein said that it was wrong to compare cruise wages to American pay. Rather, he said, the pay should be compared to what crew members would receive in their home countries—the Philippines, Turkey, Serbia or India.

"We do have a different wage scale," he said. "Wherever you are on the land, the employees are sourced from that country, they live there. And in our case, what we are able to do is, we are able to generate fantastic opportunities for people from a variety of countries around the world.

"Typically what they are able to earn from us is significantly greater than what they are earning if they would have stayed where they were," Goldstein said. "So our view, not surprisingly, is that we provide fantastic employment opportunities to people from around the world that would not otherwise exist."

Goldstein's argument is what academics call the "race to the bottom" justification, a throwback to the early twentieth century before societies mandated minimum wages, improved labor conditions and the right to collective bargaining. While those rights were codified in national laws and are enforced within national boundaries, they are laws that the cruise companies can ignore.

Twenty years ago cruise ship wages would have been a decent sum, especially for highly motivated people trying to escape abject poverty. Today, though, the wage gap is disappearing and the average monthly income in India is between $60 and $100. And a junior waiter in Singapore can earn $591 with free accommodations as well as tips. Meanwhile, wages for low-level crew members have barely risen since the 1993 congressional hearings.

The result is an ever-higher rate of turnover, with the average length of service for cruise ship employees dropping from five years in 1970 to nine months in 2000, the latest statistics available.

Mr. Goldstein, whose annual salary and compensation ranged from $2.7 million to $3 million in 2008 and 2009, argued that the statistics on wages and days off looked deceptively bad because they didn't calculate the long breaks for workers between contracts.

"The majority of people who work on board work anywhere from between four and eight months at a time. Then they have a break—a significant break—which needs to be factored into the regime because those are the kind of breaks that Lyan and I can only dream of," he said, smiling at Lyan Sierra-Caro, a senior communications executive at Royal Caribbean who sat in on the interview.

I asked if crew members enjoyed paid vacations as he and Ms. Sierra-Caro do.

"No, they aren't paid on their breaks, so they have to have money from the time they worked so it works for them," he said. "But we are proud of what they do. We think they deliver better service on the ship than on the land almost anywhere."

It seemed a slip of the tongue: comparing his crew's service favorably to land-based waiters and housekeepers but not their pay.

Ross A. Klein, a Canadian professor at Memorial University in St.

John's, Newfoundland, and the author of several books on the cruise industry, said that while these near-servitude wages form the backbone of the profits of the cruise business by keeping ticket prices low, the growing source of profits is onboard sales.

"Onboard spending is becoming more profitable than ticket sales. On average, each passenger provides forty-three dollars in profits each day to the big cruise companies," he said. "If you include all the onboard spending, it is now less expensive to stay in an upscale Caribbean resort than to sail there on a cruise ship."

That onboard revenue translates, roughly, into at least 24 percent of all cruise revenue. Along the U.S.–Caribbean routes it can jump to more than 30 percent, according to UNWTO. Booze is one of the biggest earners. In the earliest days of modern cruises, ships served some of the best and most inexpensive drinks around, passing on the savings from buying alcohol at duty-free prices, often in the country where it was produced.

Nowadays, those savings stay with the cruise lines and drinks are at least as expensive as they are on land. And ships are designed to encourage drinking, scattering bars and serving stations throughout, according to Bob Dickinson, formerly of Carnival, who said "the idea is that you should be able to get a drink wherever and whenever you want it.

"In a well-executed ship design, the most convenient way to go from your cabin to the dining room should take you past a lounge," he said. "And because most ships sail in warm waters, you also need a highly visible bar by the pool—or even in it!"

Gambling brings in nearly as much profits. Spas, Internet fees, extra costs for fancier restaurants, fees for sports and exercise classes, photographs and a DVD of the cruise—that DVD can earn at least $100,000 in revenue on a short cruise—and souvenirs all bring in money. As Mr. Dickinson wrote, "Everyone has already prepaid for their ticket and the only variable left that will determine the overall revenue (and ultimately the overall profitability) of a voyage is how much is spent on board.

"The truth is that selling goes on all of the time all over the ship," he said, "and it makes all the difference in the world when it comes to the bottom line."

Convincing passengers to spend is part of the theater of a cruise, conjuring up "the vacation of a lifetime" with unique flashy shows. This is especially true for the third big profit center for cruises: art sales.

Even though art auctions are relative newcomers to cruises, begun in the mid-1990s, they are now big business and a serious source of money. The king of the cruise art auctions is the previously mentioned Park West, a privately held Michigan firm with $300 million in sales each year. Cruise lines receive at least a 35 percent cut of every piece of that artwork. Until 2010 Park West had something of a monopoly, selling aboard Carnival Cruise, Royal Caribbean, Norwegian, Holland America, Regent and Oceania lines.

Enthusiasm is whipped up with flyers tucked into cabins, by announcements on the in-house television channel and by lectures on how to buy art. At the auction we attended, the salesman spoke convincingly about the quality of the paintings and artworks, the high reputation of the artists, and the long-term investment value of the pieces. And everything, he said, was guaranteed with appraisals of the fair market price and a generous return policy.

But over the years hundreds of customers have complained that those guarantees are sketchy. And they have tried to bring legal cases against Park West, but the gallery argued that since the sales were made in international waters, the gallery was outside the jurisdiction of the American legal system.

The customers felt cheated and started writing letters to their members of Congress and their hometown newspapers. The narrative of the complaints was always the same: back home the customers discover that the art they purchased was worth far less than they had paid and, at times, wasn't even authentic. But when they complained, the return policy evaporated and Park West refused to refund the purchase.

Those stories caught the eye of an art expert who registers and tracks artwork. Theresa Franks, the owner of Fine Art Registry website, said she published an article about Park West in 2007 and afterward her website received over four hundred complaints from other unhappy clients of Park West. Those stories, in turn, got the attention of mainstream media including CBS and the *New York Times*. In some instances, the gallery refunded money to people mentioned in those articles.

But Park West sued Ms. Franks and her company for defamation, and after a six-week trial in 2010 the gallery lost the case in federal court. On appeal, a retrial is pending. Ms. Franks also won her appeal to the World Intellectual Property Organization in Geneva to stop Park West from creating a copycat website with an almost identical name.

Eventually, some of the customers banded together and sued Park West in federal court in eastern Michigan for fraud, breach of contract, misrepresenting the value of artwork and unfair trade practices. Park West argued that the case should be dismissed because art sales on a cruise ship fell under admiralty law or the law of the sea. The court disagreed and accepted the case.

"We got standing. The court said that Michigan common law applies, not admiralty law," said Donald L. Payton, their attorney. He said all but two of the plaintiffs reached cash settlements with Park West Gallery before trial. Payton, though, is forbidden to say how much money they were paid.

Significantly, the plaintiffs also sued Royal Caribbean for its close relationship with Park West. Adam Goldstein told me in our interview that he could not comment because of the ongoing litigation. However, two months later, Goldstein wrote in his company blog that Royal Caribbean decided not to renew its contract with Park West.

Here is where the drive to increase onboard revenue collides with the theme of having the time of your life aboard a cruise. Most art buyers haven't sued Park West Gallery, as the owner points out. Passengers on vacation feel free to try things they rarely do at home—like attend an art auction. They trust the cruise line, they feel they can let their hair down and splurge.

Therein lies the easy mark. If this is a vacation of a lifetime, this is a special occasion that deserves a little extra spending, like a graduation, birthday or wedding. In that mood passengers pay as much for photographs as they would spend for a digital camera. They go to spas as expensive as a fancy resort. It's one great memorable experience.

This is what they spend beyond the price of their ticket: on average, passengers younger than 45 years old spend $357 on a Caribbean cruise of three to seven days; passengers between 45 and 65 spend nearly as much at

$345, while those over 65 watch their budgets and spend only $242 on average. And cruise lines and concessionaires have come up with ever-more-profitable ways to make money, like those Park West art auctions with their fine-print disclaimers. This helps explain how Carnival Cruise Lines could report $13 billion in revenue in 2009 during the Great Recession.

Then there are the diamonds. I was perplexed by the diamond-shopping seminars and the ubiquitous presence of Diamonds International stores, even though diamonds and other precious jewels are not mined, cut, polished or set in the Caribbean. Diamonds International stores cluster like barnacles along the cruise path, offering the same jewelry whether the stop is Cozumel, St. Maarten, Cabo San Lucas or even Juneau, Alaska. This is all calculated. The chain of Diamonds International stores was created specifically for the Caribbean to service cruise lines.

Diamonds International was founded by David Gad, an émigré who found work in the diamond trade in New York City. Eventually he was able to start his own business with an unnamed private partner and quickly opened his first retail store in the Caribbean in 1988. Its market was the emerging cruise industry. In partnership with Caribbean governments and, often, with the cruise lines, Diamonds International established their shops on piers that ensured cruise passengers would become customers on their way to the mainland. And those cruise ships heavily promote Diamonds International.

Today the chain has more than 125 stores from Key West to Aruba in the Caribbean, including four on the Pacific coast of Mexico, and 3 in Alaska. In the space of two decades this small, privately held company grew into a powerhouse and in 2007 won status on the exclusive Diamond Trading Company list as a sightholder authorized to buy bulk rough diamonds in Namibia, where the firm built a large gem-polishing factory.

The base of this phenomenal growth is Diamonds International's position as the jeweler of choice for both Royal Caribbean and Carnival Cruise lines. Each line hosts "shopping seminars" onboard, where jewelry from Diamonds International is praised for its high quality, low prices and great guarantees—all the promises Bill and I heard on our cruise. It is the only retailer that receives this blue-ribbon endorsement and exclusive publicity onboard for its jewelry and those of its subsidiaries, such as Tanzanite International.

When I asked Adam Goldstein of Royal Caribbean about the business relationship with Diamonds International, he said theirs was an "arms-length, third-party relationship.

"We don't have any stake in them and they don't have any stake in us," he said.

But, Royal Caribbean owns several ports with Diamonds International, including those in Belize and Aruba. In an interview Jane Semeleer, the president of Aruba's Central Bank, told me that her government was negotiating with Royal Caribbean and Diamonds International to upgrade the pier that the two companies own jointly in her country.

When I brought this up, Mr. Goldstein acknowledged that yes, Royal Caribbean has some partnerships with Diamonds International. Overall, he said, theirs was "an advertising, promotional relationship with us, so they are paying us effectively, without going into the details of how it is structured."

He did say that Diamonds International had won this lucrative monopoly because "customers know they can go and shop there and know that if for any reason they don't like what they bought, they get their money back. .... In the end, they are paying us to be advertising their stores to our guests onboard. And in return for that they make a promise to our guests . . . you can get your money back."

A perusal of the Internet reveals hundreds of complaints that Diamonds International does not automatically refund money for jewelry that is appraised back home at less than what was guaranteed at the ports or onboard. It is hard to say whether Diamonds International is any worse than any other jewelry chain.

On the cruise, this emphasis on buying diamonds felt out of synch with the idea of a carefree vacation. The pep-rally shopping lectures in the ship's huge auditorium added to the sense of a trip aboard a shopping mall—destination nowhere.

For all those reasons, though, cruise ships are the face of modern mass tourism. The industry has turned travel into a shopping spree. Airports have resembled shopping malls for several decades. The most glorious cathedrals and monuments are surrounded by high-end luxury stores with the same brands for sale whether in Europe, the United States or Asia.

You won't find spokesmen extolling cruise vacations as the chance to shop until you drop. More common is this description by Terry Dale, the former president and CEO of the Cruise Lines International Association, the trade group, who told me in a telephone interview that "we have passengers, customers who have wanderlust and a desire to see and experience. That is part of what we're providing them—intellectual and spiritual enrichment."

There is one more profit center for onboard revenue that seems counterintuitive. Cruise lines make significant money from what the passengers do when they leave the ship and go ashore on those excursion trips.

Cruise lines essentially apply the same system to excursion trips as they do to diamonds and artwork. The ship sells the excursions onboard, offering guarantees and then warning against taking competing excursions. Then the ship takes a nice cut from every excursion sold. On average, the cruise lines collect a commission or fee from the local tour agency as great as 50 percent of the price of the tour. In one year, Royal Caribbean earned a third of its profits from selling shore excursions.

Excursion might be a misnomer. They are designed by the hour. On a Caribbean stop, you can choose to take a bus tour of an island's beaches and historic sites or go snorkeling near coral reefs. At ports near cities like Florence and Rome, the passengers are bused to the cities for a visit to a museum or a walking tour, always with great guides and time to eat and shop before returning to the ship.

This is a complete reversal of the original idea of the passenger liners, when the voyage itself was the excursion.

Then ships docked for days at a time; in Hawaii they were met by young boys swimming alongside the hull, waiting to catch coins tossed overboard by passengers. There were days to stroll along the beach, swim in the surf, visit memorials and forests before the ship turned around to return home. Tourists cruising to Alaska in the early 1950s spent two days in Ketchikan, three days in Juneau and five days in Seward. In those days a cruise was truly a rare, once-in-a-lifetime occasion and passengers expected to spend far more time on land, exploring.

Today's cruise excursions are miserly in comparison. What do passengers actually see, understand and appreciate after a few hours whizzing past masterpiece paintings or strolling through an old European capitol with a guide reciting details of an unfamiliar history that will be forgotten by the next morning.

The advantage of these excursions, said Adam Goldstein of Royal Caribbean, was that cruise ships allow tourists to visit so many cities in such a short time, albeit for mostly half-day stops.

"On a cruise ship you can see Tallinn, Estonia, and two days and a night in St. Petersburg, and you can see Helsinki and Oslo," he said, describing a seven- or twelve-day cruise. "It's really not feasible to do that many flights in a two-week period."

This is true and many tourists find a day in Tallinn and another in Oslo more than enough. However, the people of Tallinn and Oslo are having second thoughts about seeing hordes of people descending on their cities at once. Thousands of cruise passengers herded into a few well-known waterfronts or museums do earn bragging rights about seeing the windmills of Mykonos or the Hermitage in St. Petersburg. The regular appearance of these crowds are transforming the cities and ports, helping push out locals and alter the culture and sense of place that drew tourists in the first place.

"Cruise ships have changed the face of tourism in the last ten years, and not for the better," said Paul Bennett, founder and head of Context Travel in Philadelphia. "They're like portable low-rent Hiltons that go everywhere with little concern for the garbage they leave behind or the havoc they make in the short time they invade a place. See Rome—the Vatican and the Coliseum—in a few hours and then take a bus back to the ship. We call it 'drive-by tourism.' "

Venetians call it a crisis. And Venice isn't the only port where the locals feel cruise ships have gotten out of hand. The town of Bar Harbor, Maine, decided in 2009 to restrict the number of cruise passengers allowed in a day. A few years earlier Key West, Florida, did the same thing. And the people of Moloka'i, Hawaii, effectively banned all cruise ships from calling on their port.

This antipathy derives not only from the frustration of seeing your city overrun on a regular basis but also knowing that there is little profit in welcoming them. In Venice the city spends more to cover the services used by the ships—water, electricity, cleaning—and their passengers than it receives in the taxes paid per passenger to the port. (Given Italy's murky political system, it is impossible to find out what that per passenger fee is and whether it goes into the city treasury.)

In a study with the Center on Ecotourism and Sustainable Development, the Belize tourism board found that cruise ship passengers spent an average of $44 on land, not the $100 average cited by the cruise industry. The tourism board commissioned the study out of disappointment that passengers on the cruise ships were not helping the economy as promised. The study warned of an "inherent tension between the objectives of the cruise industry and those of Belize."

By contrast, tourists who came by land to Belize spent at least $96 a day and $653 per visit. Costa Rica's figure for cruise passengers was similar to that of Belize, with an average of $44.90. In Europe, an impartial study found passenger spending in Croatia averaged about $60 in 2007.

After our cruise I spoke to Anna Dominguez-Hoare, the executive director of the Belize Audubon Society, who worries about the effect of cruise ship excursions on the fragile ecosystems of the country. Belize has one of the region's most diverse populations of birds, many of which spend the winter months in Belize's tropical forests before returning north in the summertime to the backyards of many of the visiting tourists. And while she welcomes tourism, Ms. Dominguez-Hoare says that cruise tourism has presented more problems than it is worth. She said that the small head tax paid by cruise ships doesn't begin to cover the damage that cruise passengers cause during their short stay.

"Goff's Caye has really been trampled now. Locals avoid it," she said, describing an island near the Belize port where tourists can snorkel and then feast on barbecue. "Most of the wildlife has fled [from Goff's Caye], but that is fine because these cruise tourists are less sensitive to protecting habitat of birds or monkeys, or protecting coral reef. If there is garbage strewn everywhere, you know the tourists came from cruise ships."

To her mind and those of other conservationists, keeping cruise ship passengers restricted to a few areas—sacrifice zones—could prevent irreversible damage. Ms. Dominguez-Hoare said she isn't opposed to cruise ships in theory but that the numbers are getting out of hand. Excursions of several hundred people descending on a wildlife preserve for a few hours can be disastrous. "Our parks weren't made for that kind of an invasion and the guides can't control the tourists.

"Is there some port, some destination, where they were able to find a balance?" she asked.

When I put that question to James Sweeting, the Royal Caribbean vice president for environmental stewardship, he said, "That is a very good question.

"That is the biggest challenge of my job," he said in an interview, "to convince destinations to make long-term investment in their destinations. I know a lot of government people see us as a problem, which is ironic since they are beating down our doors to get the cruise ships coming."

Both Sweeting and his boss, Adam Goldstein, said the best destinations are the tourism villages that Royal Caribbean creates itself, where passengers swim, eat and play in an artificial environment not knowing if they are in Haiti or another Caribbean nation. Also appreciated are tourism villages near a better-known area like Montego Bay in Jamaica, where passengers can bus in and out of the real country from their base camp.

Places like Cozumel become tourism villages once they open up to mass tourism from cruise ships. Ports, cities, beaches, promenades are now seen as "destinations" and rated as enjoyable if passengers can spend five hours and feel they have had a memorable "experience" captured in photos and remembered with souvenirs. The goal for the cruise lines is to shuttle tourists in and out with the help of local charter buses and tour agencies with the greatest efficiency and assured profits. For instance, our cruise offered us fifty-seven options for excursions to Cozumel, averaging from $50 to $150 per person, and all payable to the cruise ship. Local businesses on the list pay a percentage of their fee to the cruise ship—often as much as 50 percent. Moreover, as in Venice, citizen groups question what happens to the fees cruise ships pay political leaders for permission to dock.

"No Caribbean country has survived intact from the cruise ships. I think that is the worst thing they do, flooding the ports and beaches with crowds of people," said Jonathan Tourtellot, director of the *National Geo-*

graphic's Center for Sustainable Destinations. "You should see what they do to the old square in Dubrovnik."

To Adam Goldstein of Royal Caribbean, these complaints sound like snobbery.

"There is a wish, a nostalgic kind of wish in certain quarters for the days when relatively few people had the wherewithal to go and see places like Dubrovnik for one. It was small numbers of people staying in small hospitality establishments with zero congestion, no crowds, not many people there. Which would have been a really, really nice experience for those few people who had access to that opportunity," he said.

"But in the world where many, many, many millions of people, tens of millions of people, maybe hundreds of millions of people in number, when you bring China and other countries into the mix, really want to explore the world—the idea that you can keep a few places to a few people wandering through the streets with a tour guide is not realistic."

That means ports will have to figure out how to manage the congestion from thousands of cruise passengers arriving in a single day, said Mr. Goldstein. "Our goal is to bring volumes of people in an environmentally responsible way where congestion is manageable. There is no interest on our part to have unmanageable congestions."

Manageable congestion to one man is a nightmare to another. Mr. Tourtellot disagreed with cruise companies taking credit for allowing millions of people to explore the world. "They barely have time to get off the ship, go to a museum or a beach, before they're back on board speaking English to the waiter at their assigned dining table," he said.

The fundamental issue, though, is the cruise company's claim that protests against crowds that are ruining a spot is somehow "elitist." Mr. Tourtellot has toured the beaches that have been trashed and have little chance of recovery. He has watched as centuries-old historic sites are now threatened by regular visits of "managed congestion" of tour buses from cruise ships that are making billions of dollars of business.

"Since when is it elitist to show respect for a beautiful square or beach and for the people who live there and want to protect the beauty that brought the tourists in the first place," he asked.

• • •

Cruise ships do pollute the ocean.

Human activity has damaged the seas by overfishing, polluting, dumping garbage and sewage, spilling oil. The huge maritime transport industry—oil tankers, fishing fleets and recreational vessels, including cruise ships—are some of the culprits. Popular and scientific reports have chronicled the drastic reduction of the fish, shellfish and marine mammal populations. Underwater habitats and coastal vegetation are under stress or are disappearing altogether. The pollution has created dead zones in oceans around the world. Global warming has added the *coup de grâce* by raising water temperatures that bleach coral reefs and force species to seek new feeding grounds.

Against this bleak picture, cruise ships could seem insignificant; there are some four hundred cruise ships, compared to a global fleet of tens of thousands of commercial vessels. And these few cruise ships sail across vast oceans. Yet their contribution to the fouling of the seas is considerable. While the oceans are large, these cruise ships stick to a standard path whether in the Caribbean or the Baltic, disposing of their considerable waste at roughly the same stretch at the same time, year in and year out.

According to the Environmental Protection Agency, in the course of one day the average cruise ship produces: 21,000 gallons of human sewage, one ton of solid waste garbage, 170,000 gallons of wastewater from showers, sinks and laundry, 6,400 gallons of oily bilge water from the massive engines, 25 pounds of batteries, fluorescent lights, medical wastes and expired chemicals, and 8,500 plastic bottles.

Multiply this by those 400 ships cruising year-round and you have a sense of the magnitude of the problem. But there are no accurate studies of how well that waste is disposed of because the ships are not required to follow any state or national laws once in international waters.

Cruise companies won an exemption from the Clean Water Act's requirement for waste disposal discharge permits that apply to the resorts and hotels. Waste disposal discharge permits are given out by the Environmental Protection Agency, which decides what waste they can discharge and the sewage treatment required to limit and reduce the damage of pollution to water. That permit information for each hotel and resort is public, so any new pollution in a stream or coastline can be traced to the offender.

Cruise companies got their exemption by arguing they fell under the category of commercial maritime vessels, like container ships or fishing boats, where "waste discharges are incidental to the operation of the ship." In fact, they are floating hotels where waste discharge is essential to their industry. As James Sweeting, the Royal Caribbean environmental officer told me, "A cruise ship is not a form of transportation, but a form of vacation that happens to transport you at the same time."

Instead, cruise lines say they follow international standards in disposing of their waste water from toilets, showers and sinks, restaurants, spas and beauty parlors, into the oceans, or at least 12 nautical miles off the U.S. coastline. Those international standards do list environmental-safety and pollution-prevention measures, but they lack the authority of national law and are essentially unenforceable. They are issued by organizations under the loose umbrella of the United Nations, which has no navy to inspect ships or enforce the standards. Responsibility for enforcement of standards falls on the flag states like Liberia, Panama and the Bahamas, and they routinely fail to fulfill that responsibility.

Significantly, cruise lines are not required to monitor or report what they release. As a result, neither the government nor the public know how much pollution is released at sea.

International standards were devised to reign in the worst side of maritime shipping when it underwent a rapid revolution. In the 1960s new construction methods allowed ships to grow larger to take advantage of scale, which led to the invention of the cargo container. With the advent of satellite navigation and radio communication, the revolution was complete. Ships became the giants of commerce, carrying 80 percent of the world's freight and clogging the harbors. The last fifty years brought about more changes in maritime shipping than at any time in history, according to the United Nations' International Maritime Organization.

With such a dramatic increase in commercial shipping, accidents and disasters at sea multiplied, especially those involving oil tankers. In 1967 the *Torrey Canyon* spilled its entire cargo of oil in the sea off the coast of Cornwall, England, sparking the adoption of a United Nations convention to mitigate pollution from ships spilling oil or chemicals or discharging sewage and garbage into the ocean. The resulting International Convention for the Prevention of Pollution from Ships, or MARPOL, covers all ships at sea, including leisure cruises.

In general, MARPOL prohibits the dumping of oil or plastic anywhere at sea. Otherwise, ships can dump whatever they want in international waters. Once a ship is within twelve miles of the coast, it must obey local or national laws covering discharges. Only national navies and coast guards have the authority and wherewithal to enforce antipollution standards or laws.

Disasters continued. The *Exxon Valdez* spilled 32 million gallons of oil in Prince William Sound, Alaska, in 1989. The *Prestige*, a Greek ship registered in the Bahamas and Liberia, spilled 77,000 tons of fuel off the Galician coast of northwestern Spain in 2002. Despite the MARPOL convention, the owners of the *Prestige* escaped responsibility. Furious, the Europeans sharpened their own laws and stepped up surveillance of the coast.

Against this backdrop, cruise ships were largely ignored, considered harmless for carrying tourists rather than oil. The awakening came in Alaska ten years after the *Exxon Valdez* spill. The guilty party was Royal Caribbean. Their cruise ships, which sailed through some of Alaska's most sensitive harbors and coastal waterways, including the Inside Passage, were caught illegally dumping bilge water containing waste oil and hazardous chemicals. The bilge water routinely dumped by the cruise ships was sufficiently toxic that the U.S. Clean Water Act forbids its discharge within 200 miles of the coast because it endangers fish and wildlife and the habitat they depend on.

Royal Caribbean was convicted in 1999 of a "fleet-wide conspiracy" to rig their ship's piping system to avoid using pollution treatment equipment and then lying to the Coast Guard about it. The cruise line pled guilty to twenty-one felony counts and paid $18 million in criminal fines, entering plea agreements with the Justice Department in Miami, Los Angeles, New

York, Anchorage, St. Thomas in the U.S. Virgin Islands, and San Juan, Puerto Rico.

The company was put under a five-year court-surveillance environmental compliance program. Royal Caribbean denied that this was a company policy and instead blamed the rogue employees who, the company said, "knowingly violated environmental laws and our own company policy." But in a statement following the 1999 ruling, then–Attorney General Janet Reno said that "Royal Caribbean used our nation's waters as its dumping ground even as it promoted itself as an environmentally 'green' company."

Sweeting, the Royal Caribbean environmental officer who once worked for Conservation International, said the cruise industry has poured millions of dollars into solving most of these problems, something many activists fail to acknowledge. He said he is genuinely convinced that the cruise line was unaware of the illegal dumping in Alaska and "were so devastatingly shocked by what happened."

The government made new efforts to police the industry. In 2003 the Carnival Corporation pled guilty to illegally discharging oily waste from its ships, paying a $9 million fine and agreeing to pay another $9 million to environmental projects.

Environmentalists lobbied for new legislation in Congress and in state legislatures to strictly regulate the discharge of ships refuse and regularly monitor that discharge. The cruise line industry pushed back, saying they were making voluntary improvements in their waste disposal systems.

The clash between these approaches played out in Alaska, one of the oldest and most popular cruise destinations. Citizen activists there said they were tired of the ever-growing size of cruise ships, the noisy crowds filling their ports, the pollution, the dumping and Alaska's ever-shrinking share of the proceeds.

After the Royal Caribbean convictions a group of Alaskans lobbied their state government to hold cruise lines responsible for the damage they caused. Juneau, the state capital, imposed a $5-per-passenger head tax to cover costs of cleaning up after those cruise tourists. Governor Tony Knowles convened a state panel in 2000 to monitor the waste produced by cruise ships during that summer season. One of the members appointed was Gershon Cohen, a scientist and environmentalist who lives in the small port town of Haines, which limits the number of ships allowed to dock there.

As Cohen describes it, the panel tested cruise ship waste for evidence of hazardous material. What they found, instead, was untreated human sewage. "That shocked the hell out of us," he said. "We found the cruise ships were floating poop producers."

The raw sewage came from inadequate "marine sanitation devices" that were designed to treat the refuse from a few dozen people but were installed on ships to treat the waste from thousands. Cohen said the samples testing fecal coliform bacteria from the ships' human sewage were unbelievable: "One ship tested out at nine million fecal coliform bacteria counts per sample. Another tested at fourteen million, another at twenty-four million. These samples to be healthy are supposed to be at 200 or less."

Those pollutants from human sewage were threatening Alaska's marine life, its fish, coral reefs, oyster beds, and sea mammals. Since the Alaskan economy depends mightily on fishing, recreation and other land-based tourism, those findings alarmed the state leaders. The Alaskan legislature passed laws requiring that cruise ships routinely be tested to meet the state's clean-air and -water standards and levying a $1 tax on each passenger to pay for the program.

In Congress, Senator Frank Murkowski, Republican from Alaska, won passage of a law to allow Alaska to set standards and regulate "black water" waste that contains human sewage. No other state had these laws.

The cruise industry pushed back again, and convinced Senator Murkowski to win approval from the Secretary of Interior to nearly double the number of cruise ships allowed in Glacier Bay National Park during the high summer season over the strong objections of park officials.

Then Gershon Cohen and an Alaska attorney won a petition drive that placed an initiative on the 2006 ballot requiring cruise ships to apply for official waste permits with strict limits on sewage disposal. The initiative also created an ocean rangers program of marine engineers who would ride cruise ships to monitor the discharge and that would be underwritten by a new $50 passenger head tax. Despite predictions to the contrary, the voter initiative passed. Some of the requirements were later eased by Sean Parnell, the new governor, including cutting in half the passenger head tax in order to head off a lawsuit filed against the tax by Carnival and Royal Caribbean.

Maine joined Alaska in passing state laws curbing cruise ship pollution. California, with its long, varied coastline and strong environmental movement, has passed the strictest rules against any waste discharge by cruise ships. The laws were sparked in part by a Crystal Cruises ship that dumped 36,000 gallons of gray water and sewage in Monterey Bay. The cruise line was able to claim, rightly, that it hadn't broken any rules. So the town banned the Crystal Cruises ship from the bay in 2005. The California state legislature then passed a law forbidding discharge of any waste whatsoever—treated or untreated, black water or gray water, sewage waste or garbage waste, into California's coast waters by cruise ships or other large vessels. The federal government through the EPA endorsed the law in 2010, which gives the Coast Guard authority to enforce it.

Sweeting of the Royal Caribbean said the company's ships are being outfitted with advanced waste treatment systems that transform human waste into watery discharge that is "as good as or better than municipalities." At the same time, the industry has forcefully opposed the Clean Cruise Ship Act, sponsored by Senator Richard Durbin, Democrat of Illinois, which would require sewage and gray water discharges to be controlled by the Clean Water Act. The legislation would also require cruise ships to use advanced treatment systems and to sail beyond the current 12-mile limit before discharging treated sewage.

The U.S. Coast Guard is charged with enforcing existing laws and standards in American waters, but it has done a lackluster job, largely because inspecting sewage from cruise ships is close to the bottom of its to-do list. After the 9/11 attacks, when the Coast Guard was absorbed into the new Homeland Security Department, its mission has been insistently focused on "antiterrorism." In theory, complaints about ships' discharge in international waters are investigated by flag states like Liberia, Panama and the Bahamas, but they rarely follow up. The Congressional Research Service study of cruise ship pollution rated overall enforcement as "poor."

That leaves the industry as its own enforcer. Terry Dale, of the cruise ship industry group, said cruise companies obey laws and standards, often exceeding requirements, and that they "fully respect our role as environmental stewards, otherwise the future of our industry would be in jeopardy. I would take issue with those detractors who say we aren't taking it seriously," he said in a telephone interview.

In some countries, cruise ships pose such an immediate danger they are under tight restriction. Antarctica has banned large cruise ships outright, beginning in 2011. The cruise ships' heavy fuel oils were causing serious air pollution and, when spilled in an accident, causing irreparable damage. In 2007 the cruise ship *Explorer* capsized in an ice field, dumping 50,000 gallons of marine diesel fuel, 6,300 gallons of lubricant and 260 gallons of gasoline into the ocean where it rests at a depth of 5,000 feet. Cleaning up in those remote, freezing waters was close to impossible. With tourism quadrupling in the past decade to 46,000 visitors every year, the Antarctica authority decided these heavy fuel oils are too great a risk to the fragile environment.

"Without regulations, we are going to have a disaster where a lot of lives are lost and where oil spills out into the environment, and we see penguins being smothered and poisoned by fuel oil in their rookeries," said Trevor Hughes, New Zealand's head of Antarctic policy in the Foreign Ministry.

The Antarctic Treaty members are reducing the number of ships and landings allowed, imposing a ban on building tourist hotels and mandating strict rules on waste discharges from ships. Ultimately, officials and scientists said they hoped to protect the few remaining seas in the Antarctic where there was no pollution, no toxic "red tides," no alien species, no dead zones, no invasions of jellyfish, no control by humans.

But these uninhabited dramatic landscapes are catnip to tourists looking for a new experience. The demand to visit the poles has been so great that at the other end of the globe Norway enacted a similar ban in 2007 for the east coast of the Svalbard Archipelago in the Arctic Circle. The Norwegian environment minister, Helen Bjørnøy, said any ship using heavy fuel oils was forbidden to visit the area; only ships using a very high quality of light fuel oil are permitted to sail inside the nature reserves of eastern Svalbard.

"Tourism has become a big industry," she said in the announcement. "Tourism brings jobs and opportunities to people all over the world—including Norway, including the Polar regions. But tourism—especially the large-scale global tourism—is also producing growing pressures on resources, nature areas and ecosystems."

Air pollution from the ships' high-sulfur-diesel-fueled engines is a separate problem. Arriving, departing and idling in ports, the ships' fuel exhaust releases carbon monoxide, sulfur dioxide and nitrogen oxide that the Environmental Protection Agency considers human carcinogens. As previously mentioned, one ship's engine idling at the dock released diesel exhaust into the air equivalent to 12,000 cars each day. Part of the problem is the cheap, heavy diesel fuel that ships burn rather than cleaner, more expensive fuel.

Sweeting of Royal Caribbean said comparing the air pollution from cruise ships to either automobiles or airplanes was mixing apples and oranges because cruise ships are not modes of transportation.

For the 2010 Winter Olympics, city officials of Vancouver, British Columbia, required all cruise ships idling at their port to shut off their engines. Citing "cruise ship haze," the city said the ships had to use electricity when they docked, hooking up to the hydroelectric power grid to operate as hotels during the games. The Canadians did not want their games spoiled by cruise ship pollution, much like Beijing officials who ordered factories closed weeks in advance of the 2008 Summer Olympics to cut back on pollution during that competition.

The United Nations Environment Programme helped broker that compromise with Vancouver in its assignment to "green" the games. Amy Frankel, head of the UNEP office in Washington, said it was a good story. "There were no unwanted air emissions, which made sense for the environment, and the electricity should have cost less, which made sense for the bottom line."

Responding to the growing evidence of air pollution from cruise ships and large marine vessels, the Environmental Protection Agency passed a new rule that took effect in August 2012, to establish a 200-mile buffer zone around the coasts of the United States, including Alaska and the main Hawaiian Islands. Within that zone, which was initially adopted by the International Maritime Organization, these ships are required to burn cleaner fuel to reduce their nitrogen oxides and sulfur oxides that pollute the air. The EPA estimates that a cruise ship carrying 2,000 passengers on the open sea will pollute the air with the same amount of sulfur dioxide as 31.1 million automobiles every day. The new rule will prevent as many as 31,000 premature deaths every year, according to the EPA.

The cruise industry opposed the new standards, saying it would drive up fuel costs by 40 percent. Terry Dale of the cruise trade group said that cruise lines were already investing millions to improve air emissions with new exhaust scrubbers, some using seawater as well as equipping ships to plug into electric outlets while in port, which has all been voluntary. The industry will continue fighting mandatory national pollution standards and laws.

Besides renewing the national debate over cruise ship pollution, Congress also passed a law in 2010 requiring cruise ships that dock in the United States to tighten their security for passengers through the entire journey. After rising reports of mysterious deaths and injuries on board cruise ships, Congress mandated higher guardrails, and peepholes on cabin doors, on the ships and ordered that all crimes onboard be reported to the FBI. It was a rare instance in which cruise lines were held responsible under American laws for behavior in international waters rather than under those of one of the countries where the ships are registered.

Business analysts warn that things could be getting out of hand. In a recent assessment Lloyds Cruise International said that the industry's "strategy of gigantism" risked undermining the cruise experience on and off the ship. The report said that megaships "with 5,400 passengers may cut the operating cost per passenger but is too large for most ports, and arguably too sizeable to provide a personal experience or to offer either a tranquil or an adventurous holiday."

Little of this criticism leaks out. The cruise industry watches its reputation carefully with multimillion-dollar advertising campaigns, a ubiquitous presence on the Internet and underwriting the expenses of the travel press who are largely mute about the effect of the industry on the environment or the ports they visit.

The industry also has made friends in the nonprofit media, think tanks and organizations by offering them fundraisers aboard cruise ships at special prices. These cruises offer fans and donors the chance to spend up to a week listening to their favorite personalities. At the same time, the price they pay for the cruise fills the organization's coffers with tens of thousands of dollars. Nonprofits from across the political spectrum take advantage of these offers. Media stars like Diane Rehm of National Public Radio, Katrina vanden Heuvel of *The Nation* magazine and Gwen Ifill of public television's *News Hour,* have hosted cruises to the Caribbean and Europe for their organizations. More than one critic has asked if it wasn't hypocritical for organizations to blithely make hundreds of thousands of dollars on cruise ships that pay poor wages and routinely dump pollutants, the exact practices they deplore.

On the conservative side, the *Weekly Standard* and the *National Review* magazines famously made history when their fundraising cruise docked in Juneau, Alaska, in 2007. The top staff and donors were welcomed by then-Governor Sarah Palin, who swept them off their feet. When they returned to Washington, some of the editors, like Fred Barnes of the *Standard,* promoted this fledgling politician as a bright new face of the Republican Party. One year later Governor Palin was the Republican nominee for vice president.

6

DESERT FANTASIES

We landed at Dubai International Airport shortly after 10 P.M. feeling like zombies after a fifteen-hour flight from Washington, D.C. Yet once Bill and I entered the airport terminal, I woke up as if I'd just downed five espressos. The baggage area was frantic with passengers taking this first opportunity to indulge in the local version of duty-free shopping—Cartier and Chanel, Russian caviar and French champagne—before heading out into the hot breath of night. Weary passengers revved up by shopping. We drove into the city and onto Sheikh Zayed Road, the main drag. The night skyline was a pastiche of vanity skyscrapers and giant-size shopping malls with no discernible pattern or aesthetic. Not Middle Eastern or European or Asian or American; not urban or suburban; not tropical or northern. There was little evidence of quirky neighborhoods or old-fashioned anomalies, at least from the highway.

Billboards and banners advertising every conceivable international luxury brand added to the sense that you weren't quite sure where you were, only that you were surrounded by wealth. New trains—empty at that hour—on the new elevated track hugged the highway. Several buildings were entirely dark at night, which locals said meant they were empty. Driving through that surreal city, I felt as if I had stumbled onto a movie set.

Nothing quite prepares you for Dubai. I had read up on its extravagances and made a list of Dubai's nicknames: "Singapore on Steroids," "Manhattan on Speed," "Oz–Las Vegas," "Miami in the Gulf" or "Disney in the Desert." Those sobriquets are inadequate for the breathtaking scope of this tourist fantasy made from scratch at the mouth of the Arabian Gulf in what used to be forgotten desert scrub brush lit at night by stars and home to nomadic tribes who gave way to nimble traders.

Now it is a tourist's paradise. Dubai's malls are legendary in the Middle East and South Asia for selling more brand names outside of any city but London. Its nightlife with free-flowing drinks and a "united nations of prostitutes" for hire is a stunning rarity in a region best known for war and strict Islamic social and religious rules. Big-name architects built fanciful hotels here; one is underwater. Everything in Dubai has to be the biggest, the best, or the most outrageous: from the Burj Khalifa, the world's tallest building, to an indoor ski slope in the desert at the Mall of the Emirates. Travel and tourism magazines can't write enough about all of its over-the-top milestones and uninhibited night scene. Russians and Germans, Italians and Brits, Indians and Chinese, Saudis and Iranians, and Afghanis from both sides of the war come to Dubai to relax. The beaches are cosmopolitan, with women wearing bikinis. The golf courses, horse races, car races, sports stadiums, and film festivals bring in celebrities from around the world, often for a fee. Restaurants serve every cuisine imaginable.

All of this was built in a few decades, at warp speed. Everything was imported: from the people and the materials to the culture filling up the new museums in neighboring Abu Dhabi. Cost was no object: this air-conditioned desert fantasy requires more energy use per person than any other spot on the globe. Understandably, Dubai was considered a one-off original, too bizarre to be duplicated. That assessment proved totally and completely wrong. Today, Dubai is considered a model for tourism in the twenty-first century. Its neighbors in the Gulf region are trying to duplicate its success, even the conservative rulers of Saudi Arabia, who are vamping up the Hajj with glitter and high-end resorts. Foreign delegations visit to take notes. Only China has garnered more accolades for its attractions. The elite World Travel & Tourism Council gives Dubai credit for breaking open the Middle East tourist market as "one of the world's leading case examples of an economy which has positioned Travel & Tourism as a strategic priority for long-term development and prosperity."

The success of Dubai, though, is more prosaic, and basic. First, in a region drenched with oil money, Dubai (and to a lesser extent its neighbor Abu Dhabi) has staked its fortune on tourism—a sign, if we needed one, that tourism is the globe's stealth top industry. Second, and most important, this Middle Eastern emirate is a rare bare-bones example of what the *industry* of tourism looks like unfettered. Few if any major tourist spots have been built solely and entirely as a business. Here the tourist or traveler is treated like a consumer. None of the folderol about finding oneself or disappearing from the troubled world to discover anew the beauty of Mother Nature or the wisdom of an exotic culture. Examining the tourism industry in Dubai is like looking at the engine of a fancy sports car with its hood off. The parts are all there to see as well as the dynamic of what keeps the motor humming. A journey through Dubai—and Abu Dhabi—is a practical course in tourism and its future. It is a pretty frightening one, too.

This is made possible because Dubai is a monarchy, one of the seven emirates in the loose federation of the United Arab Emirates. Officially the UAE is a constitutional monarchy but without universal suffrage or full democratic elections. (Less than 10 percent of the citizens are allowed to vote or run for office and these are chosen by the sheikhs.) This means the sheiks and royal families are free to run their emirates more or less as they wish. They appoint their advisors and members of their councils and legislative bodies; they have the effective say over what laws and regulations are passed. The citizens of Dubai are more like subjects, but very well-paid subjects. The saying goes that with the UAE's discovery of oil in the 1960s, every soul in that stretch of sand hit the lottery for life. The oil wealth of the UAE means there are no taxes, no duties, free housing and subsidized utilities for most citizens.

There is the rub. There are very few Emiratis. Most of the people living and working in Dubai are foreigners—at least 85 percent of the working population in a country of over 3 million people. Foreigners run Dubai—the airlines and hotels, the consultancies and the banks. Yet they all live there on temporary visas with no political rights to speak of and no official say in government decisions. The foreign workers at the bottom rung are famously deprived of nearly all their rights. They are brought in from the poorer communities of South Asia and live in labor camps under conditions that would be illegal in most countries. Experts believe that this very cheap foreign labor was as important as oil wealth in underwriting Dubai's growth as an international tourist attraction.

Citizens without votes and foreigners without rights leave the sheikhs in charge to organize Dubai without fear of protests or popular backlash, lawsuits or sit-ins. There are no political parties to contend with or to protest the extravagance that requires the highest water consumption per person in the world and some pretty awful sewage disposal that has polluted or destroyed many of the beaches. No independent citizen groups exist to halt construction that threatens the environment or to protest the sound of jets flying in at all hours of the night; no labor unions to demand better pay and living conditions; no independent experts to impose regulations on those skyscrapers.

Dubai's leader, Sheikh Mohammed, of the ruling Al-Maktoum family, has taken full advantage of the circumstances to push the business of his emirate. In a 2007 Newsweek interview he described himself as the "C.E.O." of Dubai. He has won praise from business groups for his dedication to efficiency and growth. When the global economic meltdown brought Dubai to its knees in 2009, its high-flying status seemed doomed even after Abu Dhabi, the wealthiest of the seven emirates in the UAE, bailed out Dubai with loans of over $10 billion. Yet, while the rest of the world struggles, Dubai has rebounded, welcoming millions of tourists again—three times as many foreigners as New York City. At the end of 2010, Dubai's most expensive hotels were full during the Muslim holiday of Eid Al-Fitr and, again, for New Year's Eve.

One reason is location. Dubai is an oasis of conspicuous consumption on the edge of a region simmering in conflict. Taliban commanders from Afghanistan have been known to disappear to Dubai for a break. During the Arab Spring, when dictatorships were being challenged throughout North Africa, the Dubai hotels were filling up again with both the citizens of the countries of the Arab Spring and the tourists who normally visited the Pyramids of Egypt or the beaches of Tunisia.

So that missing sense of place that I felt that first night is all part of the business plan. In Dubai you could be anywhere and nowhere. It is a playground for tourists, after all. And wasting resources and calculating the cost to the environment isn't part of the spread sheet here. Here the industry rules with few regulations or restrictions, where the centerpiece of a journey in the United Arab Emirates is widely advertised extravagant consumption with no concern about the cost. And in our age of dramatic climate change resulting from such consumption, the basis for this tourism success story is wildly unsustainable. Dubai and the United Arab Emirates are models for the overconsumption that is threatening the planet.

Airports are the foundation of any tourism industry. Once I slept off my jet lag, I went back to take a closer look at Dubai's three enormous terminals. I walked into what can only be called temples to duty-free shopping. Even the two oldest terminals—Terminals One and Two—are polished to the highest sheen. A huge gold palm tree stood at the center of the concourse, marking a gold counter that actually sells gold in value of 18, 22 and 24 carats. Then I power-walked over to Terminal Three, which raised the shopping bar even higher. This time, the décor suggested a swank hotel, even a palace, with an atrium that climbed to the heavens. Marble and gleaming brass and endless escalators and elevators: everything to make you comfortable and put you in the mood for shopping.

Everyone could be tempted into buying something here: perfumes, fashion, toys, food, cameras, sunglasses, luggage, more gold, jewelry, liquor. Upbeat modern songs floated through the air; restaurants and cafés were full; Indian men in work clothes were buying whiskey to take home; and women in veils were spritzing perfumes. In 2010, Dubai's duty-free shops sold $1.25 billion to passengers, placing the airport up in the rarefied company of Singapore and Amsterdam airports, the top duty-free heavy-hitters.

That retail triumph is woven into Dubai's status as a major air hub. It began with geography. Dubai is at the cross roads between Europe and South Asia, the Middle East, North Asia and Africa. Over 100 airlines fly out of Dubai to 100 destinations. During the annual Hajj pilgrimage, Terminal Two is crowded with the faithful going to Mecca.

Yet fifty years ago there was no airport. Dubai was still a rough-edged port city, famed for pirates, gold smuggling and turning a blind eye to questionable imports and exports, not to mention money laundering. Oil had just been discovered. Sheikh Rashid, then the ruler of Dubai, decided to take a page from other ambitious small port cities like Singapore and become a regional center for trade, finance and especially tourism. By necessity, Dubai would not depend on its oil supply.

Those were the earliest days of modern tourism, when the industry was expanding through the airlines. This new technology of transoceanic flight was opening up the world, country by country, with new airstrips, landing rights and full-fledged airports. Cities were clearing farmland beyond the suburbs and paving runways. It was a point of pride that countries created their own national airlines to be flagships of these airways. France is the obvious example of how the old world responded. As the world jumped into the age of tourism, the French modernized the Orly airport south of Paris, built in 1932, and then in 1974 added the enormous Charles de Gaulle Airport to the east of Paris, giving Air France its own terminal.

It wasn't obvious why Dubai needed an airport. No one had heard of it and there was nothing to do there, no cultural sites to see, no reason to spend the night, much less a week on vacation. The sheikh went ahead anyway and built an airfield and terminal following the now-tired principle of "build it and they will come." He pursued an "open skies" policy of basically unrestricted landing rights in Dubai in order to attract business from near and far. And he raised the ante by stocking the airline terminal with the region's first duty-free shopping, a move that helped make the place profitable from the start and somehow fitting for the emirate with an outsize reputation as a pirate's haven. The emirate was still under nominal British rule, and these old colonial masters weren't thrilled with the idea of a new airfield. The sheikh was undeterred. At first, the new "international" Dubai airport depended on flights from the regional Gulf Air, and planes from other companies that stopped off for refueling. Once that airport was built, people did spend time in Dubai, mostly traders or diplomats, and they needed a hotel. None existed.

The sheikh pushed and an Airlines Hotel was built near the airport in 1960. By the end of the decade the Carlton Tower and the Ambassador Hotel had risen near the airport to lodge people on layovers and guests of locals. Dubai was ready to proclaim itself a "tourist destination" and in the 1970s to sell its beaches and balmy weather—the Miami or the Mediterranean of the Middle East. The large chain hotels took the bait. Sheraton and the Intercontinental built five-star hotels, and European sunbathers showed up for winter holidays on the sand and warm waters of the Persian Gulf, with palm trees and camels as backdrop.

Spreading travel and tourism beyond Europe and North America was tricky, requiring a pioneer spirit. Ed Fuller, the president and managing director of international lodging at Marriott International, told me that hotels followed airplanes. He helped mastermind Marriott's expansion overseas, especially in the Middle East, and is an informal historian of tourism. "To win landing rights in many countries, airlines had to promise that hotels would be built for the people who came on those airplanes. That's one of the reasons Hilton became an international company."

The ball was rolling. Completion of the Dubai airport led to hotels that led to more new airlines using the airport and then more new hotels for the tourists they brought in. By the end of the 1970s, Dubai's airport actually looked international, with the now-defunct British airline BOAC and the German carrier Lufthansa leading the way. By the 1980s over forty airlines were flying into Dubai. In the meantime, Dubai became independent from Great Britain and joined with neighboring emirates to create the UAE in 1971. About ten years later, as they were sorting out their future prospects, several of these gulf neighbors got into a quarrel with Dubai. The regional airline company Gulf Air, then backed by Bahrain, Abu Dhabi, Qatar and Oman, wanted Dubai to pay it subsidies and give special concessions. Sheikh Rashid wasn't happy with the demand, and when he refused to accept these conditions, the airline cut back services to Dubai.

That could have put a severe dent in Dubai's plans for tourism, so the sheikh made the wildly risky decision to create an airline just for Dubai that he named Emirates. With $10 million and the help of two British expatriate airline experts, he put his son Sheikh Mohammed, the current ruler, in charge of starting up Emirates and turning it into the region's star carrier.

That was 1986—an auspicious moment in tourism and all the stars aligned in Dubai's favor. Just as Emirates was getting off the ground, the world opened up after the fall of the Berlin Wall. By the 1990s previously closed economies were jumping into the world markets, especially in Asia: China, India, and Southeast Asia. Emirates saw an opening and got landing rights to fly into these newly developing countries, especially the second- and third-tier cities that had only known puddle-jumper airlines, what the industry called "under-served areas," which became lucrative markets when the middle classes started flying, on Emirates Airlines.

More advanced technology allowed the airline company to focus on Africa and Europe and eventually North America. Thanks to that gift of geography, Dubai now served a market of 2 billion people living within four hours by plane and another four billion within seven hours. Since the turn of the twenty-first century, long-haul jets can fly nonstop for up to 16 hours, and Emirates Airlines could offer nonstop flights to Washington from Dubai, or to Sydney and even to São Paulo.

"Dubai completely changed the rules of the game," said Richard Quest, the CNN anchor and airlines correspondent whom I met when we both spoke at a tourism conference in Abu Dhabi. Quest said it would be hard to underestimate how central the airports and airlines have been in transforming Dubai into a world-class tourism destination, how Dubai willed itself to become one of the major hubs in the airline world. In a few years, it could be *the* hub.

The very weakness of Dubai—a blank canvas, in the middle of nowhere with a tiny population, no claim on a great history or culture, and an archaic government—became its strengths in the tourist industry. And the loosening global marketplace meant Dubai had access to cheap labor and all that oil money to finance the venture.

Emirates Airlines is wholly owned by the government and spent the billions of dollars necessary to eventually buy a fleet of the best airplanes. (No airplane is older than five years by company policy.) It has been profitable from the start. Further, Emirates can offer "world-class service" at reasonable rates below that of the competition because its costs are much lower. And since citizen complaints about the noise or environmental impact of airports are irrelevant, Emirates can offer night flights, large terminals and plentiful runways unavailable in other countries where locals demand restrictions and regulations.

Labor costs at Emirates are at least 30 percent lower than those at other airlines, largely because labor laws for the lowliest workers in the emirate are considered nearly medieval in a country of such wealth—a point of special importance for construction of those hotels, palaces and stadiums. Pilots and other members of the professional staff are paid competitive international wages, which are especially attractive because there are no taxes in Dubai. The lower on the employment scale, the lower the wages, whether in housekeeping or catering. At rock bottom are the countless construction workers who built the airport and hangars. And like all foreigners, they live in Dubai on two-to-three-year temporary visas that are granted at the request of the employer. That means if your employer is unhappy with you, you're not only out of a job; you are on the next airplane out of Dubai.

Whatever works for business becomes government policy in Dubai, Inc.

Today, Emirates Airlines is ranked as the world's largest airline by passengers carried and by capacity. It is easily one of the most comfortable airlines I've ever flown on as well as one of the most convenient and inexpensive in that part of the world. Remarkably, when I had to fly from Bangladesh to Sri Lanka, the easiest and least expensive route was through Dubai on Emirates Airlines, even though that meant double the time in the air.

Alain St. Onge, the CEO of the Seychelles Tourism Board, said that Dubai is the most popular transit point for flights to his island nation off the coast of Africa. "We have more transfers from Dubai by far, more than from Johannesburg. If we want more flights, Dubai always said yes. Other airlines had to figure out the pros and cons. Dubai could say yes."

Other airlines have called foul and accused Dubai and Emirates Airlines of providing hidden, questionable subsidies for jet fuel. So far, none of the charges have stuck, although Emirates resists adding extra charges other airlines have been forced to impose, and even dropped the fuel surcharge in 2012 as the price rose.

To understand the repercussions of having such a huge and growing airline, consider the value of business done with frequent-flyer miles. Started as a marketing gimmick by American Airlines in 1981, frequent-flyer miles are now considered one of the largest currencies in the world. In a 2005 analysis, *The Economist* magazine valued frequent-flyer miles as greater than the U.S. dollars in circulation that year. British Airways said its frequent-flyer miles are one of the four biggest currencies used to buy airline tickets.

Airlines and airports are in a category of their own in the tourism industry.

Today, Dubai is the third-largest airport in the world for international passengers and poised to grow even larger. Within five years Dubai plans to complete an entirely new airport at Jebel Ali that will be the largest in the world. At that point the Gulf region will have a greater airport capacity than the combined giants London Heathrow, Paris Charles de Gaulle and Frankfurt. Already, the head of Air France is warning that this stretch of sand on the Gulf is poised to dethrone Western Europe as the globe's central air hub.

As the rest of the world struggled to recover from the Great Recession of 2008, tourism in Dubai was up within two years, with 4 million passengers flying into Dubai in one month alone. So what do all those millions of tourists do on vacation in Dubai?

First, they shop.

Leaving the airport for the city itself is part of the experience. Bill and I rented a car with a driver and headed to the city. In daylight shops beckoned you at every corner. I brought along one of the standard tour guides, *Footprint Dubai* by Zee Gilmore, an expatriate who was born in Dubai and raised in England. She gushes: "Is there anywhere else on earth that can claim to be so attuned to the whims of tourists, so wholly dedicated to the entertainment of its guests and so completely accomplished in the pursuit of pleasure?"

I vote NO—Dubai wins by a mile.

Driving down Sheikh Zayed Road, we passed ever-larger shopping malls with glamorous names I recognized from glossy magazines. This is the Middle East's version of Beverly Hills' Rodeo Drive, London's Oxford Street, New York's Fifth Avenue and Paris's Avenue Montaigne. This is why deposed rulers of Pakistan, an exiled former prime minister of Thailand

and Saudi princes make Dubai their home away from home. We opted for the famous Mall of the Emirates, where "shopping is just the beginning," and the newer Dubai Mall.

The expanse of parking lots rivaled those at a professional football stadium; we worried about getting lost. This wasn't a shopping mall, it was a city. In the desert heat of Dubai, shopping malls substitute for town squares or public parks. Locals meet their friends and families at the mall, and walk around in large circles in a mall version of a Spanish paseo, stopping for a meal, then catching a movie, all under the same roof. For tourists, these air-conditioned shopping malls are often the closest they get to meeting locals. We passed young girls eating ice-cream cones with their cell phones glued to their ears. Emirati families crowded in front of a floor-to-ceiling aquarium, the children screaming when a shark swam by. Mostly we saw foreigners. Soon we were picking out the European languages—French, Spanish, German—and judging from a woman's robes and scarves, figuring out the different Muslim nationals represented in the shopping frenzy.

And they were shopping. Over 450 clothing stores were listed in the directory. I was dizzy writing down the names of all the designer shopping bags looped like bracelets on these ladies' arms: DKNY, Cerrutti, Hugo Boss, Ralph Lauren, Missoni, Fendi. This is one of the planet's "hottest shopping spots."

We took a break at one of the 75 restaurants and cafés listed in this one mall. Our choice was Le Pain Quotidien, a Brussels-based chain, comparing the sandwich to our favorites at the outlet in our Washington, D.C., neighborhood; nearly the same taste. If we had wanted, we could have picked up a snack at one of the pricey grocery stores, too. Entertainment was next on our list. The two big choices were an amusement park called Magic Planet and the jewel in this crown—Ski Dubai, a fake indoor ski slope in the middle of the desert.

From the outside looking in through thick plate-glass windows, Ski Dubai resembles a giant snow globe, with fake snow falling, a ski lift, and real humans skiing and snowboarding. The ceiling is painted the blue of early dusk. Distant mountains rise on a painted mural. Lights are dimmed to add to the effect. Children clambered up the bunny slope, celebrating a birthday. Their parents sat on the other side of the windows drinking coffee at the St. Moritz Café and watching their children slide down in toboggans.

Suleh Sueed Abdullatif of Ski Dubai guest relations hovered nearby. He told me he had been a policeman for five years but left his job to work in the mall's snow slopes because he had always wanted to travel. His new job gave him the feeling he was in Europe. "I have never been to the mountains, but I have no need to go there now. I have it all here. This is real snow, man-made real snow," he said. "I used to do sand boarding in the desert, but it is hard on real sand. Now I go snowboarding here on my time off."

We had this conversation in English, that limited "global" English that is sufficient for a sales transaction, directions or chitchat. (I do not speak Arabic.)

Abdullatif captured the premise or promise of Dubai. The real world can be replaced with theme park artificiality. No expense is too great. Experience is negotiable. Everything can be imported or borrowed, then packaged and sold to the tourism industry. A simple slide down a small man-made slope has a superficial appeal over sports on a cold mountaintop; a flight to Dubai takes the place of a hike through the Alps, the frustration of speaking a foreign language and the adventure of living in a foreign culture.

Everything in the modern tourism industry discourages such an effort. The Kempinski hotel in the mall is a case in point. "Snow in August" headlines a story in the Kempinski glossy magazine extolling the virtues of staying in one of their fifteen ski chalets "overlooking a gigantic snowdrome in the middle of the desert; the incongruous contrast it offers between the stifling temperatures outside against the minus 1 degree Celsius that is maintained within Ski Dubai at all times . . . you can enjoy a cool experience that's unrivalled by any hotel anywhere in the world."

That is Dubai. Nothing can rival any number of the hotels built to outclass each other. The Hydropolis Hotel is the "first underwater luxury resort" built on the seabed, over 60 feet below the water; its suites have clear Plexiglas walls to view artificial bubbles and sand and "mermaids." Then there is Burj Khalifa, the world's tallest building, rising higher than two Empire State Buildings piled on top of each other. Here you can stay at the

Armani Hotel Dubai, advertised as the first hotel developed by the Italian designer Giorgio Armani. Fine dining includes Japanese, Mediterranean, Indian and, of course, Italian. Nothing Middle Eastern, though; that is not part of the "Armani lifestyle experience."

I couldn't understand why anyone would want to stay in a hotel underwater or one in the highest building on earth so, for a different brand of opulence, Bill and I visited the Atlantis Hotel. This is the second Atlantis built by a South African millionaire—the first is in the Bahamas and is advertised ubiquitously as if it were the original Atlantis surfaced from its watery grave. The Dubai Atlantis is a megaresort on Palm Jumeirah, the world's largest artificial island, which cost the government $12 billion to build from desert sand and millions of tons of rock. To the consternation of environmentalists, native sea life was destroyed during the dredging. The government said that new, foreign fishes have since colonized the waters. As we drove down the causeway, we passed new residences and villas built in an architectural style that might be called modern Ali Baba. Then through the heat haze and across a snaking narrow bridge the pink-palazzo-colored Atlantis Hotel rose into full view, an image straight out of a James Bond movie.

The hotel fosters that impression. Its opening in November 2008 was an extravaganza of fireworks seven times larger than the display at the Summer Olympics in Beijing that year and reportedly big enough to be seen from outer space. Two thousand celebrities came, including Denzel Washington, Charlize Theron, Robert De Niro and Michael Jordan, although a few declined, saying it might not be a good idea during the Great Recession to decorate the opening of a hotel that charges $37,000 a night for its penthouse suite.

We arrived on a mildly sweltering morning. Tour buses and taxis were lined up outside along the seawall. Giant bubbling fountains marked the entrance, past the security guards who were easily appeased when we said we had come for lunch. The lobby is the size of a small auditorium, defined by icing-white palm columns that disappear into an arched canopy over a 40-foot Dale Chihuly sculpture. Its crystal-blue glass twists ending with a golden flare gave the place the feel of a high-class Arabian boudoir. Gold leaf decorated murals and mosaics with seahorses and other underwater creatures. The piped-in music had an underwater sound as well, the kind you hear at a spa. Then we turned around and saw the point of the décor. There was a truly gigantic two-story aquarium, home to 65,000 fishes and sea animals, including flapping manta rays and whale sharks. (The whale sharks were later released after protests from animal rights groups.)

We slid into the crowd in front of the floor-to-ceiling glass panels, next to a Sikh family from the Punjab, a young French couple and two Russian tour guides planning a package tour to the hotel. Everyone was pointing and exclaiming "Ooh" or "Aah."

After all of the artificial and make-believe of Dubai, it was amazing to see real fish. The hotel also has real dolphins, flown in from the Solomon Islands so guests can swim with the mammals in "Dolphin Bay." In this instance, the people trying to protect wildlife wish the hotel had not pulled the dolphins out of the sea. There is also Aquaventure, a water park with a "Lost Civilization of Atlantis" water slide, a Royal Pool Beach, Zero Entry Pool, and an activity schedule rivaling anything offered on a cruise ship: hula hoop contests, touch rugby for teens, potato sack races, limbo contests, a movie lounge, video arcades, craft-of-the-day at the Kids Club, ping-pong, trampolines, a tennis academy, book reading on the beach for small children and Dubai bus tours, plus shops, cafés and restaurants. Also like the cruise ships, the staff here came from everywhere: Turkey, the Philippines, the United States, Great Britain and India.

You could spend a week at the "Palazzo" of Atlantis and never leave the resort and its 112 acres, which is the point. Ed Fuller, of Marriott, said that the all-inclusive resort, "where guests spend most of their money in your hotel," brought the greatest profits in the hotel industry today.

All that seemed in jeopardy during the Great Recession when Dubai had to borrow billions from Abu Dhabi and experts were predicting the demise of the emirate, especially its rise as a tourism haven. The prospects of Dubai defaulting again are high, in part because the terms of the loan and even the size are not public. Dubai's public debt is spread out among various government-owned investment conglomerates, including the Nakheel property firm, a subsidiary behind the Atlantis. No one knows whether the initial $10 billion bail-out was enough and whether the current recovery will be enough for Dubai to repay an $18 billion principal that is due on its state-owned entities. (The question of sustainability rests on Dubai's extravagant debt as well as its outrageous use of energy and its environmental degradation.) The leaders assured their creditors that they could go back to the basics, leaning even more heavily on tourism.

Yet the Atlantis Hotel is a success story, at least on the surface. Even though it opened during the recession and caters to wealthy clients who might have lost a good chunk of their portfolios, the hotel is in demand. During the 2010–11 Christmas and New Year's celebrations, there wasn't an empty room. Why tourists from near and far wanted to spend the holidays away from home in one of Atlantis's nearly 1,600 rooms can be answered by that James Bond image.

Dubai has done such a good job nurturing its glamorous, brash, devil-may-care image that the city made it into the latest James Bond novel, *Carte Blanche*, as the site of danger, and of course lots of luxury products. The backdrop for the movie *Sex and the City 2* was Abu Dhabi, with Carrie and her friends cavorting in an imaginary desert city. (Abu Dhabi refused permission to film the licentious story in the emirate.) In Filipino and Indian films Dubai is the Promised Land reachable by selling yourself out as a common laborer and then hoping to either strike it rich or fall in love. The Dubai Studio City complex, the Hollywood of the Gulf, attracts Middle Eastern, European, Asian and American television and filmmakers who routinely use Dubai as a backdrop.

Those films feed tourism—just check the official website for tourism in Austria. Julie Andrews and *The Sound of Music* are central to the "brand" of the country.

The appeal of Dubai stems in part from its location on the volatile edge of Middle Eastern and Asian war zones. Each new conflict brings more tourists. Some are disguised as soldiers. On our plane from Washington, we were surrounded by mercenaries or contractors who flew into Dubai on their way to Iraq or Afghanistan or Pakistan, with some serious time off in the emirate. These young men with short haircuts looked like they might have been recently discharged from the Marines and were hired on contract to take part in one of the wars—as private guards, in logistics, transport or a dozen other fields. Dubai reminded me of Thailand during the Vietnam War, when American soldiers were given short vacations from the war for R & R (rest and recuperation) and many of them spent their time off on Thai beaches and Bangkok bars, marking the beginning of the Thai tourism boom.

With its monolithic government devoted to tourism, Dubai and the UAE have cashed in on the eruptions of war and revolution in the Middle East. In the spring of 2011, Dubai hit the jackpot when thousands of tourists fled Egypt as the government faced down demonstrators demanding freedom in Cairo's Tahrir Square. This Arab Spring of revolution was a historic turning point for democracy but a headache for the tourist industry as cruise ships were diverted to Turkey and holiday makers switched their vacations from Egypt's Sharm el-Sheikh Red Sea Resort to Dubai, lifting hotel occupancy by more than 25 percent and adding thousands more shoppers to the crowds attending Dubai's annual Shopping Festival. Tunisia, where the revolts against corrupt dictatorships began, lost half of its tourism business, some of it diverted to Dubai.

In 2011, during the wave of revolutions, Dubai emerged as the top city for tourism in all of the Middle East and Africa, attracting not only the greatest number of tourists but the greatest amount of money spent by tourists.

That success has translated into an impact on the biggest single annual tourist event in the world—the Hajj pilgrimage during five days of the twelfth month of the Islamic calendar. Devout Muslims are required to make the Hajj pilgrimage to Mecca, Saudi Arabia, once in their lifetimes, as long as they are physically fit and can afford the journey. Mecca was the town where the Prophet was born and lived until he moved to Medina, where he died. With the modern ease in travel and inexpensive airfare, the pressure for permission to make the Hajj to Mecca is immense. No more than 3 million Muslims are given visas every year. (The shorter Umrah pilgrimage to Mecca can be taken at any time of the year and is not required.)

Religious pilgrims were some of the first true mass tourists in history. Worshipers traveling as a group to foreign lands to seek salvation needed lodging and food, inspiring innkeepers and Church officials to open their doors to the faithful and create new businesses and direct religious spectacles. Eventually, Christians followed three great pilgrimage routes: to Jerusalem, to Rome and to the Cathedral of Santiago de Compostela in Spain.

The Islamic pilgrimage of the Hajj has been in continual practice since the seventh century. The traditional route to Mecca was overland, from Damascus, Cairo and Aqaba, traveling south down the western edge of the Arabian Peninsula to Mecca. Or they traveled from Kufa and Basra in eastern Iraq across the desert to Jeddah as the stopping-off point for Mecca. This larger region from Jerusalem to Jeddah is the epicenter of religious pilgrimage. Jerusalem is considered sacred by all three of the desert faiths: Judaism, Christianity and Islam. For all these faiths, the "journey" is one of the most ancient and deeply felt similes. A faith journey tells of conversion and redemption. An actual pilgrimage is an act of faith.

In earlier years, making the Hajj could be a dangerous proposition. Bedouin tribes robbed the pilgrims as their primary source of income until the Ottoman Empire took over the peninsula and put an end to the attacks. Instead, they paid the Bedouins to protect the foreign pilgrims on their way to Mecca and Medina. The pilgrims who bought camels from the Bedouins and lodging and food along the route were the main source of money for the region. At the beginning of the twentieth century the Ottoman rulers built a railway connecting their capital, Istanbul, to the holy sites of Mecca and Medina. That was the railroad that was attacked by Lawrence of Arabia in the Arab revolt against the Turkish Ottomans during World War I. Then oil was discovered and Saudi Arabia became one of the world's wealthiest nations.

Today the antique Hajj railroad is gone and most pilgrims arrive in Jeddah by airplane. The Hajj has become a multibillion-dollar business fueled by the religious requirement for billions of Muslims to make the pilgrimage and the mathematic reality that no more than 3 million are chosen to make the Hajj every year.

That's the sort of situation that gives pilgrims a sense of joy to be given visas and opens up unwelcome possibilities of all kinds of sweetheart deals, if not corruption, for those making the selections.

As the custodian and protector of the holy sites of Mecca and Medina, the king of Saudi Arabia and his government are in charge of all things

Hajj, deciding how many pilgrims can come from each country, approving changes to the holy sites and building new rail systems and airports. It would be as if the government of Italy decided which Catholics could visit the Vatican and fulfill an absolute requirement of their faith as well as decide how to alter the appearance of the churches and St. Peter's Square.

The pilgrimage is so critical that Islamic countries have cabinet ministers just for the Hajj. They lobby Saudi officials for more Hajj allotments, and they set up elaborate bureaucracies for doling out who receives a spot, which travel agents work with the government on Hajj and how much it will cost—systems that often have room for hidden bribes. The government of Indonesia, the nation with the world's largest number of Muslims, holds deposits of $2.4 billion from citizens who are on the waiting list to make the Hajj at Mecca. In 2006 ministry officials were convicted of "misusing" these Hajj funds and bribing government auditors to approve the Hajj accounts. Anticorruption groups have launched a campaign to open to the public how the Indonesian government spends the pilgrims' money to buy air tickets and lodging in Saudi Arabia, acting on reports that the current closed-door system hides several million dollars in bribes. The campaign is popular since the least expensive package to make the Hajj is nearly $3,500—which for the average Indonesian is their entire life savings.

In Bangladesh, political groups successfully lobbied against "irregularities" in the government's handling of Hajj travel that left thousands of Bangladeshi pilgrims without accommodation or meals. Pilgrims will now receive regular passports, not flimsy "pilgrim cards," and the government promised that the housing will be adequate and food catering will last through the entire visit.

The temptation to make money off of devotees doesn't disappear even in wartime. In Afghanistan the minister of Hajj and pilgrimage fled to Britain after being accused of embezzling $700,000 of Hajj funds from the poor. Mohammad Sidiq Chakari denied the charges against him but refused to return to the country to stand trial.

The Hajj itself is a voyage of a lifetime. Pilgrims routinely describe their trip as a religious reawakening. Dubai has made itself an essential part of that trip. Terminal Two in Dubai is a stopover for Hajj flights, a gateway to Mecca. Emirates Airlines offers a special twenty-four-hour, seven-days-a-week telephone service in English and Arabic to keep everyone informed of any changes and to answer complaints. In 2008 the demand proved so great that Emirates Airlines added thirty flights from Dubai to Jeddah at the last minute. For wealthier travelers, Emirates has a deluxe religious Hajj package with private tours and five-star hotel accommodations.

I was in Dubai at the time of the 2010 Hajj, and could see the commotion and excitement at the airport. Like all non-Muslims, I am forbidden to enter the Holy City. Instead, I followed the pilgrimage in the local newspapers, impressed by photographs of the Grand Mosque in Mecca awash in pilgrims. It was a miracle how they all performed the rites in such packed spaces and with reverence and harmony. Photographs showed believers throwing pebbles seven times to symbolize human attempts to cast away evil. Others gave us a snapshot of the multitudes walking seven times around the Kaaba, the black enclosed stone that symbolized God's oneness and God's center at the heart of human existence. Many were reciting the pilgrim's prayer: "Lord God, from such a distant land I have come unto Thee. . . . Grant me shelter under Thy throne."

Unmentioned was the dramatic physical change in this sacred landscape. Rising in the center of Mecca, near the Kaaba, is a cluster of new luxury skyscraper hotels and condominiums, a shopping mall and a clock tower that bears a striking resemblance to London's Big Ben. This new construction was built by some of Saudi Arabia's wealthiest developers with the enthusiastic approval, and sponsorship, of the government and against the protest of religious preservationists who sought to protect the centuries-old buildings and neighborhoods that were torn down to make way for the glittering new commercial center.

Sami Angawi, an expert on Islamic architecture and the public voice of the preservationists, has written treatises on the need to save the traditional character of Mecca, its buildings, its history and its layout that treated the faithful as equals. The new development, he argues, destroys that physical declaration that all are the same in the eyes of the Lord. Instead, only the wealthy can now afford to live in the center of the holiest of holy spots, in those new luxury hotels and apartments, while the poorer pilgrims are pushed out into the faraway suburbs.

"We are witnessing now the last few moments of the history of Mecca," he said in 2005, when he realized the campaign to save the antique treasures of Mecca was lost. "Its layers of history are being bulldozed for a parking lot."

It seems counterintuitive that the socially conservative Saudi government, which forbids women to drive and puts severe restrictions on the mingling of the sexes based on Islamic tenets, would be in favor of tearing down old Mecca and replacing it with a commercial development along the lines of the luxury tourist destinations of Dubai. Isn't materialism the antithesis of religion?

Wahhabism, the dominant Islamic doctrine of Saudi Arabia, believes that historic preservation of buildings associated with the Prophet Mohammed or holy sites might become a form of idolatry. Developers seized this interpretation to win approval for the Mecca projects in what is considered a holy sanctuary, throwing up those glamorous new towers and making glamorous profits at the same time. They argue that they are creating more space for the annual Hajj and Umrah pilgrimages, which are expected to grow to some 20 million annually by the next decade. Those old buildings, they say, were hovels, and the residents were more than happy to sell them and spend the profits on new homes in the suburbs. And they are improving the infrastructure, building a light rail system from Jeddah to the holy cities of Mecca and Medina.

These are the reasonable responses you might expect from a tourist official in Dubai. The goal is to increase hotel rooms to accommodate more travelers with an emphasis on high-end visitors and rational transportation. In that sense, the religious pilgrimages to Mecca fit firmly in the model set by Dubai that is transforming the tourist industry throughout the Middle East, especially on the Arabian Peninsula.

Competition over pilgrim tourists is familiar to Palestinians. The only way foreign Christians can make a pilgrimage to the West Bank town of Bethlehem, birthplace of Jesus, is through Israeli checkpoints, including the wall built on three sides of the town. In an affront to Christian Palestinians, the Jewish state has won control over the traffic and Israeli tourist agencies reap most of the profits from the pilgrimages.

By contrast, the thousand-year-old European Christian pilgrim's route to the northern Spanish city of Santiago de Compostela is no longer a strictly religious venture. It is now an official World Heritage Site, preserving the physical way to the great cathedral that is believed to hold the relics of Saint James the Apostle. The Christian faithful now share the road with tourists—who may or may not believe anything about the religion but share an esthetic appreciation for the sacred route and a love of exercise. Somehow, this has revived the popularity of the route, and the tourist business has enriched the region's economy immeasurably.

To anyone who has made a pilgrimage, this makes sense. Whether walking alongside the Hindu faithful on a crowded, song-filled holy day to the Ganges or with Buddhists celebrating the New Year walking to Angkor or in the quiet contemplation of my Christian faith on a Good Friday walking the Stations of the Cross at St. Mark's Episcopal Church in Washington, D.C., I know firsthand that the pilgrims themselves are best at creating the spiritual landscape. The question is how much the tourism industry can intrude on their journeys before the religious character is subsumed.

We left Dubai and drove down the E-11 Highway to Abu Dhabi. Clouds of brown dust swirled across our windshield as heavy machinery clawed the parched earth on construction sites that had shut down following the 2008 recession. In those days foreigners were going broke and fleeing the country en masse, leaving their cars in the parking lots at the Dubai Airport. There were predictions of the death of Dubai. Now, the boom is back, at least on the surface, and construction cranes dominate the bleached-out sky.

As the traffic thinned, we noticed oddly painted old school buses filled with men dressed in identical dungarees. From a distance it looked like a prison bus in the United States. The windows were dirty, but from what we could see of the faces of the men, they appeared to be from South Asia. Finally it dawned on us that these were the foreign workers that built all those luxury hotels in Dubai. They were the men we saw from a distance, gaunt figures, some with scarves wrapped around their heads against the heat, climbing scaffolds and filling construction sites.

All those hotels in Dubai and Abu Dhabi, whether American chains that cost $500 a night or deluxe hotels that cost $5,000 a night, were built by men like these. And they were paid only $175 a month for their labor.

"The first-world wealth for citizens and professional expatriate workers is created through third-world wages of Asian laborers," wrote Syed Ali in his book *Dubai: Gilded Cage*. He believes the poorly paid migrant labor has been as important to Dubai's economic success as oil. Otherwise, the emirate could never have afforded its architectural fantasies.

The buses head toward an area called, logically, Labor Camp. Here these foreign workers are often housed in crowded, squalid buildings with often-fetid bathrooms and scant running water for bathing, drinking and cleaning their clothes. They are bused from the labor camp to construction sites and back again. That is their life. Camp—work site—camp—work site. Construction goes around the clock with workers bused in shifts back and forth, from morning to night to morning, working without any extra pay for overtime or staggered schedules. I could see them from a distance as small figures hoisting steel and hammering at the top of improbably high buildings. We had seen them at dusk the day before, waiting in very dirty overalls for buses to take them to the camps.

While tourists have no idea that the hotels where they are staying were built by men who are often treated like indentured servants, in the human rights community the issue has become a cause célèbre.

Dubai and all of the UAE reject international labor regulations, including the Migrant Workers Convention, and reject any role for the United Nations' International Labour Organization. Wolfgang Weinz of the ILO's tourism department said that labor unions are frozen out.

"I have no idea, honestly, what goes on there other than what I read in human rights reports," he said, explaining that the ILO cannot work in countries where workers do not have independent rights. Dubai and Abu Dhabi prohibit freedom of association to create a union, and reject international rights of migrant workers, whether male construction workers or female domestic workers.

Those human rights reports have been scathing. In the seminal investigation *Building Towers, Cheating Workers*, Human Rights Watch detailed "wage exploitation, indebtedness to unscrupulous recruiters, and working conditions that are hazardous to the point of being deadly."

A British report was even harsher, saying "the labour market closely resembles the old indentured labour system brought to Dubai by its former colonial master, the British."

Essentially, these investigators describe the working conditions as miserable. Poor family men from India, Pakistan, Sri Lanka and Bangladesh pay several thousand dollars in finder's fees to land construction jobs only to discover the pay is nothing as promised. Immediately on arrival at the Dubai airport, the workers have to hand over their passports, with visas, to their recruitment agents, essentially giving up their rights for the duration of their two- or three-year contracts. They are bused to the bleak camps to begin construction work. Often their first two months of pay are withheld until they leave. Their monthly salary of roughly $175 a month is especially pitiful considering the UAE has a per capita income of $4,070 a month, which is higher than the annual incomes of average workers in the men's home countries on the subcontinent.

Construction workers have staged occasional demonstrations in Dubai—shutting down a major highway in one instance—but to little effect. They are prisoners of the country's sponsorship system, which applies to all foreign workers. You can only work in the UAE with the sponsorship of a company. Once you lose your job with that company—and complaining about poor wages or dangerous working conditions means you'll be fired—then you lose your visa and must leave the country.

The labor camps for these workers are off-limits and so are the construction sites in Dubai and Abu Dhabi that I tried to visit. So I asked a local investigator to visit the camps for me and bring back a report as well as photographs under the terms that he remain anonymous.

The camps house not only construction workers but the taxicab drivers that ferry tourists around town. The older barracks-style buildings house eight to sixteen men in a room. "You can imagine the smell of these construction workers crammed into the room. They have one small window they don't want to open because they're stuck in the desert, far away from everything and if they open the window the sand blows in.

"These guys are semiliterate. They're together with only other guys, no women, and they don't take good care of themselves. Plus they're working all the time. It's crazy," he said. "They seem depressed."

These foreign workers may seem invisible to tourists, but they are essential to creating and maintaining Destination Dubai, and Abu Dhabi. They not only build the hotels; they are the menial porters and tea servers, drivers and deliverymen. Their female counterparts are just as critical—the housekeepers at hotels and in the homes of the professional class. And their poor treatment is starting to cause concern.

Newspapers in the Gulf area occasionally carry accounts of worker discontent. A popular article in the *National* newspaper of Abu Dhabi was the story of a Bangladeshi maid who cut off her employer's penis because she was sick of the seventy-year-old man trying to sexually molest her. Domestic workers like maids, housekeepers and cleaners in hotels and private businesses and homes depend on the fairness of their employers since there are few laws protecting them. The maid told the police she took drastic measures because she saw no other way to stop him from raping her. These domestic workers are as vulnerable as construction workers in the face of cruel employers.

When asked, locals point out that no matter how bad the situation in the UAE it has to be better than at home or else all those workers wouldn't pay the shifty recruiters to be sent to Dubai. And the remittances they send home are further proof. Somehow, most of the workers send the lion's share of their small salaries home, preferring to live miserably in those camps so that their children can be sent to school.

In the globalized world these labor practices are largely hidden and Dubai doesn't suffer any opprobrium. The city of Dubai welcomed 8.3 million foreign tourists in 2010, while the huge country of India, home of many of the construction workers, received fewer than 6 million foreign tourists.

Tourists visiting Dubai see a modern, forward-looking country with designer hotels and splashy music concerts. They have no idea of the medieval social practices underpinning this twenty-first-century lifestyle. This is "pick and choose" globalization: embracing open-skies airline policies to challenge European supremacy and bring in tourists; selectively opening borders to attract migrant workers while rejecting the other promises of globalization to improve lives with fair employment laws and respect of human rights.

This has nothing to do with the cultural differences of an Islamic nation. Tourists are told in advance that the UAE prohibits public displays of affection and all illegal drugs, puts severe restrictions on drinking alcohol and on desecration of their faith. Tourists have heard the stories of random application of these laws leading to a year in prison for consensual sex between unmarried couples or for questioning the supremacy of the Prophet.

And yet in bars and clubs, hotels and restaurants, foreigners can indulge in just about anything as long as they keep it private. Drunken, rowdy nights with young foreign prostitutes, drugs that slipped through the radar—the over-the-top nightlife of foreigners in Dubai has been described in glossy magazines around the world, with irony, wonderment and scorn. Hotel concierges, restaurant maîtres d'hôtel, locals and fellow tourists take new arrivals aside and clue them in on how to get around the public restrictions. The advice: take a taxi home if they have had even one drink, and go to bars and clubs like the York or the Cyclone to find the newest prostitutes.

Prostitution is illegal in the UAE, but beautiful women prostitutes are plentiful in Dubai, especially if you can afford thousands of dollars for a night and bottles of Dom Perignon champagne. It is part of the emirate's attraction. Business travelers expect to have a wide range of choice among women, and occasionally men, for hire. Many, if not most, of these young women were forced into prostitution, just as the young women in Cambodia and Thailand. But in Dubai they have been brought from foreign countries by gangs of human traffickers. The stories of these enslaved young women are as heartbreaking as those I encountered in Cambodia. And given the country's visa policies requiring employer sponsorships, the government clearly approves of this modern form of slavery and enables the business.

Sex tourism has become an integral element of the twenty-first-century global industry and Dubai's tourism constitutes no exception. Getting away from it all now includes the possibility of paying for sex with a stranger for kicks, diversion, or something darker. An estimated 26 million young women and men are trafficked every year to and from every continent to be placed in servitude as sex workers or laborers. As one of the most labor-intensive industries, tourism has profited mightily from the growing business in human trafficking. None of this is hidden. In the 2011 Trafficking in Persons Report, the U.S. State Department said that the UAE was a "destination for men and women, predominately from South and Southeast Asia, who are subjected to forced labor and forced prostitution."

The tourists and visitors don't seem to mind. A local businessman told me that in 2008 the big news was the deportation of 5,000 Filipina prostitutes to make way for an equal number of young Russian women, adjusting to the changing tastes of men visiting Dubai.

After a two-hour drive we arrived in Abu Dhabi, the capital city of the UAE, built on a series of islands. We crossed the bridge and headed toward the famed Corniche, a wide promenade along the beach with wide spaces for walking, jogging and cycling framed by palm trees that define the passage and catch breezes off the gulf. Driving down the Corniche, with trees and green spaces, the inevitable sight of towering skyscrapers seems less overwhelming.

This is the emirate that is making its name as the cultural alternative to Dubai. Everything is high-end here: a Ferrari Formula One sports stadium complex with the world's fastest roller coaster; Arabian stallions at the Abu Dhabi equestrian club; a modern palace of marble and gold, with gardens as large as New York's Central Park, became the Emirates Palace Hotel and includes an ATM machine that dispenses gold ingots; and, finally, an entire separate tourist island for branch museums of the Louvre and the Guggenheim that contain treasures of the world.

Those museums seemed a safe if expensive investment to affirm the elegance and stature of Abu Dhabi and give it a boost in the competition for tourists. It was an art-world twist on the UAE habit of importing whatever they wanted from anywhere in the world to bring in tourists. Eminent architects were hired. Frank Gehry designed the new Guggenheim Museum as an exuberant pastiche of modern shapes. Jean Nouvel designed a sleek spaceship-capped complex for the new Louvre. The two museums will be centerpieces of the new tourist and culture center on Saadiyat Island, along with a national museum named after Sheikh Zayed, the founder of the UAE, that will exhibit traditional Islamic art and calligraphy and showcase the nation's history.

This sure bet turned out to be a major headache, proving the old industry adage of tourism being a double-edged sword. Once you depend on foreign tourists, you become vulnerable to international standards and tastes.

At first, French critics denounced the Louvre agreement as the crass sale of their nation's "cultural heritage" or patrimony to an oil-rich emirate that wanted an instant museum. The French government responded that it was simply exporting French culture. What took the French centuries to collect, catalogue, study and curate, the government of Abu Dhabi would purchase in one contract for the cool sum of $1.3 billion. That gives the emirate the right to use the name of the Louvre, receive loans from the Louvre's vast store of art, special exhibits and instruction on how to manage the museum and its treasures.

The financial rewards outweighed the cultural complaints, especially after it was reported that the French were being nice to Abu Dhabi in return for the UAE's purchase of French armaments and Airbus airplanes for its Etihad Airways.

That controversy was a small blip compared to the announcement by American artists that they would boycott the Guggenheim arrangement to protest the treatment of workers in the emirates. Organized by New York artists along with Human Rights Watch, more than 1,100 international artists, curators and writers signed on to the boycott, saying they refused to have anything to do with a museum built by workers treated so poorly. "Artists should not be asked to exhibit their work in buildings built on the backs of exploited workers. Those working with bricks and mortar deserve the same kind of respect as those working with cameras and brushes."

The UAE's deplorable labor record was finally raised as a matter of public debate through the intervention of artists. The list includes Janet Cardiff, Thomas Hirschhorn, Mona Hatoum, Krysztof Wodiczko and Harun Farocki.

The artists have demanded that Abu Dhabi's Tourism Development & Investment Company enforce rules that forbid the huge fees that workers pay recruiters before they arrive in the UAE. Their petition also asks that workers be given the right to demand better and safer working and living conditions. Slowly, the UAE and the Guggenheim have acceded to the demands, beginning with hiring an independent monitor to insure that workers weren't paying onerous recruitment fees. And while the artists are serious, their boycott does not threaten the final outcome.

The effort will improve the lives of the workers on the tourist project, but it has had darker consequences as well. At roughly the same time, Abu Dhabi signed a contract with a private American firm to create an elite battalion of foreign mercenaries. The contract specifies that these foreign soldiers and police are to be trained in crowd control to put down labor unrest or any other form of protest by unarmed civilians. The wave of civilian political revolts against authoritarian regimes in Tunisia, Egypt, Libya, Syria, and nearby Bahrain during the Arab Spring apparently made the rulers of Abu Dhabi nervous.

In the middle of a multibillion-dollar building campaign, with a calendar filled with festivals headlined by world-class sports car drivers and hot entertainers like the Jonas Brothers and Prince, the government of Abu Dhabi decided it was time to host its first Green Tourism conference in November 2010. "Green" has become an essential part of every national tourist campaign. I was invited to speak on the keynote panel.

We gathered at the new conference center and were ushered to a private majlis, or audience, with Sultan Bin Tahnoon Al Nahyan, the chairman of the Abu Dhabi Tourism Authority and singular sponsor of the three-day event. True to Middle Eastern custom, the room was one oblong of generous chairs arranged to allow everyone to enter, acknowledge each other and then sit for desultory conversation. The sheikh was the last to arrive and he took the empty chair waiting near us. When it was my turn to speak, I asked: "What inspired you to hold a green conference for Abu Dhabi tourism?"

With utter charm, the sultan looked around at his senior aides and asked, "Why? Why not?" We all laughed and it was time to open the conference. Richard Quest, the CNN anchor, was the master of ceremonies and said this was "the first time such a conference has been held in this part of the world, and for that very reason it takes on a new importance." He then introduced the sheikh, who said the issue of sustainable tourism "defines our industry and the times we live in," that green tourism is not a "niche concept" but one that requires "a seismic shift in the way we do business."

He revealed the results of a recent market survey showing that two out of every five tourists is willing to spend more money for an environmentally friendly destination. "In other words," he said, "there is a high-end market waiting for us to deliver."

That was the tension throughout the conference: how do you keep making all that money from tourism, keep that industry at the top of its game, while decrying its ill effects. Ministers of tourism from New Zealand and Thailand underlined how their countries depend on tourism for 10 percent of the gross national products—the biggest industry for both countries, bigger than lamb in New Zealand, bigger than rice in Thailand—and the extraordinary efforts required to keep attracting all those tourists.

During a break Suraphon Svetasreni, the head of the Tourism Authority of Thailand, told me how the government designed a program to keep tourists coming even in the time of war. After demonstrators took over Bangkok's international airport in 2008 to force a change in government, he designed a crisis program. He put it into play in 2010 when new demonstrations broke out and Bangkok suffered through seventy days of urban violence. Fires destroyed several blocks in the city's swank districts. While the government and armed forces battled the rebels from their own crisis center, Mr. Suraphon set up a parallel tourism crisis communication center.

With members of the Thai Tourism Industry Association and Thailand's hotel association joining him, Suraphon launched a virtual campaign on Facebook and YouTube showing you could still have an idyllic vacation despite the fighting. Airplanes were rerouted. "We used social media, and sent out photographs of people on the beach in Phuket and in Bangkok, in the parts where there were no problems—showing it was okay to come to Thailand," he told me.

The tourism trade in Phuket actually doubled from the previous year, proving, he said, that you can work around a revolution as well as a global recession. "Tourism is strong," he said. "No one wants to give up their vacation."

During the first morning panels several of the local hoteliers extolled the "green" standards of Abu Dhabi and Dubai for lowering energy usage and costs with new technologies. Gerald Lawless, executive chairman of the Jumeirah Group, described his hotels as "luxury without guilt." He was referring in part to the Burj Al Arab, the luxury seven-star hotel built to resemble the sail of a yacht that incorporates ingenious energy-saving, cooling and lighting technology. But it was built on an artificial island that pretty much wrecked the natural environment of that beach and is part of an overall destination that produces more carbon per capita than any other spot in the world.

As at most conferences, some of the best conversations took place outside the official discussions. Several foreign nonprofit tourist operators complained of "green-washing" by the hoteliers. During the lunch break Ashraf Faisal Hegazy, an architect who heads the sustainability committee of his Dubai architecture firm said that the "green" standards in the UAE were far too weak, "almost meaningless."

"Their use of water, energy, their glass walls and air conditioning allowed under these standards are all out of place in our desert," he said. "And Abu Dhabi is allowing the building of more and more massive new hotels that strain the infrastructure."

Hegazy argued that architects and engineers should apply lessons from the original desert dwellers, building with pillars and screens that caught breezes and took advantage of cool mornings and evenings without air-conditioning. "You don't need it—that was proved in New Mexico," he said.

About 20 miles outside of Abu Dhabi, a multibillion-dollar project called Masdar is attempting to do just that but on a mammoth scale that has become the norm in the United Arab Emirates. Promising to be the first carbon-neutral city in the world, the architects and engineers are using modern technology and ancient urban desert design like narrow streets and latticework screens that fight off the heat and glare of the sun. Eventually this refuge should show the way to a desert life after the oil economy runs dry. Masdar is part of the larger Masdar Initiative to develop alternative energy in the UAE, investing in solar, wind and nuclear.

The poor environmental record of tourism in the UAE was rarely mentioned at the conference meant to advertise that Abu Dhabi was intent on becoming known as a "green" destination, however loosely defined. For the last three years, the UAE has had the worst score in the Living Planet scientific report showing each nation's per capita "environmental footprint." Produced by the World Wildlife Fund, the Zoological Society of London and the Global Footprint Network, this survey measures the annual resources consumed and waste produced. On the graph the UAE's carbon consumption stands as tall as the skyscrapers that attract the tourists and pollute the country. What is most remarkable is that this small desert nation consumes more resources per person than the United States, which ranked fifth, or Saudi Arabia, its neighbor on the Arab Peninsula, which ranked twenty-fourth.

What does that reckless consumption look like? You can find many of the problems caused by that waste in the water. Dead fish in the rivers, ruined beds of coral, raw sewage on the beaches, ever-saltier water in the seas.

The dead fish can be found floating in the Dubai Creek, victims of the pollution in the river that flows through the city and celebrated as one of its tourist attractions. In 2009 the number of dead fish exploded to more than 100 tons. Most were pulled out and buried in overflowing landfills. Many were strewn along the beaches where the gulf flows into the creek. The stench from the decaying fish was overwhelming; many were undersized and the few that were breathing appeared to be paralyzed. Marine life has had a hard time surviving during this rush to build a major tourist destination. During the dredging to create the artificial island that is home to the Atlantis Hotel, the only known coral reef off of Dubai was destroyed as well as the turtle-nesting sites. (In his presentation, Gerald Lawless noted that his Jumeirah hotel group started a turtle rehabilitation center in Dubai and has returned twenty-five turtles to the sea.)

Those beaches have also been bathed with pungent tides of raw sewage, toilet paper and chemical waste material. The problem is simple. There aren't enough sewage plants to treat human waste, so it is retrieved from septic tanks, hauled away in trucks and dumped into drains that go straight to the sea. It is cheaper for hotels. The construction of a second sewage treatment plant has helped, but raw sewage still courses through the sea and onto beaches. Garbage and sewage from the millions of tourists simply outpace the infrastructure.

This has become a common problem in resort areas around the world. Bali, the ultimate paradise, is now inundated with sewage and garbage from the millions of tourists who test its limits. All these tourists produce waste—human waste, garbage—that goes into illegal dumps or is thrown into rivers and the ocean. As in Dubai, there just aren't enough public collection and waste disposal sites. Everything suffers and yet more and more hotels are going up on the island. Olivier Pouillon moved to Bali, married a Balinese woman, and started a family and tackled what he considered the island's worst problem: garbage from all the tourism. He set up his own nonprofit in Bali to encourage hotels and the local government to do something about the growing burden of that waste. He told me that it needs to be regulated just like "pollution, methane and carbon pollution from hotels and resorts. These resorts pump out trash and pollution like factories."

Trouble in paradise takes on a whole different meaning when truckloads of human shit are dumped into the sparkling blue seas.

Several government speakers at Abu Dhabi's World Green Tourism conference accented all the positive work underway, implying that their emirate was trying to learn lessons from the mistakes of Dubai. Her Excellency Razan Khalifa Al Mubarak, of the Environment Agency of Abu Dhabi, promised that she is putting "environmental protection at the forefront and not waiting until all you can do is mitigate the damage."

To that end, she painted a picture of the UAE as home to "huge" numbers of birds and wildlife with the "unique ability" to survive in the harsh conditions of the salt marshes or the Empty Quarter of the Arabian Desert and home to fish sheltered in the intricate coral reefs of the Persian Gulf. This starkly beautiful landscape, she said, has shaped Emirati culture and is the spirit of Bedouin poetry whether in verses about hunting with falcons or camping in the desert. And, of course, it is the backdrop for parts of the Koran.

"We are people of the desert. We are people of the sea," she said. "We have a fantastic natural heritage."

What an elegant Scheherazade for the conference. Her stories of Abu Dhabi and the Emirates spoke of days from long, long ago when there was no pollution, no destruction of wildlife habitat, and no tourism geared toward consuming, consuming and consuming. At most, the princess made an oblique call for action; otherwise, she said, "we lose our heritage."

Many of those birds and wildlife have already lost their homes, sacrificed to the construction of more hotels and resorts. The falcons were saved—falconry is now on UNESCO's cultural heritage list. Margit Gabriele Muller, a German veterinarian, directs the preservation effort at the Abu Dhabi Falcon Hospital, which has won awards for saving more than 30,000 of the endangered birds.

At an earlier conference in Abu Dhabi, Paul Vercammen of the Sharjah Breeding Centre for Endangered Arabian Wildlife warned that the remaining wetlands of the UAE were either "developed or earmarked for development." That leaves shorebirds like the bald ibis, the slender-billed curlew and the sociable plover on the critically endangered list of threatened species by the International Union for Conservation of Nature.

And since the Arabian Peninsula is also at the crossroads for migratory birds from Europe and Asia to Africa, this destruction threatens those birds as well. The only answer that these scientists have come up with is the creation of protected areas fenced off from developers who want one more glamorous resort spa at the expense of the nearly extinct Arabian leopard and the Arabian oryx whose lithe body and curved horns are the emblem of the region. The governments are slowly agreeing and creating the equivalent of protected parks, drawing on the native concept of *hema*, one of the world's oldest systems for conserving and protecting rangeland, which was critical in a nomadic society. The Sir Bani Yas Island wildlife preserve south of Abu Dhabi is also an inspiration, initially under the protection of Sheikh Zayed, and now a respected reserve as well as a draw for tourists.

The crisis has nearly overwhelmed conservationists because "perhaps more than any other region in the world the Arabian Peninsula has seen massive social and environmental change in only the last 50 years," according to the report written from a decade of these workshops. The culture of Bedouin poetry had no influence over owners of five- and six-star hotels.

Nothing is safe from the developers. Along the shore, just west of Abu Dhabi where we were meeting, the salt flats, or *sabkhas*, that were part of that old nomadic world are disappearing. To hoteliers these inhospitable stretches of white salt-crusted water are a nuisance that need to be destroyed to create attractive beach properties. To geologists, these flats — the largest of their kind in the world — are not only essential to preserve a healthy shore life, they are a rare record of sea levels from prehistoric times. Graham Evans and Anthony Kirkham, scientists who have been studying the sabkhas since the early 1960s, have been leading a campaign to convince the government to preserve these flats.

"We have seen what has been going on and we feel horrified," said Professor Kirkham in an email. "Unfortunately, recent dredging and infill of the lagoons, road building, pipe laying and other civil engineering projects are rapidly and irrevocably changing both the lagoon and groundwater salinities and destroying this coastal area."

The two scientists believe that "a carefully preserved part of the coastline and its adjacent sabkha plain would undoubtedly attract considerable attention from both visiting scientists and educated members of the public especially if it is backed up by a good museum display explaining the coastline, its history of development, and its relevance to the petroleum industry.

"However, time is short and the whole unique area will soon be lost to the world unless some action is taken very soon."

The speakers at the Green Tourism conference were captains of business and well versed in the high cost of tourism to the natural world all around them. Richard Riley, the CEO of Abu Dhabi National Hotels, said that tourism is "exceptionally heavy on resources and development" and, as a result, these industry leaders "have a role in the protection of biodiversity." His solution, though, wasn't close to what environmentalists believe is necessary. Riley's answer was to train his employees to reduce energy use, and reduce the impact of tourism on climate change. Not particularly radical, especially for a country that is overwhelmed by water bottles discarded by the millions.

Richard F. Smith, an engineer and chair of carbon-critical buildings for the Atkins Group, an engineering and design firm in the UAE, was not so timid. He told his peers that they had to get serious. The designer of the technological breakthroughs for the Burj Al Arab Hotel, Smith said that only 10 percent of the tourism industry is committed to carbon reduction.

"If the tourism industry were a country, it would be the fifth biggest carbon emitter in the world," he said.

No one disputed that astonishing figure.

"The learning curve is very steep and the needs of the future are always under assault from the pressures of today," he said before recommending serious changes that included reducing travel itself—the ultimate heresy in the industry.

"A sea change in our behavior has to come," he said, suggesting fewer vacations, travel closer to home, more video conferences, perhaps government regulation of travel. No one else at the conference recommended curtailing travel and tourism; several said it wouldn't be necessary. Smith turned out to be something like the skunk at the picnic.

It was left to Ralf Stahl to mention the basic issue of all that water being used for tourism in the middle of the desert. His topic was artificial landscapes, like golf courses. The UAE has over a dozen championship golf courses, and Dubai has become an unlikely "golf destination" in one of the world's driest regions. To water just one of those expanses of green grass requires the equivalent of the water consumed in one year by a city of 12,000 people. The UAE doesn't have that volume of water so they retrieve it from the ocean and put it through desalination plants, one of the reasons why the Middle East has half of the world's desalination plants. Environmentalists say this is a disaster in the making.

Stahl said that golf courses and all heavily irrigated landscaping have to be reimagined, if not replanted with local plants that require far less water and provide shade as well as soil treated to retain water. "The proper planting cuts water usage in half," he said. "It makes sense for a business because it cuts cost, too."

He proposed a carefully supervised rating system to insure that water is managed efficiently and some system of punishment if it is not.

The water problem goes beyond the difficulty of supplying enough fresh drinking water. (The UAE is also one of the biggest consumers of bottled water.) The tourism demands are overwhelming to the point of far-cical. The new Iceland Water Park is 120 acres of artificial pools, slides and 'rivers' tied together with the theme "Let's Freeze the Desert." Naturally it claims to have the largest man-made waterfall in the world, the 120-foot-tall Penguin Falls, which requires 100,000 gallons of water every minute to create the fall.

Without government subsidies for water and energy, these projects wouldn't be profitable.

I almost skipped the last session which, after a confusing beginning, brought a coda to the conference and the UAE's contribution to the tour-ism industry. The panels dealt with a concept called "Emiratization." When I first heard it, I thought the speaker was saying "amortization," and I wondered whether you could amortize tourism the way you amortize your mortgage. "Emiratization" means convincing native Emiratis to join the workforce in all fields and become masters of their economy.

In this instance "emiratization" meant simply convincing the native Emiratis that they should work in the tourism field. Among the most pam-pered people in the world, many citizens of the UAE need not work. The panel concentrated on coaxing the natives into the workplace, setting up "ambassador" programs to find out what jobs most interested prospective employees, then to teach and train these locals about tourism and their native heritage.

"We receive complaints from tourists that there are no Emiratis in our hotels," said Ghanim Al Marri, who joined Jebel Ali International Hotels in 1993, becoming the first native to work in the hospitality sector. Very few have followed him.

"We need locals in hotels who know our own style of welcome and hospitality," he said.

Education was one of the answers to this dilemma, and the audience that morning was filled with local students studying tourism under visiting foreign instructors such as Brian King of Victoria University in Melbourne, Australia. The question is, who is teaching these Emiratis their own culture and style?

The reality is discouraging. One of the biggest losers in this push toward tourism has been local culture, beginning with the Arabic language. The youth of the Emirates have been described as "linguistically rootless," with mediocre English and bare literacy in Arabic. An early study in 2003 by the Abu Dhabi Policy Agency found that one-fourth of males and one-fifth of females were actually illiterate in Arabic, with the figures far worse among the young. Blame was assigned to all the public English of the tourism world and the foreign workers, beginning with the Asian maids who are raising the children. As the language disappears, basic Arab cultural forms and habits disappear as well.

Tourism is hollowing out the culture. For all of its outward insistence on its Arab moorings, the twin cities of the UAE are losing their moorings as they become global cities for tourists. Anthropologists have been predicting such a fate for tourist destinations for centuries. From the first field studies in Africa, Asia and the Pacific Islands, anthropologists warned that tourism was turning local culture into a commodity to entertain foreigners and that, ultimately, as foreigners demanded standard hotels, standard meals and standard comforts (including the speaking of English), that local culture would lose its authenticity and then disappear.

"The first question we ask is what effect tourism has on the culture and identity of host communities," said Professor Carol Greenhouse, chair of Princeton University's Department of Anthropology. "Is the culture bolstered and enhanced or is it perverted and deformed?"

She told me during an interview on campus that while tourism is now considered an essential right of the middle and leisure classes, that doesn't remove the responsibility of understanding what they are doing to the countries they visit. "Tourism is creating a monoculture of shopping malls, hotels, karaoke bars and restaurants—a cultural fusion that is erasing native culture."

As if to prove her point, while we were attending the Green Tourism conference, Abu Dhabi was host to the Formula One races, held near the new Ferrari World red dome "wonderland." Besides its otherworldly racing track that skirts yacht basins so the wealthy needn't budge from their ships, Yas Island has concert arenas and the world's fastest roller coaster. Hotels were packed. Foreign celebrities—King Juan Carlos of Spain and Sir Richard Branson—attended and Abu Dhabi was declared "firmly on the map" of hip places for the world's jet set.

That is the bargain that the UAE has made. In return for becoming one of the most desired tourism destinations in the world, Dubai and Abu Dhabi are now global cities with little left of their desert heritage, their environment or their hold on the future should all those foreigners leave.

PART FOUR

NATURE TOURISM

Zambia, Costa Rica and Sri Lanka

7

SAFARI

Maybe it was those long afternoons spent at the zoo when my children, Lily and Lee, were young. We lived within walking distance of Washington's National Zoo, where we became friends of the baby giraffe, the elephant and the wildcats, but were always wary of the reptiles. The pandas kept to themselves, so we didn't loiter outside their home. Instead, we meandered through the walkways of the zoo's private universe sheltered alongside Rock Creek Park. It was so civilized we rarely got a whiff of the rank circus smell from large animal excrement. Eventually those endless hours spent looking at animals in well-appointed enclosures rearranged my images of wildlife. The raccoons and possums that prowled our backyard at night were wild. The animals in those cages were not.

That could be one reason why I never jumped at the suggestion of going on an African safari. I'd read Isak Dinesen's autobiographical novel *Out of Africa* about her life in turn-of-the-twentieth-century Kenya and saw the movie adaptation starring Meryl Streep and Robert Redford. This was beautiful, romantic Africa seen through the eyes of privileged Europeans who killed buffalo, lions and antelope, who eventually understood the harm being done and, too late, mended their ways. Public television specials on Africa showed the opposite picture of wild Africa, with aerial footage of animals galloping across the savannahs, unmolested by humans while they stalked and ate each other. I avoided the continent until I began writing this book and realized one of the pillars of the global tourism industry is the African safari, with cameras or rifles, in search of those animals I saw in the zoo.

"Safari" is an Arabic word meaning "journey." It found its way into the Swahili language and was adopted by British colonialists to mean a specifically African journey or adventure. Beneath the surface, the idea of a safari is loaded with the baggage of European colonization begun in the late-nineteenth-century "scramble for Africa" that didn't fully end until the 1960s and beyond. The Europeans conquered some 10 million square miles of territory, tore apart traditional African nations and tribes, reassembling the land into thirty colonies ruled by white foreigners: British, French, German, Belgium, Portuguese and Italian. They extracted great wealth and treasure and subjugated the natives in a rivalry for empire.

The Europeans also treated the immense continent as their private hunting ground, killing Africa's magnificent animals for trophies and sport at such a rate that some Europeans began to worry. Something had to be done to save the elephants, lions and native antelopes from European rifles and extinction. The authorities' solution was to set aside vast parks where the animals could roam free. Those parks were carved out of land that had been hunting grounds and tribal lands of local African people, setting up more reason for resentment. Then the colonialists left and by 1980 the African nations were independent.

Today those parks are the foundation of African tourism. Nearly 50 million visitors go to Africa annually, and the majority who travel to sub-Saharan Africa are drawn initially or exclusively to the wildlife parks. Package tours can include a weekend on the beach after a safari, and a few nights in a stunning city like Capetown, South Africa. But without the animals, most tourists are unlikely to travel those long distances when other beaches and beautiful cities are closer and less expensive. The top sub-Saharan African tourist destinations all rely on parks: South Africa, Tanzania, Mozambique, Zimbabwe, Botswana, Kenya and Namibia. To attract more tourists and encourage them to spend more days and money on the continent, the industry offers packages of visits to three and four wildlife camps in different countries, trumpeting what officials call their sublime "nature base" tourism. One visit to the Johannesburg airport, the massive air hub of the region, says it all. The shopping area of the terminal is kiosk after kiosk of safari-themed clothes, toys, gadgets and books. It is called, naturally, "Out of Africa."

Despite some attractive marketing, the parks are not on firm footing. The checkered history and modern pressures have created considerable problems: poaching, corruption, deforestation and, above all, encroaching human settlements. The promise is singular for the industry: without those animals, the industry would shrink, and with it the $76 billion in revenue tourism brings to the continent every year. When adding up all of the money spent indirectly because of tourism, the figure rises to $171 billion. For several African countries, money from tourism is the largest source of foreign exchange receipts, gross domestic product and new jobs.

No other continent is so dependent on preserving nature for its tourism as Africa.

Flying into Zambia is a trip back in time. The Kenneth Kaunda airport in the capital of Lusaka has lost some of its sparkle since it was built in 1967. Today it has the feel of a well-worn pair of shoes, nicely buffed. The terminal was blessedly quiet. People chattered and laughed in the lounges. The pace was easy. The taxi stand was beyond the parking lot. I loved it. But the atmosphere did not suggest much of a tourism business.

The city of Lusaka resembles its airport. It has the appeal of a provincial capital going through a small renaissance. Modern buildings and apartments have been built alongside old colonial homes and offices along wide tree-lined boulevards. The sidewalks are still cracked and uneven, and the smoke from cooking fires can burn your eyes in the evening. There is also an unmistakable smell of change in the air. A landlocked nation in southern Africa, Zambia has become the forgotten, almost homely country in a flashy neighborhood. Fabled South Africa to the south is the giant of the continent. Zimbabwe, directly south, was once a wealthy dynamo, until its president, Robert Mugabe, ran it into the ground. Botswana and Namibia are far better known for their wilderness tourism.

Zambia is slowly recovering its footing in the region. Since the government opened up its copper industry to foreign investment, the economy has been booming, growing at 6 percent every year, with copper earnings making up more than half of Zambia's gross domestic product. Much of the new money underwriting this transformation is Chinese. The Asian giant is a new player in Zambia's mineral industries, including its precious gemstones, joining the dominant Canadian, Australian and Indian companies.

Mark C. Storella, the U.S. ambassador to Zambia, argues that Zambia is an overlooked country. "It has a stable and functioning government, has never had internal armed conflicts and is a showcase of democracy in southern Africa, especially after the September 2011 elections that saw another peaceful democratic transfer of power."

Tourism is a laggard next to the mining industries. Zambia has some of the largest wildlife parks in Africa, but they have been mismanaged and were never publicized well in the larger tourism world. Today, Zambia's tourism officials are trying to raise their country's profile and slowly balance Zambia's dependence on minerals. Last year, tourism made a small leap, contributing nearly $1 billion to the economy, but copper is king, providing 65 percent of exports. The tourism receipts are also minuscule compared to the $41 billion that South Africa pulls in from tourism every year.

Tourism, though, is on the rise, and foreign visitors coming on safari are a mainstay of the culture of Zambia, like oil in Texas. I discovered this at a mass at St. Ignatius Church in Lusaka, where a choir sang inspired hymns throughout the service. Father Chilanda built his sermon around the gospel story of the apostles fearing for their well-being once Jesus left the earth. He used a tourist to symbolize modern man. Then he put the tourist in danger, falling off Zambia's Victoria Falls while he was trying to take a photograph of the tumbling waters. Father Chilanda said: "Miraculously, the tourist broke his fall by grabbing a branch."

Then the tourist heard a voice calling through the blue sky, saying: "Let go, I'll catch you." The tourist asks "Who are you?" When the voice says he is God, the tourist refuses this promise of salvation from an invisible God and instead says, "I'll wait for someone else." The congregation laughed. Where would priests be without the feckless tourist to act as the fall guy?

More than a few Africans and tourist experts asked me why I was headed to Zambia and not Kenya, or South Africa. As it turns out, Zambia benefits from being off the beaten track. I was promised a safari where I wouldn't have to worry about spending days in the wilderness without seeing a lion or, even worse, finding myself in a traffic jam of Land Cruisers and vans searching for one. I wasn't going to a park that specialized in luxury tents rather than elephants. Zambia is still wide open, with more than a hint of the Africa that the Europeans fell in love with a century ago.

As soon as my Land Cruiser drove through the welcoming park gate of the South Luangwa National Park in northern Zambia, I knew I had made the right choice. All doubts disappeared. This wilderness area of more than 5,600 square miles of the Luangwa River valley—about half of the size of the state of Massachusetts—truly is in the middle of nowhere. My first animal sighting was a clutch of hippos cooling off in the shallow end of the Luangwa River, small birds pecking their backs for insects. The river is described as the park's lifeline. Its waters attract the sixty species of mammals that find sanctuary here. Farther up the road, elephants were munching on the trees, and just before we turned into the Mfuwe Lodge driveway, two young puku bucks stopped to stare at us, then leaped into the bush.

The Mfuwe Lodge, with its thatched roof, high ceilings, open-air dining space and African fabric covering pillows and couches, was evocative of the wilderness without falling into the kitsch trap of trying to duplicate the set of Out of Africa. What caught my eye, though, was the deck that led straight to the edge of a lagoon. Baboons were climbing down the opposite bank. Herons and egrets were padding through the marshy banks. I couldn't believe it and blurted out, "Look, baboons."

"You'll see more baboons here. They sleep in the trees at night around the cabins," said Deborah Phiai, the receptionist who checked me in. She is a twenty-four-year-old graduate from City College in Lusaka who majored in tourism and immediately took a position at the lodge here. Three of her classmates also were hired for what she said are coveted jobs. She walked me to my room and continued telling me about her career in tourism. "Working at the lodge, I saved enough money to build a house in the village, and now two of my sisters are living with me. My father is very proud," she said.

I found it odd to receive an unsolicited endorsement of the lodge from Deborah. It took a while for me to understand that while Zambia's tourism industry provided as much as 5 percent of the jobs in the country, few pay well enough to allow local young people to better themselves like those at the Mfuwe Lodge and bush camps. Ms. Phiai was simply grateful.

On the short walk to my cabin she gave me two basic instructions. After dark, walk only with a guide carrying a flashlight. Animals are everywhere. Second, watch out for the tiny frogs that love to hide in water jars and showers. They are harmless but alarming when they leap up in your face. Naturally, when I opened the water thermos in my room, I screamed when the precious pale-emerald-colored frog leaped into my glass. Now knowing better, I waited at the dinner hour for the rap of a guide to escort me back to the lodge for dinner.

A pleasant buffet under an African sky dense with stars was all I remember of that first evening. I was escorted back to my cabin and immediately fell asleep. Then around four in the morning I heard the sound of some very loud cows grazing on the rough grasses outside my window. I woke up confused. Cows, here? I turned on all the lights and peered through my screened windows at the very large, glistening rumps of two hippopotamuses. They were chewing up the grass at a deliberate pace, oblivious to me or the lights shining on them. I went back to bed.

It was a sweet time in the valley. The months of rains had ended, leaving the savannah and mopane woodlands green and the Luangwa River full. The roads had dried out. Young lion cubs and zebra ponies were beginning to venture out slowly under their mothers' sharp supervision.

At first glance, Luangwa was a testament to the proposition that tourism can save more than it destroys. I had been told by experts of all ideological persuasions that African wildlife safaris are the poster child for the good side of tourism. Without tourists paying to see the wild animals, the parks would disappear, and without those parks the beasts and birds of Africa would lose much of their habitat, plowed under to make way for human farms and cities, and the surviving animals would be slaughtered for food. Africa would look the same as everywhere else; and the animals would be isolated in zoos until they became extinct.

That was the refrain I heard in the United States. A more complicated story unfolded at South Luangwa.

On my first morning I climbed into a Land Cruiser with two tourists at six-thirty. Steve was our guide and driver. We hadn't been on the trail more than ten minutes when we came across two lionesses sleeping soundly while their cubs played nearby, batting each other with their paws and pouncing like animated stuffed toys. Steve pointed to a carcass hidden behind a tree: "That's their kill—a waterbuck. They've been feasting and are now lazy." He zeroed in on one slumbering lioness with a fantastic muzzle brimming with whiskers. "That is Alice—her hunting ground is near the lodge area. We know her well."

After gazing at these sleek cats we veered off into a network of one-lane dirt roads across a never-ending savannah. The morning air was cool and brisk; the smells were musky and voluptuous. Up ahead two impala bucks were chasing a female. Overhead, a colony of vultures was clustered in a tree. Two hippos were half-submerged in a vast lagoon, gorging on the green lettuce heads of Nile cabbage that covered the surface. Three slender pukus, an African antelope, bounded away, out of our sight just as a flock of bright green parrots with tangerine faces flew overhead. "Those are Lilian's lovebirds," said Steve.

He pulled off the road and drove onto the plain, where warthogs were digging up the ground with their curved tusks and square snouts in search of bulbs. A mother and her piglets joined them, trotting in front of our Land Cruiser with erect tails and determined ugly faces. Baboons were watching from the sidelines, grooming and eating and keeping an eye out for food to steal. Further ahead a lone giraffe was munching leaves on the top of a spindly tree. Finally we came upon a herd of zebras grazing near a clear river. When they turned around, their wet brown noses gleamed in the morning sun. A mile further on, monkeys were sharing a grassy plateau with impalas. To complete the picture a white stork deftly marched on his stilt-high legs into a neighboring stream, plunged his beak into the muddy waters and came up with a fish. It was breakfast time on the savannah.

Three hours passed in five minutes. I had walked through the looking glass into an entirely complete "other world" where humans and their edifices were sidelined, ceding primacy to these African beasts and birds and their wilderness homes. In minutes the forested plains no longer looked exotic. It seemed preternaturally normal for giraffes and zebras and lions and storks to go about their business of hunting, grazing and chasing after mates. We tourists watching from the Land Cruiser were the anomaly.

After a swim at the lodge's pool, lunch and a nap, I packed an overnight bag and drove to Kapamba, one of the six remote base camps operated by the Bushcamp Company that also owns the Mfuwe Lodge. Together, the lodge and camps form one of the few resort areas permitted within the confines of South Luangwa Park. I left midafternoon with Steve and Calvin, a second guide who was needed at Kapamba. The trip would take four hours driving south-southwest as we left the rim of the park for the remote interior. At that time the sun's rays melted into dusky rose streaks across the darkening sky. One of the main roads had been flooded out during the rainy season, forcing us to take a detour climbing over a range of rugged hills. To the west a small herd of elephants was lumbering toward a copse of trees where several of the leaders had begun tearing down branches to get their daily fill. Each requires 300 kilograms of forage daily, which sounded like a lot, but it is less in proportion to their weight than the diet of mice. We stopped to gaze a few minutes. Their solid gray bodies, with their noble trunks, blended into the scenery as comfortably as buffalo herds in North America.

Calvin threw cold water on my reverie: "Forty years ago there were a hundred thousand elephants in the park. The government culled fifty thousand and the poachers killed thirty-five thousand until there were only fifteen thousand left. The poachers didn't stop, and then the population was down to four thousand until the World Wildlife Fund paid for an antipoaching patrol. We are back up to twenty thousand elephants. But they are all small-tusked. The poachers killed the large-tusk elephants and their genes have vanished."

As we drove up the hills, the forest thickened and the air cooled. We had left the open plains and meadows. I zipped up my jacket as Calvin apologized for the bumpy road. "We call this an African massage."

We were cresting the hill when Calvin silently signaled the driver to come to a stop.

There, at the edge of the forest, was a dark chestnut antelope that slowly turned his head to stare at the intruders. What a face: black with bold white markings that clearly inspired more than a few tribal masks. It was framed by majestic horns curved backward.

"A sable," said Calvin.

"My first," said Steve, who raised his hand with his fingers separated in a victory sign.

I was mesmerized. I didn't pick up the camera. I just stared. He was so magnificent. A bull in his prime with the face of a magician.

Then he was gone. "Do you realize how fortunate you are?" said Calvin. "I've only seen a sable twice in my life and Steve never, and we both have lived in Zambia all of our lives."

It was pitch black by the time we arrived at the camp. At the sound of our Land Cruiser a gate swung open and flashlights led the way to what seemed like extraordinary luxury in the middle of the bush. Calvin and Steve talked of nothing but the sable, while our hosts—two Zambian men and one young Englishwoman—showed me the open-air common room and my cabin. An English couple was staying in the second of four cabins. We ate supper on the deck overlooking the Kapamba River, and I went directly to sleep in my wonderful tented bed. For the second night, though, I heard noises.

This time it was a thunderous, low pitch growl. A lion? And this time my bedroom was open to the wilderness, with only a decorative iron gate between me and that increasingly loud, growly noise. I turned on my solar-powered flashlight and aimed it at the noise with pathetic results. The light disappeared in the African darkness. As the creature grew closer, I listened carefully and discerned a thumping burp before the growl. It is probably an herbivore, I thought, and my fear drained away. I picked up a book and read for an hour until the sounds disappeared and I went back to sleep.

Zillah, the young English hostess, asked me over coffee the next morning if I had heard the young bull elephant that had ravished several trees in the camp during the night. I laughed and told her about the lionlike growl outside my cabin. No, it was a hungry elephant, she said, and waved me off on the 6:30 A.M. walking safari. We were three tourists led down to the river with a guide and a ranger scout armed with a rifle in case we were threatened by an animal. Dew was heavy on the grass and clung to our ankles. Mist rose from the Kapamba River. I could have stayed there for the rest of the morning. Our guide pointed across the river to a lilac-breasted roller bird perched on a half-buried tree stump across the sandbar. "We'll start from there," he said.

Walking in a single file, we saw fewer animals and far more birds. As the sun rose, the earth came alive with new smells and colors. Traveling by foot, we appreciated the dimension of the wilderness and, up close, the true size of the animals. Elephants were tanks with trunks. Zebras were impressive horses.

As we walked, our guide asked us to keep one eye on the ground, to follow the soft calligraphy of the tracks left by a civet cat or examine the wet dung of water buffalo. It smelled like a pile of carcasses.

"Look up," said the guide. A male impala was leading a herd of nearly a dozen females through the forest. Scenting us, he leaped into the air flying ahead with the females following. A ballet troupe exiting stage right.

"They could have been scratching their horns here," the guide says, pointing to an 8-foot-high cone-shaped termite hill. "The male impala has scent shards in his hooves. His footprints leave his musk scent for females to follow."

Further ahead was the impala dung and signs, according to the guide, that a leopard had been rolling in the heap. "The leopard does this to disguise his scent. He wants to smell like an impala when he hunts for antelope."

So much to learn from dung! Lifting our eyes, we caught glimpses of the sharp-beaked kingfisher and then, as the four-hour walk was coming to an end, I saw the African hoopoe, a cousin of my favorite bird of India. He had the silhouette and similar coloring, with a black-tipped orange crest that waved like a ceremonial turban. Then I heard his faint plaintive cry of *hoop-hoop, hoop-hoop-hoop*. I was happy to go back to breakfast.

Waiting for me was Andy Hogg, the Zambian founder and director of the Bushcamp Company. Before I had a chance to say a word, Hogg turned to me and asked, "Did you really see a sable yesterday?"

I laughed and said I had never even heard of such an animal before yesterday, and then I described what I saw, including the shock of seeing that dramatic mask of a face at dusk.

"That's a sable," he said. "That's good news. We rarely see them in this park."

Hogg is a member of a small fraternity of European-Africans that forms the backbone of much of the international safari tourism business. No matter the difficulties of their position, especially as white Africans, these men and women seem attached by their roots to the parks of south and east Africa. Hogg was born in the Copperbelt of Zambia in 1964 when it was still known as Northern Rhodesia. His father was an Anglo-American businessman and his mother a schoolteacher. "We lived near the swamps with herds of lechwe antelopes and shoebill storks," said Hogg by way of explaining his attachment to the land here and why he can't seem to leave.

After independence a wave of nationalism swept through Zambia and much of the economy became state-owned. Facing financial ruin, Hogg's family left in the 1980s and moved to Johannesburg, South Africa. Hogg finished his schooling in Cape Town and received a certificate in hotel management from the local Protea hotel chain. With those qualifications he hoped to return home to Zambia and land a job in a safari camp.

Thanks to his Uncle Jerry, Hogg got his foot in the door with an entry-level position at the safari camp and resort of the legendary Norman Carr, one of the founding fathers of the African national park system.

Carr was the role model for Hogg and countless other young safari entrepreneurs. He practically invented the business. Born in East Africa in 1912, Norman Carr lived during the height of colonial life—great wealth and decadence—immortalized in the true-crime book White Mischief. Carr reveled in his colonial privileges as a game warden. He loved to hunt and on his twentieth birthday he proudly killed his fiftieth elephant. A decade later, at the start of World War II, Carr's life changed forever. He served in North Africa as an officer with the King's African Rifles, and on his return home from that bloody conflict, he underwent a secular conversion. He gave up killing wild animals as a "medium for expressing my prowess" and instead dedicated himself to protecting them.

To that end he established Zambia's first national park in Kafue in the Luangwa Valley and trained local Africans in wildlife conservation. He centered his project on local communities since, without their support, the animals would be hunted down and the bush cleared for farming. Carr was far ahead of his time.

He tested his ideas in 1950, approaching the paramount chief of the region around Chipata, in what is now northern Zambia. The chief was doubtful that foreign tourists would pay money simply to watch African wildlife rather than kill it as foreigners normally did, but he gave Carr the go-ahead. After building six rondevaals, or African roundhouses, of mud and wood for sleeping, Carr opened his walking safari tourism business.

The basic requirement for safari tourism was safe national parks that protected the wild animals from poachers and secured the property from encroachment by farmers and villagers anxious to cut down the trees for firewood. That required paying farmers living in the area to relocate and respect the park boundaries. Using his close ties to government officials, Carr was instrumental in setting up national parks as well as training rangers and wardens. When Zambia became independent, he worked with the new president, Kenneth Kaunda, who went on walking safaris with Carr. Over his lifetime Carr was credited with helping set up parks in Malawi, Zimbabwe and Zambia, where he settled permanently. More than 30 percent of Zambia's land has been put under protection, although the quality of that protection has been cyclical, ranging from woefully inadequate to decent. That, too, is part of the legacy of Carr and the other European-Africans who went from hunter to protector.

Carr was an elderly gentleman in his seventies when Jerry Hogg found a job for his nephew Andy as a paid volunteer at the Chinzombo Lodge run by Carr's Save the Rhino Trust. Hogg remembers his first miserable salary. "I made exactly fifty kwacha a month as a volunteer."

Hogg became a full-time staff member at the Chinzombo Lodge in South Luangwa Park and learned critical lessons about conservation as well as tourist management. Over the next ten years he became an entrepreneur and leased two camps in the park. Then in 1999 he teamed up with Andrea Bizzaro, an Italian-Malawian, to found the Bushcamp Company. Her family had leased the Mfuwe Lodge as soon as the government opened it up for private management in 1996. But the Bushcamp Company, like safari camps throughout the continent, faced daunting problems. Many of the wild animals—the very basis for African tourism—were under the threat of extinction.

In the intervening years, while Hogg was learning his trade, the newly independent African nations were grappling with a multitude of issues, including how to manage the national parks and protected areas they had inherited from the colonial era. More than a few countries lacked officials with the expertise to manage the parks. And all were under extraordinary pressure from within and without. Some African leaders questioned the need for parks. With independence, villagers were demanding the right to recover tribal lands that had been forcibly taken from them to establish these parks. In their eyes the government had stolen the land that had been their homes for generations, and they wanted it back. Absent official permission, they started hacking away at the bush, recovering the land on an "informal basis" and cutting down trees for firewood and charcoal.

And there were many more people who needed land to farm and firewood to burn. The continent's population had exploded to over 750 million, doubling from just a few decades earlier and putting pressure as never before on the African wilderness. Even though Africa is the second-largest continent, today its population is less than India's. For centuries this thin population meant the sub-Saharan savannahs and forested areas were vast enough for humans and beasts.

Despite the popular image created by *Tarzan, Lord of the Jungle* only 8 percent of Africa is rainforest or jungle. A modest proportion is arable land, while vast areas are desert, semiarid, or water-short, with poor soils. Exploding population growth puts pressure on this limited space; subsistence agriculture and limited use of fertilizers has meant low crop yields and farmers searching for more land to cultivate. Against this backdrop, the protected wildlife areas have taken on increasing importance and the ability to protect them made much more difficult.

The rise in human population mirrored the decline in elephants according to several scientists. For most of African history, elephants and humans were competitors, and for most of that history elephants won the battle for land and water. That changed dramatically in the middle of the twentieth century, when as many as 3 million elephants roamed the continent.

Authorities in Kenya kept the best record of how that flipped. In 1925, when the colonial system was entrenched and new national borders had been drawn, wildlife was abundant and the elephants freely roamed 87 percent of the savannah in East Africa. Fifty years later, after the colonial government ended and Kenya had been independent for a dozen years, elephants had lost half of their lands and then half again, now restricted to a meager 27 percent of the savannah.

During the 1980s an old scourge reemerged. Poachers were back in force. Many of the continent's largest national parks were wrecks. Governments hadn't paid for upkeep, the corps of trained scouts and game wardens had been depleted. Those who remained behind were often poorly paid. This made Africa's great herds vulnerable to poachers. No longer just locals looking for a meal or a pair of ivory tusks to sell on the black market, poachers were now organized in gangs with high-powered rifles and well-trained scouts. They were able to hunt and kill 100,000 elephants a year, a rate not seen since the Europeans first arrived in droves at the turn of the twentieth century. The market for ivory soared with the newly available elephant tusks and rhino horns.

Ironically the movie *Out of Africa* was released in 1985 at the height of the massacres. While moviegoers thrilled at the panoramic shots of antelopes stampeding across the plains of colonial Kenya and of elephants charging hunters in the colonial days of East Africa, the real live elephants in Kenya were being decimated. From 1975 to 1989, Kenya's elephant population dropped 83 percent.

This wholesale slaughter of elephants moved from a conservation issue to one of economic importance. Tourism was being devastated at a time when African countries were counting on that industry to earn foreign exchange. Between villagers encroaching on the wild parks and gangs poaching for ivory, elephant herds were disappearing.

It finally occurred to officials that elephants, one of the most iconic animals on the planet, were being threatened with extinction. Alarmed, officials banned the international trade in ivory in 1989 in order to save the elephant and the rhino, through the Convention on International Trade in Endangered Species of Wild Fauna and Flora, or CITES.

To insure that poachers were stopped, several African nations took drastic new measures to protect and recover their herds. In Kenya the government turned to Richard Leakey, a white Kenyan born to one of the most illustrious families of paleontologists in the world. Leakey was appointed director of Kenya's Wildlife Department in 1989 even though he had limited experience in the field organizing safaris and had been running the National Museums of Kenya. He was given the task of revitalizing the parks and saving its beasts, especially the elephants. As it happens, Leakey's experience and the approach he developed are a microcosm of the battles waged by conservationists across eastern and southern Africa. They had to face down well-armed poachers and inept or corrupt governments while rebuilding the wildlife parks and wildlife services. They were saving a natural order of savannah and wildlife and a way of life. Their governments' motivations were less clear.

What is certain is that the salvation of the tourism industry in Africa would depend on the success of a handful of wildlife administrators. After taking over the wildlife service, Leakey said the economic health of the country depended on these animals. "The slaughter of our elephants is economic sabotage: elephants are the flagship species of our wildlife and the basis for Kenya's biggest industry, tourism."

To make his point, Leakey ordered the unthinkable. To show that Kenya would no longer tolerate poaching elephants or selling their ivory tusks, Leakey held a public bonfire and burned 2,000 tusks government park rangers had captured from poachers. Normally the government sells the ivory and deposits the money in the treasury. To destroy the tusks was the equivalent of burning $3 million. Kenyan President Daniel arap Moi was initially taken aback but quickly agreed and actually lit the pyre. That act would show that Kenya was serious. The photograph of the president and the crackling bonfire was published around the world.

Then Leakey started grappling with the mundane and profound problems of managing modern African wildlife parks. Roads had to be repaired and rangers trained, equipped and clothed. Vehicles and gasoline were purchased, air transport arranged. Staff morale improved. And Leakey had to raise money to solve many of these problems. The government had earlier stripped the parks service of its independence, including the right to keep their revenues from tourism fees. Instead, the money went into the general budget and the government set the parks budget. How to pay for the parks' upkeep has proved to be an ongoing issue. Like his predecessors, Leakey had to turn to foreign nonprofit groups, the World Bank and a number of official donor agencies in the United States and elsewhere for funds, despite his distrust of the strings often attached to the grants. While the tens of millions Leakey raised, combined with his tough management, went a long way to restoring the physical and human infrastructure in the parks, the problem of maintaining that infrastructure was not solved. Revenues from park admissions and constrained government budgets fell well short of meeting the costs.

Most African parks have been underfunded since they were established. Admission and licensing fees pay from one-third to one-half the costs at most parks, with the exception of South Africa's Kruger and a few other internationally known preserves. The fewer the resources, the more likely that poachers will kill animals and locals will cut down trees. Harold Wackman, who was the World Bank's country director in Kenya and works on conservation with Leakey, said that "tourism may be the biggest industry but tourism admission fees will never cover all of the costs of maintaining parks that are a huge benefit for all of us. We have to find another way to do it."

Tellingly, Leakey's most difficult challenge was rooting out corruption. A secret government investigation had implicated several senior officials in poaching and the illegal ivory trade. Corrupt officials drained resources. And corrupt officials undermined Kenyans' confidence in the park system itself. Through patience, new hires, transfers and political maneuvering, Leakey made progress. Then in 1993 en route to a meeting in Kenya, Leakey was badly hurt in the crash of a Cessna airplane he was piloting. He survived, but both of his legs were eventually amputated and his health was seriously compromised. An investigation failed to explain how his airplane's engine had lost power so quickly, and to this day Leakey cannot rule out the possibility that powerful figures profiting from corruption may have been behind the accident. One year later, he resigned after his department was severely weakened, an action taken at the suggestion of his political enemies and rivals. A few years after that, as the parks began to deteriorate again, Leakey was rehired.

Nothing has been easy about saving elephants. Governments clashed with guardians. Some turned to high-revenue private hunting. Others outlawed it. Nonprofits disagreed with the tourist industry. No one had a secret formula for recovery. In every country and sometimes at every park, there were bloody clashes between humans over the animals. Just north of Andy Hogg in the North Luangwa Park, an American couple made it their mission to protect the wildlife and succeeded for a while until they ran afoul of the government and were accused of murdering interlopers. Ardent conservationists, they were thrown out of Zambia.

This was the reality for most parks in sub-Saharan Africa. Humans were as dangerous as the wild animals that roamed far beyond the parks onto the grasslands, and forests with the tasty "sausage" trees and were hunted by local villagers. In Zambia wild animals are as likely to live beyond the park boundaries as in them.

Andy Hogg lived through that recent history with one foot in the tourist camp and the other squarely with the conservationists. Most days he said he can't distinguish between the two. With his trimmed graying beard, intense eyes locked in a permanent squint after a life in the African sun, Hogg has more than a hint of Hemingway about him. He is solid and square and practical about almost everything except his attachment to Zambia's wilderness. He works nearly nonstop. There are few days off while at the park—Mfuwe Lodge is open all year, while the bush camps are seasonal. When Hogg is not at the park, keeping accounts in his office at the lodge or roaming through the 9,050-plus square miles of unfenced wilderness, he is traveling to promote the lodge.

"Normal people couldn't sustain this pace for this reward. If I were married with kids, I couldn't afford to run this," he said. "If I had put this much effort and time into any other business, I'd be rich."

In fact, he said, he loves his work and can't imagine another life. "Obviously there are a lot of positives or I wouldn't still be here," he said, gesturing at the bush around him.

The qualities that made South Luangwa so remarkable are the same that make it so maddening. The park is one of Africa's last unspoiled expanses in part because Zambia is such a backwater, protected from some of the worst pressures of modernity. At the same time, this backwardness has meant that the government won't make the investment necessary to maintain the park.

In the last few years, Hogg has had to create much of the improved infrastructure. "We just put in seventy kilometers of all-weather road," he said. "Unfortunately, lately we have ended up financing just about everything else."

The parks are managed by the Zambian Wildlife Authority, known as ZAWA, an underfunded organization with a mostly impressive professional staff but burdened by politically appointed leaders who are too often corrupt. Hogg is careful about describing his relationship with ZAWA, since this is the organization upon which all tourism depends. "Some of the guys are fantastic," he said. "But if the leaders at the top knew what they were doing and had some money to do it with, this place would be incredible."

In a country as poor as Zambia that may not be surprising.

Zambia, though, has benefited from several decades of foreign aid, which has had a direct impact on its tourism industry. One of the more generous countries has been Norway. Over the last fifteen years, the Norwegian government has given Zambia at least $715 million in development aid, including money to underwrite wildlife conservation and management in South Luangwa National Park.

In effect, the northern country famous for fjords, tundra, reindeer and the Arctic midnight sun saved this semitropical park with its herds of great mammals and four hundred different bird species. And they did it for the tourists, as well as the environment and conservation, of course.

In assessing its aid to South Luangwa, the Norwegian government said it is pleased with its investment. Thanks to money to improve the park's ranger corps, wholesale poaching of elephants has ended. "Wildlife populations have been protected and stabilized, through greatly improved patrolling effort and success," said a government report issued in 2007. Tourism is up. Local communities benefited from the aid, and villagers have shown greater respect for the park, especially since the increase in tourism has improved their lives and provided new jobs through spin-offs like handicraft industries.

But the Norwegian government wasn't happy with the way the foreign aid was often spent and the recent difficulty in getting a full and open accounting of the funds. For instance, the report notes "political interference in ZAWA by powerful individuals." That is a pointed reference to political appointees who could not account for the money given by Norway. When Norway asked for an audit that showed how its aid had been spent, ZAWA delayed and delayed. There were other problems, including roads that Andy Hogg complained were so poorly maintained. "The relatively large expenditure on roads across all phases, and their ongoing low quality despite these efforts, could be judged inefficient as well as ineffective," said the report. That is a polite way of saying that the money for roads disappeared into the pockets of officials or was paid to cronies who did a crummy job. And also that thinly stretched government budgets had other priorities to attend to, such as health and education.

Enough was enough and recently Norway announced it was phasing out its aid for South Luangwa. But Trond Lovdal, the first secretary at the Norwegian embassy in Lusaka, said that his country was proud of its work in South Luangwa. Norwegian aid protected animals, insuring South Luangwa would remain a sanctuary which, in turn, attracted foreign tourists. Those tourists would help underwrite the park as a sanctuary.

"Norway's continuous and long-term support of the park has been one of the reasons for its relative success," he said.

Andy Hogg said that the Norwegian aid did help create a mini tourist boom, but it hasn't been enough. Hogg came to the unhappy realization that he needed a considerable sum of money to upgrade his lodge and camps and attract high-end tourists. He put his company up for sale. Fortunately for him, a generous angel came to his rescue. He sold the company in 2008 to an anonymous benefactor who immediately invested enough money to upgrade the camps and lodges. Hogg hired an interior designer from South Africa to work her magic on the camps and lodge and paid for the repair and upgrade of roads. Hogg has signed a nondisclosure agreement that prohibits him from saying who bought the company. He could only say that the new owner is an American philanthropic businessman who wants to make a profit "but only to plow it all back into the company."

"For him, it's not about making money. It's about doing it right. His sister came here and fell in love with the place," said Hogg.

It didn't take long asking around in Lusaka to establish that the philanthropic businessman was Paul Allen, the cofounder of Microsoft and a Seattle billionaire. His sister Jody Allen runs his foundation and initially agreed to talk to me about Paul Allen's involvement in Bushcamp Company, but at the last minute she decided against commenting on the family's purchase of the lodge and camps. Publicly, Paul Allen prefers a "no comment" to my questions about his ownership and what he hopes to achieve in South Luangwa Park.

Allen has shown a fascination with Africa. His foundation supports a trust to save the scruffy, almost ugly wild dogs of Africa. These wolf-type predators have their own role in the African wilderness. Farmers are afraid of their packs and have killed off enough to put them on the endangered list. Allen also gave $25 million to Washington State University, his alma mater, for a global animal health project specifically targeted at Africa. Generally, his conservation efforts have centered on the Pacific Northwest, from protecting old-growth forests to figuring out how to establish the proper balance between fishing and preservation on the Pacific Coast. South Luangwa seems to parallel those interests, especially his strong belief that private enterprise can do more for conservation.

Without mentioning Paul Allen by name, Hogg said that the two men agreed that responsible tourism was critical to saving South Luangwa. "Without tourism, a park like this, where the government puts in so little, things simply wouldn't work."

Hogg's predicament is a microcosm of what is facing the African tourism industry. First, he needed foreign aid to repair the park as a whole and private philanthropy to keep his company afloat. With Allen owning the Bushcamp Company, Hogg has fewer worries about the bottom line. He is paid a salary and can concentrate on the company's ten-year plan. The lodge and camps are being improved to the highest level. Mfuwe has won the award for best lodge in Zambia. The second part concerns the community, getting the locals involved in the park and seeing how their lives are directly improved through tourism. "In the United States people realize they have to manage the wildlife. In Zambia, it's let nature take its course," said Hogg.

It is up to Hogg and his company to convince the local community that it is in their best interest to maintain the park by creating programs for their benefit. In the broadest sense it is an educational campaign with all sorts of incentives to resist the impulse to cut down trees or kill animals for meat. The greatest incentive is providing jobs at the lodge and camps. The Bushcamp Company employs 170 staff members as well as seasonal workers. The wages are the best in the area and the benefits are unusually generous. For the local staff at the lodge, Hogg pays $500 in education fees for one child in each family. Next year he will pay the fees for two children per family. "In a remote area like this, it's hard to make ends meet," said Hogg.

The lodge also promotes the native fabric industry near the park, which in turn employs dozens of locals. To prevent deforestation they underwrite a solar cooker project and a large tree-planting program. "We started off paying the men to replace the trees. When they didn't show up, the women came and said they would plant them for free. Now, the kids at schools are volunteering to plant trees. Last year, they planted 7,000 trees."

The company helps two local schools by renovating their buildings, sponsoring orphans, buying school uniforms and supplies, paying teachers' salaries and, most important, sponsoring wildlife clubs for the kids. "The children learn about the wildlife as their heritage. They come to the parks to see and get to know the animals. They draw them. They bring their parents."

The company has invested in local vegetable gardens and a beekeeping business, buying back the produce and the honey for the kitchens at the lodge and bush camps. These programs are typical of high-end resorts in parks whose owners realized that the local community has to be part of any conservation program. "All of our investments in the company and the community come to ten million dollars total over the years," said Hogg.

Manda, the company's senior guide, drove me back to the lodge from the Kapamba bush camp. He talked about his experience at South Luangwa, of his apprenticeship and studies for the guide certificate, even the perils of his profession. "In one year—2002—a hippo threw himself on top of three tourists. I got him off and they all survived. On another walking tour a male elephant pushed some Americans into a dry riverbed. He trumpeted, then ran away. Later that year an aging buffalo threatened a tourist. It was my worst year."

That danger in the wild, which the human species has yet to conquer with its machines and weapons, is as inspiring as the sunsets.

Beyond the park, Manda said he and the other guides are ambassadors of sorts to the villages surrounding South Luangwa, bringing the children into the wild savannahs on Land Rover tours. "The first time I brought the schoolchildren to the park, I nearly cried that they had never seen a zebra ever even though they lived just outside the park." We slowed as, if on cue, two zebras trotted across the road.

"People see that as a guide I have earned enough money to build a house just outside the park, with a borehole well, electricity and plumbing. People understand from this the importance of tourism, of caring for the park," he said.

All of this was brought into sharp perspective on my last morning tour in the park. My fellow passengers in the Land Rover were three young Americans who served in the Peace Corps in other parts of Zambia. Renee was from San Francisco, Adam from Reading, Pennsylvania, and Joseph from Southern California. I had noticed them at the lodge because they looked and acted as if they had been hitchhiking across Africa and the lodge was their first taste of the good life in quite some time. I was wrong about the hitchhiking part.

"I was working in the Copperbelt for the last two years," said Renee. "I never saw wildlife. It was a different country than this."

The young men agreed and said, "Man, a different country."

Adam, who helped farmers install ponds and raise fish, said he had seen only one monkey in his two years in Zambia. "One of my farmers saw the monkey first. He shot it right there and killed it and ate it. They eat everything. I ate it with him."

The three pulled out their bird guidebooks and pointed to a red bishop in a tree. Mostly they were silent, drinking in an Africa they said was foreign to everything they had known in Zambia.

The Honorable Catherine Namugala, minister of tourism of Zambia, opened the conference with a regal bearing, a commanding voice and a broad smile. The late-morning audience was alight with young women in bright textile skirts and young men in white shirts attending the 5th International Institute for Peace Through Tourism Africa Conference. We were 440 delegates from 36 countries as well as Zambian students and guests invited to discuss tourism and climate change. The conference center at Lusaka's Intercontinental Hotel was full.

"Welcome," said Namugala, and she introduced Rupiah Banda, the president of Zambia. Everyone stood as the large man walked to the podium.

It wouldn't be an understatement to say that Lusaka, Zambia, is rarely host to international tourism conferences or trade shows. The first city that comes to mind is Berlin, the host of the gold-standard ITB International Tourism Bourse, the leading tourism trade show in the world. Singapore hosts the Asian version. In the United States, New York and Las Vegas are meccas for tourism conferences and shows.

Lusaka isn't even on the B-list of tourist conventions. So this conference was a welcome moment in the tourist spotlight for Zambian officials, who were determined to make the most of it. President Banda gave the proceedings a Zambian flavor by first welcoming tribal chiefs in the audience—before the foreign ambassadors, members of Parliament and assorted dignitaries—and expanding on an earlier comment to take a poke at an issue of tribal rivalry that set the crowd laughing. "We are all cousins," he explained to us visitors.

Then the president switched to his text and the thrust of his speech. He hoped, he said, that the conference would showcase Zambia's tourism and investment opportunities. Zambia's economy is one of the fastest-growing in the world thanks to tourism and minerals. "We are pleased with this recognition of our efforts to put Zambia on the world tourism map."

Zambia was in the midst of an election campaign that Banda wanted everyone to know would be different from other African elections, which

had been marred by violence and corruption. Zambia's would be a peaceful transition, he promised, saying "tourists will only come to countries at
peace."

The scene-stealer was Kenneth Kaunda, who at eighty-seven years of
age is one of the last living fathers of African independence and the first
president of independent Zambia. His is the name on the Lusaka airport.
The old lion began his talk by singing "We shall fight and conquer, in
the name of Great Africa," a song about peace and unity that became an
anthem of the anticolonial struggle. Later he adapted it as the theme for
Zambia's fight against HIV/AIDS after his son died of the disease. He had
played with the lyrics again for us and sang a new version about peace
through tourism. By the last chorus of "We shall fight," people were singing along and stamping their feet. This was not normal fare for a tourism
conference. A Zambian student sitting next to me laughed and said their
first president, whom he called KK, always sang. "We love him."

Namugala took over after the photographers left and business began,
saying to the foreigners that "we will work together, but our problems
need to be owned by Zambia. Then we will seek support from cooperating
partners. But we own our problems and our partners don't tell us what our
problems are."

"Most Zambians worry about being at peace and about prosperity
rather than wildlife," she said. "We have to make people believe wildlife is
a resource that can generate income, that it is not a nuisance."

Known in international circles as a polished speaker about the environment, Namugala delivered her message clearly and often: "We know that
now with the challenge of climate change, tourism as a key sector is being
undermined. We also know that tourism is one of the few key sectors that
can impact on poverty. We feel very strongly that we need to be prepared
for the challenges that climate change is now causing on this critical industry. It is very important for tourism and the more important need to
develop tourism as a sector that can reduce poverty."

The cosponsor was the small Vermont-based International Institute
for Peace Through Tourism, founded in 1986 by Louis D'Amore, who still
heads the organization. One of its themes is that every tourist is a potential
ambassador of peace.

We delegates were guests of the sponsors and lodged at the Intercontinental Hotel, the main venue for most conferences and meetings in Lusaka as well as the main watering hole for the elite and the strivers of the city. The floor above mine was entirely taken up by Chinese visitors, who held private dinners with important Zambian officials. Business was in the air.

After the first day of panel discussions we gathered around the tree-shaded patio for cocktails, tribal dances and gossip about tourism. Caristo Chitamfya, the media manager for the Zambia Tourism Board, told me that fifteen years earlier he had quit his job in broadcast journalism in order to produce weekly shows for Zambian television to tell his countrymen and -women about their parks and animals.

"My goal was to show Zambians what is in their own backyards. So the people in the north would know what was in the south and the south in the east," he said. "We had to change the perception of tourism as only for foreigners who are white. Yes, the parks were originally only for colonial English. We were excluded but no longer."

So he produced shows focusing on local tourism, showing Zambians which parks to visit, prodding them to get out and "own" their parks. "When I began, people would call in and ask, 'Is that in Zambia?' They thought it looked too wild to be Zambia," said Chitamfya. "And, yes, we know it worked because more Zambians are going to their parks."

Standing right beside him was Evelyn Mvula, a fifty-four-year-old Zambian native who proved his point. She had been invited to the cocktail party with her friend Rhoda M. Gander, also a Zambian native who has worked in tourism for thirty years.

Mvula said she saw her first lion in a French zoo in 2000 and didn't go to a wildlife park in Zambia until she was thirty-three years old. "I only went because I was working with some visitors from Johannesburg. When we got close to an elephant, I ran, I ran to the car. The foreigners looked up and asked, 'Why are you running? The elephant won't hurt you.'"

Mvula giggled and told another embarrassing story. "When I was a child, I had a pen pal in England and I would write and say an elephant was walking by my window—I lied."

Gander had a different yet also typical history with parks and animals.

She said she saw her first wild lion when she was a child of seven visiting her grandfather, a tribal chief. "We grew up with lion folk tales but not with many lions." They were as effectively cut off from their cultural heritage in Zambia's cities and farmlands as we Americans are from the German forests and French castles that figure in our fairy tales. The big difference is that their lions and zebras still inhabit their land as well as their imaginations, and the government wants them to replenish their ties with visits to the parks.

We were watching a dozen provincial dancers perform an abbreviated wedding dance by the pool, their feet pounding out the rhythm with their ankle bracelets. "Look at the dance — it is like the folk tales. It tells the story of our lives with the animals," said Gander. "There is no question in my mind that tourism has saved our wildlife. We need to save more animals with stiffer penalties for poachers."

Mvula shook her head and said it wasn't that simple. "There is a struggle for the land between the animals and the people."

That last warning was a subtheme of the rest of the conference whenever Zambians held the stage. A majority of Zambians are rural and depend on subsistence agriculture. Their small holdings keep shrinking as the population grows and the plots are divided and subdivided. They want the land inside the parks or they want some of the rewards they believe they deserve from the parks.

Namugala refereed some of these discussions. She also appealed to the foreigners in attendance for understanding and aid. Zambia is sometimes given money for issues that are not the government's priority, she said, and not for what they need. One of the country's biggest expenses is the cost of maintaining nineteen national parks and thirty-six game management areas. She mentioned high-level negotiations with the United States to refurbish the country's largest park in central Zambia. The request was later denied because the government couldn't prove the park would make economic sense in and of itself, which is not the primary reason for preservation of national parks whether in Zambia or the United States.

So Zambia has fallen back on the biggest, quickest money-earner — selling licenses to kill the animals. It is one of the few African nations that still allow hunting and it charges high trophy fees to foreigners: $10,000 for a hippo and $60,000 for an elephant. Sport and trophy hunting have been part of conservation in Africa for decades. This is called "consumptive" revenue and it has come under close scrutiny. There are disputes about its value.

Namugala said that "sustainable hunting earns us 85 percent of our tourism revenues." A World Bank study by Adam Pope said there was not enough reliable data to confirm Namugala's claim. His data showed that non hunting activities surrounding visits to nature parks, including the Victoria Falls, are responsible for the majority of tourism revenue. One of the conclusions was critical of "an element of short-term opportunism in niche ventures." Animal rights groups argue that the trophy hunters kill more animals than necessary to cull herds and they are depleting the stock.

Then there are the complaints from local communities that question whether they receive their share of the bounty from foreign hunters. In theory, local communities are supposed to receive half of revenues from the park and game preserve revenues, with the other half going to ZAWA, the wildlife authority. By local communities, the government generally means the subsistence farmers who live in the buffer zone around the parks, which are generally unfenced. Often these subsistence farmers do not receive their promised share, a common problem around the world. In dozens of studies of native people who have been moved off their land to create conservation areas, the benefits of these new areas go to people who did not make the sacrifices.

While there is no single formula for getting it right, governments like Botswana, Namibia and South Africa have provided fair compensation through coordination of conservation and tourism, including hunting. The Zambian government has fallen down on planning and making routine public accounting of how the park revenues have been distributed, making it impossible to know whether corrupt officials have funneled large sums of money to their own bank accounts, as foreign donors like Norway fear. That raises the basic issue of whether the people who benefit from the parks, including the international tourist industry, have shared with those who made the sacrifice of giving up their homes and land for the parks.

Without clear records, Zambia will have a difficult time raising more foreign money to help conserve the parks that support their tourism industry. The debate will continue to rage about how to involve locals in managing the parks with jobs and training that protect the environment and the animals while balancing that effort with rangers who can keep away others who would destroy the park.

The evil villain at the conference was the thriving poaching business that stretches from Africa to China, where ivory is now worth $700 a pound. At times, little distinction was made between the Chinese and the poachers. The horns of rhinos and tusks of elephants are prized by Chinese for carvings and, when ground into a powder, as a medicine that falsely promises longevity and, for men, virility. There is so much money to be made that thieves are sawing off the horns of stuffed rhinos in European museums for sale in China.

Environmental groups have conducted lengthy investigations of elephant poaching in Africa, showing that Chinese groups are underwriting the killing and then illegally importing the tusks. The Convention on International Trade in Endangered Species in Wild Fauna and Flora (CITES) forbids the trade in new ivory from elephant tusks, so poachers and their networks have devised sophisticated ways to kill the animals and serpentine routes to smuggle in the tusks and then disguise them as old ivory that is legal to sell in China.

Esmond Martin, one of the leading investigators of the illegal ivory trade, completed a study in 2011 showing how China has become the main market for illegal ivory in large part because the authorities do not enforce rules even though China has been a member of the CITES treaty for thirty years.

In 2008, CITES made an exception and allowed the sale of old ivory in China while continuing the international ban on any new ivory that was taken from live elephants. But in China, where authorities do little to control the ivory market, this created a giant loophole that has triggered the illegal killing of thousands of elephants in Africa. According to Martin's report, in the Chinese city of Guangzhou, 61 percent of the 6,500 retail ivory pieces surveyed were illegal and lacked proper identification. "Several vendors openly said their ivory was new and illegal. This suggests that official inspections and confiscations have not taken place in most shops."

"What you have in Africa is an unregulated ivory market where the majority of buyers in those markets are foreigners. They're not African," Martin wrote. "The Chinese aren't actually killing elephants but they're organizing it and that's even worse."

This matters to Zambia, Kenya, Tanzania, Mozambique and the other African countries struggling to improve their parks and tourism.

Others have confirmed the report. Writing in *Vanity Fair* a few months after the Martin study, Alex Shoumatoff described his investigation traveling around Africa—to Kenya, Gabon and Zimbabwe—tracing the path of Chinese-supported poaching. In Amboseli in southern Kenya, poaching was unheard of until Chinese contractors moved in to build a new highway as a foreign aid project. Soon poaching returned. Conservation groups using DNA sequencing of smuggled ivory determined where the contraband came from.

This is poaching on a global scale that threatens to put elephants on the extinction list. Yet there is little sign that the tourism industry is actively involved in this issue even though, from a strictly monetary perspective, tourism has a lot to lose if nothing is done. What would happen to African safaris without elephants, or tourist brochures without an elephant backlit by a setting sun?

For their part, the Chinese have largely denied their role in the illicit trade. Richard Leakey told me that when he asked Chinese officials why they didn't crack down on trafficking in ivory from poached elephant tusks, he was told that China wouldn't get serious until Africa did. They told him Africa needed stronger penalties. "In China, you are executed if you kill a panda," Leakey said.

Vietnam, another Asian country whose citizens trade in illicit rhino horns and elephant tusks, has been more forthcoming. In September 2011 a group of Vietnamese officials flew to Johannesburg, South Africa, to discuss how they can better help stop the trade in their country. In China, it has been nongovernmental groups that actively campaigned against the poaching of elephants and buying ivory; they have broadcast films showing the damage done by the trade and the foolishness of believing that ground tusks can make an aging man more virile.

The Chinese are the new power brokers in Africa and exert an influence both appreciated and feared. China's wealth has helped fuel the continent's rebound over the last decade, and in 2010, China became Africa's largest trading partner, accounting for $129 billion of business. Overall, the money has financed exports to China of African resources, largely minerals and oil. At the same time, the Chinese government is spending 41 percent of its foreign aid in Africa, building highways, hospitals, ports and sports stadiums. A South African journalist at the conference accused the Chinese of acting like neocolonialists when the discussion touched on indirect Chinese support of elephant poaching.

Zambia was once one of China's closest friends on the continent, with ties that go back to the first presidency of Kenneth Kaunda. The Bank of China opened its first southern Africa branch in Lusaka. In 1975, China built the Tazara Railway to connect Zambia's copper mines in the deep interior to the port of Dar es Salaam in Tanzania, a 1,155-mile stretch of track over difficult terrain. It was the largest foreign-aid project in the country at the time, costing $500 million.

In 2010 the Zambian government announced that China had invested more than $1 billion, money that created 15,000 jobs. That same year the ugly side of Chinese investments broke into the news when coal miners of Sinazongwe, in southern Zambia, protested against their Chinese employers, demanding better pay than their $100-a-month salary and better living conditions. (Many lived in mud-walled huts that lacked plumbing or electricity.) In response, the Chinese guards fired into the crowd of protesters, injuring eleven workers. The mood among the average Zambians changed. News reports listed the indignities and exploitation of workers at Chinese-operated mines. Zambians had to work two years before they were given safety helmets and many said they were never given other safety equipment. China's reputation has never quite recovered.

Yet the Chinese didn't give up, and one of their new offensives was to promote Chinese tourists coming to Africa. The Chinese government opened its first official African office in Cameroon in 2010 with a partner office in Shanghai. The Chinese are promoting themselves as "the future of African tourism" and are marketing exotic trips to Africa to "the new generation of 50 million Chinese outbound tourists."

The highlight of our conference was a day trip to the Victoria Falls.

We flew to Livingstone, named after the Scottish missionary and African explorer who was the first European to see the falls. He is honored in Zambia for his strong stance against slavery. The falls are easily the top tourist spot in Zambia, a point made by Minister Namugala, who was relaxed away from the microphones. She wanted the important foreign officials, especially from the United Nations World Tourism Organization, to see the modern luxury hotels recently built near the falls. Before we had lunch at the Sun Hotel, Namugala told me she saw herself as a businesswoman as well as a government official. "I made money from gas stations and fast-food joints. I like making money and I like helping people, helping my home village and women, old ladies. I love old ladies."

She went over to greet a row of women wearing native costumes waiting to sing at a ceremony to plant a tree to celebrate peace through tourism. Their music lifted our wilting spirits on that hot day. Afterward we walked to the falls. As majestic as advertised, the falls seemed of a piece with the green landscape, pastoral where the Grand Canyon is rugged. "Welcome to Mosi-oa-Tunya—the Smoke that Thunders—one of the seven natural wonders of the world," said Namugala, using the Zambian name for the falls. After lunch we took a short Land Rover tour through the small Mosi-oa-Tunya National Park where we saw a rare rhino and her calf.

Namugala proved herself an excellent businesswoman. A few months later, the U.N. World Tourism Organization announced it had chosen Victoria Falls as the site of its general assembly in 2013, only the second time an African location had been selected. Namugala had prepared her country's bid, arguing that this would be a perfect showcase for African safari tourism. Zambia's cohost will be Zimbabwe, which shares the falls with Zambia.

That partnership bid ran into political trouble since Zimbabwe is led by Robert Mugabe, whose human rights record has made him one of Africa's most despised leaders. When the UNWTO announced that Mugabe would be an informal "leader of tourism" for the conference, there was an immediate outcry. But even the opposition in Zimbabwe was pleased with winning the honor of holding the international tourism gathering. For them, tourism is outside of politics. It's good business.

But Namugala will not be the host of the event. President Banda was defeated in the September elections, which were as peaceful as he promised. In one of Africa's smoothest democratic transitions, Michael Sata, the winner, was installed as president the day after his election, and he appointed a new minister of tourism.

Sata had won by campaigning on a strong anti-Chinese platform, saying he would protect workers' rights in the mines. But at the end of October, one month after his election victory, Sata sent former President Kaunda to Beijing to visit Chinese officials and reaffirm that Chinese investment was still welcome in Zambia but that a few issues needed to be sorted out.

Greg Carr is an American multimillionaire who may save African tourism. He is one of a handful of private philanthropists who are rescuing African parks and wildlife as part of the daunting goal of saving forests, open spaces, wildlife and the planet. In that battle, tourism is seen as one way to stave off harmful development.

Carr may be the most ambitious of the lot. He is spending nearly $50 million to underwrite the recovery of Gorongosa National Park in Mozambique, an expanse the size of the state of Rhode Island in the southern end of Africa's Great Rift Valley. Created in 1960, Gorongosa was, briefly, one of southern Africa's premier wildlife parks until war broke out to wrest independence from Portugal. The fighting turned into a civil war and lasted from 1977 to 1992. Over 1 million people died.

Some of the worst battles took place in Gorongosa, where soldiers lived off the wild animals, killing 95 percent of many species for their meat. Fighting also tore into the landscape. By the time Carr signed his agreement with the Mozambique government in 2007, the animals of Gorongosa National Park were nearly gone. The herds of 14,000 buffalo and 3,000 zebras had all but disappeared. Conservationists found only 15 buffalo and 5 zebras. The elephants had fared just as badly. Three hundred elephants remained of a herd of 2,200. Only 6 lions survived from a population of 500. Hippos could be counted on two hands.

When he offered his help, Carr received rare control from the government over managing the restoration. He oversaw the building-up of the vegetation so that herbivore animals like elephants, hippos and zebras could be imported from neighboring southern African countries. He built up the ranger corps so the animals would be protected from poachers. As the park has rebounded, predators like lions and cheetahs have come back.

A rare success story and a mammoth undertaking, the Gorongosa project has been chronicled on film and in print. *National Geographic* produced an inspiring film about Gorongosa entitled *Africa's Lost Eden*. It opens with lush panoramas of the expansive Lake Urema at the center of the park, where birds and warthogs, crocodiles and elephants, lions and antelopes had regained a foothold. Carr doesn't show up until midway through the program, when elephants arrive from South Africa's Kruger National Park. "Have you had any sleep," he asks the caretakers as they gently unload the elephants onto the open savannah where their job is to procreate and eat as much of the grasslands and trees as possible.

An unassuming man who would not stand out in most crowds, Carr grew up in Idaho near Yellowstone National Park. (He is no relation to Norman Carr of Zambia.) In the film, Greg Carr says that Yellowstone Park's recovery inspired him in Gorongosa. Yellowstone, too, had been hunted out when President Theodore Roosevelt designated it as the first national park in the United States. After the vegetation recovered, the animals returned, newly protected from humans. (Paul Allen has also said that living in Seattle, surrounded by the wilderness parks of the Pacific Northwest, is a big reason why he is involved in conservation philanthropy.)

The story of Gorongosa was told in lyrical detail in a twelve-page *New Yorker* profile by Philip Gourevitch. In this article Gorongosa has yet to recover from the trauma of war. Many of the traditional people who live there view Carr as a white man trying to steal their land. On the highest mountain they are stripping the trees that are essential for capturing water for the valley, yet they refuse to allow Carr to reforest the area. At the same time, new groups of hippos and elephants are flourishing and the neighboring villages are benefiting from the park. Carr's foundation has built health clinics and schools and funded new agricultural projects.

The article asks whether this one man from Idaho could save an entire African ecosystem. The answer was "maybe."

I met Carr on one of his visits to Washington and asked him whether tourism was a critical part of the plan. "Yes, a big part," he said. He is searching for professional tourist groups to build luxury lodges that respect the environment and offer well-guided tours of the wildlife, a vision that sounded a lot like the Mfuwe Lodge in Zambia. Carr said that the license for the lodges would require giving back 10 percent of profits to the park. When combined with park fees, he said, the money should be sufficient to cover most of the expense of maintaining Gorongosa.

But the experience of other philanthropists suggests that African parks can be a constant money drain that modest tourism cannot satisfy. Nicky Oppenheimer, the chairman of the De Beers diamond company and scion of the wealthiest family of South Africa, owns the Tswalu Kalahari Reserve in northern South Africa near the Botswana border. Oppenheimer has poured millions into returning the 250,000 acres of farmland and highland back into the wild; in his words, "restoring Kalahari to itself." With a net worth of over $6 billion, Oppenheimer and his wife Strilli can afford the investment and are willing to operate at a loss.

They succeeded in attracting lions, hippos, antelopes and other wildlife to the savannah and high desert and restricted tourism on their huge property to two lodges. The Motse Lodge charges $960 a night for "bare-foot luxury," which is an understatement. Butlers are as numerous as guides. Visitors can ride on horse safaris or opt out and order a gourmet lunch al fresco in the midst of this immense private reserve where cheetahs, antelopes and seventy-five other mammal species abound. The effort is so extraordinary that the Oppenheimers have won the prestigious World Wildlife Fund's Lonmin Award for environmental conservation as well as prizes from Condé Nast Traveler for responsible tourism.

The Oppenheimer reserve underlines how the open spaces and wilderness are becoming the biggest luxury on the crowded planet. After a lecture in Washington, Oppenheimer told me that despite all the hurdles, he believes that preserving and expanding wildlife parks is "absolutely vital."

"South Africa is way ahead of the game on that. We know it is incumbent on us to set apart what is required for the animals," he said. "Wild animals are more important than almost anything else in the world; certainly more important than minerals."

Conservationists are divided over the long-term effect of allowing tourists into wildlife areas. In Kenya, Richard Leakey, the former wildlife head, said he sees tourism as offering only the short-term benefit of preventing development. Eventually the best protection would come from educating the African public to love the animals and protect them. Huge areas of parks would be put off-limits to that most invasive of species, the human being.

"Ecotourism is an oxymoron," he said. "Tourism is a short-term benefit, but in the long term humans and wildlife don't mix."

The islands of Galápagos have learned that hard truth. Darwin's original wildlife laboratory is a U.N. World Heritage Site and one of the most popular tourist destinations on the planet. The millions of tourists have trampled native species and brought with them invasive plant species that are strangling the island. Simply raising common hens to feed tourists fried and baked chicken has spread avian diseases. Wild birds have been stricken with canary pox virus and penguins with avian malaria.

After pleading by environmentalists that tourism was imperiling the wildlife paradise, the government of Ecuador has agreed to place restrictions on the number of tourists on the islands to protect the land and wildlife and recover from the previous years' onslaught. Beginning in 2012, only four cruise ships can land during any two-week period. Once on the island, tourists are allowed to stay no more than four days and three nights. And they will be spread out over more islands rather than congregated on three main islands.

The Galápagos restrictions were spurred, in part, by restrictions imposed further south at Antarctica. An agreement reached by the nations with ties to Antarctica allows only 100 tourists on the shore at any time and completely prohibits all cruise ships with more than 500 passengers from entering Antarctica's waters. But Ecuador seems of two minds about tourist restrictions. At the same time, the country is planning to build a new airport to welcome more visitors and boost the $500 million it earns annually from tourists.

Since the days of high-riding European colonials, tourism in Africa has been disparaged as an industry that caters to white foreigners who look down on black Africans as "exotic" natives at best. That cultural and racial chasm has been chronicled in numerous anthropological studies. In his description of Maasai dancing staged for tourists in Kenya, the scholar Edward M. Bruner captured this in a series of vignettes.

> The Sundowner (Hotel) presents Maasai men dancing in the context of an "Out of Africa" cocktail party near an upscale tented safari camp on the Mara reserve. The Maasai performers mix with the tourists, who are served drinks and hors d'oeuvres by uniformed waiters. Globalizing influences are apparent, as Hollywood pop culture images of Africa and blackness are enacted for these foreign tourists as they sip champagne, alternately chatting among themselves and dancing with Maasai, all the while on safari in the African bush.

Now that cliché is being overturned. African-Americans in search of their ancestry and roots are becoming the sought-after tourists on the continent. In some respects this is part of a larger trend. Cultural or heritage tours became big business around the globe in the last twenty years, thanks to the Internet, which makes it possible to find ancestors and to travel to countries that invite Americans to come and search for their families.

But most of the African-American tours are in a class by themselves, tied to the original sin of slavery. They often have no documentation showing the nationality of their ancestors or even their names. So their tours often begin in West Africa, where governments have opened up the former European slave forts on the Atlantic Coast and created museums and tours to educate the world about the centuries-long slave trade. In 2007 in celebration of its fiftieth year of independence, Ghana promoted itself as a must-see destination for African-Americans, urging them to visit the slave-trade sites along its coast. St. George's Castle in Elmina is one of the most visited former slave forts, where tourists can see the slave dungeons, the punishment cells and the auction room.

It's impossible to know how many of the nearly 50 million foreign visitors to Africa in 2011 were following a heritage tour. African nations are wooing them out of national pride as well as financial gain. Tours originating in Senegal and Gambia promote themselves as introducing visitors to the region where Alex Haley traced his family in the bestselling *Roots*, a book that caused such a sensation in the United States, especially after it was turned into a television mini-series that broadcast the full story of the African slave trade into American homes. "Roots" is now shorthand for the heritage tours of African-Americans.

Paulla A. Ebron, a professor at Stanford University, studied the phenomenon by traveling on a "Roots" tour sponsored by McDonald's, the fast-food giant. In her words, the "McDonald's tour moved the tourists and refashioned them as pilgrims."

There were ninety-six Americans on the tour; the majority of them African-American women between the ages of thirty and forty-five. Most of them had won the trip in a contest sponsored by McDonald's for African American History Month. William Haley, the son of the author of *Roots*, traveled with the group. These tourists-turned-pilgrims were motivated in part, she wrote, because "African Americans are as deeply involved now in the search for history and memory as they have been at any period in U.S. history. The stories of collective trauma and of African cultural healing move people very deeply, even if they take the form of advertising jingles."

They followed the emotionally charged slavery route and talked about the irony that this exceedingly personal trip was sponsored by the multinational corporation. They were not on the champagne safari circuit. Instead, they were on a pilgrimage and the continent they saw was "exactly what they already believed Africa to be: a poor, struggling, hot, spiritual, creative place, full of sound and color."

They felt their homecoming, their pilgrimage, began when they toured the island of Gorée. They were in awe, she wrote, at "the slave fort, the place where it all began." Now a UNESCO World Heritage Site, Gorée was one of the most infamous forts where slaves were held and sold, then shipped off on the murderous "middle passage" voyage across the Atlantic to be sold again in the new world.

This is not Africa as seen in tourism brochures, but it is part of an international trend of mostly Americans traveling around the world to find their roots. Greece, Japan and China are three of the countries with special bureaus to help their overseas communities to come "home." These tourists spend hundreds of millions of dollars every year to see where grandmother or great-grandfather once lived. I traveled to Germany to see the northwestern village of Lohne, where my family lived for hundreds of years. And on an August vacation Bill and I found out that my family's Irish branch came from Nenagh, County Tipperary, thanks to baptismal records there.

The most famous modern "Roots" trip to Africa or possibly anywhere else was taken by Barack Obama just before he entered Harvard Law School. He told the story of his first trip to Kenya in the final chapters of his best-selling *Dreams from My Father,* which became a key part of his appeal during his successful campaign for president of the United States. His is a classic story. As a first-generation American on his father's side, he had been in touch with his father's Kenyan family for most of his life.

He called the trip a pilgrimage. "It will be just like 'Roots,' " a friend told him at a going-away party even though Obama was tracing the roots of his African father, who had come to the United States as a university student, many generations removed from the days of slavery. It became a homecoming for the future president. In Nairobi he met a parade of relatives whom he got to know better over the weeks. He also discovered the bias they held against wildlife parks. When he told his half-sister Auma that he wanted to take a safari, he got an earful about white colonials who care more about one dead elephant than one hundred black African children. "How many Kenyans do you think can afford to go on a safari?" she asked. But in the end she agreed and went with her clearly American half-brother to the reserve, where Obama saw herds of zebra, giraffe and wildebeest; camped on a riverbank; and studied the stars. He was awestruck watching hyenas feeding on the carcass of a wildebeest. At the end of that day he wrote: "I thought to myself: This is what Creation looked like."

8

BECOMING GREEN

On our fifth day sailing, I woke up early to see the sun rise over Costa Rica. The captain saw me standing at the bow of the ship and said, "Look down." Just below the water's surface a small school of dolphins swam alongside the ship, catching a ride in its wake. They undulated and leaped. They flashed what looked like dolphin smiles, and at times it seemed as if they were leading us. Then just as quickly they disappeared.

"They've probably gone to get something to eat," said Dan Dion, the captain of the *Sea Lion*.

Dolphins at starboard, brown pelicans dive-bombing into the sea and white hawks circling overhead were common on our eight-day voyage aboard the ship. On our daily trips ashore we were disappointed if we didn't see capuchin or squirrel monkeys swing overhead or a shy agouti—a rodent the size of a small lamb—munch in the undergrowth. Sometimes we circled rocky islands in inflatable zodiac boats, binoculars pasted to our eyes to spy on birds fighting midair over food or nesting on the rocks, all to a deafening symphony of squeals and cries.

Bill and I had come to Costa Rica to see "ecotourism" at one of its birthplaces. Ecotourism is a clunky name for a movement begun several decades ago to put the brakes on industrial-strength tourism and return to a form of travel that doesn't spoil or disfigure a country's landscape, people or society. When I first told friends I was writing a book about the tourism industry, they assumed I would concentrate on ecotourism. In many people's minds, ecotourism is to regular travel what local organic farming is to factory farming. And they think it is sweeping the planet; it is not. In the most optimistic measures, ecotourism or its sister practices of geotourism, sustainable tourism and responsible tourism make up no more than 8 percent of travel. The reason is simple: its aims often clash with industry goals for high volume and profits. And that makes it very difficult to pull off, even in Costa Rica.

To measure those differences and difficulties, Bill and I visited Costa Rica by ship, aboard the *National Geographic's Sea Lion* on a voyage organized by Lindblad Expeditions. I wanted to compare an ecocruise with the commercial cruise we had taken aboard the Royal Caribbean *Navigator of the Seas* in December 2009. During our cruise in March 2011 we first passed through the Panama Canal from the Atlantic side to the Pacific Ocean and then headed north up the coast from Panama to Costa Rica.

Every day we either went ashore to hike in the forests or snorkeled in the sea or zipped around the islands in a zodiac motor boat. To find pristine areas, our ship followed an itinerary of protected parks—national parks, private parks, regional parks.

The ship carries only sixty passengers and offers no room service, no casinos, no nighttime entertainment and no television in the cabins. That doesn't mean we suffered at all. The meals were extraordinary and the company amiable. We were also pleasantly exhausted from the day's excursions. Above all, we were surrounded by nature, exuberant nature.

We also could have booked into an "ecolodge" in the middle of a jungle and taken excursions hiking through Costa Rica's rainforests, climbing around its volcanoes. Alternately we could have chosen to get drenched white-water rafting in its rivers, surfing on the Pacific Coast or simply relaxing on its beaches. The country advertises itself as "Costa Rica—No Artificial Ingredients."

It's not that simple, but as a slogan, it's not entirely wrong. What is missing is the ups and downs in Costa Rica's recent history that not only gave birth to ecotourism but created a counter-movement that gave Costa

Rica the highest rate of deforestation in the entire Western Hemisphere for nearly two decades.

Ecotourism may sound like a squishy, feel-good concept, yet there are new international guidelines defining what it means to be a responsible, sustainable tourist company or destination. Those guidelines were recently hammered out by the Global Sustainable Tourism Council made up of representatives from United Nations agencies, private companies and environmentalists. I took along that list of guidelines.

Isabel Salas was our expedition leader. A biologist trained at the University of Costa Rica, she has the air of a female Indiana Jones, a no-nonsense curiosity about the natural world of her native Costa Rica and a gentle sense of humor. Her professional specialty is the social and sexual life of the howler monkey, the swift dark simian with a small gorilla face and a voice from the grave.

Our guides were as much a part of the ecotourism phenomenon as the landscape. They fulfilled the requirements to employ locals in high positions and provide visitors with knowledge about natural surroundings, local culture and cultural heritage. (This was the opposite of our Royal Caribbean trip, where they offered seminars on shopping for diamonds and other jewelry and nothing about Mexico or Belize where we docked.)

Four of the five naturalist guides were Costa Rican—the fifth was from Panama. They were scientists and locals; they could see the flash of a bird's wing in the thickest forest, then tell us not only the name of the bird but its mating habits, favorite food and where it fit in the life of the rainforest. After a day's adventure—hiking through the jungle, swimming in the bay or touring the islands in our zodiac boats—we would catch our breath, change into dry clothes, and gather for informal discussion led by Salas or one of the other naturalists. With slides and movies, postings of the birds and fishes, they would review what we'd seen and experienced that day and preview what was in store the next. It was somewhere between an exquisite hike and a sweaty classroom, at least what I wish my science classes had been like.

We crossed into the Panama Canal our first night of the voyage, our ship a bathtub-size toy boat compared to the mighty tankers and freighters that surrounded us. Each step up the watery ladder of the canal's locks was masterfully climbed as the ships rose to the height of a man-made lake created when the United States dug the canal bridging the Atlantic and Pacific oceans in 1914. The next morning we crossed that lake and docked at an island called Barro Colorado, a rare wilderness officially managed by the Smithsonian Tropical Research Institute. We would hike up the side of one of the hills with guides who are scientists at the institute. They told us that the island is normally off-limits to visitors; Lindblad is the only organization permitted to bring tourists to the island—another benefit of signing on to the *Sea Lion*.

That first hike was a stretch, getting our legs accustomed to climbing trails in the tropical heat while showing enthusiasm for small wonders like the ants crossing our trail in single file, each holding a corner of a green leaf that waved in the heat like a geisha's fan. Even with the thick canopy of trees we were literally dripping with sweat. Then, when I felt like fainting, we heard our first troop of howler monkeys. Two adults and two children perched on the highest branches of a tree swung into action at the sound of our footsteps, answering our arrival with their deep-throated howls that flooded the woods.

That night we passed through the canal, and in the morning we were on the Pacific Ocean, taking slow Zodiac boat rides around rugged rock islands in the Las Perlas Archipelago, where fishermen once dove for pearls. Now these desolate outposts are nesting homes to thousands of frigatebirds, pelicans and brown and blue-footed boobies. Against the clear blue skies off the Pacheca and Pachequilla islands, they swarmed in search of food and mates. When the males weren't vying for the attention of females with aerial acrobatics or deep dives into the sea, the birds were engaged in aerial combat. The elegant black frigates maneuvered like cocky fighter-jet pilots encircling the slow-moving brown pelicans until the frightened pelicans dropped the food from their pouches and the frigates swooped in to steal the fish.

That night we watched the sole movie shown during our trip: David McCullough narrating a PBS special based on his book about the building of the Panama Canal. I felt like I was part of a *New Yorker* cartoon about politically correct travel. Yet the three teenagers aboard stayed until the very end. After dinner the passengers walked on the deck and stared at the stars, gathered in the lounge below or retired to their rooms. No nights of karaoke or dance contests.

Before leaving the Panamanian coast we dropped anchor in the Gulf of Chiriquí at Coiba National Park. A rare refuge for threatened species like the crested eagle, this park is known as a spectacular site for scuba diving, with 760 species of well-protected marine fish, 33 species of shark and acres of live coral reefs. We snorkeled in the warm waters, weaving our way through schools of yellowtail surgeonfish, rays, zebra morays, the pencil-thin trumpetfish, and—my favorite—the spotted boxfish that look as if they were wearing organza party dresses. It was like swimming in an aquarium. Never had Bill or I been so close to nature and so at ease. We were outnumbered by these glorious fishes, guests in their world.

This was the moment when I understood the huge appeal of ecotourism. We were the only boat in sight. Only ships that leave the area as they found it receive approval for passage from the Panamanian national park system. In this case, that meant leaving the waters and beaches pristine and unspoiled, without polluting sewage or fuel or crowds. By definition, that excludes large modern cruise ships.

We had sailed into paradise. If we had arrived a few years earlier, we would have found something closer to hell. Until 2004 the island had been the heavily fortified penal colony known as Coiba Prison. Panama emptied it after eighty years of operation in this isolated area and turned the islands and marine area into a national park.

Lunch was a picnic on the beach, followed by two more hours to swim and snorkel. By the time we returned to the ship, the sun was beginning to set in bands of soft pink and yellow and my arms felt like worn rubber bands from the hours chasing fish.

Our next stop was Costa Rica, birthplace of ecotourism.

Isabel Salas said environmentalism is bred into her fellow citizens. "We grow up with conservation, knowing the names of trees and animals," she told me over morning coffee. "We've had so much time to think about conservation, not like our neighbors with their wars. We've had no army since 1948."

That year President José Figueres Ferrer abolished the military and redirected its funds to the police force, education, cultural preservation and the environment. Salas can be forgiven for bragging about that prescient move. Thirty years later it helped save Costa Rica from being involved in the bloody wars that engulfed its northern neighbors. This wasn't the only time Costa Rica had been the odd country out in Central America.

Costa Rica was the poorest of the Spanish colonies in Central America, relegated to the sidelines of history for several centuries. Christopher Columbus mistakenly named the area Costa Rica or rich coast in the belief that gold was buried in its hills. He was wrong. The volcanic mountain chains that rib the narrow country are home to multiple microclimates and countless species of flora and fauna but not gold. So the land proved uninviting to Spanish investors and entrepreneurs who preferred Nicaragua.

Eventually, in the mid nineteenth century, the colonialists cleared some land for coffee plantations, and coffee beans became Costa Rica's chief cash crop. But much of the land remained a wilderness. About the same time, European scientists started arriving, drawn to Costa Rica by popular scientific books about the extraordinary diversity of species in the small nation's jungles—then and now an extraordinary biodiversity that has become the country's distinguishing attribute.

Among these foreigners were two German physicians who moved to Costa Rica to practice medicine. Carl Hoffmann and Alexander von Frantzius were naturalists who had watched the woods in their own country cut down for lumber and energy during the age of industrialization. The two physicians spent their weekends hiking through the jungles of Costa Rica and exploring its mountains. They collected specimens in a thorough, scientific fashion, helping raise awareness of the breadth of Costa Rica's wildlife. Dr. Frantzius catalogued the country's mammals and Dr. Hoffmann did the first extensive study of the country's bats. Their names live on in places like Cerro Frantzius and animals like Hoffmann's woodpecker.

Their greatest achievement, though, was teaching natural history to the young students of Costa Rica, initiating the studies that eventually made Costa Rica the center of academic tropical research in Central America. Dr. Frantzius used the backroom of his pharmacy as a classroom and laboratory, educating the country's first tropical biologists and researchers. By teaching Costa Ricans the science of the forest, the two physicians and the European and American scholars who followed them, taught them the value of the wilderness. This in turn reinforced Costa Ricans' resolve to reject blandishments in the early twentieth century to clear-cut forests to create more plantations. Their answer was that the forests were worth more standing than if they were cut down for lumber or cleared for cultivation.

These foreign scientists in turn trained more and more Costa Ricans, who became great naturalists themselves, until the country grew to become a center of the conservation movement in the Western Hemisphere. Alberto Manuel Brenes Mora, one of the brightest young Costa Rican naturalists trained in the early 1900s, was a pioneer in the study of the country's 1,200 species of orchids.

By 1940 the country had created the University of Costa Rica from four schools of higher learning. In the decades that followed, the university excelled in the study of tropical rainforest preservation, and success followed success. The Organization of American States established an institute for agricultural sciences in Costa Rica to teach wildlife management and forest conservation. There, Leslie Holdridge, the pioneering ecologist, taught some of Costa Rica's finest naturalists. (He was so dedicated to conservation that he purchased a tract of rainforest named La Selva to better study tropical systems.)

One of his star pupils was Gerardo Budowski, a Venezuelan student who exemplifies how academics led naturally to ecotourism. After Budowski completed his studies in Costa Rica, he earned a doctorate in forestry in 1961 at Yale and returned to Costa Rica to teach and practice conservation. He was recruited by the United Nations to take part in the then-new program of conservation and ecology. His achievements eventually included becoming the president of the International Ecotourism Society in 1992. This scientific tradition, begun nearly one hundred years ago, is responsible for educating Costa Rica's large pool of conservationists and naturalists like Isabel Salas.

To this day Costa Rica can boast a stunning diversity of flora and fauna in a country slightly smaller than the state of West Virginia. Costa Rica has more species of birds than the United States and Canada combined, more butterfly species than the entire continent of Africa, and as a "biological superpower" boasts 200 reptile species, 208 mammal species and an astonishing 35,000 insect species.

More astounding, small Costa Rica is home to 5 percent of the world's biodiversity, thanks in considerable degree to its conservation habits. The national parks and private reserves cover more than one-fourth of the country. Forests are known in Costa Rica as the "lungs of the cities" that keep the air and water clean and protect the soil. Proportionately, Costa Rica has more protected lands—national parks and private reserves—than even the United States.

The marriage of ecotourism to the natural sciences was a natural fit. Ecotourism could not exist without the forest, the birds, the animals, the wild landscapes. And in theory, money earned from ecotourism protects the wilderness. This concept wasn't an easy sell, not even in Costa Rica. Many people saw "ecotourism" as a thin basis for modern economic development. I got a hint of the close calls in recent Costa Rican history that nearly buried the prospects of ecotourism.

Late one afternoon we were slowly circling the forested Golfo Dulce Bay in our Zodiac speedboats, hoping to see monkeys come out after the heat of the day. On this outing José Calvo, another Costa Rican naturalist, was our guide. Birds were roosting in the trees. Calvo thought he heard the cry of a howler. He lifted his binoculars to a thick blue-green patch of trees and saw them—a troop of howler monkeys with an elusive squirrel monkey by their side. "An orphan," said Calvo. Somehow the howlers managed to munch on the tender leaves of trees above the mangroves while bursting out their fantastic screeches. On one branch a baby clung to her mother's back. We applauded him for finding the monkeys.

"When I was growing up, you could see monkeys everywhere. There were pet monkeys on the street corner doing tricks. Especially capuchin monkeys because they are so smart. They train easily. Today you never see them anywhere. So many were killed that now it's illegal to capture them," said Calvo. "It's also illegal to cut down the mangrove forests."

That protection came only after years of a tug of war over what made the most sense to improve Costa Rica's economy. At first, the monkeys and forests lost in Costa Rica's race to improve livelihoods and figure out what kind of country it would become. After an early spate of conservationism a new president changed course in the 1970s and 1980s and removed several key regulations, opening the way for ranchers to buy up and clear land for cattle. The ranchers had their eye on the growing appetite in the United States for beef: Americans were consuming hamburgers at a remarkable rate. Fast food was no longer just a convenience food but a staple. Costa Rican policy-makers and ranchers wanted to cash in on the trend and export beef to the United States.

Chain saws and bulldozers cleared nearly one-third of the land for pastures in those two decades, earning Costa Rica the distinction of having the highest rate of deforestation in the Western Hemisphere. Beef became the country's major export: 36 million tons were sold to the United States in 1985. The shift to intensive cattle ranching not only changed the economy but the country's self-image as well, from a wilderness sanctuary to a home of modern ranchers. The period became known as the "hamburgerization" of Costa Rica.

The conservationists didn't give up. They already had a solid foothold in the country with the national park system Costa Rica created in 1960 patterned after that in the United States. It was augmented by private reserves scattered around the country. At the beginning these private tracts had been purchased by foreigners entranced by the country's beauty. Among the pioneers in this movement was a group of American Quakers who left the United States in 1951 in protest of their country's role in the Korean War. Pacifists, they immigrated to Costa Rica because it had abolished its army three years earlier. They bought 3,000 acres of cloud forest in the Tilarán Mountains of Costa Rica's north central highlands in the belief that the weather was ideal for dairy farming. They had cut down half of the forests for pasture when they realized in horror that in doing so they had jeopardized their water supply. So they left the other half of their land in wilderness: cooled by mist and wind much of the year, the cloud forests were thick with foliage every shade of green. Moss enveloped stones and dripped from branches. All of it was fed by cold streams as clear as glass. They named it the Monteverde Cloud Forest Reserve.

Following the Costa Rican tradition, the Quakers invited scientists to do research at the Cloud Forest Reserve. The scientists, in turn, spread the word about the beauty of the area and soon tourists arrived. The first bed-and-breakfast inns opened in the early 1950s. From this modest beginning Monteverde became one of the birthplaces of ecotourism in Costa Rica. The reserve grew, through land leases for scientific research in the 1970s and land purchases by American philanthropists for conservation purposes. Today it covers over 26,000 acres. Ecotourism grew along with it.

The preserve inspired an adjacent preserve. In the late 1980s a Swedish schoolteacher visited Monteverde and was upset at the noticeable degradation of the forests on the edge of the preserve. She went home with a mission. She convinced the young students in her school to help her raise enough money to buy up land to act as a buffer for Monteverde and save that paradise. The nine-year-old students collected enough Swedish kronor to buy 35 acres; once news of the campaign spread, children from Japan, the United States and Europe canvassed their family and friends, eventually raising millions of dollars and creating the Children's Eternal Rainforest, which encompasses 17,500 acres.

Now the tourists were arriving by the thousands. Just off the reserve, boutique hotels called ecolodges were built that adhered to the conservation ethic of low impact on the environment and centered on the natural wilderness surrounding them. Multiply Monteverde by the hundreds and you have an idea of how nature tourism became an important industry for Costa Rica. Since ecotourism required more and more protected wilderness, that industry piggybacked off of the government's push to build a national park system throughout the country.

In the 1980s, events beyond its borders threatened this peaceful progression. Nicaragua, its northern neighbor, was being torn apart in a civil war that pitted a leftist government pledged to helping peasants against rightist rebels who saw the government as an extension of Cuban communism and sponsored by the United States. Soldiers from both sides sought refuge on the Costa Rican side of the border. War was also exploding in El Salvador, except in this case the rebels were leftists fighting a rightist military government. Assassinations of civilians were common, including the notorious murder of the Catholic Archbishop Oscar Romero. Costa Rica worried that the wars could spill over as they had in Vietnam and engulf their country one way or another.

Costa Ricans elected Óscar Arias Sánchez as their president in 1986. Sensing the mood of his country, Arias set off to help end the war. He presented a peace plan to resolve the conflicts, relying, he said, on Costa Rica's moral authority as a neighbor without an army. The plan led to a peace accord the next year and Arias was awarded the Nobel Peace Prize.

Somehow, that prize helped affirm Costa Rica's identity. The country was developing a reputation as a peaceful, conservationist-minded niche nation. Costa Ricans confirmed that direction for their country when the price of beef fell in the 1990s and Costa Rica's cattle ranches became less profitable. Agriculture seemed less attractive, and over the next five years, traditional farming and ranching lost their premier economic position to the new leaders: tourism, especially ecotourism, and computer and bio-medical technology. The small country has averaged over 2 million foreign tourists every year, quite a number considering that Costa Rica's population is 4.5 million. And most of those tourists come from the United States.

Becky Timbers was seated in a lotus position every morning as she welcomed us at sunrise for thirty minutes of stretches. We gathered on the covered upper deck, passengers of varying skill and flexibility, to be gently led by Timbers through a series of modified yoga positions. She had the nimbleness of a ballet dancer. Bill, on the other hand, got stuck on some of the first positions. But he didn't give up. This was his first attempt at anything resembling yoga, and although he swore yoga wasn't for him, the fresh morning air and calm nature of the class convinced him otherwise. Throughout the cruise he showed up every morning for the stretches before breakfast.

Timbers is from Vermont, a college graduate with an itch to travel. She started out as a steward, or housekeeper, and worked her way up to the ship's "wellness expert," which involves, among other things, holding classes and giving massages.

Most important for the standards of sustainable tourism, or ecotourism, Timbers is an American, as are all of her fellow crew members from the captain to the stewards. *National Geographic* is headquartered in the United States and the vast majority of the passengers are American. So, in contrast to the large commercial cruise ship companies, the *Sea Lion* is registered and flagged in the United States. Its port home is Seattle. The ship recruits Americans, pays American wages and follows American regulations and standards. The wages are significantly higher than those on big cruise ships. Timbers said she is paid $140 a day on a six-month contract, and added that, as a steward, she was paid roughly $100 a day, or twice as much per day as a steward on a Royal Caribbean ship earned in a month.

The *Sea Lion* fulfills the guidelines' requirement that locals are hired and paid living wages: an American ship with American crew also employs Costa Rican and Panamanian naturalists. It is not flagged and registered in a country like Liberia to avoid environmental and labor laws.

"It's hard to get these jobs," Timbers said. "I was lucky."

The mood on the ship reflected that difference. The crew was not obsequious; there were no complaints about wages and pleas for high tips to supplement a miserable wage. And on our vacation it mattered to Bill and me that we were around people who were properly compensated for their hard work.

Translating the sustainable ecotourism requirements for the cruise meant local hires at the home port and local hires for the countries we visited. On that score, Isabel said she was just as pleased with her role. "I have been with Lindblad Expeditions since 1997 and I believe we Costa Rican naturalists are best at guiding visitors to our country."

How much did all of this sustainable ecotourism cost?

On the face of it, this was a much more expensive trip. It cost $4,800 for each of us for eight days with everything included—food, all of our expeditions on shore and the premium for traveling through the Panama Canal. Tolls to go through the canal can be steep. The *Disney Magic* cruise liner paid $283,400 in toll fees in 2008. Our small cruise ship was charged far less, but the toll was passed on to us in the higher expedition cost.

For the same amount of money Bill and I could have stayed in a deluxe suite aboard the Royal Caribbean *Allure of the Seas* for a seven-day cruise in the Caribbean at $3,349 per person. (Instead we stayed in a room with balcony for a five-day cruise.) There is no question that we couldn't afford this trip very often, compared to commercial cruises.

For us the *Sea Lion* was the bargain. There was no comparison between the experiences aboard the Royal Caribbean ship, which was largely a crowded floating hotel, and those on the *Sea Lion*, which actually took us on a voyage to foreign countries with the greatest of luxuries in the twenty-first century—actual experiences in the disappearing wilderness. We could have stayed in an ecolodge for far less money, but then we wouldn't have had the breadth of the seagoing experience.

There was more than a touch of luxury aboard the *Sea Lion*, especially at mealtime. The dining room was no more than comfortable, an "intimate" space with old-fashioned round tables covered in standard-issue white linens and the sound of the sea seeping through the portholes. The décor was 1950s practical, nothing like the high-end dining room on the Royal Caribbean ship. But the food—that was something else. Gary Jenanyan, the executive consulting chef for *National Geographic* and Lindblad Expeditions, traveled on our cruise, supervising spicy huevos rancheros for breakfast and a light pineapple cream for dessert later at dinner. Whenever we landed near a local market, he sent a crew member off to buy fresh fish, vegetable and fruits. More than a few of the meals would have earned praise in a restaurant guide, reflecting Gary's decades-long service as head of the Great Chefs program at the Robert Mondavi Winery and personal chef to Mondavi. Instead, the local food earned more good marks for buying and cooking local.

We weren't assigned seats at mealtime. Instead, we mixed and eventually spoke with most of the other passengers and found a few whose company we especially enjoyed. This was a self-selected group of people from around the country who consciously chose a vacation because it was a rare trip through a wilderness. There was the tree farmer from Moweaqua, Illinois, who saved much of his old-growth forest and sold what others considered waste lumber on the Internet, making a very nice living. Also on board was a National Park forest ranger and her chemist husband, who chose the voyage because "*National Geographic* believes in protecting the land and leaving it as you find it." A British entrepreneur came on the trip to take photographs of wildlife for his professional website. Finally, we met a nurse whose husband had just abandoned her, forcing her to sell her home alongside a national park in North Carolina. She told me it was worth spending $4,000 on the voyage: "I came on this trip to see paradise before I have to start my new life."

On the fourth night of our trip we sailed to the Osa Peninsula on Costa Rica's Pacific Coast, one of the most celebrated ecotourist spots in the country, with beaches that qualify as a slice of paradise. We began the next morning with a wet landing, climbing out of the Zodiac boats as best we could on the beach. The smell of the sea was as sharp as metal, pure salt and humidity without an overlay of pollution.

Once on the beach, we had a choice of riding horses or hiking through the jungle. Horses were waiting for us on the sand. Bill and I chose a morning hike.

The peninsula is in the southwest corner of Costa Rica. It is shaped like a crab's claw, sheltering the Golfo Dulce to the east, where we had visited a tropical garden the day before. This time we were traveling around the western side of the peninsula, up the lush Pacific Ocean shoreline with mangroves dripping into the sea and untamed beaches framed by dense jungles. The foliage was a study in every shade of green and blue. This was the magnificent Corcovado National Park, which covers nearly half of the Osa Peninsula. Experts have called it the crown jewel of the Costa Rican park system. Few other spots on Earth can claim more diverse flora and fauna than Corcovado. The park is home to the last old-growth rainforests on the Pacific Coast of Central America and naturalists compare it favorably to the Amazon Basin and the deepest forests of Malaysia and Indonesia.

Keeping it that way has not been easy. This is also one of the few areas in Costa Rica where gold was found, centuries after Christopher Columbus misnamed the country. International mining companies bought up much of the land surrounding the park and 'oreros,' or gold panhandlers, continued working in the forests, polluting the streams and killing the wild animals for food. International logging companies were about to clear-cut wide swaths of the area until Costa Rica named it a national park in 1975, earning then-President Daniel Oduber the Albert Schweitzer Award for preserving the habitat of animals in the park.

Over the next decades, the government, supported by money and expertise from philanthropies as varied as the Corcovado Foundation, the Nature Conservancy, Catholic Relief Services and the World Wildlife Fund, has tried varying strategies to protect the park. First, officials created jobs for local Costa Ricans in ecotourism to discourage logging or gold panhandling. Then they hired more park rangers to make sure poachers and panhandlers stayed out. So far, they have saved the hermit crabs, tapirs, jaguars, pumas and ocelots and the local villagers have been able to prosper from tourism.

As one conservationist said, Costa Rica is a laboratory in ecology, not an "eco-topia."

After lunch we sailed farther up the coast and landed at San Pedrillo on the northern tip of the park for our afternoon hike. We climbed a steep, rutted path that wound with sharp angles up the hills, leading to a waterfall. Sweating, we dove into its shimmering pool and splashed for half an hour surrounded by rainforest. Sounds perfect and it nearly was, but this was a group of strangers thrown together, so there were bound to be a few irritating encounters among us. One passenger monopolized our guide by speaking to him in colloquial Spanish that few of us could follow. There was a small rebellion to end that. At another point a passenger decided she could answer our questions better than our Costa Rican guide. The guide diplomatically cut her off.

The Osa Peninsula is something of a showpiece for ecotourism on Costa Rica's Pacific Coast and is routinely used as an example of best practices as well as a reason to prevent the rest of the coast from being developed with chock-a-block high-density motels. To make that point, the Center for Responsible Travel, headquartered in Washington, D.C., published a survey in 2011 showing that Costa Ricans working at ecolodges as housekeepers, kitchen staff and groundskeepers earn an average of $709 each month, nearly twice as much as other workers in the region, whose average income is $357. And the people working in ecolodges were far more likely to be from the Osa region than those in other jobs, who were imported from other regions and willing to work for less money.

The survey also questioned the tourists. The majority said they came to Osa to enjoy the wilderness and said they considered themselves people who "were concerned about traveling in ways that are socially and environmentally responsible." They said their vacations in Osa were a "good value," and would have been willing to pay more than the $42 fee charged to visit Corcovado National Park. That study and many others have linked Costa Rica's successful ecotourism industry with the fact that Costa Rica stands out as the wealthiest nation in Central America, with a high rate of literacy and good health care system.

Foreign hotels and tour operators have taken note of the popularity and profitability of Costa Rica's ecotourism market and have bought up considerable land there to build their own hotels. I witnessed how valuable that tourism has become during a maneuver at the highest diplomatic level. In 2003, Costa Rica was one of five Central American countries negotiating a new trade agreement with the United States called the Central American Free Trade Agreement or CAFTA. Just as the agreement was to be announced at a public press conference, Costa Rica bowed out, in part because the United States refused to drop its demand that Costa Rica open up its tourist trade to foreign corporations, giving up some control of its coastline and its emphasis on ecotourism. That public standoff was my first introduction to the power of ecotourism. (In fact, that was the first time I had ever written the word "ecotourism" in an article.) I was covering the negotiations as the *New York Times* international economics correspondent and I had never seen a country walk away from a U.S. trade deal at the last minute. The other four countries signed the accord. Costa Rica waited one year before signing, after negotiating the removal of the threat to its tourism industry.

Back on the ship the crew had organized a display of local handicrafts for sale in what they called the "global marketplace." On sale were baskets handwoven from native grasses by indigenous women; jewelry crafted by local artists; and blouses and shirts sewn by native seamstresses. I bought a necklace for a gift.

This was straight out of the how-to list for responsible ecotourism: "The Company offers the means for local small entrepreneurs to develop and sell sustainable products that are based on the area's nature, history, and culture."

Our last day was a reminder of how fortunate we had been sailing through the wilderness with few other humans nearby. During the night we had sailed past the old banana-exporting port of Quepos and anchored in Drake Bay opposite the Manuel Antonio National Park. This is one of Costa Rica's smallest preserves as well as one of its most popular. We learned why when we landed on its shores before nine o'clock that morning, ahead of the hundreds of tourists expected that day and in time to see the monkeys playing around in the cool of the morning before the heat sent them off to siesta.

The capuchin monkeys swung around to greet us on the first leg of our hike. There are no fierce predators threatening these and the other mammals at the park, and plenty of tourists feed these irresistible creatures. Our fellow travelers were helpless in the face of the capuchins, with their famous monk-colored coats, long sinuous tails and sensitive pale faces. They snapped photographs and took videos of the capuchins, muttering that the monkeys were so "curious" or "intelligent" or "playful" or "adorable" until the guides said "Enough" and we continued up the path.

Capuchin monkeys and the colorful toucan birds are practically mascots of the Costa Rica park system. Thanks to them and the other wild critters, the number of foreign visits has skyrocketed over the last thirty years. The National Parks Service was only created in 1977, yet foreign tourism took off immediately. From 1985 to 1991, visits to the park quadrupled from 63,500 to 273,400 foreign tourists. A few years later in 1995 tourism eclipsed coffee and bananas as the top income earner in Costa Rica. Today the wilderness parks help draw the more than 2 million foreign tourists to Costa Rica every year. While Costa Rica is universally praised for its decision to live in "peace with nature," pioneer ecotourism, prohibit oil exploration and protect its tropical rainforest, that doesn't mean that all of the tourism hotels and lodges in the country are so respectful of nature. To sort out which places were truly "ecotourist" establishments, the government created a Certification for Sustainable Tourism program that evaluates and scores all types of hotels in the country.

On our hike back down to the beach, the monkeys put on a show for our last walk through the jungle. Howlers screamed to the heavens and capuchins swung over to the trail, jumping from tree limb to tree limb until they disappeared inside the green forest wall of trees and vines. How could you ever tire of these jungles, especially when you had a comfortable ship anchored off the coast to welcome you after the daily excursion with a warm shower, comfortable bed for a nap, and a delicious meal?

That night at dinner we sat at a table with Isabel and with Mike and Judy, a couple from Seattle—my old hometown—and discovered we had friends in common. At breakfast on Saturday we said goodbye to Jane, an artist from Stow, Massachusetts, whose cabin was near ours on the small boat. We climbed into a bus for our ride to San Juan and our flight home, passing new villas along the way that were second homes for foreigners, a key concern in Costa Rica as it is in France and Britain.

Waiting at the airport, I reviewed all the categories for sustainable tourism. The *Sea Lion* passed them all. Its greatest triumph was in category D: "Maximize benefits to the environment and minimize negative impacts." The *Sea Lion* actions were impeccable, especially for "conserving biodiversity, ecosystems and landscapes." No wildlife were captured, consumed or traded. The naturalists were so keen on this rule that we were forbidden to collect shells. Isabel gave a shout-out to Riley, a teenager from Texas, who photographed a quirky collage of shells in place and left them scattered on the sand rather than pocket them.

Beyond our individual journey, the company supports local environmental groups as well as the daunting goal of creating a "panther path," a wide swath of protected areas from Mexico through Panama to give the great panthers room to survive. Its website contains a "commitment to sustainable travel" section describing how it does business and the local groups it supports.

After this experience I think I trust the *National Geographic*, but how about all the other groups and hotels that say they are sustainable, or "green," in Costa Rica? Upscale hotels like the Four Seasons Resort and Spa in northwest Costa Rica charge as much as $2,000 a night, advertising "eco-activities," a neighboring dry tropical forest and two "unspoiled beaches" along with an Arnold Palmer Golf Course, a spa, paddleboats and tennis. Is this ecotourism? Or is it more like the J. W. Marriott Guanacaste Resort and Spa built in the same region on the Pacific Ocean, with classic spa, gym and restaurants, yet claiming only to be luxurious, not an ecoestablishment.

In most surveys tourists say they will pay a little extra for vacations that respect the environment. Governments have given subsidies to hotels to make them environment-friendly. This adds up to big business in calling yourself "green." Not surprisingly, hotels and destinations around the world are now advertising themselves as just that: green.

Companies now talk about the triple bottom line—profit, people and the planet—especially in the tourism industry. At Abu Dhabi's World Green Tourism conference a debate broke out over the definition of "green."

"How can some of these places pretend they are green? Building more hotel rooms that use less air-conditioning; that's not green, it's using less energy. Being green is much more than that," said Gopinath Parayil, founder of Blue Yonder, an ecotourism venture in South India that has more awards than it can count. "This is more green-washing."

When it was his turn on stage, Parayil showed how his travel group helped revive traditional Kerala arts and music, clean up rivers, restore four-hundred-year-old homes and recover local history—all the while making a profit.

The hotel executives were just as confident singing the praises of their operations by defining "green" to fit their own situation. The tourism industry is filled with confusing claims of environmental stewardship based on little more than changing towels less frequently and therefore saving water.

Groups have tried giving out certificates for green tourism, responsible tourism, geotourism and ethical tourism in a piecemeal fashion, and it has been difficult to know who is backing these certificates. Some "green labels" are patent lies; others are simply disingenuous, because there is no certificate or uniform standards to distinguish who is genuine. Businesses that adhere to high standards fear that if such a certificate is introduced, they will be undercut by competitors who lie about their environmental credentials.

A group of tourism experts and international organizations set out to solve this problem and found a champion in Ted Turner. He agreed to underwrite the creation of the certificate that would be as respected as the Michelin star system for restaurants.

Few people could have been more welcome than the glamorous businessman from Atlanta, with deep pockets and an impressive record as an innovative entrepreneur, founder of CNN, the first cable news network, as well as Turner Classic Movies, owner of the Atlanta Braves baseball team—the list is endless. He used his wealth for conservation and philanthropy. Turner bought 2 million acres of land in the United States, putting most of it under conservation easement; he is the single largest private landowner in the U.S.

Turner headlined a press conference in Barcelona in October 2008 at which the certificate effort was announced. Standing with officials from U.N. agencies, environment groups and businesses, Turner said he was putting his money and prestige behind the world's first gold standard for ecotourism, or sustainable tourism.

Turner portrayed the new initiative as a commonsense approach that was in line with good business practices. "Sustainability is just like the old business adage: you don't encroach on the principal, you live off the interest. Unfortunately, up to this point, the travel industry and tourists haven't had a common framework to let them know if they're living up to that maxim," he said.

He then promised that a new "Global Sustainable Tourism Criteria" would change that. Turner honored his pledge through his own United Nations Foundation, which has a small project on tourism. Along with the Rainforest Alliance, the United Nations Environment Programme and the United Nations World Tourism Organization, the U.N. Foundation was crafting the criteria.

Erika Harms, the foundation's tourism expert and the force behind the criteria project, was named the executive director. When I asked her how she became interested in tourism, she said it came naturally—she was from Costa Rica.

"We grew up seeing tourism in a different light. Ecotourism was in its nascent state then. It meant no trashing a place. Instead, it was 'go, see, help preserve these pristine places.' Originally it was pitched to backpackers. Spartan small hotels with plumbing and electricity fulfilled your basic needs with no luxury. Families prepared the meals. There were no restaurants per se," she said.

Harms earned a law degree in Costa Rica, and after working in business and as an environmental consultant, she moved to Washington as the deputy chief of mission and consul-general at the embassy of Costa Rica. Then she joined the U.N. Foundation.

Harms has zeroed in on the need to weed out the real ecotourist establishments from the fake. The average person looking for a responsible way to travel didn't have a clue which claim was genuine.

"There were so many missing elements in certification programs before: culture, community, destination and habitat. You could destroy a mangrove to build your hotel and still receive a Green Globe certificate," she told me in 2008 in the first of several interviews.

In September 2009, less than a year after the Barcelona announcement, Harms held a reception in Washington to celebrate its creation. "We developed the criteria with industry, always with industry. That is how we collaborate. It didn't take that much money. . . . It was only about solutions," she told me.

"The concept of tourism has changed with industrialization, yes, and standardization," said Harms. "You don't see any difference anymore between one place and another. It's easier to build that way and provide standard service, but how can you preserve a sense of place and culture? The complexity of the tourism industry works against sustainability."

"Unless you create some tie to a place and its people, you won't have demand for sustainable tourism," she continued. "Our certification program will help all tourists find the places that are still authentic."

That sounds high-minded and slightly boring. It is the opposite. Behind the phrase "sustainable tourism" is the wish to keep all of the intriguing, messy and exotic differences in the world. The rules and regulations of sustainable tourism are meant, ironically, to avoid a world that looks the same.

The criteria for certification were unveiled, reviewed and revised by 2011, with nearly universal praise. That was the criteria I used to evaluate our voyage in Costa Rica.

Business understands the value of that label. People will search for it and often pay more money for its reassurance, which means big profits can be made by being on the ground floor in the certification scramble. "We are more like the police that recognize and enforce the standards," said Janice Lichtenwald of the Global Sustainable Tourism Council.

Companies are lining up to become official certifiers. Green Globe, which is privately owned, has already adopted the sustainable tourism standards and hopes to be able to certify hotels with the "Global Sustainable" label.

"Green Globe and other companies will make money from this, yes they will," said Lichtenwald. "There is a consumer desire for labeling—they expect it."

Hotels, resorts and tour operators are willing to pay companies to certify they are on the side of the angels, that visitors on vacation know they are not destroying the environment, or playing on a golf course that had been home to poor peasants a year earlier.

This drive for certification and sustainable tourism grew out of the environmental movement. The leaders of the ecotourism, or sustainable tourism, movement are not the fire-breathing types. There is no one like Ralph Nader, who stubbornly forced the government to demand safety features in the automobile industry. The tourism reformers are professors, writers and tour operators who wield ideas, gently. They write, lead groups, give awards and, when asked, will help a country, a community or a hotel figure out responsible tourism. One of their biggest difficulties is to explain that tourism is the classic double-edged sword that, unless properly managed, can ruin a place as easily as save it.

Over the last two decades, several tourism activists saw the gross problems that tourism was creating in the hyperactive world of cheap travel and the Internet. Jonathan Tourtellot, writer and editor at *National Geographic*, coined the term "geotourism."

Tourtellot was familiar with the work of Héctor Caballos-Lascuráin, the Mexican who coined the term "ecotourism" to describe using tourism to enjoy and protect relatively undisturbed natural areas. Tourtellot wanted to broaden the concept to protect destinations in a holistic fashion—its people, culture and society as well as its natural landscape. "Geotourism" fit the bill, he thought, a name that encompassed the globe. He defined it as travel that "sustains or enhances the geographical character of a place—its environment, culture, aesthetics, heritage, and the well-being of its residents."

"The industry had become all about promoting tourism and very little about stewardship. I wanted to go back to the origins of tourism—meaning to tour, to see and appreciate what is already there, the local culture, the sense of that particular place," said Tourtellot. "Tourism today is about resorts, spas, golf courses and theme parks that were built to bring in tourists and was subverting the very idea of place," said Tourtellot.

He founded the *National Geographic*'s Center for Sustainable Destinations. Then he wrote a Geotourism Charter in 2006 with a set of "stewardship principles" for destinations to adopt. In the first years Honduras, Norway, Guatemala, the Douro Valley in Portugal and the City of Montreal asked to sign on to the program. He also helped create a Geotourism Map Guide program in which locals submitted their thoughts about what was most attractive about their locales for tourists and then created a map and blueprint for sustainable tourism development.

Tourtellot's most controversial move was to break the tourism taboo and print articles describing the worst as well as the best of tourism. And he published the list in the *National Geographic Traveler*; it was hard to miss. Tourtellot and his colleagues decided to select a theme every year; for instance, coastal areas. Then they polled hundreds of experts to decide which are the best and worst shores in the world, or which are the best- and the worst-kept World Heritage destinations, or which are the best- or worst-kept national parks.

For the first time in anyone's memory, famous destinations were graded professionally and the results published as the cover story of the November/December 2010 issue of the *Traveler*. Georgia's Sea Islands were on the top and South Carolina's Myrtle Beach at the bottom. South Carolina's newspapers published the findings and deplored that their sandy strand was declared one of the world's worst along with crowded, foul beaches in Vietnam and Spain.

Don Hawkins, a respected tourism professor at George Washington University, told me that he first thought Tourtellot had overstepped the boundaries. Then he saw the reaction and changed his mind. "The Thai tourism authority asked, 'How can we fix this?' And they did. It worked."

Tourtellot and the *National Geographic* teamed up with the Ashoka Changemakers organization to create a "geotourism award." I attended the first-ever award ceremony, hosted by Tourtellot. The geotourism prize comes with a $5,000 check for each of the three winners for transforming tourism to "celebrate places and change lives."

The auditorium at the *National Geographic* headquarters was packed with tour operators and hoteliers and students from around the globe. The general public had voted online for the finalists. The atmosphere was a cross between the Academy Awards and student civics prizes. For me one of the lessons from the event was the supremacy of Costa Rica as a superpower of responsible tourists. That first year the top winners came from Costa Rica, Nepal and Ecuador. The finalists included tour groups from Bhutan, Tanzania, Thailand and Latvia. Two years later, the theme in 2011 was tourism "on the edge" or saving fresh water and coastal destinations from degradation. Once again one of the three top winners came from Costa Rica.

Martha Honey is another early activist who credits Costa Rica for her lifelong passion for ecotourism. A journalist, she lived with her family in Costa Rica in the 1970s and eventually wrote the book *Ecotourism and Sustainable Development: Who Owns Paradise?* which explores sustainable-tourism policies around the globe. As cofounder and codirector of the Center for Responsible Travel (CREST), Honey oversees research and convenes conferences on responsible tourism. She also has become a leading figure in "philanthropy tourism," which encourages tourists to give back to the people and places through donations and volunteer work. Her ideas have gone mainstream, encouraging new philanthropy and funneling volunteers to established programs like Habitat for Humanity which builds homes around the globe.

She said the first question she asks about tourism is "Who benefits?" Too often the answer is not the local people.

"The big worry today is the conglomerates and hotel chains that are consolidating more and more. The Internet is countering that power by making a more equal playing field."

Honey welcomes the push for a sustainable-tourism label and new criteria but warns that "the problem is the programs are all voluntary."

On the other side of the Atlantic, Harold Goodwin is something of an éminence grise of the sustainable-tourism movement with a different vision. He prefers to work directly within the industry to effect change, eschewing outside activism. As a professor, he founded the International Centre for Responsible Tourism at Leeds Metropolitan University in Britain and is a familiar figure on the international conference circuit.

His inspiration is Jost Krippendorf, a Swiss academic who examined the politics of tourism in the 1970s and argued that the industry needed to help the environment, culture and local communities. Goodwin believes that there is no single global industry. "There is not an international market for tourism," he wrote to me in an email exchange.

Goodwin argues that sustainable tourism has to be created in "each originating market," or the homes of the tourists. In other words, educate the tourists and the companies they use to travel. To that end, Goodwin concentrates on working with the industry and governments and not with nonprofit groups or activists. "The private sector is achieving far more than the NGOs," he wrote, dismissing programs such as community-based tourism, ecotourism, carbon offsetting, global sustainable-tourism criteria as "superficially attractive" but unproven.

Through his teaching, Goodwin says he has trained tourism professionals who work around the world to transform the industry from within by creating tourist operations that put sustainability into practice. He gives Responsible Tourism awards to what he considers good examples of responsible tourism. He also hosts an online forum called Irresponsible Tourism where people can complain about the bad apples.

The tented auditorium was draped with ropes of fresh branches. The Brazilian night had fallen and strings of lights sparkled in the cool evening. Columns holding up the tent were covered in leaves, fruits, flowers and more branches. Dirt swirled on the floor. The motif was Amazon rainforest. The glittering invitation-only gathering was the 9th Annual Summit of the World Travel and Tourism Council, held in May 2009 in Florianópolis, Brazil.

The dinner crowd included the titans of the tourism industry, who mingled with the political elite from Asia, Europe, the Americas and Africa. As they gathered at the buffet lines, the guests resembled a society photograph in a glossy magazine: well dressed, well heeled and enough beauties, both male and female, to create a buzz. This was the annual summit of the movers and shakers, and the theme behind the rainforest décor was responsible, sustainable tourism and green tourism. In the buffet line I met Thea Chiesa, of the World Economic Forum of Geneva; at dinner Costas Christ, chairman of the judges of Tourism for Tomorrow Awards. The industry definitely saw itself as protectors of the planet, not exploiters.

This is the organization founded in 1991 by James Robinson III, the CEO of American Express, who teamed up with the U.N. World Tourism Organization to produce the Satellite Accounts system that governments use to measure income from tourism.

At the time of the Brazil conference, the satellite system reported that the industry contributed $5.474 trillion to the world economy in 2009, more than 9 percent of the world's GDP and the biggest employer in the world with 235 million jobs. (Academics and economists dispute some of the industry's claims, although most agree that tourism is the largest service sector industry and the largest employer.)

Some of those attending were government tourism directors from China and South Africa; the secretary-general of the United Nations World Tourism Organization, and business executives from American Express, Carlson Hotels, Accor Hotels, IBM, Orbitz, Marriott, Gap Adventures, Jones Lang LaSalle, Abercrombie & Kent, the Jumeirah Group and Silversea Cruises.

At the conference the industry leaders spoke as if they were leading the charge toward reform. Green was the theme. It was held at Costão do Santinho, a luxury resort on Brazil's Atlantic Coast, with a nod to Brazil's rainforest. The WTTC Tourism for Tomorrow Awards for best sustainable-tourism practices were integrated into the annual conference for the first time.

I was able to attend the conference thanks to Kathleen Matthews,

Marriott's executive vice president for global communication and public affairs. We started out together as young journalists in Washington—she was an ABC television correspondent at the local Washington station when I was a *Washington Post* reporter covering local politics. Now she is an advocate of sustainable tourism within the industry. When I first interviewed her about Marriott and tourism, she said she couldn't keep up with all of the requests she received from the tourism reformers to meet with their groups.

Marriott was one of three finalists for the top prize of Global Tourism Business Award at the WTTC conference. The company's entry was its underwriting of more than 1.4 million acres of pristine protected Brazilian rainforest to offset the carbon emitted in the corporation's daily business—part of its evolving sustainable-tourism program to alter how the company administers its 3,000 Marriott hotels to improve the environment.

The awards ceremonies were dazzling. Rajan Datan, a BBC television host who appears on the program *Rough Guide to the World*, roamed the stage as if this were a deluxe variety show, introducing each of the nominees and showing videos of their accomplishments. Spotlights crisscrossed the hall as the winners were announced with applause and smiles.

Marriott won the big prize. Accepting the award was Ed Fuller, president of Marriott International. In his acceptance speech and in his comments to reporters afterward, the Marriott executive sounded more like a reformer than the reformers. "We are very proud of our award for sustainable tourism. We are actually stewarding these 1.4 million acres of rainforest," he said. "Clearly sustainability is the long-term strategy for tourism. It's good business. And it is for everyone in the business. The focus of sustainability is to get everyone involved. Europe has been the leader. We have to do more."

Interspersed with the awards were panels to discuss the state of tourism. The recession and its deeply unsettling bite into business was the top concern of the executives.

"After 9/11, political leaders asked everyone to travel again. We're seeing the opposite now in this recession," said Hubert Joly, president and CEO of Carlson, the hotel and hospitality corporation. He recounted how U.S. travel industry leaders had to plead for a meeting with President

Obama in March to delicately request a more positive position on business travel and to underline how much travel and tourism contributes to
the economy, especially during down times. Yet, said Joly, "none of the
governments are including travel and tourism in the conversation about
economic recovery."

Fernando Pinto, the CEO of TAP Air Portugal, agreed. "We are the
cash cows," he said, expanding on the underlying theme that their business
doesn't receive the respect it deserves. The snubs from political leaders was
a variation on the old insult that travel and tourism are frivolous pursuits
and travel executives not serious businesspeople. And the answer to that
quandary was the familiar refrain: "We have to act like an Industry—not like
'Travel and Tourism,' but we have to behave like an industry," said Charles
Petruccelli, president of Global Travel Services at American Express.

The environment was the second-most-talked-about issue. Unlike
other environmental awards ceremonies, there was no overall consensus
about how much the industry was responsible for the problem or how hard
it was working to reverse environmental degradation. What the participants
did agree on was that tourism depends on the health of the planet.

"If there are no monkeys, no birds, no rainforests, where would our
tourists go?" said Alex Khajavi, the CEO of Naturegate, an airline and
tourism company, when he accepted an award at the summit for innovative sustainable tourism. This was more than the expression of the triple
bottom line. It was an acknowledgment that the planet may be a higher
priority than profits.

A major political decision had already been taken when the now-
hundred-member-strong WTTC selected Brazil as the site of the summit.
It was the first time a South American country had been chosen for the
prestigious gathering. Brazil, though, isn't just a South American country.
As one of the countries known collectively as BRIC (Brazil, Russia, India
and China), it is one of the four major developing nations whose wealth is
shifting the centers of power and influence around the world. And, with
the conference's emphasis on sustainable tourism and the environment,
Brazil and its endangered Amazon Basin was an ideal choice.

Grateful for this honor, Brazilian President Luiz Inácio Lula da Silva
opened up the conference with a stirring address. It was a singular perfor-

mance by one of the sharpest leaders of this era. President Lula, as he is known, explained how the tourism summit would add weight to Brazil's bid to hold the 2016 Summer Olympics. "This is the first in a series of events we intend to celebrate during the next eight years," he told the crowd. "This event is being held in our continent for the very first time. In five years, we will host the FIFA World Cup and, with a little help from God, in 2016 we will host the Olympic Games."

It is rare for the head of state to attend a WTTC summit, much less give the opening address. Three years earlier, when the summit was held in Washington, D.C., the WTTC was pleased to have Secretary of State Condoleezza Rice address the group. President Lula, though, knew what he was doing. He was flattering these influential business executives by elevating the WTTC meeting to the level of the Olympics. He said tourism deserved it. "I am saying this so that you understand we are not working in tourism because it is beautiful or because it helps us win elections. We intend to help the tourism industry because we understand it is an extraordinary industry for cultural, economic and social development."

In the high-stakes lobbying campaign to host the Olympics, the president, a former labor organizer, was enlisting the elite of the travel industry—an essential partner at these sporting extravaganzas—to return to their capitals and spread the word that Brazil was worthy of hosting the 2016 summer games. Sports are an integral part of tourism. Few industries follow the bidding for international sport events like travel and tourism. It was of a piece with President Lula's stubborn push to hoist Brazil into the top ranks of the world's emerging powerhouses, and it worked. The executives could see for themselves that Brazil was capable of organizing a fabulous summit for them.

"A big embrace and thank-you," said President Lula.

At the close of the summit Jean-Claude Baumgartner, the president of the WTTC and summit host, said he was pleased at the outcome. He had set the agenda: trends and crises in the industry, including fears of pandemics, and the special emphasis on sustainable tourism. A former Air France senior executive, Baumgartner said he saw tourism as a natural advocate for the environment.

"What is important now is that we get out of this economic crisis and that we protect our fragile planet," he said. Baumgartner quietly slipped away with Ed Fuller, Marriott International president, after the summit and traveled 1,800 miles across Brazil to tour the Marriott-sponsored preserve. Thanks to Kathleen Matthews, I was able to travel with the group. The forest was over halfway across the enormous country. We flew four hours northeast to Manaus, the famous turn-of-the-twentieth-century rubber capital that lost its wealth when the British stole rubber plant seedlings and planted them in Malaysia. Now the legacy of that long-ago era is confined to the historic town center, especially the city's century-old opera house. Today, Manaus is on the tourist map as the main jumping-off point for the Brazilian Amazon.

The next morning we climbed into small private planes and flew through thick layers of impossibly white clouds toward the rainforest preserve. Even though we were just south of the Equator, the air was moist and pure. The forest canopy grew green and thick as we left the city farther behind. When we landed on a small airstrip, I caught my breath in the clean tropical air. It was sweet and soft.

For the last leg of the journey we boarded speedboats. The sun had risen and blue skies stretched as far as we could see. I stopped counting the shades of green that defined the mangrove coves or the ropes of vines leading deeper and deeper into dense tropical forests. We saw no humans and no sign of humans.

The river was a tributary of the Amazon and seemed as wide as the Mississippi. Bird songs did battle with the roar of the outboard motor. Then we saw the settlement of the Juma Sustainable Development Preserve and our boat swerved over to the bank.

"Watch your step, hold on to the railings," said Virgilio Viana, the director general of the Amazonas Sustainable Foundation and our host for the day. We still slipped, walking up the steep stairs on the riverbank, our first initiation into life in that humidity where everything is wet and slippery nearly all the time. The pungent jungle smell was a combination of smoke, wilderness and the cloying sweetness of decay. We walked through the small settlement in the jungle clearing, marching down the main street of red tropical soil, past simple new houses, a church, primary school, health clinic and a playground.

We reached the project campus, where Dr. Viana briefed us. A serious evolutionary biologist with the looks and showmanship of Francis Ford Coppola, Dr. Viana had cobbled together this vast preserve with the financial support of the state government of Amazonas and private industry— chiefly the Bradesco Bank of Brazil, the Yamamay clothing chain and now Marriott. He said he went to private industry for money because he needed a lot of cash and he didn't have time to rely solely on foundations. (He does receive funding from a Spanish foundation.) The rainforest was disappearing too quickly.

"Until 2003 the state was handing out chain saws and encouraging people to clear the land and become farmers," he said. "We haven't had a lot of time to turn the situation around."

The initial result was impressive: a 70 percent reduction in deforestation. A big reason for the success was the method. The native peoples are paid a salary to play their traditional role as "guardians of the forest." They extract palm oil, harvest Brazil nuts and keep out anyone trying to cut down the trees.

"There are sixty-six indigenous groups here, only two are dangerous, and many different realities," said Dr. Viana. "Ethically and morally they should be paid for their environmental services. That's our approach— education and income, not policing."

After a lunch of grilled local river fish that melted in our mouths, we walked a few paces into the rainforest with several local foresters. "Dense" doesn't begin to describe how every centimeter teems with life. Thick trees climb so high into the sky I couldn't see their tops. Ferns and vines crisscross the bushes and trees in no pattern. We tucked our pants into our socks to keep out critters.

We stopped in front of a particularly thick, tall tree, and the men gathered bowling-ball-size nuts that had dropped from its branches. With an impressive knife, one of the foresters cut open the shell and out fell a dozen or so Brazil nuts. He took one, sliced off the thick skin and gave it to me to eat. It was soft and sweet like the meat of a coconut, with the taste of a scented fruit. Not at all like the Brazil nuts that we crack open at Christmastime. Another group arrived. This time they were visitors from Mozambique, also foresters who shared the same colonial language of Portuguese and the same imperative to save their tropical forests. They were taking notes.

After an hour we headed back to the compound, where the adults were making handicrafts and the children studying in their common room. We had to leave before sunset. Fuller said Bill Marriott was attracted by the enormity of this vision and by Dr. Viana's modern business approach. After a thorough review by independent accountants Marriott contributed an initial $2 million to the project. It will never become a tourist resort or provide any income for the corporation.

"This preserve works. It does what it says it would do and offsets some of our carbon footprint," said Mr. Fuller. That matter-of-fact appraisal reflects the consensus among the elite ranks of the industry that tourism has to improve its environmental record.

We trod carefully down the permanently damp stairs and climbed back into the boats. As we pulled out, a flock of parakeets rose above the trees, their cries echoing unimpeded in silence. In that clean evening sky, the sun turned a blood-orange before it disappeared behind the curve of the earth.

Brazil won in its bid to host the 2016 Summer Olympics. The games will be held in South America for the first time, in Rio de Janeiro. There was no doubt about Brazil's commitment to visitors and tourism. President Lula wept at the announcement, saying, "Today is the most emotional day in my life, the most exciting day of my life."

The Juma Reserve has won official recognition by the United Nations REDD program to reduce carbon emission from deforestation and forest degradation. Marriott has helped build seven community schools in the reserve and is funding more programs through contributions from Marriott hotels in Brazil.

The tourism industry continues to give awards: for best hotel advertisements, websites, package tours, country destination, theme park advertisement, resort brochure and now for protecting the environment and culture. The World Travel and Tourism Council's Tourism for Tomorrow Awards that Marriott won are the equivalent of an Oscar. The *Condé Nast Traveler* magazine gives World Savers Awards for social responsibility in education, health, poverty, preservation, wildlife and the top prize for "doing it all."

Prizes aside, the industry will have to have a 25 percent adherence to those standards before it gets close to fulfilling the promises of "green vacations."

9

POSTCARD FROM SRI LANKA: WAR, REVOLUTION, TOURISM

Sri Lanka was an island paradise wrapped in barbed wire when I visited six months after the civil war ended in 2009. That conflict had lasted twenty-five years, effectively shutting down what had been a promising tourism trade. The questions were, how long would it take for the country to revive tourism or for investors to rush in and buy prime property at fire-sale prices, and, would tourism help the divided communities recover from those decades of loss and horror? Families were still searching for their missing; the country was waiting for a full and probably illusive accounting of the human and material cost of the conflict. In this atmosphere confidence in the future was in short supply.

On the thirty-minute drive from the airport our car had to pass inspection at three heavily armed guard posts. Rising above the skyline of tropical cement buildings and streets crowded with motorcycle taxis and bicycles were giant billboards of the president, Mahinda Rajapaksa, smiling like a movie star and wearing his trademark red scarf over a flowing white shirt. When we reached my hotel—the five-star Cinnamon Grand—I wasn't surprised to see barbed wire choking off access to the esplanade facing the sea.

The moment I checked in, I understood a basic consequence of the long war. My premium suite was a bargain. The Cinnamon Grand is the city's premier hotel, with beautiful gardens and a swimming pool, in the best part of town. Yet it cost only $151 a night, breakfast included, less than half of what I had paid the week before in the far less lovely city of Dhaka, Bangladesh. The cavernous lobby was bustling with locals—with the war over, everyone was hosting a dinner or a dance party; we tourists were in the minority.

My day job that first week was teaching journalism workshops on behalf of the U.S. embassy, culminating with a public lecture. My topic was postwar tourism. In the audience were two men who became my tourism gurus: Hiran Cooray and Geoffrey Dobbs. Cooray is the chairman of Jetwing, Sri Lanka's foremost tour agency and a member of the commercial aristocracy of the island. His family is descended from Sri Lanka's small Catholic community, which was first converted by Portuguese colonialists. Dobbs is from an English family that has a few colonialists in its past. He has the demeanor of a casual entrepreneur who almost accidentally put together a collection of high-end boutique hotels that are famous worldwide, not just in Asia. (He is also the brother of an old friend and colleague of mine from the *Washington Post*.)

Both Cooray and Dobbs were intrigued by an experiment, mentioned in my talk, that had occurred in Guatemala, where the government and tourism experts used new tourism to help once-warring communities work together. The results had been mixed, but I suggested that the idea could be transplanted to the island of Sri Lanka. Both Cooray and Dobbs had given their time, money and leadership to help the southern part of the island recover from the 2004 tsunami and knew from that experience that Sri Lanka's communities were capable of rebuilding tourism from the ground up. Cooray thought Sri Lanka might be able to replicate the Guatemala experience of inviting former warring neighbors to design a new look for tourism.

Dobbs was dubious about using tourism to bring together the Tamil and Sinhalese communities. The war was so long and the wounds so deep, he said, "We'll need a czar here."

The Sri Lanka civil war pitted the minority Tamils, who are mostly

Hindus, against the majority Sinhalese, who are Buddhists. After suffering under a government campaign of intimidation and repression, the Tamils launched a war in 1983 for a separate homeland in the northeast corner of the island. The fighting dragged on until 2009, with increasingly vicious fighting. The Tamil Tigers used suicide bombers. The government routinely ignored human rights and tortured and killed people they considered suspicious. Even the war's end was a nightmare of ruthless overkill, and the United Nations called for an inquiry into war crimes.

I had seen that war five years earlier, when the capital's Bandaranaike airport was covered in filthy shrouds of heavy plastic to hide damage from an earlier rebel attack. Only three international airlines were willing to fly in then—and one of them was SriLankan Airlines. I presumed that tourism had largely died in Sri Lanka during the war, as it had in Cambodia.

Somehow, though, throughout those years of terror, intrepid tourists remained loyal and came for sunshine holidays, sticking to the safety of the southern coast. At the beginning of the war half a million tourists visited every year. At war's end that figure hadn't changed: 500,000 tourists had traveled to Sri Lanka in 2008.

Then peace arrived and the island was up for grabs. Libby Owen-Edmunds, a thirty-one-year-old Australian and a tourism consultant in Colombo, met me for coffee at the Cinnamon Grand Hotel. She told me her phone started ringing in June 2009, a few weeks after the government declared victory. Private helicopters were ferrying investors, ready to spend money, over the sandy white beaches of the former rebel base, circling the area and evaluating which area would make the best new resorts. The land grab was on. Rumors of high-level corruption and murky real estate deals were in the air.

"Hedge fund guys were already touring by helicopter, offering $10 million for 100 acres. . . . I must have gotten a call a week, or email, from a big tourist industry, wanting land for investment. Prices are going up by the day," she said. "I'm so nervous about what this will mean for the east and north of Sri Lanka. There is so little infrastructure, and if we aren't careful, we'll reinvent ourselves in the worst way."

The government had already issued "offering[s] of land for tourism development" for projects in Kuchchaveli, territory that had been held by the rebels in the northeast for more than two decades. The government was selling property along the coast in a new "tourism zone" that included some of the island's most beautiful unspoiled beaches, which had been off-limits throughout the war.

That is the new lightning-fast cycle: war, revolution, peace, tourism, often overlapping. The phenomenon of tourists caught in crossfire is no longer rare. From Egypt to the Philippines, tourists have been shot at and killed in uprisings. Sometimes they are the targets. In Bali, terrorists specifically bombed a tourist hangout in 2005 and killed 202 people. In Thailand, rebels seized the Bangkok airport in 2008 and shut down tourism at the height of the season to force a change in government.

Now, governments understand tourism is part of the equation during and after an upheaval. In Sri Lanka the government is encouraging deals to bring back tourists and create new wealth.

Cooray, the chairman of Jetwing, invited me to his home in the exclusive Lake Gardens district of Colombo. Built near the sea, the home is filled with Sri Lankan art and handicrafts and surrounded with a garden of native plants. Over dinner of exquisite home-style Sri Lankan cooking with his wife Dharshi and his young sons, Cooray told me: "You can't understand the relief in May when the war ended. Without victory, we would have been finished."

No one knew when the war would end, he said, whether their country could survive, whether their businesses would collapse, whether their families could get by. Where tourism had once been the top moneymaker, employing the most people in the country, it had slipped to third place, behind the garment industry and remittances sent back home by Sri Lankans working abroad as common laborers. "The hunger for money . . . just to stay alive. Tourism had suffered for thirty years. Some people were begging."

Cooray was the rare optimist. "Tourism should be the major industry for our postconflict recovery. It's in our blood. It helps everyone on the island."

To his mind, Sri Lanka now had a rare opportunity to redesign tourism. Because of the war, Sri Lanka had been spared the worst aspects of the global tourism boom of the previous decades. The coasts were not marred by high-rise cement hotels, the mangrove coasts and rainforests were largely intact, and the souvenir shops were filled with local handicrafts, not imitations made in China. By skipping that era Sri Lanka might be able to slide into a better future. "Done right, tourism could help save our environment, our wild spaces and our coast."

The salient phrase was "done right."

Bernard Goonetilleke, chairman of Sri Lanka Tourism, welcomed me to his bare office along the esplanade in Colombo. His mandate was to encourage projects and optimism. A former ambassador in the Sri Lanka foreign service, Goonetilleke was newly appointed to his job, which required recalibrating the island's image as well as building up its infrastructure, training Sri Lankans in tourism and lobbying the government to regulate tourism growth that enhances the beauty of the island rather than turning it into a cookie-cutter version of the beaches of Thailand.

His simple rule of thumb: "No hotel should be taller than a coconut palm tree and the beaches remain public property."

Goonetilleke knew that international corporations were lobbying to buy up the beach property that until a few months ago had been battlegrounds. He worried that Sri Lanka's poor human rights image would dampen the return of tourists. Europeans, in particular, have been adamant that the Sri Lankan government show greater respect for human rights and democracy.

It was as if ghosts haunted the island, a theme of the novel *Anil's Ghost* by Michael Ondaatje, the island's esteemed author of *The English Patient*, who now lives in Canada. In the chilling prose of human rights reports, those ghosts are confirmed as victims of grave abuses and murder.

It turns out that most tourists don't check out a country's human rights record before taking a vacation. My husband Bill joined me for a week-long trip around the southern half of the island, famously shaped like a teardrop, where we ran into pockets of tourists from surprising parts of the world, none of whom were concerned about human rights.

We rented a car with a driver, the only practical alternative in this land of rutted, unpaved roads and questionable signage. Then we headed southeast, along the coast road toward Galle, the walled city first built by the Portuguese.

Driving along the palm-fringed coast road, we marveled at what was missing: no chain stores, no international designer boutiques, no fast-food joints and no ATMs. Women still dressed in traditional pastel-colored saris and shopped at small greengrocers and roadside stalls. This part of the island was spared during the civil war, which was fought largely in the northeast. Driving along, we saw extraordinary wildlife, from purple-faced langur monkeys to peacocks, butterflies, brilliantly colored parakeets, and, from a distance, leatherback sea turtles. We traveled past spectacular stretches of beaches and lush tropical forests. Traffic was spare. Trucks and antiquated buses hogged the center lanes, careening on worn tires. Three-wheeled motorcycle taxis, or tuk-tuks, hugged the periphery. Ours was one of the few private automobiles on the road.

By the time we arrived in Galle, we felt as if we had traveled backward in a time machine to 1975. Our first stop was Dutch House, a former colonial mansion that was transformed into the island's first boutique hotel by Dobbs. He was waiting for us at this eighteenth-century hideaway.

With top ratings and awards from magazines like *Condé Nast Traveler* and *Hip Hotels Orient*, Dobbs operates in an atmosphere light years away from the mass tourism market that has nearly died out on the island. His business secret was to attract the top-end tourists while staying within the local economy, buying local and hiring local. This frugality preserved the unique beauty of his hotels while saving him money and buffering him from the ups and downs of war. Through war and the tsunami, Dobbs said he never lost money. His high-end travelers were largely Brits and other Europeans who came and went, vaccinated from the war in the cocoon of Galle. Peace is expanding his roster. A South Korean film crew interviewed Dobbs while we were there. The reporter asked Dobbs: "Koreans don't know Sri Lanka—what is its charm?"

Where to begin listing the charms of this island? Arthur C. Clarke, the British science fiction writer and futurist, moved to Sri Lanka for its extraordinary beauty and because it is "a small universe; it contains as many variations of culture, scenery and climate as some countries a dozen times its size."

With peace, all of the island's protected areas are open for scuba diving among the tropical fishes or viewing wild elephants, leopards, sloth bears, langurs and countless birds in one of Sri Lanka's four large national parks. The cultural heritage is as staggering, with its seven World Heritage Sites and countless temples. Its literature, dance and arts are part of the rich South Asian culture—as is its cuisine. But it is not overwhelming, as India can be. Galle is often compared to Marrakesh. Both are magnificent walled cities lovingly restored by foreigners and resented by locals.

But Dobbs said it wasn't so much this beauty but its near devastation by the 2004 tsunami that convinced him to settle permanently in Galle and give up his primary home in Hong Kong. He had been celebrating Christmas in Galle with his mother, his brother Michael and Michael's family when the tsunami's huge waves struck. Michael Dobbs wrote of the near-death experience in the *Washington Post*, saying that he was swimming in the ocean when he was surrounded by waves 15 feet high in what "seemed like a scene from the Bible." Miraculously everyone in the Dobbs family survived. Geoffrey Dobbs then devoted himself to helping the island in the aftermath.

To aid the recovery of local tourism, Dobbs started the Adopt Sri Lanka charity that repaired 125 guest houses, the traditional hostels for Sri Lankan travelers. To promote new international tourism, especially the high-end tourists, he founded the Galle Literary Festival, luring authors like Germaine Greer, Alexander McCall Smith and Simon Winchester to read and mix with locals and tourists. Soon after, he founded the Galle Film Festival and is planning a Gourmet Galle food festival.

It's hard not to sound like a tourism brochure when describing how Dobbs redid the Dutch House or the Sun House, Dobbs's other boutique hotel, across the road. Both are straight out of a film by Merchant and Ivory. He remained faithful to the colonial proportions of the Dutch House, keeping the verandahs that catch the breezes and filter the light during the hottest hours of a tropical afternoon. The interior lawn and gardens are home to a mongoose, who entertained us at breakfast. A pool is discreetly hidden on the back slope. We could see why so many British couples chose this mansion for destination weddings, even during the war. At dusk we gathered in the great room for drinks amid polished antiques and comfortable sofas that were the antithesis of the overdecorated hotels of London or New York.

During our stay we met other Americans and Europeans visiting Galle, but we were the only guests at his four-suite hotel, except for election night when an old friend with a home in the middle of town repaired to Dutch House to be safe in case there were riots during this first postwar balloting—a reminder of the toll of war.

It was difficult to leave and head out for rougher territory. Dobbs wished us well: "The roads are rubbish—you'll be pushed and pulled in all directions."

Our next stop was the hills that cluster in the center of the island. Our route took us back on the coast road, stopping at an extraordinary three-story-tall Buddha built by Japan in memory of the people of Sri Lanka who lost their lives in the tsunami. Farther up the road we saw the small guesthouses—Bright Sunshine Guesthouse, Mali Guesthouse. At a pizza parlor named Rotty, I talked to the forty-four-year-old owner, H. H. Pluma, who bemoaned the death of the foreign hippie trade that dipped when war broke out and disappeared after the tsunami. "I had to go work abroad in Dubai to make ends meet," she said.

Posters along the highway celebrated the government victory with paintings of Sri Lankan government soldiers posing with the macho air of a Rambo movie. Homemade signs offered land for sale, and several promised new casinos for tourists. When we turned off the main road to climb into the hills, we understood Dobbs's warning. A drive that should have taken a few hours required an entire day of swirling around potholes and deep trenches. The scenery, though, was breathtaking. Gentle water buffalo lumbered through paddy fields. Higher up we were surrounded by terraced tea plantations. After a series of hairpin turns we saw the mist-covered hills and arrived at Kandy, the former royal capital and the favored hill station under the British colonialists.

Kandy is centered on a lake, and surrounded by the best of Sri Lanka and Britain: botanical gardens, a royal palace, the sacred Buddhist Temple of the Tooth and wedding-cake hotels. There is more than a hint of lost grandeur. We left the city and continued our climb to Hunas Falls in the jungles above Kandy. We stayed in a Jetwing hotel that was only one-third full, and in the morning we took our coffee out to the balcony to watch a troupe of gray langur monkeys swing and somersault in the trees. Then we tried to count the finches, sparrows, swallows and crows flying through the air. In the breakfast room we ran into different tourists who had stayed loyal to Sri Lanka despite the war. They came from the Persian Gulf region. I was the only woman in the dining room who was not wearing an abaya or a head scarf. These tourists—couples and families—told us they came to the lush green hills of Kandy to escape the desert heat at home. Airlines from the Gulf were among the few that had continued flying into Colombo throughout the war, and Sri Lanka's small Muslim community welcomed the tourists to their mosques.

We ran into them again later that morning when my husband played a round of golf on a six-hole course laid out on a nearly vertical slope. I tagged along in sandals and had to scrape the leeches off my ankles afterward. After a few days walking in the hills around the Hunas Falls, we paid our bill. Another bargain: our two nights with breakfast and dinners totaled $169.93.

It was easier driving down the hills toward the plains and we reached the coast before dusk. We spent our last day in Sri Lanka at Negombo, the beach resort area just north of Colombo and close to the international airport. This was pure mass tourism. Think Thailand in the 1980s. Europeans who bought Sri Lanka package holidays during the war ended up here. The beaches are hardly the best on the island, but they were safe. Buses took the tourists into Colombo by day and returned them at night. On the beach and on the dinner menu the first language was German. We stayed at another Jetwing hotel, and the manager said that Germans were the most loyal visitors to Negombo. A beach holiday at low prices was a big reason.

We left the next day. On the drive to the airport we saw a Buddhist shrine and a Christian shrine, with the portrait of Jesus displayed much as the statue of Buddha. From this direction, we were required to show our papers at only one military guard post. The lasting impression was an island frozen in time. The infrastructure is terrible. The possibilities are endless. I was reminded of the anomaly of the demilitarized zone that divides North Korea and South Korea. For sixty years it has kept out people—developers and tourists—and is now one of the more pristine wildlife preserves in the world, a refuge for birds and bears and endangered plant species despite the fact that it is seeded with land mines. Korean conservationists are in the awful position of worrying what peace might do.

As Cooray said, "this is the perfect opportunity—either we make the right tourism that lifts up all the communities—Sinhalese, Tamil and the minorities—or we ruin it—ruin the landscape, the beaches and the communities."

One year later Cooray sent me an email saying he was encouraged that the government still cared about sustainable development. Tourism had grown an astonishing 46 percent in a single year—with almost 1 million visitors. "Hoteliers are finally regaining the confidence to put money back into tourism," he wrote. His life had also changed. He became the first Sri Lankan named as chairman of the Pacific Asia Travel Association. "Peace fever," as he called it, was as high as ever. Foreign governments and international companies were lobbying the government for fast-track approval of their tourist developments. Cooray wrote that "this puts unwanted pressure on the government and this worries me as they may side track regulations (to protect the environment, habitat, etc.) in order to expedite development."

Come back, he said, and we can see which tendency won.

PART FIVE

THE NEW GIANT

China

Tourists learning tai chi on the grounds of the Temple of Heaven, Beijing

10

GOLDEN WEEKS

For the tourism industry, image is everything. Ephemeral, illusive image can boost or sink tourist traffic. Businesses from luggage companies to hotel chains to government tourism agencies spend millions to find an appealing "brand," one that idealizes the "journey" or the "destination" or the "discovery" without mentioning the crass notion of making money.

A country's image is not the sole property of a tourism ministry. Countries suffering frequent natural disasters, violent dislocations from political uprisings and revolutions, and rule through a heavy-handed police force are not high on any tourist list. China fits all of those negative categories. Even today, the police can walk into a hotel or restaurant and whisk away a guest without a warrant, simply saying the guest is a suspect.

When Chinese leaders opened their country slowly to tourism, they turned the image question inside out. Tourism would improve China's poor political image, which in turn would make the country more attractive to tourists, beginning a virtuous loop of image enhancements that would become a money machine.

In the 1980s, when the opening began, China's image was utterly unfit for a tourist campaign. Thirty years earlier China was so impoverished that American children were told to finish all the food on their plates or they'd end up like the starving children of China who had nothing to eat. The country was also a major "red" enemy, vilified by the United States for its communism. Mao Zedong proved to be the exceptional leader who won China's civil war, defeating Chiang Kai-shek, America's aloof ally. Mao then instituted a radical revolution that was largely hidden from the West.

Every war the U.S. fought in Asia after 1950 was against an ally of Communist China, first in Korea and later in Vietnam, Cambodia and Laos. When the Vietnam War drew massive protests on campuses and city streets, some of the students wore Mao caps to underline their anger at the war. Scholars and journalists, meanwhile, were trying to assess Mao's rule without direct access to the country, tallying up the benefits of health reforms and the damage done by Mao's Great Leap Forward and Cultural Revolution in the number of lives lost from starvation and political deaths.

In the popular mind, China had become the land of Red Guards marching by the thousands in Tiananmen Square waving Mao's Little Red Book. All those decades of revolution competed with the traditional image of China, with its Confucian scholars, blue and white porcelain, scroll paintings, shimmering silk robes and the snaking Great Wall.

In the 1980s, Chinese leaders radically changed direction and jumped into the global economy. The goal was nothing less than to make China one of the world's new superpowers. The Chinese leader Deng Xiaoping declared that "poverty is not socialism. To be rich is glorious." Factories sprang up along the coast and then in the interior. They made automobiles, computers, televisions, furniture, toys and clothing, especially clothing. Whole cities were devoted to the manufacturing of socks or underwear or sweaters. Thanks to very cheap labor and technological breakthroughs, from container ships to the Internet, China could ship around the globe and wipe out competition on every continent. Once a leader of what was known as the Third World of struggling nations, China leapfrogged into the club of wealthy ones—admired in some quarters, feared in others.

Overlooked by most was the role tourism played in China's grand strategy. From the beginning of the seismic economic reforms, China's leaders believed that tourism would be critical to its economic development and play a major "diplomatic" role, winning over foreign tourists with China's preeminence as one of the world's greatest ancient cultures and wowing them with its modern transformation. They would control that message by overseeing nearly every aspect of tourism. China took to heart the boast of the tourism industry that every foreign visitor was a potential citizen ambassador to the world.

No one better exemplifies this approach than Deng Xiaoping, China's supreme leader who opened up the country to the world. Shortly after he wrested power in late 1978, Deng gave five talks on the central role of tourism. The titles don't translate well: "Tourism Should Become a Comprehensive Industry," and "There's a Lot To Be Achieved Through Tourism." But the overall message was strong. Tourism was essential to China's new "open door" policy to rejoin the world and become appreciated and respected again as a major power. Deng saw big financial gains and even set the seemingly impossible goal for China to earn $10 billion from foreign tourism by the new millennium. China reached that goal four years ahead of schedule in 1996.

Thirty years later, during the 2008 Olympics in Beijing, Deng's dreams were fulfilled several times over. This was China's coming-out party. The Chinese spent $40 billion on stadiums for the Olympics and infrastructure. The International Olympic Committee earned $1.7 billion from broadcast revenue for advertising. The city of Beijing moved more than 1 million people out of their homes to make way for the Olympic site. World-renowned architects designed the "Bird's Nest" Olympic stadium, the "Water Cube" National Swimming Center, the "Z crisscross" television tower and the "Eggshell" National Grand Theater. Beijing added a fifth ring road, dubbed the "Olympic Avenue," around the city; the sixth was completed one year later. Around the world 4 billion people watched some of the games; the biggest hit was the elaborate opening ceremony with drums, dancing, acrobats and a cast of 10,000 that would have put Hollywood to shame. The word "fireworks" doesn't begin to do justice to the curtains of coordinated light that flooded the sky. The performers were polished and acted in astonishing unison. They repeated a similarly spectacular closing event after the world had watched more than eleven thousand athletes straining for a gold medal. Finally, China won fifty-one gold medals, topping all other competing nations.

There were more than a few problems: severe government censorship, pollution and the heavy-handed reconstruction of Beijing that turned it into a modern "Anywhere" city. But the Olympics went off without a hitch. The world applauded China's vitality and its modern image framed by reminders of its old culture. (Unfortunately, the Olympics were held as the global economy went into a recession, and it took several years before tourism rebounded, negating the short-term benefits the government had expected.)

Despite all of the hoopla over the Olympics and the daily reporting about China's economic miracle, many of today's tourists to China are surprised, if not starry-eyed, at what they see. For example, I met three couples from suburban Washington, D.C., on a cool October morning for tai chi lessons on the grounds of the fifteenth-century Temple of Heaven, a masterpiece of architecture and landscape gardening now surrounded by the city of Beijing.

It was the last day in Beijing for Herb and Ellen Herscowitz, Donald and Susan Poretz, and Arthur and Amy Kales. They are all professionals; the men are medical doctors highly regarded in their fields. They are near retirement age and grew up with all those contradictory images of China. They subscribe to the *Washington Post* and the *New York Times* and read the articles about China's modernization, yet they were flabbergasted at what they had seen on their first trip to China.

"The size of the buildings, the way people dress is unbelievable. So is the hustle, the commerce, even the airport. When we landed it was like being any place in the U.S., only not as crowded," said Susan Poretz.

"We can't believe how modern this country is. And we haven't seen any police. I thought this was supposed to be a police state," said Arthur Kales.

The three couples began their tour visiting the must-see classics: the Great Wall and the Forbidden City. They ate Peking duck at a restaurant where they had had to order the duck one week in advance.

Amy Kales said, "I thought the people would be solemn, dreary. They aren't."

Another Washington couple was just as impressed after their three-week trip to China. Rick and Jewell Dassance are retired and spent months diligently reading travel books on China as well as histories and novels.

They thought they were prepared for their first visit to China. Instead, they said they were blown away by the country.

"I don't know what I was expecting—I think I thought China would be like Senegal, you know, a Third World country where you might be staying in a nice compound but right outside is squalor. But I didn't see squalor. The roads were good, the plumbing, electricity. I wasn't prepared to see that level of development. I wasn't aware of the magnitude of the changes. It was so educational for me," said Rick Dassance.

His wife Jewell said the size of the country shocked her. "The sheer number of people in those cities was unbelievable. I started calling the cities and their apartment buildings concrete forests. I know, I had read about China's modernization, but to see it in reality is a different experience.... Now I know it in my bones."

Those reactions, transforming tourists into political emissaries, are what Deng Xiaoping had in mind thirty years earlier when he summoned his aides and told them tourism could change his country's image.

China is the new center of the universe, the new Middle Kingdom. Mention China and experts spew superlatives. The country is skyrocketing in popularity, and the Chinese people are becoming the most sought-after tourists of the twenty-first century, spending lots of money and taking full advantage of their new ability to travel the world. The statistics point to even more record-breaking accomplishments. China will replace France as the most popular tourist destination in the world no later than 2020. China climbed to number three in 2011, according to the U.N. tourism organization, and earned $45 billion from foreign tourists, the fourth-highest amount in the world. If Hong Kong, with its high-end shopping for tourists, and Macao, with its gambling casinos, were included in that total, the sum would nearly double to $86 billion.

The flood of Chinese tourists visiting foreign countries for the first time is just as phenomenal. Tourism ministries swoon over this China "outbound market" that has grown 22 percent each year, on average, for three years, ranking fourth in the world by 2011. The U.N. tourism organization expects China to be the number-one source of tourists about the same time as it becomes the number-one destination for foreigners. And over the past five years Chinese tourists have become among the biggest spenders on overseas vacations, surpassing the British by shelling out $55 billion in 2010. Because they tend to save money on hotels and airfares, they are only third in the overall rankings of big spenders, behind German and American tourists.

Behind all of the hyperexcitement about Chinese tourism is the often-forgotten fact that Chinese tourism came out of nowhere. For most of the twentieth century China wasn't part of the tourism industry. The Chinese government had no interest in opening their country to foreign tourists or allowing the Chinese to travel overseas. The Chinese had to wait until 1997 to win the right to travel abroad in tour groups, and then they were allowed to visit only a few government-approved destinations. It wasn't until 2009 that the government gave the green light to true overseas foreign travel and dropped some of the tightest restrictions. The Chinese middle class was earning the money to travel but lacked the time. In 2000 the government finally declared guaranteed paid national holidays celebrating Spring Festival (or Chinese New Year) in late January or February, and the country's National Day in October. The two long holidays are known as the "Golden Weeks."

This is the story of how the tourism industry has changed China and how China is changing the industry.

My first short visit to China was in December 1978. The streets of Beijing were dimly lit, the air dry and dusty. My cheeks felt like cold sandpaper when I walked outside. Evening rush hour was announced by crowds of bicyclists streaming home, their tires swishing through the shadows, their bells pinging in a staccato rhythm. There were few hotels for the rare foreign visitors; I stayed at the Friendship Hotel, a Chinese-modern establishment built in 1954 with grand proportions. I was a journalist heading to Cambodia on assignment, which in those days required a layover in Beijing. I had time to explore the city.

Hidden behind that sleepy façade was a city in political turmoil. A French colleague, the journalist Francis Deron, took me to the heart of the public debate, cutting through the city's distinctive hutongs, or alleys, in a circuitous route that ended at a bus station. Plastered across a high wall were protest posters written in bold black characters asking for individual rights and freedoms, and democracy. This was "Democracy Wall," where small groups of Chinese men were engrossed in conversation and glancing over their shoulders. Later, at an informal market, I bought a scroll painting of sparrows on bamboo from an artist who asked Francis what I was doing in China. We had to shake off a small crowd following us. On the way back to the hotel it dawned on me that we had seen very few traces of the old palaces or temples. In India, the cities are a mishmash of Hindu temples and Muslim mosques, walled forts and marble palaces, alongside modern villas and new office blocks; the ancient and the new butting up against each other.

I had seen only a glimpse of the calculated destruction of the city's heritage—what Chinese artists and preservationists have called "death by a thousand cuts."

Ideology drove the first wave of destruction. It is hard to exaggerate the exhilaration that the Chinese Communists said they felt at their victory in 1949. They had defeated their Chinese rivals led by Chiang Kai-shek and shaken off the United States. Under the leadership of Mao, the Chinese People's Republic was a single-minded experiment to fashion a new socialist society of equality in a country that had been ruled largely by imperial dynasties. The initial idealism sparked needed reforms in the health system and the redistribution of land in favor of poor farmers.

When Mao Zedong entered Beijing to enthusiastic crowds, the city was encompassed by 25 miles of thick crenellated stone walls with sixteen multistory gates, many guarded by stone lions. Outside the walls were moats and farms. Inside the walls was a city planned to reflect the harmony of heaven. Set at the edge of the great northern plains, Beijing, or the North Capital, was a well-planned city of "palaces, peony beds, lotus-filled lakes, dragon walls, carved lions embodying the antithetical yet complimentary principles of yin and yang," according to earlier visitors like Arnold Toynbee. The Imperial Palace, known as the Forbidden City, sat at the geographic and celestial center of the city, surrounded by other palaces, temples, vast Asian gardens, archways over the wide streets and a labyrinth of hutongs leading to traditional houses built with central courtyards mimicking the larger harmony of the city. As charming as Paris and as mysterious as the Sphinx, Beijing was considered one of the world's great marvels.

Within ten years most of that ancient Beijing that had been built over five hundred years had been torn down on orders of the government. The reason was political. The city's plan followed the feudal order of imperial China and the new leaders wanted a socialist city.

"The very map of Peking was a reflection of the feudal society, it was meant to demonstrate the absolute power of the emperor. We had to transform it, we had to make Peking into the capital of socialist China," said Professor Ho Renzhi of Peking University to the journalist Tiziano Terzani.

It was the equivalent of tearing down central Rome because it represented the Italian past of empire and medieval feudalism. First, the Chinese Communists tore down the "pailos" or arches, in marble and painted wood that were built across the major streets in honor of revered citizens of China. Next, the walls came down. In 1950 the Communists ordered the famed walls removed at night, to avoid citizens' anger. Liang Sicheng, one of China's best architects at the time, wrote that "it was as if my own flesh was being torn off, as if my skin was being peeled away." He was denounced for his right-wing tendencies and died in disgrace.

This cultural suicide continued. In 1958 the government officials surveyed the city and declared that 8,000 monuments and buildings were of cultural value and worth saving. Yet political powers overrode that survey and only 78 of those structures were allowed to remain standing. Some were removed to make way for small-scale factories and industries; others for dormitories, apartments or barracks. Centuries-old temples were razed as unnecessary as the country geared up for the Great Leap Forward and, in their place, were built 1,400 factories in the center of Beijing. The Abundant Tranquility Temple and the Sleeping Buddha Temple were destroyed to build new roads. Palaces were turned over to work units and the military.

The authorities tore down thousands of Beijing's courtyard houses, which had defined northern Chinese architecture since the twelfth century. Every storybook about old China is illustrated with paintings of modest homes with curved roofs, windows of paper inside lattice frames, with a small garden enclosed by walls. In place of those temples and palaces, walls and gateways, the new Chinese authorities built massive modern public buildings with exposition halls and enormous conference rooms in a style that was bland at best, and at its worst was grotesque. This modernization purposefully eliminated centuries of culture in order to remake Beijing into a symbol of socialist China. Acting more like officials in Dubai than in Paris, the Chinese tore apart the city, turning it into a chaotic shell, without the exquisite references and planning of old Beijing.

Then in 1958, Mao organized the Chinese in a campaign to make a Great Leap Forward to become a modern, self-sufficient economy. All private landholdings ended and farms were melded into large public communes. Local, even backyard, factories went up all over the country. The experiment collapsed in three years. The economy was in shambles; agriculture was devastated with such poor harvests that China suffered a famine that left tens of millions dead. The backyard factories produced shoddy goods and wasted precious energy.

At first, Mao admitted he had made mistakes. Then, in 1966, he reasserted his power, calling for a Cultural Revolution to radicalize the country through its youth, targeting his rivals in the Communist elite. The young Red Guard went after those in authority, the potential rivals of Mao, and pushed China into further chaos.

Most of this was hidden from the rest of the world. From the beginning, Chinese Communist leaders wanted to shut out foreign influences that had been so detested during the nineteenth and early twentieth centuries and to cut off their economy from the capitalist system. For their part, the western countries, especially the United States, sought to deny legitimacy to the new, Communist China and recognized Taiwan as the "real" China. This deep physical and political division was known as the "Bamboo Curtain" in Asia, erected by China but reinforced by the West.

Through this tumultuous period, there was no tourism to speak of. Foreign visitors were largely delegations from friendly nations or foreign political parties who visited to nurture alliances. The government created the China National Tourism Administration (CNTA) and the China International Travel Service in 1956 to organize these largely diplomatic visitors in a new campaign to "Spread Chairman Mao Thought, Assist World Revolution." Western Europeans were allowed to visit China, albeit under strict controls. The numbers were minuscule: over the next decade only 19,000 foreign visitors from 38 countries came to China, a nation of 740 million in 1966.

Some of the foreign visitors were experts sent to help Chinese development. Others were foreign students from other Communist countries or overseas Chinese students from Southeast Asian countries. Even this small trickle of visitors ended with the Cultural Revolution when the Red Guard took aim at foreigners. Most foreign experts left and several foreign embassies were burned to the ground. No more foreign students were accepted.

In 1971, when China regained its seat at the United Nations that had been held by Taiwan, the country slowly opened. The CNTA could only handle a few thousand tourists at a time, organized in groups with official sponsors; there were exactly 2,500 beds for foreigners in Beijing in the mid-1970s.

It was equally difficult for the Chinese to travel in their own country. Every trip required official permission, which was given sparingly for official business, family visits or medical treatment. During the 1950s most Chinese travelers stayed at canteens, or simple guest houses, which offered a desk, a bed, a wash basin and a common toilet. In the 1960s cities like Beijing built small hotels for elite Chinese visitors, mostly political bureaucrats visiting the capital on official business. Given that history of isolation and even xenophobia, as well as the strict restriction of movement within the country, Deng Xiaoping's early call to open China to foreign tourists came straight out of the blue.

In October 1978, Deng was in the throes of a high-stakes power contest to succeed Mao Zedong, who had died two years earlier. Deng took time out to deliver the first of what were described as five "directional talks" about the importance of tourism. These small talks are rarely if ever mentioned in the many books that describe how China engineered its monumental reversal from radical communism to aggressive state-controlled capitalism in the tidal wave of reforms that propelled China from poverty to superpower status in less than four decades.

To underline his seriousness about the subject, Deng delivered his next talks about tourism in January 1979, soon after he emerged from the critical meeting that consolidated his power. He gave talks about the importance of tourism in the new China to top government officials, to the small government tourist bureau and to state industries. Saying that China had wasted too much time and resources on heavy industry, he said "we should start to develop industries that would accelerate capital circulation and help earn foreign currency, such as light industries, manufacturing, trade and tourism."

"Our country is huge, with many cultural relics and heritages. If we receive five million visitors, with per capita tourist expenditure at $1,000 we could earn foreign currency of $5 billion in one year," he said adding in another of these talks that "we can earn more money quickly through tourism."

Tourism met both of Deng's basic requirements for China's economic transformation, called "Opening and Reform," to develop China's economy in a more capitalist mode while remaining under Communist rule. In Deng's talks he said that tourism could do both and enhance China's world image.

He envisioned tourists coming to China to see the country's landscape, go dancing, play billiards and stay in hotels that had yet to be built. He said tourism would require foreign investment and foreign partnerships, bring in foreign tourists and their money, and create "huge employment opportunities for youth."

"We should build hotels," he said. "In the first stage, we can make use of Overseas Chinese and foreign investments. Afterwards, we can develop on our own."

For one talk on tourism, Deng trekked up China's Yellow Mountain (Huangshan), the subject of countless landscape paintings and poems. In the official photograph of his visit, Deng, who was only 5 feet tall, poses on the trail wearing dark Bermuda shorts, a white tee-shirt and white socks bunching up around his ankles. That image was slightly shocking for a leader who normally wore buttoned-up Mao suits. Deng was conveying his idea of a tourist at leisure, down to resting on a hiker's cane. His message was simple. China's leader was endorsing tourism at Huangshan, one of China's most renowned mountain landscapes. Everyone was expected to fall in line behind him and build up the industry.

Another surprise in these tourism talks was Tibet. Deng singled out Tibet as a key attraction in his vision of Chinese tourism. "We should develop tourist routes to Tibet. Foreigners are interested in Tibet. . . . We should build hotels in Lhasa," he said, conjuring up images of planeloads of tourists drawn to exotic Tibet and spending their money in new hotels built by the Chinese.

China's rule of Tibet has prompted bitter condemnation since Chinese troops marched into the Himalayan country in 1950 and asserted it was part of China. Tibetans have rebelled intermittently ever since against Chinese Communist rule over their strict Buddhist culture; Tibetan monks burn themselves in protest against Chinese heavy-handedness. Tibet's exiled Dalai Lama received a Nobel Prize for his peaceful protest against Chinese rule, and movie stars have joined the global Free Tibet movement to force the Chinese to listen to international public opinion.

Tourism is the one policy that has diluted this opprobrium over China's handling of Tibet. It took two decades to realize Deng's vision of building a modern rail link to whisk tourists to the Himalayan kingdom, but once that was accomplished, nearly 2 million tourists have visited Tibet every year. They are entranced by the pagodas and palaces carved on the rooftop of the world. And their Chinese guides give the tourists a happy version of the recent history that tourists accept as something close to the truth. To the list of reasons why China refuses to give Tibet greater freedom and autonomy, add tourism and the $300 million spent every year by the 3 million visitors.

Deng's tourism talks were farsighted in predicting the downside of China for tourists. The main problem, he said, was pollution, and this was in 1979 when China's pollution problems were minor compared to what China faces today. Deng used the example of Guilin, a city encircled by mountains and divided by two rivers to underline how China's industrial growth threatened the environment and, therefore, tourism. "Water pollution in the Lijiang River is very serious. We must do everything to prevent it. Factories that caused water pollution should be closed. Mountain and water scenery in Guilin is the best in the world. If the water is not clean, how can tourism be sustainable?"

He also said the Chinese had lost their instinct for hospitality and become inept if not boring when it came to entertaining foreign tourists. He wanted China to build cinemas and entertainment spaces and be welcoming to tourists. "Who will pay money and come for a visit if service attitudes are not good and the place is dirty? Even if some may have come, they would not have satisfaction." The answer was training, he said, for interpreters, guides, service staff and management teams. "There should be programs to train tourism professionals. The service staff should learn foreign languages, and tour guides should know tour regulations."

In the top-down political structure of the government, Deng's five tourism talks were translated into a set of basic principles for the tourism bureau and other government agencies. China became a member of the United Nations World Tourism Organization in 1983 and immediately impressed officials there. China asked for help to make domestic and international tourism a central part of its economic development and to boost its chances of becoming a global power. That same year, China held its first international tourism conference. "I believe it was one of the first international conferences on any subject that China held after it opened up," said Patrice Tedjini, head of the UNWTO's archives and its informal historian. "China understands tourism."

Barbara Dawson, a tour operator in Colorado, was an American delegate to that conference. She and her Canadian husband were pioneers in China travel and had shepherded their first tours in 1979. "We took a group from the Atmospheric Research Center at the University of Colorado at Boulder. We had to negotiate everything with a national guide, local guides and a Communist Party person. They wanted to show us factories and communes. We wanted to see art and culture," said Dawson. "We loved it; these were trips of a lifetime."

The Chinese invited delegates from countries on every continent to this conference to explain how they were open for tourism and how they hoped to learn from the delegates how to run a modern tourism industry. It was cold for early spring and Dawson remembers a stiff wind blowing in sand from the Gobi Desert. All that made the prospect of China's tourism future more exciting.

"There were a lot of banquets and speeches. It was like a coming-out party," she said.

She still has the conference souvenir of a silk brocade box filled with an ink stone, brushes, writing paper and a chop or seal to be engraved.

Dawson was hooked. As a dedicated tourist agent, she watched China's metamorphic transformation, measuring progress by the number of airlines flying into China and the number of available hotel rooms. In 1983 there were three airlines available: Air Canada, Philippine Airlines and Singapore Airlines. There were only three good hotels for foreigners: the Beijing, the Friendship and the Evergreen. Lindblad and Abercrombie & Fitch were the only tour groups working in China. The Chinese guides were often ham-fisted, and the government controlled the message to tourists as if they were political delegates. "They wanted us to know that China was different from Russia—the Soviet Union—that China was socialist and Russia was Communist," said Dawson.

Deng scored his first impressive economic victory in 1984 when China had the single largest grain harvest in its history. The lives of Chinese improved and their treatment of tourists improved as well, Dawson said. "This made my life so much easier," she said. "The Chinese were able to see greater horizons, and became so much more perceptive, tourist professionals."

That year the Great Wall Hotel opened in Beijing, the first of what would become a boom of modern chrome-and-glass hotels that hasn't abated. The hotel was a Sino-American venture. Dean Ho, now of Unison Building Systems in Shanghai, helped put together the deal. He represented a private investor in the project that included the Beijing branch of the China National Tourist Office as the equity partner, a model that continues today. The hotel, he told me, proved "highly profitable" both for the foreign investors and for the Chinese who were the majority owners. "One hundred percent funded by American dollars, one hundred percent filled with foreign tourists who paid in American dollars while all local labor costs were paid in the Chinese currency renminbi," he said.

Foreign tourists still traveled in groups with itineraries largely under the control of the official state tourism agency: the visitors had no choice over their hotels or restaurants, and their tour guides were trained by the government to deliver a narrow political message.

Nothing better exemplified this than the June 1989 bloodbath at

Tiananmen Square, when the Chinese People's Liberation Army broke up a popular, nonviolent demonstration by young Chinese asking for democracy. The soldiers, under orders from Deng Xiaoping, used lethal force and murdered thousands of citizens, leaving their bodies littering Tiananmen and the nearby streets. The world was outraged, but most of the foreign tourists in China were oblivious. If they weren't in Beijing, they didn't know anything had happened. All the news had been blocked out, and the guides were told to stick to the standard praise about their country's progress. "A tour group in the south kept traveling and didn't know what was going on in Tiananmen until they called home to check on their families," said Dawson. "I don't think the Chinese will ever give up that kind of control."

That episode exemplified China's political quandary as it focused on economic gains while papering over any questions about human rights or protecting the environment. The government wanted to create a tourist market inside China by wooing foreign investors. At the same time, the Chinese government wanted to censor the image presented to the foreigners through their system of guides and marketing, with a uniform interpretation of China's recent past, an enthusiastic presentation of contemporary life and little room to hear an alternative view.

China had to become much more accommodating. Itineraries expanded far beyond the once bare-bones tour of Beijing, Shanghai and a train trip to Hong Kong. China gradually allowed tourists throughout the vast nation from Harbin in the north near the Russian border to Guilin in the south near Vietnam. Other rules were relaxed. Tourists could eat in private restaurants along the bund in Shanghai. Bars were opening in Beijing and Shanghai.

"All of a sudden, China was the place to go. Sometimes I thought there were more travel writers in China than tourists—each trying to get stories saying they were the first to get to go somewhere that had been closed off for forty years," said Dawson. "The airlines saw the market. They expanded. Everyone saw the opportunities. It was a tremendous experience going through all of that."

Equally important was the Chinese government's fundamental decision to open up travel for Chinese people within China. The strict rules preventing the Chinese from moving around their country were dropped, and for the first time since the revolution the Chinese could hop on a bus and see the mountains, or the cities, or the sea, or the Great Wall. Officials undertook what amounted to a "tourism reeducation" campaign to expand the definition of Chinese travel beyond the traditional visits home during the lunar New Year, to find work, to serve in the army, or to study, but not to simply enjoy themselves. In those early years "leisure travel," or tourism, was a foreign concept.

The Chinese entering the new middle class needed little encouragement. In the 1990s, Chinese tour buses carried these newly minted tourists along newly paved and widened highways, trailing dark diesel fumes behind them. Parking lots the size of football fields were cut into national parks and near historic sites. Provincial and local governments threw up auditorium-size canteens to serve mediocre meals and sell souvenirs. Some tourists had to be told not to spit, or shove to be first in line. Many were unaccustomed to modern flush toilets. All seemed happy.

To keep up the momentum, the government subsidized much of this travel and built up the new "destinations." National holidays were given for Chinese New Year and in autumn.

To tie it all together, the government named these vacations "Golden Weeks." Now enshrined in law and custom, these weeks have proved golden for the tourists with precious time off and for the local industry with golden profits. From 1995 to 2005, travel within China rose by more than 50 percent, which, in a country that was then nearing 1 billion people, added up to millions of dollars spent on bus tickets, admission fees, new travel outfits, souvenirs and those requisite photographs. By 2010, Chinese tourists had spent $123 billion traveling around their own country in 1.5 billion getaways.

This was a dress rehearsal for the next stage in China's tourism ambitions: letting these new Chinese tourists venture outside their country. The door was open ever so slightly in 1983, after the International Tourism Conference in Beijing, when the Chinese were allowed "family visits" to their relatives in Hong Kong and Macao so long as these overseas families paid all the expense. Chinese were forbidden to exchange their renminbi into hard currency for overseas travel. A few years later, family visits were allowed to relatives in nearby Southeast Asian nations.

It wasn't until 1999 that Chinese tourists were given passports to travel abroad just for fun. Restrictions were built into these first "leisure" tours. Chinese tourists had to travel in groups with Chinese tour operators and deposit at least $3,000 in cash as a surety bond that they would return to China. Those first years, some Chinese were "lost" and didn't get back on the airplane. When that happened, the tour company was warned it could be removed from the Chinese government's approved list.

Australia and New Zealand were the first two countries to win "approved destination" status to receive these first Chinese tourists, a privilege that turned out to be a mixed blessing. They accepted China's special visas for tour groups and were willing to work with the Chinese tour operators that brought them over and organized their trips in a program entitled "Provisional Regulation on the Management of Outbound Travel by Chinese Citizens at Their Own Expense." The program was full of missteps those first years and the Chinese bureaucracy was horrendous. The Chinese tour operators were often cutthroat. And those Chinese tourists weren't sure what they were supposed to do in these foreign countries.

Australia and New Zealand were the guinea pigs for the rest of the world. George Hickton was the brand-new CEO of Tourism New Zealand those first years of the experiment. New Zealand was experiencing an explosion of tourism—growing by 60 percent from 1999 to 2009 after long-haul airplanes were able to fly directly to the island nation from the United States.

It was a remarkable era, and Hickton found himself in the role of educating these Chinese tourist consumers and reining in the cut-rate Chinese tour operators. Hickton smiled when remembering the headaches of those years—a Chinese opera of naive tourists exploited by tour groups who acted like pirates, cheating their countrymen and women at every turn.

"They brought in low-market tourism at the cheapest price and gave them the worst experience," he said.

The rip-off began with the price. Many tour-bus operators charged less than $50 a day to attract as many tourists as possible. But $50 didn't go far in New Zealand. So instead of seeing New Zealand's breathtaking land-scapes and fine vistas, many of these Chinese tourists were holed up in un-inspiring hotels and fed miserably. They were shuttled around in crowded buses to shopping emporiums where they were strongly encouraged to buy tacky souvenirs because the tour operator got a commission from the sales. After a few years of such tours, New Zealand had earned a poor reputation among Chinese tourists. Hickton said he and the New Zealand tourism agency were concerned that they had no control over the questionable Chinese tour operators who won the concession to run these lucrative overseas tours from the Chinese government's tourism bureau.

"We couldn't afford to be swamped by the high volume of poor tours," he told me when we met at a tourism conference. "We had to reject a few of the Chinese tour operators."

New Zealand's only recourse was to renegotiate the tourism agree-ment with China, resulting in a new 2010 "code of conduct" that revised the "approved destination agreement" to eliminate most of the shadier practices. New Zealand had no choice. Tourism was becoming the single largest export industry—ahead of even lamb and butter. If New Zealand hadn't overhauled the Chinese tours, it could have infected the country's tourism campaign, which markets itself with the slogan "100% Pure New Zealand." In the end, New Zealand recovered and the Chinese revived their opinion of travel there.

"It wasn't easy," said Hickton, adding quickly that it was worth the ef-fort, since China has surpassed Japan as one of New Zealand's top sources of tourism, growing from 20,000 to 120,000 visits a year in the last decade.

China soon added other countries to its approved list. Each agreement required the approval of the Chinese Ministry of Foreign Affairs, the Min-istry of Public Security (the national police) as well as the national tourism administration. Malta, Germany and Hungary were the first European countries to join the list in 2002 and 2003. The next year twenty-one Eu-ropean countries were added, including France, Belgium, Austria, Greece, Italy, Norway and the Netherlands. By the end of the year African coun-tries like Ethiopia and Zimbabwe were approved to accept Chinese tour groups. By 2011 the list had grown to 135 countries, including the United States and Canada.

Now the competition was on to woo the newly wealthy Chinese tourists. Several European nations commissioned the U.N. Tourism Organization to undertake a study of these Chinese outbound tourists. The findings confirmed many rumors about the Chinese and added surprising details.

The profile that emerged confirmed the obvious: Chinese tourists live for shopping; it takes up as much as 65 percent of their travel budget. They are so intent on buying things that they are tightwads when it comes to paying for airfare or a hotel. They sign up for cheap hotels in the suburbs and supereconomy airfare in order to spend more money shopping. At the same time, they complain that those cheap hotels are far from the nightlife and that the food is lousy. Generally, they craved Chinese food when they were abroad. Other than shopping, Chinese tourists enjoyed learning about famous European writers and artists, especially visiting their homes that had been turned into museums: Claude Monet's home in Giverny; Beethoven's home in Bonn. They liked the boulevard life of lazy afternoons whiling away the hours at a café, getting lost in crowds along the grand boulevards and seeing the art and architecture of Europe's great cities.

They shop for brand names, luxury clothes, jewelry, luggage and whisky, anything with prestige. To that end, Chinese tourists are becoming the world's newest big spenders. The money is impressive. Worldwide, Chinese tourists spent nearly $55 billion in 2011. This level of spending can alter tourism markets. In France the steadily rising flow of Chinese tourists has been the equivalent of a small stimulus package in the time of the global recession, with the Chinese spending over $900 million in 2011. Thanks in part to their travels, the Chinese are learning to love wine—especially French wine—and have put China in the top five wine-consuming countries in the world, besting even Great Britain.

One study found that while Chinese tourists typically spend 8 percent of their discretionary income on a single trip within China, they can double that amount on a trip abroad, often traveling with a list of goods to buy for their friends. In London, they have surpassed shoppers from Russia, the United States and the Gulf states as the biggest spenders, according to tax-refund records of luxury-goods stores there.

France comes out on top of survey after survey as the country the Chinese most want to visit. Chinese tourists know France by its icons: the Eiffel Tower, the Arc de Triomphe and the Louvre. They associate the French with elegance, history, romance and luxury. And the French were among the first to see the potential of wooing Chinese tourists. France was one of the first countries to translate its official tourist website into Chinese. French tourist officials prodded businesses to prepare for the Chinese before the first tour groups arrived in 2003, recruiting Sino-French chefs to prepare Chinese food, finding Chinese-speaking tour guides and especially Chinese translators for department stores.

Today the Chinese version of the grand tour of foreign countries looks more like a grand shopping spree. Chinese translators are poised at cosmetics counters, lingerie departments and handbags. Chinese speakers are available for personal shopping, and some stores have special entrances for Chinese tour groups. While this is nothing new for France—the French were just as accommodating for the Japanese when they first began traveling in the 1960s—the volume of the Chinese tourists has outpaced earlier waves of new foreign tourists.

Cultural clashes are inevitable. Christian Delom, the senior French tourism official, said his agency is "monitoring" the Chinese tour operators to make sure they are following the rules, similar to the stance of New Zealand's Hickton, who found those operators gouging the planeloads of their fellow Chinese tourists. At the same time, the Chinese government is training the tour operators and the Chinese tourists themselves, giving them handouts reminding them that they are cultural "ambassadors" of China and should behave accordingly—no shouting, no spitting and no disputing prices at luxury stores.

Matteo, our guide in Venice, repeated universal fears that Chinese tour operators were ruining legitimate Italian businesses by dropping off their tourists at stores and pizza parlors newly purchased by the Chinese. "They serve 'pizza' that doesn't taste like pizza," he said. Matteo also pointed to the stores that sold Chinese tourists "Venetian glass" that was made in China.

Chinese tourists and their money is topic number one in the global tourism industry. Rashmi Sharma is a jeweler and owner of the high-end Jewels of Africa boutiques in Zambia. She said Chinese visitors buy some of her most expensive pieces, so much so that several Chinese businessmen want to become her partners. "I don't know what I'll do," she told me at her store in the Lusaka Intercontinental Hotel. "They are very good businessmen."

In New York, business owners were offered a two-day seminar on how to attract Chinese tourists into their stores. The fee to attend was $900 a person. ChinaContact, the organizer, promised to reveal the latest data tracking Chinese tourists' "brand perceptions, travel habits, purchase preferences and service expectations." Senior executives from luxury companies like Cartier, Tumi and Bergdorf Goodman would share their secrets. One of the big enticements was the latest calculation that showed Chinese tourists spent $7 billion overseas during the 2012 Chinese New Year. The pitch was simple: in 2015, only three years away, the Chinese would be the single largest source of international tourism.

Roy Graff, the host of the event, was ecstatic with the turnout: "The guest list read like a walk up the entire 5th Avenue of New York—top fashion, jewelry and cosmetics brands, luxury hotel chains and marketing agencies came to listen and learn about China's wealthy consumers."

11

THE CHINESE MARKET

China is at the center of the tourism gold rush. Everyone wants a piece of the action. International hotel chains unimpressed with anemic economies in Europe and North America are multiplying their properties in China every year. Young European, Asian and American tourism professionals manage and train the Chinese in tourism. They stay within the bounds set by the government tourism officials because the rewards can be stunning.

The wealth being accumulated is astronomical. As of 2011, China had 271 billionaires and 960,000 millionaires. Asia now has more millionaires than Europe and could surpass North America shortly. And tourism is one of the great cash cows for the Chinese economy; by 2020, when China is expected to become the number-one destination, tourism will provide over 10 percent of China's GDP. To keep up with all those tourists, China is expected to need 5,000 additional new passenger airplanes at a cost of $600 billion.

Typical of the tourism professionals lured to China is Javier Albar, a Spaniard with a degree in hospitality from Oxford Brookes University in Great Britain. He has spent most of his career in Asia, in South Korea and Hong Kong before becoming general manager of the Beijing Marriott

Hotel City Wall. It is Marriott's biggest hotel outside of the U.S., and when I met him in Beijing in October 2011, he said he wouldn't want to be anywhere else.

"China is a different animal from any other country today," he said. "It went through the revolution of Mao Zedong and all of those terrible things. Mao actually did several good things. He united the country and he set the ground for the growth of today. Now the country is becoming wealthy, the young are impatient; there are problems of expectations and inequality; everyone wants to get ahead. After what has happened over the last thirty years, who knows what will happen in the near future. The country is very alive. And I want to be here."

The first and most important requirement for doing well in the Chinese tourism industry is having the right connections to the government. China is a one-party state where top officials, their cohorts and their children—known as princelings, or the "red nobility"—play the decisive role in cutting through the bureaucracy to win the licenses and permissions necessary to do business. In all areas the most important decisions are made behind closed doors, a situation that has led to calls for better and more open legal structures and supervision of business dealings. Since the government retains control over the tourism industry in China from the top to the bottom, connections are essential.

"You can have all the resources, the expertise and professionals working for you, but you are nothing without contacts," said Albar. "Connections bring you to the table."

For Marriott International, those connections came overnight with the 1997 acquisition of the Renaissance Hotel Group. The principal owner of Renaissance was the New World Development Company, a Chinese real estate and hotel powerhouse run by Dr. Henry K. S. Cheng. With that purchase Marriott went from running nothing in China to managing forty hotels and became connected to Dr. Cheng. His political ties go to the top of the Chinese government, and he is a member of the standing committee of the Eleventh Chinese People's Political Consultative Conference of the People's Republic of China. With that political heft and his wealth, Dr. Cheng's views are heard at the very top of the government. He is the ideal patron required for any international tourist group.

With that partnership Marriott has a presence in China, adding hotels and attracting tourists, conventions, business travelers and local Chinese events. Bringing local Chinese business into his hotel is part of a larger ambition, said Albar, to transform the Chinese into fans of Marriott when they travel abroad.

"Our number-one objective here is to attract inbound travelers to China to stay at our hotels. Our number-two objective is to influence Chinese outbound travelers to choose Marriott when they travel overseas," he said. "The market is that strong."

As an example he cited a twenty-four-year-old Beijing couple that held their wedding reception at his hotel. "It was elegant—food, flowers. When they went to the U.S., they booked at a Marriott. They went to France, they booked at a Marriott."

Like every other tourism professional in China, Albar knows his profits depend on capturing a share of the outbound as well as the inbound China trade. Marriott announced plans to open its hundredth hotel in China by 2015, a schedule that will require opening one hotel every month for three years.

The competition is fierce. International-brand hotels—those owned by the Chinese but designed and managed by an international chain—are opening faster in China than anywhere else on the planet. "China, China, China" is the mantra for major chains like Hilton, Intercontinental, Four Seasons, Hyatt, Ritz-Carlton, Marriott and Starwood. In the five years ending in 2012, the number of international-brand hotel rooms grew 62 percent, and that's just the beginning of the boom.

By 2014, Hilton will have quadrupled the number of hotels it manages in China. Hyatt Hotels Corporation is doubling the number of hotels it manages in China. The Starwood brand, which includes Sheraton hotels, is building its largest resort hotel in Macao, and industry projections show that China could become its most important market soon, outpacing the United States. All of this adds up to a 50 percent increase in international-brand hotel rooms by 2015—a thought that raises fears of one big hotel bubble that will burst and send occupancy rates plunging.

David Barboza, the Shanghai bureau chief for the New York Times, who has lived in China for over a decade, has seen hotel business shoot through the roof. "They are doing very well with room rates up and labor costs still low. They give you great service with no labor costs to speak of—about the same as in Mexico."

A few years ago the Chinese government published figures showing that the average monthly wage for Chinese chambermaids was $97 and for hotel receptionists, $133. (In Hong Kong a receptionist was paid $1,305.) At the same time, international-brand hotels were charging $125 a night for a room. While wages have gone up—analysts say to around $200 a month on average—so have average hotel prices to $225. China's five-star hotels are no longer one of the world's great bargains.

Low wages are an essential source of those handsome profits. When Deng opened up the economy, he outlawed strikes in 1982 and kept Chinese unions under government control. In return, the unions have kept labor costs down, attracting foreign investment as well as flooding the global market with inexpensive goods. It is a public secret that union officials expect discreet cash payments from hotels and other services for tourists as a token of gratitude for those low labor costs.

Barboza said that in the mind of the government, the tourism sector has been a huge success and there was no reason to change its formula. "The Chinese state rakes in the money with licenses and monopolies and partnerships. Why would officials give it up?"

All these blue-sky predictions are hard-won. The day-to-day reality of running a hotel in China is complicated. During my four-day stay at the Marriott City Wall, I could see the cultural gaps and disconnects. At lunch one day at the hotel's dim sum restaurant, I waited half an hour with no sign of my food. When I asked my waitress why none of my dishes had appeared, she answered, "You should have ordered something else." At breakfast one morning a hostess interrupted a man filling his plate at the buffet, asking him to sign a check with his free hand so she could check off his room number. He wasn't happy.

Albar said Marriott has worked overtime training new Chinese employees to be sensitive to sometimes extreme cultural misunderstanding.

"China is a completely different game than the other Asian countries, where hospitality is second nature," he said. "The Chinese are animated people of wonderful character but little concept of hospitality, of putting guests first. Maybe it is communism. There are small things. You have to explain that when opening the door to bring in the luggage you have to watch out and not hit the guest in the nose."

"There is also the bigger issue of saying thank you and please. Some Chinese consider saying thank you and please as somehow degrading. It's understandable. These people have had to be fighters, survivors. We are saying now, your job is to help others, not compete with them."

The gap reaches to the top. When Albar arranged for an international summit on women to be held at his Marriott hotel in 2010, the government balked. At least eight hundred delegates would be attending from around the world. "The government said it didn't want the summit at my hotel, that it was too close to the central railroad station and that wouldn't give a good impression. I had to go through higher government authorities to win clearance. The compromise was to have arrival cocktails at the People's Hall," said Albar. "Before, the hotel for a summit would have been fully under government control. Now officials are learning new ways. They say they want Beijing to have more conferences—they have to learn how we do it."

As yet, there are no Chinese hotel chains and few mainland Chinese managers at the international hotels. Albar's senior staff members are natives of India, Singapore and Malaysia.

"Some industries are more difficult for the Chinese to understand at this stage, especially ones like tourism that involves foreigners and their food, drink, behavior, entertainment," said Albar. "In a decade, that could change."

At first glance, this makes little sense. Chinese culture is great in part because of its cuisine and the enjoyment of food, drink and conversation. By the eighteenth century, China was crisscrossed with eating clubs, restaurants and inns. Chinese tea shops were crowded with travelers. Food stalls served prized snacks of the season—cakes, salt eggs, watermelon, sea scallops. Restaurants were known for their specialties, some for their service by beautiful young women. Buddhist temples served artful vegetarian meals on festival days. Chinese banquets could last days. The food was served on porcelain, the finest in the world, and eaten with chopsticks.

Jonathan D. Spence, the noted historian of China, points to the journal of the British ambassador to China in 1793, who wrote that "the poorest classes in China seem to understand the art of preparing their food much better than the same classes at home."

During the Communist revolution the culinary and hospitality arts withered in China's blizzard of change. Their revival has been tied to the economic boom. Like everything else, those Chinese habits and arts are being filtered through the desire to appeal to a global standard. The bridge for this has been overseas Chinese from Asia and North America. With their knowledge of the modern world as well as the old Chinese culture, these Chinese managers from Hong Kong or Singapore have helped lead the budding tourism industry with their practical abilities and their insight into what works in the Chinese context. Now, thirty years after the initial opening, native Chinese are taking their places in the tourism business.

One example is Zhang Mei, a rare woman entrepreneur in the Chinese tourism industry. She is the mirror image of Javier Albar. Zhang Mei is a young Chinese woman who founded her own company, a high-end boutique tour operation that has won accolades from experts like *Condé Nast Traveler*. Zhang and Albar agreed on most aspects of the tourism industry in China: its tremendous opportunities, the extraordinary role of government and the industry's problems.

A native of the town of Dali in Yunnan Province, Zhang attended college at Kunming, the capital of Yunnan, and then Harvard, where she earned a master's degree in business administration. She was unhappy at her first job in banking.

"So I took a sabbatical and traveled around the world: Northern Europe, Scandinavia, Switzerland, and South Africa," she said. "I went to Tibet and Nepal in the Himalayas, which was probably the peak of my life."

She ended up in her home province where, she said, she was struck by its stunning scenery and its potential for tourism. "After I had seen the rest of the world, I realized how beautiful Yunnan was and how great it would be for tourism."

Impressed by the possibilities, Zhang resigned from her job, and in 2000, at the age of thirty, she started her own luxury tourism agency called

WildChina from a small office in Beijing. "All of a sudden I became this take-charge entrepreneur. From there the snowball started rolling."

Today she is a well-spoken, handsome woman who runs a company of fifty employees from her office in the diplomatic section of Beijing. Zhang said WildChina has a 25 percent profit margin, but she is anxious to "jump into the next class and grow the business." With her solid base in the United States, she is broadening to include countries throughout the Asia-Pacific region and Europe. Recently she added French and Spanish translations to her website.

Her top goal is to win official approval to operate tours in the United States for Chinese travelers. She sees the same pot of gold that Albar at Marriott sees: the money that can be made as millions of Chinese tourists travel for the first time.

I spent three days shadowing Zhang Mei as she plotted her next move while keeping an eye on her tour company. Zhang said WildChina's popularity requires that she stay one step ahead of what until now has been pretty lousy competition. She is constantly reimagining tours, adding restaurants and fanciful twists on iconic visits. For a famous movie-star client, she turned a visit to the Great Wall into a sunset dinner party, serving supper on white tablecloths with the sun disappearing over the hills. "It is a way of seeing the familiar from a different angle—a wild moment," Zhang said.

The three Washington-area couples I met taking lessons in tai chi were her clients. Their three-week tour took them eventually to Shangri-La in the mountain valleys of Yunnan Province bordering Tibet. They went from the plush comforts of Shanghai to the austere beauty of snowcapped mountains, Buddhist monasteries and no heat or indoor plumbing. They told me they felt as if they had gone from modern to medieval times, the reaction that Zhang cultivates to show old and new China.

So far, Zhang has been lucky that her competition is largely from the Chinese government. Most of the thousands of Chinese tour agencies that appear to be independent are owned by the government and focused on serving a mass market. They compete by offering the lowest prices. That means buses with fifty people or more traveling to the big-name sightseeing spots and eating at designated food halls where the cooks prepare food with bland foreign taste buds in mind. The tour guides have been schooled by the government and speak from the same memorized script. The goal is to offer the biggest tour at the lowest possible price. The profits won't come from the trip itself but from tips and payoffs given by the souvenir shops and restaurants that are part of the tour. Even the government tour guides have to rely on tips.

A few years ago the American Political Science Association organized such a tour of China through a travel agency owned by the government. Michael Levy, who taught political science at Georgetown University, went on the trip along with his wife Bonny Wolf, a food writer. For Wolf, the trip was a nightmare. On her first visit to one of the great culinary countries of the world, she was starved for real Chinese food.

"Every day was planned to the minute," she told me. "We could tell when we were stopping for lunch when we saw the parking lots filled with other buses. These tourist halls served horrible food. I remember the Great Wall for its horrible food. The Peking duck in Beijing wasn't any different than the Peking duck I can eat in Arlington, Virginia."

The low point was Shanghai. They were told they would dine at an American-style restaurant with a choice of eggplant parmesan or meatloaf. "That's when I had enough and led a rebellion. I talked to everyone on the bus and we all agreed we had to go to a real Chinese restaurant."

The guide said there would be no refund for their prepaid meal. More important, she said she needed permission from Beijing—a thought that seemed to make her nervous. For half a moment, Wolf said she worried: "Would the Chinese put us in jail because we went to a good restaurant?"

The guide relented—Beijing didn't need to know—and the group went to a first-class restaurant where everyone was transfixed by the food. The much-feared bill cost $5 per person.

Zhang avoids tourist restaurants at all costs, quite literally. A tour of five or six cities that would cost $1,500 per person in a government agency tour package can cost around $4,850 through WildChina. While that is triple the government rate, it is reasonable for Americans and Europeans making a once-in-a-lifetime trip and expecting fine food, local flavor and experiences, and good hotels. This is the business principle undergirding WildChina, said Zhang: "We don't do assembly-line travel."

WildChina views the practices of government agencies as a template for what not to do. Government tour groups give a small base pay to guides and drivers in the expectation that they will earn much of their income from kickback payments from tourism restaurants, jade and porcelain factories and from tips from the tourists themselves.

"We don't subscribe to that for multiple reasons. It's not good for the guides, the drivers or the tourists," said David Fundingsland of WildChina.

Instead, the agency selects and trains their own guides and drivers, whom they pay a high base salary: $90 a day for the guides in a country where the official average daily wage is $16. Moreover those salaries are supplemented with tips from clients and bonuses based on feedback from the clients. Kickbacks are not allowed. WildChina also has a "no-shopping" policy. Clients can shop if they want on their downtime without a guide. WildChina organizes meals at restaurants owned by locals, not chains. Local involvement extends to regular volunteer projects like building latrines and donating tents to the nomads of Yunnan Province.

"When the earthquake hit in Sichuan, we sent tents and equipment to the nomads we had trained to serve and work in camps and enjoy tourism. They had lost everything," said Fundingsland.

Despite the higher costs, WildChina has those profit margins of 20 to 25 percent, far better than most Chinese government tour operations.

"Our institutional clients—like the Peabody Museum, the University of North Carolina—want us to do the coordination for their work and their pleasure, from the general to the thematic, and they trust us to provide the logistics for their meetings, equipment for trekking, as well as the side trips for their enjoyment," he said.

Zhang knows American tastes. She is married to an American writer and journalist, and she lived in Los Angeles and Washington with her family of three children for more than five years. Now, as she ramps up her business, Zhang is attending high-end tourism conferences, speaking on panels and employing a public relations firm in the United States to get out the word and raise the profile of WildChina.

"If I have enough stickiness to the brand, people will come to our website," she said.

But her steady focus is on securing rights to launch outbound tours for

Chinese traveling overseas—the Holy Grail of the industry that Europeans, Americans, Australians, Arabs and Africans are all fighting for. One day Zhang lunched with the man she calls her "patron," a major official in a government travel agency that acts as the umbrella for her agency. She will apply for an outbound license through his umbrella agency. "We're required to have that state license to operate," she said before running off to meet him, refusing to say his name.

Nellie Connolly, WildChina's head of marketing, reviews what drives sales for WildChina on the Internet, word of mouth, awards from magazines like *Condé Nast Traveler* and the *National Geographic*, travel shows, Facebook, Twitter, and the WildChina blog. "We don't buy advertisements," she said. "We rely on travel writers."

After reading those blogs and articles as well as the awards citations, I saw that while WildChina is challenging the government business model, it is staying very much within the political limits set by government officials. The extreme example is Tibet. WildChina has championed travel to Tibet, most recently describing it as a "bucket list destination" with not even a hint of the sporadic bloody protests there. In an email sent out in March 2012, WildChina told would-be clients, "There is something very special about visiting the birthplace of the Dalai Lama, witnessing monks in worship, soaking in the panoramic views of the Himalayas and having your first sip of yak butter tea. . . ."

Six days earlier, two young Tibetan women had burned themselves in protest against Chinese rule. One year before, twenty-four Tibetans committed suicide as political protest. The situation was so tense in 2008 and early 2009 that China banned foreigners, including tourists, from visiting Tibet, canceling all foreign tours. The Chinese are trying to maneuver around the politics and hold on to the tourism that makes up 20 percent of the economy. The government built a road to the village where the fourteenth Dalai Lama was born but forbids tourists from entering the house where he lived. To this day, it is a crime to own a picture of the Dalai Lama.

In the Chinese tourism game there is no other choice but to stay within the bright lines of political correctness drawn by the government. On my last night in Beijing, Zhang invited me to her home, where I met her three lively children. Her husband was away on work. There is nothing extravagant about her lifestyle save the car and driver required to navigate Beijing traffic. When we started discussing Zhang's future plans, her youngest daughter said, "Mommy likes to travel but she loves to be with us more."

We delayed the conversation until Zhang walked me to a cab. "Wild-China is privately held and now it is comfortable for me, a small cash cow. But the dream is too small. If outbound takes off, then I could combine the two and be ready to take it public and to grow. I'll need some pretty big growth to break through. That's what I'm working on."

That description of her goals paralleled my last interview with Albar. Marriott, he said, was building its brand in China and through China. "We require a thirty-year, iron-clad contract for every hotel we manage here with the highest standards—far stricter than the Chinese standards. We turn down more opportunities than we accept. We can't get it wrong in China—this is the new world."

After my stay in Beijing, I joined my husband Bill in Shanghai, where we began our travel through China as tourists. There is a fierce modern-day rivalry between Shanghai and Beijing in most spheres. Shanghai plays the role of New York City—the economic hub of the country, a trading giant that faces the sea, and the biggest city, one with swagger and attitude. If the comparison were a direct parallel, Beijing would be Washington, D.C., the staid, single-minded capital of the United States. But Beijing has more of the feel of Berlin, with its heavy history and its search for a modern identity as the newly emerged power center of the Asian continent.

The Chinese government challenged both cities to land the Big Event that could transform their appeal and reputation and attract more foreign visitors. Beijing won its bid for the Summer Olympics in 2008. And Shanghai was selected as the host for the World Expo in 2010, becoming the first city in a developing nation to host the Expo since the tradition began in London in 1851.

Top Chinese officials decided which city would be the candidate for each of these events and aggressively promoted them. Shanghai, the economic engine of China, was the logical choice to vie for the World Expo, which is known as the Economic Olympics in tourism circles. Staging those two events within two years was a major statement of China's intent to enter the top tier of cosmopolitan nations. The Shanghai Expo cost $55 billion, excluding the new infrastructure, more than the $40 billion spent on the Beijing Summer Olympics.

Wu Yi, the head of China's commission for bidding on these events, made the case that "more and more tourists come to China for its time-honored, splendid culture, and more and more foreigners become friends of China for its honest, warm-hearted people."

Like Beijing, Shanghai razed a huge swath of the city to clear over 1,200 acres of land on either side of the Huangpu River that divides the city. Then Shanghai spent $45 billion to add seven new subway lines to its city system to move crowds to the Expo grounds, more than doubling its reach, and to improve or construct major highways and other infrastructure around the area. For its landmark, the World Expo 2010 Shanghai built a massive red-lacquer Chinese Pavilion with a roof built using traditional fretwork brackets. The pavilion hosted extravagant spectacles of Chinese dancers and acrobats in colorful costumes—the same entertainment that wowed foreigners at the Beijing Olympics.

Some 246 countries, cities, companies and organizations took part in the Expo, either building full-blown pavilions or staging exhibits. By the time it closed down in October, at least 73 million visitors had walked through the grounds. Those numbers set a record for all expos; the vast majority of visitors were Chinese, many of them residents of Shanghai, who were eligible for free tickets.

The foreign pavilions at the Expo were high-class tourism advertisements to entice the Chinese to visit India, Germany or Botswana. The Denmark Pavilion was a crowd favorite. The Danish had sent its statue of the Little Mermaid on its first trip overseas to grace its pavilion, drawing nearly 6 million Chinese, more than the actual population of Denmark.

The second stage in the transformation of Shanghai into the top tourist spot began in 2011 with the construction of China's first Disneyland in the city's suburbs. As the largest tourism joint project with a foreign company, the new Disneyland is intended to make Shanghai a "world-class tourist destination," just as Disneyland Paris has become the single most visited attraction in France.

The first phase of the resort will cover nearly 1,000 acres and eventually cost more than the Expo. The resort will be roughly equidistant between Shanghai city and its international airport; 300 million people live within a two-hour drive of the site. Once the entire complex is built, the developers hope attendance will surpass the 45 million annual visitors to Disney World in Orlando. A resort of this size means tens of thousands of new jobs—and newcomers—for Shanghai, a prospect that helped convince the Chinese government to sign on to the deal after a fifteen-year courtship by Disney. While we were in the city, the Disneyland construction site was off-limits, but newspapers were filled with reports of the new subway link under construction and the renderings of the design that would be familiar to anyone who has visited Disney World in Orlando or Disneyland in California.

Bill and I stayed within the traditional tourist zones in Shanghai, at a hotel in the old French Concession in strolling distance of the Bund. On this trip we booked only hotels that were Chinese-owned and -operated, avoiding international chains. That proved more difficult than we had imagined. Albar was right when he said that over 90 percent of hotels in China were now managed by chains. Shanghai, though, is blessed with beautiful Art Deco buildings that have been preserved as hotels. Some believe they escaped the wrecking ball because they are western-styled, erected by Europeans and wealthy Chinese in the 1930s.

This was the era when Shanghai gained its reputation as the Paris of Asia. The blend of western architecture with Chinese sensibilities is the backdrop to all of those smoky images of Shanghai bankers and mobsters, traders in tea shops and women wearing the satin Mandarin dresses, or cheongsam. Dozens of these beautiful buildings still line the Bund, the stretch along the Huangpu River, which divides the city and empties into the Pacific Ocean. (It was christened the Bund by English entrepreneurs using the Hindi word for "levee" or "dam.")

We stayed at a mansion-hotel, the Heng-Shan Moller Villa, a fantastic confection of Swedish and Chinese architecture built in 1936 by Eric

Moller, a Swedish shipping magnate. The Moller family gave up the home in 1950 after China became Communist. It served as the headquarters of the Shanghai branch of the Chinese Communist Party Youth League throughout the Great Leap Forward and the Cultural Revolution, keeping intact the impressive stained-glass windows, staircases and paneled foyer. In 2001, the government gave it to the Heng-Shan Group of Shanghai, which refurbished and restored it as a hotel. Although the group added some questionable outbuildings to the garden, its eccentric Euro-Chinese décor was preserved, along with the large garden, an unheard-of luxury in downtown Shanghai, where millions of cars clog the streets and fill the nights with honking horns. We listened to birdsongs from our open windows every morning.

It was a brisk walk to the Bund, which is now the sine qua non of Shanghai tourism. The riverside quay has been transformed into an expansive modern promenade where Shanghai families come on the weekends and buy their children toys and snacks while tourists climb onto sightseeing boats to view the city. Across the boulevard stand those Art Deco buildings that have won preservation status as classic masterpieces.

To understand why the Art Deco buildings were preserved while the far older Chinese masterpieces of Beijing were razed, as well as other puzzles of modern Chinese tourism, we met William Patrick Cranley and his wife Tina Kanagaratnam, two of the founders of Historic Shanghai. They were our hosts for Sunday brunch at M on the Bund, the literary watering hole of Shanghai at the top of the old 1921 Nissan Shipping Building, now restored.

It was a bright, windy day along the river. Cranley and Kanagaratnam had moved to Shanghai fourteen years earlier and said they quickly became enamored with the city, especially the Art Deco buildings from the 1930s. In their downtime—he is an academic, she is in public relations—they became tour guides for visiting foreigners, requiring them to dig deep into the city's history and discover the Byzantine ways of the country's tourism industry.

"The first visitors were often people with family ties to old Shanghai—from the foreign concessions, Jewish families, Chinese families, French, American, British," said Cranley.

"Some came with only one photo and said, 'this is my house, please help me find it,'" said Kanagaratnam. To her surprise, she did find a house or two.

Now Cranley operates several basic tours for private groups or tour companies, often customizing them. His Art Deco walking tour takes visitors to the jewels along the Bund—the Fairmont Peace Hotel, the Park Hotel, the Bank of China Building—and then down the narrow lilongs of the city to see one of the greatest collections of Art Deco buildings in the world. Another popular walking tour covers what is left of Shanghai's once-thriving Jewish quarter. This is not to be confused with the official Chinese tour agency's "Jewish Historic Tour," which is a standard two-week trip through China with an afternoon stop at the old Jewish quarter of Zhengszhou and one day looking at Jewish sites in Shanghai.

Cranley's tours, though, are basically illegal.

"Tourism is a state-protected business in China. Those of us foreigners who give tours are technically illegal. We're not licensed. So that means we can't register as a business or open a bank account under our name Historic Shanghai," said Cranley. "So we don't make waves and we operate below the radar."

That doesn't mean that the authorities are ignorant. They tolerate the tours because they bring in business, often high-end tourism. For ten years Cranley and Kanagaratnam and their partner Tess Johnston, the doyenne of Historic Shanghai, have been sponsoring the Shanghai Literary Festival, which is publicized in the media. The target audience is English-speakers, which gives them the breathing space. The festival headlines some Chinese authors like Qiu Xialolong, the author of a popular English-language detective series set in his native Shanghai. Cranley said they sold 7,000 tickets to the festival in 2011, largely to locals but also to people who came from Beijing and Singapore: "They're all English-speakers but it is hard to tell if our audience is overseas Chinese or local Chinese."

Historic China's other goal is to save historic buildings from being demolished, an increasingly difficult proposition since those buildings sit on very valuable land. This is the axis where the needs of tourism run smackdab into the logic of Chinese development. The quickest way to make money in China is to tear down a building—historic or not—then sell the increasingly valuable land and build something else. The argument that those buildings are an essential core to the tourism trade is often ignored by the powerful interests tied to the government. With so much at stake behind the scenes, Cranley said it is sometimes better that foreigners like him lead the campaign rather than Chinese.

"That's our challenge. We can't really lobby, and all preservation is done by the state, so we have to operate through the media or with Twitter campaigns to prevent another building from being torn down on the Bund," said Cranley. With that aim in mind, he and his partners are sponsoring the World Congress on Art Deco in 2015 to spotlight and preserve what is left of Art Deco buildings in Shanghai. It is a gamble to convince the government there is room in Shanghai for the historic Bund as well as Disneyland.

All of this maneuvering has been done against the backdrop of the rapid buildup of tourism that exploded in 2000 when domestic tourism was unleashed and foreigners discovered China's strength, especially after the Asian financial crisis.

The Golden Weeks announcement of guaranteed vacation "put it all together," said Cranley. "Now we have to deal with our success. We're all experimenting to find the sweet spot where tourism is working for China and where Chinese tourists feel they are free as tourists."

Bill and I met many of those Chinese tourists at the site of the First National Congress of the Chinese Communist Party, when the party was officially founded, a critical milestone on the road to revolution. The house in the French Concession is an essential stop on the "Red Tourism Highway." The crowd entered the stone home with a degree of respect I hadn't seen before in China. Inside, visitors stood quietly before a tableau of mannequins representing the initial thirteen delegates with Mao Zedong at the head, a gathering of modern China's founding fathers.

It is one of the premier sites along the "Red Tourism Highway" that began six years earlier to recognize China's Communist traditions and to make tourism "more consistent with the times and reality." Six billion Chinese have visited one of those sites, accounting for roughly 20 percent of domestic tourism, generating millions of dollars and creating nearly 1 million jobs.

On our last day we met a native of Shanghai whom I will call Pan. She is fourth-generation Shanghai, the great-granddaughter of one of the first Chinese Methodist ministers. Her family once owned a comfortable home near the Bund but lost it after the Chinese revolution. When private property was restored, they were not given back their home. We ate at one of her favorite new restaurants, where she chose a feast for us of spicy river fish and dumplings with sweet bean curds from a menu the size of a small cookbook.

As she described her young life—graduation with honors from a Chinese university, study abroad in Great Britain and then home to Shanghai, where she teaches English—Pan said the city had lost its unique flavor and that she is wary of the surge in tourism and the Chinese workers attracted from the countryside.

"None of these people you see on the street are from Shanghai. It doesn't matter anymore if you are fourth-generation Shanghai like I am or well educated. Shanghai now belongs to outsiders."

Initially, I wanted to travel on one of China's new fast trains for a segment of our trip, but a series of fatal accidents frightened me. The government has invested billions of dollars in new high-speed rail links, the longest one between Beijing and Shanghai. These bullet trains will eventually connect major cities around the country, a commendable attempt to reduce carbon emissions by offering an alternative to airplanes and cars. It was a huge leap from China's earlier rail system, built more than a hundred years ago to carry freight around the vast country.

But the Chinese rushed the construction of the system, ignoring complaints from foreign and Chinese experts about safety issues. Then in July 2011, a few months before our trip, a new Chinese fast train had a spectacular collision with another train that killed 39 people. By comparison, Japan's high-speed rail has been operating since 1964 and has never had a fatality. Eventually, China will repair the damage done by taking shortcuts but I wasn't prepared to take a chance. We stuck to airplanes.

We flew to Xian, an old imperial capital of little modern significance until 1974, when some farmers hit a strange object while digging a well. They alerted the local government, and soon the world knew that they had discovered one of the great archeological treasures of China—an army of terra-cotta soldiers, horses and chariots buried in a necropolis, not unlike an Egyptian pyramid, to accompany an emperor after his death. Xian was Bill's focus on the trip. A retired army officer, he was enthralled with the idea of seeing a replica of a third century B.C. Chinese army.

On landing we were once again struck by the enormity of China. The air terminal of Xian was larger than Dulles, our home airport in Washington, D.C., yet it was too small for the city of 9 million. A second terminal was under construction.

Waiting for us was a middle-aged Chinese woman who introduced herself as "Linda." With her pleasant, no-nonsense manner, her hair barely combed and her clothes thrown together, she gave the impression of an intellectual who was badly cast as a tour guide. A travel agent back home had organized this part of our trip, following proper procedure by using a Chinese government tour group to book our hotel, guide and car. We asked "Linda" what her real name was. "Lin Xi," she answered, adding that all the guides are required to use foreign names with tourists. "Chinese names are difficult," she said.

She smiled and said we would have to wait. Our car and driver had been reassigned and our substitute car was caught in traffic. Twenty minutes later a vintage Red Flag automobile pulled up. We climbed inside the trash-strewn backseat, which smelled of years of chain-smoking drivers.

Undeterred, Lin Xi got into the front seat, and as we drove into town, she announced that she would tell us her life story. Born to a farmer father and teacher mother in 1966, Lin Xi said she remembered hearing people shouting, "Long Live Chairman Mao, the Communist Party and the People's Republic of China."

"They didn't care about their lives, only about politics," she said. "We were told that the Americans were imperialists and that Europeans were the running dog of the American imperialists. We prepared for war with you—can you imagine? Now I am your tour guide."

She was bitter that her education was so bad that "we were not expected to have academic excellence, only political excellence." And she was bitter about the lies she was told. "We did not know the outside world. We felt we were in heaven because we had a watch, a sewing machine and a bicycle. We were told others didn't have as much as we did."

She said that when Chairman Mao died in 1976, "the Great Man Deng Xiaoping opened us to the outside world. Before, we had been told we were the best in the world, and we learned that was wrong, that three-fourths of the world lived better than we did."

Her life improved as the economy grew at 10 percent a year. Then, she said, it was almost destroyed by the protests at Tiananmen Square in 1989. "At first, I supported the students and sent them money. Then I realized that the students lived in an ivory tower. If they had won, China would have collapsed and the world would have had to feed us."

She nodded her head to signal the end. "Just now I have told you how China's changes have changed my life in my lifetime."

Bill and I had the feeling that not only was this Lin Xi's standard script delivered for every tourist who traveled with her but that it had been approved by her political superiors at the China Youth Travel Service, the government bureau where she worked. Her "personal story" didn't waver from the Communist Party line that condemned the radical policies of Mao Zedong without criticizing him and that cast Deng as the modern savior. It even included a confession by Lin Xi and an acknowledgment of her mistakes.

This turned out to be only the first chapter of her "personal story," which she continued to deliver at appropriate moments during our three days together, each episode emphasizing the positive economic and political improvements of the New China, each revolving around her discovering of the wisdom of the government.

We arrived at the Tang Paradise Hotel. Bill and I were pleased that we had insisted on a Chinese-only hotel policy. The hotel had the multilayered roof of a mythical Chinese palace. Inside, the white walls were accented with red lacquer and black fretwork. I asked Lin Xi the age of the hotel, wondering whether it was built in the nineteenth or twentieth century. "It was built in 2005," she said. "This is a history park, not real history."

The hotel sits at the far end of a 165-acre theme park with extensive gardens and lakes built to tell the glories of the Tang Dynasty, one of the more sophisticated in Chinese history—encouraging the arts, refining the civil service examination and allotting farmland on a relatively equal basis. The history park focused on grand replicas of temples, pavilions and miniature palaces, all supposedly built in the Tang style. Admission to the park is $14; those staying in the hotel enter for free. It was a signal example of the tourism industry's promotion of replicas over actual historic buildings, a Chinese take on the Disneyland model.

The next day we were off to the Terra-Cotta Army of Xian, speeding along an eight-lane expressway. Lin Xi recited the history of Qin Shi Huang Di, China's first emperor, and how he ordered the construction of this army to accompany him to heaven. "He strongly believed in the afterlife and kept his tomb very secret. He had three thousand concubines. He made his tomb like his life. Two hundred concubines were buried alive with him and the terra-cotta soldiers."

We pulled off the main highway and drove past parking lots the size of an American football field; most were half-full of tour buses. This was the intersection of domestic and foreign travel writ large. The Chinese government had built the parking lots and an outdoor market of souvenir stores lining the wide path to the terra-cotta pits for the 2 million people who come each year. We smiled at the hawkers selling miniature statues, sheepskin rugs and nuts wrapped in a cone.

In front of the museum built at the entry of the first pit, Bill turned to Lin Xi and explained that he was a retired U.S. Army officer and had been looking forward to seeing the terra-cotta soldiers for years. He told her he wanted to study the statues for their "tactical formation and the integration of combined arms." She smiled and walked us through.

This first emperor of Qin, or China, unified much of the country in 221 B.C. with extraordinary military aplomb. The pits holding his eternal army held clues to how he won battle after battle. Clay soldiers are lined up in trenches, each with individual faces and positioned according to rank. Bill explained to me how one could read the sophistication of the army by the arrangements in battle formations that clearly showed the tactics of the day. Foot soldiers were followed by cavalry and then charioteers—these were pulled by clay horses lined up four abreast. Bill paced the perimeter of each of the three pits, marveling at the details, pointing out the flank security on both sides and taking photograph after photograph so he could study the soldiers at leisure when we got home.

Lin Xi was growing impatient. She drew alongside me and said it was time to leave. We would be late for lunch. "Could you please ask your husband to follow me?"

I walked over and told Bill our time was up. He went over to Lin Xi and told her in the gentlest terms that he would happily skip whatever else she had planned so he could spend more time with these clay ghosts. She laughed: "You are breaking the record of the Australian man who spent two hours here!"

Bill and Lin Xi reached a compromise, and one hour later we strolled out of the pit and arrived for the last seating at an auditorium-size dining hall. Lin Xi showed us to a table, pointed to the buffet lines in an adjoining room and disappeared. The food was neither good nor bad, neither Asian nor Western. After the meal we left Xian's Terra-Cotta Army, walking past the phalanx of souvenir stalls, and climbed into our car.

My eyes were burning. I rubbed them until I could open them again and looked outside. The leaden sky had been blocking the sun since we arrived. I asked Lin Xi when it was going to rain and rinse away the heavy, foul-smelling air. "The pollution is pretty bad here," I said.

"No," she answered. "This is mist. Xian has always had yellow mist. We say that dogs bark at the sun, not the moon. Seeing the sun is rare. You can call this fog, if you like."

I started to challenge her when Bill gently touched my arm and put a silencing finger to his lips. Lin Xi had her playbook that required all good tour guides to deny the country's abysmal pollution.

We had been lucky until Xian. It rained most of the time I was in Beijing, and during our long weekend in Shanghai a strong wind off the river swept much of the filth away from the city. But now we were in the interior of China, in a city ringed with factories, caught inside the pollution that blankets much of the country.

After seeing the soldiers we drove back into the city, past block after block of twenty-story look-alike concrete apartment buildings, all obscured in the soupy atmosphere. We had arrived at our next destination—the magnificent, brooding city walls of Xian, the longest left standing in the country. "The walls date from the Ming Dynasty and stretch eight miles," said Lin Xi. "It took eighteen years to dig the moat and build the walls."

At the top of the walls Lin Xi suggested we bicycle around the top of them. I started coughing, and coughing, and then sneezing. The air was impossible. I was reminded of the series of stories preceding the 2008 Beijing Olympics of athletes questioning whether they would compete in air that could harm their lungs. The marathon world record holder, Haile Gebrselassie of Ethiopia, dropped out of that event rather than compete in China's polluted air. Their complaints forced the Chinese government to make rare admissions that air pollution is a public health problem; to improve air quality for the Summer Olympics, the government ordered the temporary suspension of factories surrounding the city and instituted a policy to stagger the use of automobiles in the capital—a policy that has remained in force. After the Olympics the government reverted to their old habit of denying the true dimensions of the problem publicly, while in private taking extraordinary precautions for their own health, purifying the air in their own homes and offices with expensive filters.

Some tourists can be fooled by the stories of fog and mist from their tour guides; others become ill during their trips and post warnings on websites like VirtualTourist that caution tourists to wear face masks or avoid China during certain seasons. The heavy smog disrupts air traffic and creates serious traffic jams—all part of a tourist's experience of the country. The official China National Tourist Office avoids the subject altogether; its photographs show nothing but clear blue skies over Beijing, Shanghai and points west.

While we were in China, the official newspaper, China Daily, reported that more than half of China's wealthiest people—those with assets over $9 million—said they planned to immigrate to a wealthy, cleaner nation like Australia or the United States for the sake of their children and a better standard of living. The government denies the extent of pollution not only to tourists but to its own people. Last year residents of Beijing fed up with the lies told by their government turned to the U.S. embassy and its accurate reports on the air index to decide whether they should hazard the smog that day. By denying that pollution even exists, the Chinese tourism industry is making matters worse for itself and for the tourists. At the end of our trip pollution was my biggest complaint.

Lin Xi suggested that we attend a dinner-theater presentation at the

Shaanxi Grand Opera House. "This is a famous Chinese cultural event. Dinner is four cold plates, then four plates of hot dumplings, tea and hot rice wine," she said. "Then the theater of Tang Dynasty music and dance, the peak of Chinese culture."

Bill said he was game. Lin Xi said she would buy our tickets; each would cost 320 yuan, the less formal name for renminbi. She put out her hand. Bill pulled out his wallet, counted his money and shook his head. He didn't have enough cash to buy the tickets. He could use his credit card when we got there. Without skipping a beat, Lin Xi ordered the driver to make a series of turns and—violà—we were in front of a bank ATM machine. Bill climbed out with Lin Xi right behind him. She squeezed into the glass-enclosed booth, and when the paper money slid out of the machine she blocked Bill's exit until he handed over 640 yuan. Then she smiled.

There was no doubt that we had just witnessed how Lin Xi makes her money. She needed the cash to buy the tickets herself and get her cut. If we had used our credit cards, she would lose that cut and a good share of what she expected to earn that week.

The parking lot in front of the Opera was crowded with tour buses. Lin Xi escorted us inside to a table in a large, multitiered hall facing the stage. She introduced us to our waitress and then wished us a pleasant night. Looking around at the mix of foreign and Chinese tourists, Bill announced, "This is a Chinese version of a Las Vegas supper club."

The curtain rose. The bright pastel costumes were Chinese; the women's dresses were form-fitting and showed ample midriff; their dark hair was crowned with elaborate combs. The music had a hint of American show tunes. A heavily madeup man dressed as a Tang emperor was the emcee. The curtain rose and fell on a dozen different songs, from springtime cherry blossoms to a moonlit rendezvous. A Chinese version of a dance of seven veils was followed by a bird chirping. It was hard to believe that the show was a presentation of the arts as "passed down from the Tang Dynasty," as the emperor-host had promised.

We followed the crowd out to our car while most of the theatergoers climbed onto their buses. And we checked the price of the ticket: 198 yuan a person. That meant Lin Xi pocketed 244 yuan. We didn't say a word.

The next day we flew to Chengdu, celebrated as the home of the panda.

A French Catholic missionary named Armand David is responsible for transforming an elusive, humble bear into China's most beloved creature. The Chinese paid little attention to the black and white panda until David brought a specimen back to Paris in the late nineteenth century and declared he had discovered a new species of bear. Westerners were fascinated by the panda, while the Chinese largely ignored it. That changed during the first decades of the People's Republic of China when the government latched on to the panda as a fitting symbol of modern China that was free of the baggage of its imperial past. (The panda was rarely if ever portrayed in classical Chinese art.) Soon the panda was featured on postage stamps, as the mascot of new industries and as a popular toy. As the Chinese opened up to the world and were maneuvering through the intricacies of Cold War diplomacy, the panda proved an irresistible way to woo nations. Pandas given by China became the superstars of zoos in the Soviet Union, Europe and the United States.

As Panda popularity skyrocketed, alarm set in when the Chinese realized that their precious panda was an endangered species. Their habitat had been eaten away by logging and industrialization. The Chinese turned to the World Wildlife Fund, beginning a collaboration that is immortalized in the panda logo of the WWF. The small Wanglang reserve and the massive Wolong reserve of 494,000 acres were established as the giant panda's home in Sichuan Province. The pandas became a national treasure and the penalty for killing one is the death sentence.

Once Deng set his sights on building China's tourism industry, it was natural to make the panda one of the country's biggest draws. The Chinese were the first to fall headlong in love with panda tourism. Once domestic travel opened up, the panda reserves and base camps were overrun with Chinese tourists. In the twenty-first century, with foreigners arriving in droves, panda tourism grew fivefold. It is now one of the biggest moneymakers for Chengdu.

The power of the panda cult was demonstrated after the great 2008 earthquake in Sichuan Province. At least 70,000 people were killed in that disaster; many were children buried alive in shoddily built schools. Grieving parents bitterly protested publicly about the corrupt contractors who cut corners building the schools in order to increase their profits. Yet the government failed to fully investigate and, instead, punished the activists demanding an accounting.

By way of comparison, the government and conservationists moved swiftly to save pandas from the rubble of the enormous earthquake. In a video called *Out of the Rock Comes Life*, the pandas caught in the earthquake are shown being transferred to new temporary homes, where two cubs named Ping-Ping and An-An are born, grow up, play with the workers and are then returned to their homes in the wilder reserves. Four months after the earthquake panda tourism was back at near-peak numbers in the least-affected areas. And on the first-year anniversary of the quake, the province handed out to tourists $1.9 million of special "panda cards" for discounts and free entry to attractions.

Conservationists have been equally adroit at using the panda in their Sisyphean struggle to protect and expand China's wild habitat. In the name of saving the endangered panda, Chinese conservationists have convinced the government to set aside hundreds of thousands of acres of land, closing them off to logging and development to make safe homes for monkeys, wild goats like the golden Takin goat-antelope and thousands of bird species. They reverted back to their wilderness state in the mountainous regions of Sichuan, even in areas that had been heavily logged. In a few years clean water was running through the valleys, flowering plants and shrubs grew back, and the air was fresh. The forests began to resemble the exotic woods described by Marco Polo centuries ago with their golden pheasants. Part of the unspoken bargain for creating and keeping these reserves was opening up areas for tourism.

Just before I left Beijing to join Bill in Shanghai, I attended a panda photo exhibit with Zhang Mei. Her WildChina company has several tours into panda reserves and contributes to their preservation—part of her sustainable-tourism program. Xiang Ding Qian, a park ranger at the Changqing Nature Reserve in Shaanxi, spent seven years taking color photographs of the wild, shy bears, capturing them swinging through trees in the snow and waddling through bamboo forests in the summer. A visit to the Chengdu panda reserve has become an essential part of most foreigners' tours of China.

Nana was our tour guide in Chengdu. A moon-faced young woman in her early twenties living with her mother, Nana said she had no interest in politics. She loves movies and considers Denzel Washington the world's best actor. She said she loved fashion and wore a pink leatherlike jacket with form-fitting gray pants and an organza gray scarf with pink polka dots. She had no real memory of Deng Xiaoping and knew little of the Cultural Revolution. She was the exact opposite of Lin Xi.

Yet Nana, too, introduced herself to us by telling us her life story, which took no time at all. Then she went straight to a business proposition. "You are going to the Panda Reserve tomorrow. For one hundred seventy dollars you can hold a baby panda. Cash only in American dollars, no Chinese yuan, no credit cards."

After our night at the opera it was easy to pass on this offer. Nana tried again, saying how happy people were to hold the panda babies. We still declined. That night, when we asked to eat at an authentic local Sichuan restaurant, she found us a great one nearby and then walked there with us to insure we ordered correctly.

The next day as we crawled through the thick traffic of Chengdu—a city of 14 million people in one of the more industrialized areas of central China—Nana said she had studied two years at a government tourism school and passed the government exam, which is largely based on memorization: what to tell the tourists about the history of the region, the customs, the sayings and the areas of cultural interest.

She told us what they were instructed to say about the people of Chengdu: "We are like the pandas—we enjoy life and we are lazy and we like to eat. We like to go to teahouses and sit and talk all day."

Then she told us she had a new offer for our panda visit that morning. We could now pay in Chinese yuan and with new, lower prices: 500 yuan to clean a panda cage and 1,000 yuan to hold a Panda baby. We said no again.

The Chengdu Research Base of Giant Panda Breeding resembles Central Park given over to pandas. The walkways through the forest are lined with open-air enclosures for panda teenagers rolling around gnawing on bamboo like it was sugarcane; for adult pandas sitting like Buddhas in the thicket, their backs turned to the humans yelling at them; and the Moonlit Nursery House, enclosed pens where dozens of miniature-size baby pandas were sleeping in giant cribs, some in the arms of humans willing to pay $170 to cuddle them.

It was remarkable to see pandas climbing on gymnastic equipment made to look like a forest; pandas swinging on old tires; pandas hugging the legs of their keepers; pandas wrestling each other in one big ball of black and white fur. Yes, the air was as polluted as it had been in Xian. And the crowds grew throughout the morning until everyone was jostling at the low fence to get the best snapshots. Everyone seemed happy to be in such a predicament. Who knows if it is tourist propaganda, but pandas do make people smile.

This panda reserve in the Chengdu suburbs is just the first stop for a true panda aficionado. A popular two-week panda tour includes visits to the Wolong Reserve, the Wanglang Reserve and a valley even farther north near Tibet, with treks in the wilderness as well as enclosed panda viewings. Instead, we opted for the Buddhist tourism trail, beginning with our stay in the Buddha Zen Hotel in Chengdu's historic district.

Set in a side street near the 1,000-year-old Wenshuyuan Buddhist Temple, the hotel had the smell of a 1930s Chinese melodrama, with small rooms portioned off by sliding doors. A Buddha statue adorned with flowers sits in the entry, perfumed by burning incense sticks. An inner courtyard with a small Zen garden muffled the city noise. There wasn't a single European-style stuffed chair in sight—only comfortable Asian wooden chairs and stools around tables. A group of young cartoonists from Malaysia were standing around a large tablet left in the lobby for calligraphy, laughing. They were taking turns dipping the brushes into an ink stone to draw silly portraits of each other.

Our room had a balcony overlooking a quiet side street. The neighborhood was a mixture of new shops in old storefronts and colonial-era clubs and homes with gardens hidden behind an old walled community. The Wenshuyuan Buddhist Temple complex had been returned to a house of worship, with Buddhist faithful wearing designer jeans praying and consulting with monks draped in deep scarlet robes.

I asked the concierge whether our hotel dated from the 1920s or the 1930s. Her answer was "It was built five years ago."

"This is a new hotel?" I asked, clearly disappointed. She answered, yes, but it was built according to the old traditions. By this time, I wasn't sure that it mattered. Finding a reasonable facsimile of an old-style Chinese inn—not a grandiose theme park version of a Tang palace—was enough for me. The promises and the deep paradox of tourism in China that advertises itself as one of the world's oldest civilizations was captured in this country's impulse to tear down its old buildings and replace a few of them with replicas.

It rained the next day, clean sheets of rain for the entire two-hour drive to the Leshan Giant Buddha. We passed long stretches of rice paddies with stucco farm homes built around courtyards, interrupted by another stretch of factories sending billowing smoke in the air. Then another stretch of green rice fields, tethered goats, fish ponds and white herons flying overhead until a series of large billboard advertisements blocked the view. We arrived at the city of Leshan and made our way to the river.

Registered as a UNESCO World Heritage Site, the Buddha was carved into a rock cliff along the river sometime in the eighth century. Now a major tourist site, the government has spent over $5 million to repair the Buddha and its surroundings. We were in a group of Chinese tourists and hopped on a government motorboat tour. As the boat pulled out, Bill and I stayed on deck. Within five minutes the truly giant Buddha came in view; it is described as the largest in the world. The Buddha was carved sitting as if on a chair—not in the traditional lotus position—giving him a stiff appearance that matched his height of 233 feet. The boat sputtered past him and then turned around, idling directly in front of the statue. The young women hostesses announced on the loudspeaker that for a fee they would take special photographs of the passengers. Many did line up to be photographed looking as if they were praying to Lord Buddha. Then we were driven back to the quay. The tour lasted exactly thirty minutes. Bill said that the trip was "a long run for a short slide."

It was also another example of how the UNESCO heritage brand can so easily become a kiss of death, transforming a cultural landmark into a tourist trap. Good for tourism business, not for the monument.

• • •

When Bill and I were flying home to Washington—a fourteen-hour journey—I realized that no other country has affected me like China. It is hard to fathom how much of the future of the world's tourism industry is in the hands of the Chinese. With its pastiche of official top-down control over tourism, its nascent bottom-up entrepreneurship, the built-in corruption and mandatory propaganda lessons, China is hardly a model for a business that protects and enhances locations and provides a steady, above-board profit.

Part of the short-term logic behind the model is the sheer number of tourists coming and going to China; especially since the government has given "Golden Weeks" of paid vacation to its population of 1.37 billion and a directive to them to see the world. The other foundation is China's basic economic model. The Chinese penchant for tearing down the old to be replaced by "anywhere" architecture or ersatz "olde China" fuels growth in that system, but it also diminishes the country's long-term appeal to tourists.

Then there is the pollution. It is a health problem and a symptom of the wide environmental damage wrought by China's industrialization. Tourism can't be neutral in the face of the polluted air, water and landscape that Deng had predicted; while Marriott and WildChina have offset programs, they are symbolic of what needs to be done rather than a solution. The speed and size of tourism's growth makes it difficult to imagine how the industry will reduce rather than exacerbate the problems. While tourism officials argue that in the new world, everyone has a right to travel, China presents you with a vivid picture of what happens if that travel isn't well managed with the future in mind.

The Chinese government's tourism policy has succeeded in several ways. Tourism has helped spread the image of China as a new, modern nation. Compared to the draconian image of Communist days, China appears open to tourists who speak no Chinese and have three weeks at best to traverse this continent-size nation. They don't notice the plainclothes policemen patrolling Tiananmen Square for potential dissidents or understand the tight political and cultural censorship. They do not use the Chinese Internet and have no idea of the severe censorship that blocks entire websites with anything critical of China—all in the name of "harmony." Nor do they see routine police arrests, without warrants, of dissidents and protesters . . . the list is long.

And the Chinese government has realized its other goal during this long period of experimentation and is making handsome profits, as Deng also predicted, but those are difficult to trace.

The stakes are equally high for foreign countries that are counting on the Chinese tourists to improve their business futures by traveling abroad in great numbers and spending equally large sums of money. As Jonathan Tourtellot of *National Geographic* said, "If the Chinese get it right—if they figure out the right balance—then tourism is great. If the Chinese get it wrong, we're all cooked."

PART SIX

THE OLD GIANT

USA

The classic tourist view from the Lincoln Memorial
to the Washington Monument

12

AMERICA THE EXCEPTIONAL

When the Becker family took its first vacation west of the Missouri River, my father plotted our itinerary around visits to national parks. We left our old home in western Iowa and drove from park to park, like a game of hopscotch, heading toward our new home in Seattle, Washington. The Badlands were our first stop. That endless moonscape of sharp, jagged buttes, dizzying rock spires and cliffs was my introduction to wilderness. There wasn't a town or farm or house as far as you could see—a revelation, since we six Becker children had spent our entire lives on the tamed Iowa prairie. Climbing and falling and pushing each other on the cliffs, we enacted our version of "cowboys and Indians." Then it was back in the car and the Black Hills. We made the obligatory stop at Mount Rushmore, which was a shrine, not an adventure.

Farther down the road, we saw them: the magic of buffaloes. Their heads and horns were enormous. They were shaggy, frightening and familiar, dark buffaloes come to life, pawing the ground, running in herds and kicking up dust. The whole Black Hills were straight out of the western movies, except the greens were deeper, the sky higher and the lakes mirror-clear, reflecting the clouds.

Our powder-blue Buick managed the long stretches, then the twists and turns from the Dakotas across to Wyoming and Yellowstone National Park. We arrived when it was already dark, pitch black, since there were only stars to light the way, and we checked into a log cabin for the night. When we woke up, we were in another world. An entirely other world: snowcapped mountains, evergreen forests, thundering streams, the Old Faithful Geyser that smelled of rotten eggs, hidden valleys, wild animals—bears and more bison—yellow wildflowers on the trails. Decades later I still remember shivering with excitement taking my first gulp of pure, sharp mountain air.

Later, after we had crossed the spine of the northern Rocky Mountains, I woke up from a nap in the backseat and stared at this remarkable billboard. "What's that advertisement about?" I asked. "Where?" said my mother. I pointed directly ahead, and the rest of the family burst out laughing. I was staring at Mount Rainier, its snow cap pink from the setting sun, rising so high with such grand, majestic proportions that my brain couldn't believe it could be real. Forever after, Mount Rainier has been my favorite national park.

Most American and many foreign families have a story like ours about a wondrous vacation at a national park. The U.S. National Park System is a gift to Americans, to the world, and to tourism. National parks are at the top of the list of reasons why visitors love the United States. We invented some of the greatest ideas for recreation, and they've been copied worldwide. The U.S. National Park System inspired the parks in Africa and South America.

Disneyland ushered in the era of modern theme parks now popular in Europe and Asia. Las Vegas was one of the original made-for-entertainment cities. New York is in a class by itself; Times Square is the center of entertainment, business, fashion, the media, publishing, theater—every creative impulse in the modern world. The United States gave birth to airplanes, led the way in air travel, modernized hotel chains, the "experience economy" for travel—the list is endless.

Yet even with some of the most extraordinary landscapes and sophisticated cities in the world, as well as one of the most vibrant cultures; with states like California that are the equivalent of a country, from the northern redwood forests to San Francisco and the wine regions, down to Los Angeles, Hollywood and Disneyland; foreigners no longer flock to the United States. In the last decade, as travel and tourism became the world's favorite pastime, the number of international visitors to the United States has flattened; it hasn't gone up or down.

The United States lost out on the tourism explosion. The numbers tell the story. In the first decade of the twenty-first century, travel and tourism grew by 52.1 percent worldwide. Few other businesses can match that. Yet, the United States dropped in popularity, its number of visitors barely budged, increasing by only 1.5 percent. Things were slightly better on the money side of the ledger. The foreign visitors increased spending from $82 billion to $103 billion in the same period. Over all, though, the United States' share of the world market had dropped so steeply that France grabbed the top spot as the most popular destination in the world.

The reasons for this decline center on America's ambivalence toward the government's role in travel and tourism, which is tied to the general attitude toward governance.

American leaders have traditionally resisted centralized federal planning as is done in Europe and Asia. Many American politicians believe that such planned economies stifle individual endeavors. Instead, American lawmakers are freelancers, examining issues and passing laws often in isolation, on their own merits, without fully considered regard for a policy's impact in the larger scheme of government. (The one exception is defense policy, which has a four-year planning and budget process.) While the governments of the other top tourism nations accept their role in organizing, regulating and promoting tourism, the United States does not. Other governments have websites in multiple languages to help foreigners plan their visits; the United States did not until 2012.

The United States is just as ambivalent about its own citizens' role as tourists. It is also the only wealthy nation that does not require employers to give their workers a paid vacation. In contrast, more than two dozen wealthy nations like Canada, Japan, New Zealand and most western European nations offer at least two weeks and as many as five. It is the law.

In the United States a series of political decisions enmeshed in both partisan politics and then the overwhelming response to the September 11, 2001, attacks had unforeseen consequences that sent travel and tourism plummeting. For the last decade American politicians have been reluctant to scale back the barriers erected to heighten security after 9/11, which in turn have had a negative impact on foreign travel to the United States.

The industry struggled along, pleading with the government for recognition, lobbying Congress and contributing to campaign funds of politicians, just like other industries and interests. Some individual companies or sectors have kept their influence in Congress; the cruise industry is the prime example. But overall, the industry has had to rethink how it will do business in the United States in the future. They've come up with both enterprising and surprising answers. Medical tourism is one of the new markets they have carved out as the cost of medical care and medical insurance rose in the United States and sent Americans scurrying for help. Mostly, though, the American industry shifted its attention overseas, to countries whose governments were actively promoting tourism. China is the main focus for hotel chains, and increasingly, for casinos. The Disney empire is a power unto itself. And individual states and cities have risen to the challenge of promoting themselves without significant federal help. Throughout, the question of regulating the industry is embroiled in the larger partisan debate in Congress.

Finally in 2012, President Barack Obama put into effect some of the new policies that the industry had requested, helping to continue its recovery. That is the complex story of American tourism in the twenty-first century.

Representative Connie Morella, a Republican from a suburban Maryland county in the Washington, D.C., area, lost her seat in Congress in 2002. She had been a member for sixteen years and was rewarded for her service by President George W. Bush, a fellow Republican, with her appointment as the U.S. ambassador to the Organisation for Economic Co-operation and Development, an international organization of some of the world's wealthiest countries, headquartered in Paris.

She arrived in 2003 with high hopes. While she expected to find herself at odds with fellow member countries during some of the debates—that was part of the job description—she felt she knew her party well and could reasonably support her country's positions. And she was ambassador from 2003 through 2007 when the U.S. war in Iraq was heavily criticized by some of the more prominent member nations, including France.

One issue, though, puzzled her. When budget reviews were underway and money had to be cut, her instructions from Washington were singular. Reduce or eliminate the money for tourism research.

Tourism was the last issue Ambassador Morella considered a flash point on the diplomatic agenda. But the other member nations put a high premium on their tourism industries; not only as critical for their economies but requiring precise coordination and regulation by their governments, which in turn meant serious up-to-date research.

The United States not only disagreed with that position but actively tried to undermine it. She told me that every time the OECD budget came up for a vote, her instructions from Washington were: take money out of the tourism research account. The instructions were routine as clockwork, she told me.

"The United States consistently puts tourism as a low priority but the other countries would never allow those budget cuts. Tourism was too important to them," said Ambassador Morella. "That is one of the few positions I didn't understand. Tourism is so important, especially in the nation's capital. Why wouldn't we support it?"

The answer to that question stretches back to the federal system, which divided the role of government between the states and the central government. When Americans started traveling for leisure in the early twentieth century, they mostly visited other parts of their continent-size country. The individual states took charge of promoting and then regulating tourism. After World War II, as tourism flourished, Florida advertised itself as the "Sunshine State." Virginia named itself the state for lovers. And New York State used the song "I Love New York" to appeal to tourists. That Chamber of Commerce approach worked in the early years, and tourism became a serious industry in nearly every state and the District of Columbia. The industry was divided about the desirability of more centralized federal coordination; many were happy to leave responsibility at the state level.

In 1961 the federal government created the U.S. Travel and Tourism Administration within the Department of Commerce, to mixed reviews. Republicans, and some Democrats, wondered why tourism should be promoted at all. Despite a big cut in its budget in 1977, the tourism administration reached a modus vivendi with Congress and established its presence to promote U.S. tourism overseas through its own offices and in coordination with U.S. embassies abroad.

The partisan showdown began in 1995 when the Republicans became the new majority in the House of Representatives and selected Newt Gingrich as their Speaker of the House. Gingrich issued a "Contract with America" during his election campaign that promised to reduce government spending and reduce the size of government itself. As the new Speaker, he picked many targets; he saw government's role in tourism as a candidate to be done away with. It was one of numerous direct challenges to the policies of the Democrats in Congress and especially those of the Democratic President Bill Clinton.

The president and his vice president, Al Gore, had been keen on creating what they called "smart" government, using new technologies, especially the computer and the evolving Internet that they said promised vastly improved performance at cost savings. (Gore was the champion of this geek approach.) Tourism was on their list of industries to be enhanced by "smart" technology, and in October 1995 the president held the first White House Conference on Travel and Tourism. He invited 1,700 American leaders of the industry that was responsible for adding $417 billion to the national economy in 1994.

The White House conference was built around a new public-private strategy for tourism timed to take advantage of the 1996 Summer Olympics in Atlanta, Georgia. The administration wanted to follow the example of Spain, which had profited from heavy promotion of the 1992 Summer Olympics in Barcelona, lifting tourism to that country. But the United States was the only country of any significance without a nationally coordinated tourist program or a top-echelon tourism agency. The White House conference was geared to kick-start the industry through government help.

President Clinton opened the event with a thirty-minute address, first telling his audience that it was "about time" that their industry was honored with a White House event. The crowd cheered and gave the president a standing ovation. Then Clinton spoke of the particular moment in history as a "very important time."

"This industry holds much promise for the future of America. It has a lot to teach us as Americans as we stand at the dawn of a new era, moving from an industrial age to one that will be dominated by technology and information and our ability to relate to one another," he said. "We've moved at a breathtaking pace from the divided world of the cold war to a global village. And we know that trade and tourism and travel, all these things are tailor-made for what we do well and what the 21st Century will value."

He recited the impressive economic achievements of U.S. travel and tourism: the second-largest employer in the U.S.; adding $22 billion to the country's trade surplus in 1994; and $78 billion spent by foreign visitors that same year. He took credit for his administration's first projects to help tourism: a special commission that helped to revitalize the airline companies and an overhaul of the Federal Aviation Administration to modernize and update its equipment and technology.

"As the circle of freedom expands around the globe, the tourism industry will keep growing all around the world," he predicted.

Then he warned that tourism would not be without its problems: questions would be raised about safety from terrorism; how to keep the air and water clean so that the environment would be welcoming to tourists; how to target specific foreign tourists like the (wealthy) Japanese to visit the United States; and how to smooth the way at the border for legal visitors to feel welcome and not be hampered by unnecessary bureaucratic hurdles.

Then he outlined his new strategy for tourism aimed at increasing the number of international tourists, according the industry a greater voice in policy-making, and improve infrastructure. He closed with a reminder that the Atlanta Summer Olympics would be the proving grounds for this new public-private cooperation. "Billions of people will be watching Atlanta," he said. "I want to be sure we have done all we could so that these people have a deep, yearning desire to come to America."

Once again the audience was on its feet, clapping. Finally the tourism industry would receive the respect it deserved. The strategy called for private industry to work with the government, which would collect data showing tourism's economic power; promote the United States as the "international destination of choice"; and once foreign visitors were here, to insure that they would have "an experience second to none."

Gingrich, a representative from Georgia, would not be deterred. He pushed through Congress a budget that essentially zeroed out the tourism office. On the eve of the 1996 Summer Olympics in Atlanta, the United States essentially abolished the thirty-five-year-old tourism administration in the Department of Commerce along with most of its work in U.S. embassies. Greg Farmer, the undersecretary of commerce for travel and tourism who was overseeing the effort said: "It's an absolute outrage that we're not promoting ourselves during the Olympics."

Farmer's job was abolished along with the travel administration; a tourism office was reconfigured within Commerce as a smaller agency largely concerned with gathering travel and tourism statistics. Representative Toby Roth, Republican of Wisconsin, who was cochairman of the congressional caucus on travel and tourism, accurately predicted the outcome of his party's move to abolish the travel office without a true alternative. "Our share of the world market will keep dropping."

The United States also withdrew from the U.N. tourism agency in 1996. When the agency was elevated to full-fledged status as the U.N. World Tourism Organization in 2003, the United States refused to rejoin, citing budget pressures. Under the cloud of the Republican mandate, all meetings of the Tourism Policy Council were suspended, ending the confab that brought together the secretaries of major government departments like Transportation, Interior, Labor, and Housing and Urban Development to coordinate policies to enhance tourism. In advance of the White House conference, the TPC had created a system for coordinating the thirty federal agencies that affect travel and tourism—the first such system.

Among the unanswered questions was, why did the Republican Party single out tourism at such a pivotal moment when the government was finally coordinating a single coherent policy to take advantage of the phenomenal growth in travel, which was the second-largest employer in the country, the largest service export, and which contributed 6 percent directly to the country's GDP? For instance, the Republicans left unchallenged funding for agriculture that continues to receive multibillion-dollar subsidies, and the official charged with promoting trade merited a cabinet-level position. But the Republican resistance to a government role in tourism has held, as Ambassador Morella discovered in Paris ten years later.

That first White House conference on tourism turned out to be the last. Tourism was tarnished by partisan politics and became shorthand for the Republican Party's insistence that government get out of business affairs. President Clinton's only consolation was that his predictions about the promise of tourism and the perils proved prescient.

Then terrorists struck on September 11, 2001, commandeering commercial airplanes and flying them into the World Trade Center Towers in New York, the Pentagon in suburban Washington and a field in Pennsylvania. The attacks changed American and government attitudes for the next decade. It was the first time since Pearl Harbor that foreigners had attacked the United States. (American terrorists had blown up the Alfred P. Murrah Federal Building in Oklahoma City in 1995, killing 168 people.) With new laws and policies the administration of President George W. Bush built a fierce protective ring around the country, a fortress America.

Barriers to entry went up in the form of new requirements for visas; extensive questioning and often searches at airports and land borders; and the construction of a 14-foot-high wall dividing much of the United States from Mexico. The country united in an understandable instinct to protect the country after 9/11. However, the new barriers seemed to grow out of proportion and fueled a debate that went far beyond the United States.

Naturally tourism, the one business that depended on foreigners visiting the country, was knocked flat. Already weakened from the end of government help in coordinating and promoting tourism overseas, the American travel and tourism industry suffered collateral damage of major proportions after 9/11: $94 billion in lost revenue in the first five years after the attack and 200,000 lost jobs.

I was a correspondent in the Washington bureau of the *New York Times* on September 11 and was reassigned to cover the aftermath and the new Department of Homeland Security. In those early months and years, as the country debated whether to go to war with Iraq, the morality and legality of the use of torture, and where to imprison or try suspected terrorists, I do not remember a single moment of thought given to tourism. It would have seemed almost irreverent, if not irrelevant, in the atmosphere of imminent danger that enveloped the country after the attacks.

For three days after the attack, all aircraft, including commercial flights, were grounded. (It was a rare moment when the skies cleared across the United States and scientists were able to measure how much pollution was caused by air travel. The temperature was improved by over 1 degree centigrade in only three days—"from a climate perspective that is huge," said David Travis, a professor at the University of Wisconsin, Whitewater, who tracks vapor trails from aircraft and published his team's findings in *Nature*.)

Once commercial flights were back in the air, the routine for inspecting passengers changed dramatically. It was part of what President Bush declared was a "War on Terrorism." Congress, in near-unanimous votes, expanded federal powers and spent billions of federal dollars to prevent other criminals from attacking targets in the United States. One obvious focus of attention was screening passengers, since the hijackers had commandeered commercial airplanes and used them as missiles.

A five-year-long trend of easing entry to countries around the world came to an abrupt end in the United States. To protect the country from future attacks the Bush administration created the Department of Homeland Security. With a budget of $50 billion, it became the largest new department since the New Deal of President Franklin D. Roosevelt. Included in the department was a new Transportation Security Administration responsible for screening passengers and luggage at U.S. commercial airports.

The TSA is enormous. It employs over 43,000 screeners, more employees than the Departments of Labor, and Housing and Urban Development, combined. And those screeners are charged with examining identification papers, airline tickets and luggage of everyone boarding an airplane in the United States. Thrown together quickly, the TSA has become a lightning rod for complaints about its methods of screening, dictated by the government. When combined with a tightening-up of visa requirements by the State Department, the new policies have had an unanticipated and profoundly unwelcome impact on tourism.

During the first five years of the new policies that began in late 2001, the number of foreign visitors to the United States plunged by 17 percent. That drop translated into $94 billion in lost revenue as well as $16 billion in tax revenue. In other words, more foreign tourists visited the United States in 1997 than in 2007. At the same time, record numbers of foreign tourists traveled the globe, increasing at a 5 percent annual rate from 682 million to 898 million.

The American tourism industry started to worry about this "lost decade."

"For sixty years what had determined whether people traveled was the economy; after September 11 we knew that wasn't the case," said Geoff Freeman, the chief operating officer of the U.S. Travel Association, the trade group that represents the travel and tourism industry. There were all kinds of rumors about the source of the problem: foreigners were afraid to travel in the United States, or they were angry about the American war in Iraq and the American xenophobia from well-publicized stunts like changing the name of French fries to freedom fries.

To understand the problem, the travel association conducted a survey to find out why foreign tourists were staying away. The answer proved simple and unambiguous and had nothing to do with geopolitics. The would-be tourists were furious about the difficulty they now faced getting a visa to the United States and the treatment they received once they arrived at an American airport. Tourists were questioned on arrival in minute detail about why they wanted to visit. "Rude," "disrespectful," and "annoying" were some of the better words used to describe their treatment, according to the survey. Foreigners not only did not feel welcome; they felt they had to prove they were innocent of unmentioned tendencies, to border guards who acted as if every foreigner could be the next terrorist. In short order the United States was taken off millions of tourist lists.

The evidence of that finding was plentiful in foreign newspapers and websites confirming the worst. Travel to the United States meant a "spirit-crushingly frosty reception," according to an article in the London *Sunday Times* entitled "Travel to America? No Thanks."

"A preflight interrogation, epic queues at immigration, thin-lipped questioning from aggressive border guards and an outside chance of a rubber-gloved rectal rummage are all part of the fun," the article continued.

The *Guardian* of London printed an article in its Travel section in February 2008 with the headline "America—More Hassle Than It's Worth?" The writer, Ed Vulliamy, described new requirements for entering the United States and asked: ". . . for us travellers, it means that the already onerous task of getting to America will be complicated to a point that makes Italy seem an even more attractive option. Who the hell wants to apply online for permission to visit the US before even buying a ticket?"

The article was so popular it elicited 9,155 responses in four days that covered 36 printed pages before the comments were closed down. The last entry was representative: "I think there's a poetic justice lurking behind the new flight security measures demanded by the U.S. administration, and all the other American efforts to protect themselves from the inevitable. What they achieve mainly is to further isolate the Americans from the human beings on this planet. Everybody wins."

The British had already voted with their feet against travel to the United States. Instead of hitting the high spots of America, the British had increased their visits to India by 102 percent, to Turkey by 82 percent and to New Zealand by 106 percent. The rantings on the Internet were the tip of the iceberg.

Travel blogs were replete with stories from travelers of other nationalities unwilling to put up with the indignities and humiliation that they say is part of travel to the United States. German tourists even compared the U.S.-built wall along the Mexican border to the Berlin Wall, with the Americans cast in the role of the East Germans.

Tourists also expressed the fear that one small slip-up could land them in jail. The story of Rick Giles, a tourist from Canterbury, New Zealand, ricocheted around the Internet. Mr. Giles had spent six weeks in jail in Detroit for mistakenly overstaying his visa by six days in July 2007. When he was finally released, he was deported home, where he told the local newspaper that at first he thought the confusion was "amusing.

"But after a week that went away. I felt angry and closed in and that lasted the rest of my time there."

Another visa victim whose fame spread across the Internet was Valeria Vinnikova, a young German woman and star squash player who landed in jail for misreading the expiration date for her visitor's permit. She had come to the United States to see her fiancé, Hansi Wiens, the squash coach at Dartmouth College. When she asked for a renewal, officials at the border station in Maine discovered the mistake, handcuffed her, shackled her ankles and took her to jail with the intention of deporting her. The squash community was up in arms; a Vermont public radio station, newspapers, and local protests as well as high-powered lawyers hired by Mr. Wiens convinced the Department of Homeland Security that Ms. Vinnikova could be released. She and Mr. Wiens did marry, and as Valeria Wiens, she was the top Dartmouth woman squash player in the 2010–2011 season.

Most of the uproar over these ham-fisted violations was coming from countries with the wealthiest tourists. The tourism industry's study confirmed that the tourists avoiding the United States were those who were the highest spenders. After the new security policies were imposed, there was a 20.7 percent drop in German tourists, a 19.2 percent drop in French tourists, a 7.6 percent drop in British tourists, and a 23.3 percent drop in Japanese tourists.

These foreigners still took vacations, but to China, India and Turkey, or to Morocco and Brazil, and in record numbers. The decline in the value of the dollar in the last year has helped attract more European visitors, happy to take advantage of the bargain-basement prices for an American vacation, and helping bring tourism back to the level reached before the attacks. But half of the tourists traveling to the United States came from Canada and Mexico, visitors who on average spend about one-tenth of what other foreign tourists spend.

For the foreigners who needed a visa to visit the United States, the frustration was the highest. After the September 11 attacks, the United States required would-be tourists to be interviewed in person at an American embassy or consulate, which in continent-size countries like Russia can pose a significant burden. Russians often had to travel over 1,000 miles to be interviewed with no promise of a visa. The wait for an interview appointment could be months long. In India and Brazil two months' wait for an interview was routine. China had a similar backlog. In Singapore it was over one month. This was for all travel: an essential business trip or a honeymoon in Hawaii. All of that pales in comparison to what was required of men from Muslim-majority countries. They had to fill out questionnaires with details about people they planned to see, their relatives and their bank accounts, besides supplying photographs and being fingerprinted.

This new policing of the American border stood in stark contrast to the opening of borders across Europe, Asia and Africa; with the growing sophistication of the Internet, some countries approve visas online. It was as if the United States was closing off its border, with ramifications far beyond the travel and tourism industry.

In 2008 the State Department added new requirements for visas but promised to reduce to one month the average time it took to process a request. In addition, most visa applicants were newly required to be fingerprinted through a biometric finger scan. Susan Jacobs, the senior policy advisor for the State Department's Bureau of Consular Affairs during the Bush administration, said the travel industry was complaining too much. "We're not in the business of encouraging tourism," she told me. "These are small irritations, but once people get used to them it won't be an irritation at all," she said.

Ambassador Jacobs said the government had created a "secure process where people are treated properly" and where they know what to expect. But a visa did not mean automatic entry. "The way the law is written, a visa is only permission to apply for entry at a point of entry. That means we can turn away a visitor. Even Americans are checked when they come back," she said.

No one—not the Secretary of Homeland Security or the lowly airport inspection officer—wanted to be blamed for allowing a terrorist into the country.

Many American foreign service officers disagreed with Ambassador Jacobs but had to do so anonymously. One diplomat told me that the new visa policies were undermining support for the United States. He said: "Tourists are the best public diplomats, period. Like clockwork, they fall in love with a country on a visit no matter what their previous views. They go home and say how wonderful the U.S. is. Not anymore. More and more aren't coming. We've lost all of that good will."

The 2007 survey revealing foreign attitudes changed the travel industry's view of government policies. "Now, instead of being neutral, the government is putting obstacles in the path of our industry," said Freeman.

"Homeland Security seems to be asking: 'how do we discourage people from traveling today?' The travel industry thought that the government would roll back some of the security measures. It didn't happen. Among us, this has been a wake-up call."

His group hired Tom Ridge, the first Secretary of Homeland Security, to plead their case for "reasonable and efficient" changes at the border to make visitors feel welcome. Ridge had been an affable but largely figurehead secretary in office; President Bush's inner sanctum had made all of the national security decisions, which he then carried out. As an outside lobbyist, he could not make a dent in the iron curtain drawn around the protocols and decisions at the airports and borders that were driving away the most desirable tourists. Ridge did not stay very long with the group.

The Bush administration created an advisory board on tourism in 2005 composed of industry titans, including J. W. Marriott, Jr., chairman and chief executive of Marriott International, and Glenn Tilton, chairman and chief executive of UAL Corporation, the parent company of United Air Lines. But the board failed to convince the administration on most issues. So after quietly accepting the status quo, the industry group switched their strategy and lobbied hard to get the government back into promoting tourism. Top executives from the Travel Business Roundtable, Walt Disney Parks and Resorts, the Air Transport Association and InterContinental Hotels Group, among others, appeared before Congress to ask for help to combat the wave of negative feelings about visiting the U.S. with policies to promote a positive image and win back foreign tourists.

Several members of Congress listened and wrote legislation to create an Office of Travel Promotion within the Department of Commerce headed by an undersecretary for travel promotion. The bill also would create a public-private promotion program run by a board or representatives from industry, the states, the federal government, and higher education. The program would not only advertise U.S. tourism to foreign audiences but also "correct misperception overseas regarding U.S. travel policies."

It still didn't work. The administration of President George W. Bush said no. In a letter to Congress, a Bush administration official wrote that it "believes that tourism promotion activities should be financed and undertaken by the private sector and, where they desire, by states and local governments." The administration also opposed any elevation of tourism in the Commerce Department, saying that "travel and tourism sector issues are already well served within (Commerce's) existing structure."

Shortly after that rejection I met Freeman at his office and asked about his achievements after several years of trying to break through to the Bush administration. "Achievements—holding off the worst, trying to change the atmosphere from policing foreigners to welcoming them," he answered.

Isabel Hill, the deputy director of that small Office of Travel and Tourism Industries within the Commerce Department, said she could understand why the tourist industry is concerned. But, she said, the tide did begin to turn, slightly, in 2007, when revenue from tourism returned to pre-September 11 levels of $1.2 trillion.

Hill told me that the 2007 letter rejecting the tourism bill meant that her office had no mandate for marketing or promoting the United States to foreign tourists through a national tourism website or even information from U.S. embassies overseas. "I'm not against the idea," she said. "Personally, I see the case for a brand advertising campaign. There is also a case to be made for the administration's position."

As part of its retrenching, the industry took stock of where it stood. In a report called "The Lost Decade" that essentially covered the Bush administration, from 2000 through the end of 2008, the U.S. travel and tourism industry had lost 68 million visitors; $509 billion in spending revenue; 441,000 jobs; $270 billion in trade surplus and $32 billion in tax revenue.

Then in 2009, Barack Obama, a Democrat, was inaugurated as president. At first, the industry was disappointed with the new president and his response to the 2008 recession. His stimulus package failed to mention their industry and suggested cutting back on business travel. Every major tourism trade group signed on to an emergency cry for help: "We are extremely concerned about the unintended consequences of unnecessarily restricting corporate meetings, events and incentive travel programs."

Valerie Jarrett, senior advisor to President Obama, invited thirteen industry leaders to the White House to meet with her and Lawrence Summers, an economic advisor to the President. The group had just settled in when, to their surprise, the president walked in. "We had no idea he was coming," said Freeman.

The president shook hands all around and said he understood why they were concerned.

Bill Marriott, chairman and CEO of Marriott International as well as the unofficial éminence grise of tourism in Washington, was the first to speak for the group. He explained that they were concerned about the drop in international visitors as well as the downturn in business travel for meetings and events since the president encouraged cutbacks on travel. Now, they were asking the president to become their ally.

Much of the conversation required stripping travel of its emotional power, all of the romance and pleasure, the discovery and freedom trumpeted in advertisements, and instead, have the president and his aides view it as they do one of the most important businesses in the country. "You could see the light go on," said Freeman. "Finally we were able to make our case that foreigners coming to the United States and spending money here would not cost the taxpayers a dime. That we weren't asking for a handout. It would be a free stimulus package. We wanted the president to encourage travel."

The president said he would not be able to do that but after the meeting he stopped arguing for a reduction. At the end of the meeting, Jonathan M. Tisch, chairman and CEO of Loews Hotels issued a statement saying, "We are pleased to have the support of President Obama and his team, and look forward to working with them in the days ahead."

A few months later President Obama lived through a searing moment when he came to understand the high cost of telling foreigners they are not welcome in the United States. His hometown of Chicago was one of the four finalists to host the 2016 Summer Olympics; the city had spent millions to prepare its bid. In October of 2009, President Obama and his wife Michelle traveled to Copenhagen to lobby for Chicago. The popular young couple was greeted as near-royalty in Europe, raising their confidence that Chicago would host the Olympics.

Then the president sat down with the Olympic delegates to argue their case. Some of the delegates said they doubted that all the Olympic athletes and foreign visitors would be allowed to enter the United States; and that those who did might be humiliated by the border guards. Syed Shahid Ali, a member of the International Olympic Committee from Pakistan, told Obama that, for many people, entering the United States can be "a rather harrowing experience." The president answered that the country would welcome visitors and told the committee: "One of the legacies I want to see coming out of 2016 is a reminder that America, at its best, is open to the world."

To everyone's surprise, Chicago was the first city cut from the list. Rio de Janeiro won over Madrid and Tokyo. For the first time, a South American country would host an Olympics. The president saw how, with the border and visa changes following 9/11, the United States had effectively eliminated itself from winning bids for international events like the Olympics. The world's fears about the United States border policies became public during Brazil's successful bid for the 2016 Summer Olympics.

President Obama had learned firsthand the effect of years of foreigners feeling humiliated at the hands of border inspectors that had made travel to the United States so unbearable for many. And he had failed his hometown in his first months as president. The industry saw an opening. "When IOC members are commenting to our President that foreign visitors find traveling to the United States a 'pretty harrowing experience,' we need to take seriously the challenge of reforming our entry process to ensure there is a welcome mat to our friends around the world, even as we ensure a secure system," said Roger Dow, the president of the U.S. Travel Association.

A few months later the president and the Democratic Congress came through for the industry. First, Congress passed the Travel Promotion Act in early 2010. Democrats were in control of the House and the Senate. Nevada's Harry Reid, the Senate majority leader, was tireless in promoting the legislation that his state, especially Las Vegas, saw as the foundation for its future. President Obama signed the bill in March 2010, stressing the importance of travel and its potential to help lift the country out of the recession. At the White House ceremony, Obama praised the members of Congress and industry leaders for "working on this for a very long time."

"Obviously we all believe America is the best place to travel," he said. "Our ability to highlight the incredible bounty of this country, the spectacular sights and scenery and people is something we should all be encouraging. With this bill we will."

The president was beginning to see travel in a different light. The new bill reversed over fifteen years of the federal government's refusal to play a role promoting the industry as nearly every other country does. Travel and tourism was winning back the political support it briefly enjoyed at the White House Conference in 1995.

The new act created a national website where foreigners could learn about tourist possibilities in the United States—state parks, music festivals, and beach holidays—and how to plan their trips, all in their own language. (To begin with, the site will be translated into French, Portuguese, Japanese and Chinese.) The country that literally invented the Internet and modern computing finally had a barebones national travel website a decade behind the rest of the world, but at least the United States was back in the game.

This new tourism website is underwritten by a new fee charged foreign tourists, not the American taxpayer. It took two years, but in May 2012, the Discover America website was in business. For the first time since the dawn of the computer age, foreigners could go to one website and find what the United States had to offer. No more guessing at things like the name of the national railroad (Amtrak).

With the door open this far, the industry pushed even harder. They were too close to their goal of catching up from that lost decade. Now the association lobbied for the last piece of the puzzle: to improve the visa process by making it easier to apply, and to reduce the waiting time for approval. Freeman explained why in basic business terms. "We always had a good product—the United States. With the website we had the ability to promote and market our product. But our customer still couldn't buy the product. They couldn't get a visa. What we needed was a streamlined, efficient, and safe, visa process."

The president's council on jobs and competitiveness had singled out tourism for its potential to create jobs and recommended a move on visas. Secretary of State Hillary Clinton made Thomas R. Nides, a deputy secretary and former executive at Morgan Stanley, her point man on the issue.

Nides spoke the same language as the tourism businessmen and he was an old friend of the Secretary; he had been a big fundraiser for her when she ran for president. A plan emerged to increase staff in consulates and embassies to work on visa applications, to streamline the process and to reduce the waiting time for visas to weeks rather than months.

The figures for granting tourism visas to the United States in growing markets such as Brazil and China improved by up to one-third. "Secretary Clinton put in charge someone who literally changed travel for us—Tom Nides was that important to us," said Freeman.

Proof of that effort was an announcement halfway across the world at the U.S. consulate in Shanghai. In one year the U.S. embassy and consulates in China had issued 800,000 visas, breaking previous records. U.S. Consul General Beatrice Camp marked the occasion by making a short speech at the visa office, standing before rows of Chinese waiting in seats for their turn for a visa interview. She told a few jokes, promised that the consulate was on its way to answering visa requests in a timely manner. And to celebrate she held a drawing for the people standing in line, giving away three free trips to Hawaii and Guam to the lucky winners.

By year's end, the State Department processed 46 percent more visa applications in China and 59 percent more in Brazil—the two countries whose wealthy middle class is itching to come to America. This was a sea change. Backlogs of visa applications were clearing out; a new attitude and process was being felt in U.S. consular offices. For many diplomats this was a welcome relief, since they believe that tourism does help relations between peoples. When she returned from Shanghai, I had lunch with Beatrice Camp, and she said it was one of her great joys to help Chinese see the United States with their own eyes. "Person-to-person diplomacy does work."

The government was picking up speed, expanding on the president's proposal to open up the country to tourism to create jobs.

During the 2012 presidential race the U.S. travel industry found itself in the unaccustomed position of getting everything it wanted. In January, President Obama showed up at Disney World in Orlando, Florida, where he joked about his big ears in the shadow of Mickey Mouse. He announced a committee to create a federal task force on tourism to attract millions more tourists to places like Florida, which would be an important state in the November elections.

In April he welcomed Brazilian President Dilma Rousseff to the White House and announced that the United States was opening two more consulates in Brazil to lure more tourists to the United States. Those planeloads arriving from the south, along with those coming to the United States from China, were seen as instant stimulus packages. On average, every Brazilian visiting the United States spent $5,400; every Chinese spent $6,243.

In May 2012, President Obama tied together his tourism initiatives into one 33-page-long National Travel and Tourism Strategy. "We want the world to know there has not been a better time to visit the U.S., and America is truly open for business," said John Bryson, Secretary of Commerce, in a telephone press conference.

The strategy is the first of its kind. It reverses nearly every policy instituted since 1996, when Newt Gingrich engineered the elimination of the U.S. Travel and Tourism Administration, and the policies of successive Republican officials who believed government did not belong in tourism. The strategy also addresses the steep drop in foreign tourism after September 11. It notes that the "security requirement instituted in the aftermath of the September 11, 2001 attacks, although effective at ensuring the safety of travelers and the nation may have contributed to an impression among some that the United States does not welcome international visitors."

New Yorkers who have to navigate through summer sidewalks crowded with foreign tourists may be skeptical about this claim of a dearth of visitors. As the government has reformed visa and border policies, New York City has seen tourism rise to over 10 million a year. (This is a city of 8 million.) Europeans have been known to fly into New York to scoop up bargains in the stores as well as party all night, and while they may not make up for the numbers of Europeans staying away, many New Yorkers think there are already too many.

The government promises to employ a dozen or more new "welcome strategies," from basic politeness at airports, to hiring people who speak foreign languages, to streamlining border inspections. The inability of

Americans to speak foreign languages is a perennial problem for the industry. And all of the federal government's efforts would be coordinated through a revived national travel and tourism office at the Department of Commerce.

Timed for peak summer travel season, the new strategy has immediate and long-range goals. Hopefully the new and diverse promotion campaigns would spread the word that the United States has reformed its ways and won't unduly harass foreigners at the border and that improvements in visa application procedures will convince the wary that the United States does want them to visit. By 2020, the United States wants 100 million foreigners to visit annually and to spend $250 billion while they are here, creating innumerable jobs and opportunities for Americans. By the time all of the more than fifty recommendations are put in place, involving the federal, state and local governments as well as private firms, that goal may not seem so outrageous.

To say that the industry was ecstatic would be no exaggeration. They would not have dared to ask for such a blueprint even one year earlier. Now they were handed this gold-plated promise that travel and tourism was being elevated to a national priority and that the economic recovery would depend on it. "The travel industry is very, very excited about this," said Roger Dow of the Travel Association. "We've been talking about this for sixteen years."

Those changes required nothing less than a ten-year distance from the September 11 attacks, the killing of Osama bin Laden in 2011 and the economic recession of 2008 to deflate the atmosphere of fear in order to open the way for the government to focus on jobs and rebuilding the United States.

In the world of partisan politics, enthusiasm for the policies of the Obama administration and other Democratic officials has yielded very mixed political and financial support for the Democratic Party. During the "lost decade" of the administration of President George W. Bush the industry reduced all campaign contributions. In the 2008 campaign Barack Obama received more than John McCain. For the 2012 campaign, the industry's contributions have split 54 to 45 in favor of Republican candidates over Democratic candidates, according to the Center for Responsive Politics, which tracks contributions.

Thanks to a few major donors, the travel industry has given the majority of its support to Republicans. During the primaries, the biggest money went to the man who had done the most to disappoint the industry. The campaign of Newt Gingrich, who as House Speaker forced the closing of the federal government's tourism office, received $21 million from the family of Sheldon Adelson, a casino magnate from Las Vegas. Adelson gave that enormous sum to a pro-Gingrich super PAC during the 2012 Republican presidential primary, saying Gingrich shared his strong support for Israel.

Gingrich was defeated by Mitt Romney, the former Massachusetts governor, who during the same period in early 2012 received over $2 million from the Marriott family, of the hotel fortune. This was an old tie based on the shared Mormon faith of the Romney and Marriott families and a friendship between the patriarchs. Mitt Romney is named after the elder Marriott, and he sat on the Marriott board of directors for ten years.

With an industry that has elicited such extreme ideological views from the political parties—Republicans zeroing out a government role and erecting a border security system that has intimidated visitors, Democrats offering federal help and dialing down border hostility—the industry is taking no chances. After watching the cloud of fear lift around airport security and seeing their industry treated as an economic engine, Freeman, of the travel association, said his group wants this helpful attitude to continue. Already his staff has traveled to Boston to huddle with Romney's campaign staff. "We have to be prepared if the Republicans win." Obama won.

Las Vegas is a good vantage point for surveying the state of play of tourism in the United States after the rest of the world pulled ahead during that "lost decade" and with hopes pinned on a stronger role for the federal government.

Las Vegas is at the top of nearly every survey of the American tourism industry. Sometimes Las Vegas ranks first as the most-visited; other times that honor goes to New York City or Orlando, Florida. Unlike the other two cities, Las Vegas is pure tourism. It has no other reason for existing than offering "adult fun" for the masses.

The gangsters Meyer Lansky and Bugsy Siegel built up the town in the middle of a forlorn desert in Nevada, with casinos, resorts and mobsters. Lansky underwrote the initial casino phase with millions of dollars from the illegal drug trade with Mexico. Siegel added outrageous excess to the city by building the Flamingo, the first in what would become a long line of resort palaces with casinos, glitter and a whiff of Hollywood posh; all financed with underworld money and muscle.

Naughty Las Vegas was also sophisticated Las Vegas, with the best shows in the country. Frank Sinatra, as troubadour to the mob, brought along his friends in the Rat Pack: Dean Martin, Joey Bishop, Sammy Davis, Jr., and Peter Lawford, brother-in-law of President John F. Kennedy. In its heyday the Beatles played Las Vegas; Elvis Presley was a regular in his sequined white jumpsuits; Wayne Newton and Engelbert Humperdinck became synonymous with the midnight shows; Céline Dion sings to sold out crowds whenever she appears and Bette Midler sang through the recent recession at Caesar's Palace. Barely clad showgirls with feathers and spangles accompany the acts and fill the house.

In the background were the big gamblers at the roulette wheel, blackjack tables, poker tables and slot machines, betting money on the dice and cards and filling the coffers of the resorts. Every other state outlawed gambling; Nevada embraced it and Las Vegas was the gambling capital of the country.

Those days are gone. Native Americans have revived their fortunes by opening gambling parlors on their reservations. States with deficits are competing for tourists to come play the slots.

Above all, what altered gambling in Las Vegas was the opening up of China. For nearly five hundred years the Chinese territory of Macao, a former Portuguese colony, had been the Monte Carlo of Asia. Chinese and European gamblers lost fortunes at baccarat and roulette in casinos with the smoky ambiance of a Graham Greene novel. When the Communists won the Chinese Civil War, they outlawed gambling. This was an extraordinary decision in a country where gambling is woven into the culture. For literally four thousand years the Chinese have been gamblers, as hard-driving in the casinos as they are in their business dealings and with all of the intricate superstitions of a gambling culture. In popular Chinese movies like *Kung Fu Mahjong*, gamblers wear red underwear for luck when they hit the mahjong tables in Macao, the tiles clicking like castanets, and hope for the lucky number 8.

Macao was transferred to China as a special territory in 1999, the same status as nearby Hong Kong, and the flow of Chinese from the mainland increased dramatically. Three years later Stanley Ho, a Hong Kong billionaire, lost his monopoly on Macao casinos. Overnight the door was open to the biggest gamblers in the world.

Sheldon Adelson, the Las Vegas gambling tycoon and financier of Newt Gingrich, leaped at the prospect. In short order, he secured permission from Beijing to construct a casino, which opened in 2004 as the Sands Macao at a cost of over $250 million. The response was so extraordinary that he then built a "strip" of landfill connecting two small islands in the territory, where he built the Venetian Macao, an enormous replica of the Las Vegas resort. Adelson became one of the world's wealthiest men on the strength of the high-stakes gambling in his VIP lounges in Macao.

Steve Wynn, the better-known Las Vegas casino billionaire, soon followed and opened the Wynn Macau, a far more elegant resort but with the same accent on the high rollers. By 2006, gambling in Macao had outpaced that in Las Vegas. Now, with $33.5 billion in wagers in 2011, it is at least five times larger than the money gambled in Las Vegas. That trend will only widen if and when gambling is allowed in China proper and those 1.37 billion Chinese have the opportunity to tempt fate and gamble at home.

That specter helped convince Singapore to open its island city-state to gambling and casino resorts before it lost out on the Chinese hunger for wagers; Adelson opened the Marina Bay Sands in Singapore in 2010. This was a dramatic reversal for Singapore and its founding father Lee Kuan Yew, who had vowed to keep out the gambling disease in his majority-Chinese nation.

In terms of big-time gambling, Las Vegas has been left in the dust, so to speak. But it looks the same. The strip is still the strip: cars cruising up and down the four miles of casinos, tourists crowding the sidewalks and waiting in line at the fine restaurants and the tacky hamburger joints. "Hot babes" are advertised on billboards and in handouts. Photographs of bare-chested men offer a new definition of a "girl's night out." Inside the casinos, the habitués are in position at the slot machines early in the morning, coffee and cigarette in hand. Gamblers still come but not many really big spenders.

The city has found a replacement. It is the more prosaic business of MICE hosting meetings, conventions and exhibits. In the tourism trade this is anything but glamorous. On the other hand, unlike gambling, it is not encumbered with mobsters and under-the-table money laundering, with hit men or gangs. And in typical Las Vegas fashion, the city is now the number-one choice for conventions in the United States and in the world. (As boosters like to say, more people flock to Vegas every year than to Mecca.)

Every month the serious business of conventions is the subject of a public board meeting of the Las Vegas Convention and Visitors Authority. It is treated with the same importance as a city council meeting. When I attended, it was standing room only and the talk was of growing competition.

"This city is under attack," said Charles Bowling, a board member from the industry side as the president and CEO of the Mandalay Bay Hotel and Casino. "We are under attack from other destinations. I travel around the country—in Chicago, Orlando, and they are asking 'how can we steal business convention business from Las Vegas?'" he warned his fellow board members.

The topic under discussion was the announcement that for the eighteenth year in a row Las Vegas ranked number one in the country for conventions. The board was reviewing its strategy to renovate, improve and enlarge the vast Las Vegas Convention Center and its "convention district." The press release crowed that the 19,000 conventions and meetings held in the city every year brought in $6.3 billion to the local economy and supported 58,000 jobs.

Both Chicago and Orlando have made extensive and expensive renovations of their conference centers. Rahm Emanuel, Chicago's new mayor, was quoted in the *Atlantic* magazine as saying Chicago planned to take back its old spot as number one for conventions that it had lost to

Las Vegas in the 1990s as well as several billion dollars of business over the years.

Carolyn Goodman, the mayor of Las Vegas, told me in an earlier interview at her office that Emanuel should look no further than his city's dreary weather and its scattered hotels and property. "Who is he kidding?" she asked. "We have beautiful weather and everything is close. We have magnificent convention space. The quality of our care and service is the highest in the country because we have good union jobs."

She made the obvious but often-forgotten point that tourism cannot be outsourced, which is why cities are fighting over the MICE business.

At the board meeting Mayor Goodman was more strategic. "With casino business moving out, our single most important business is conventions. Hotels, resorts, and gaming—they are moving all over the country. Conventions are the backbone for us now," she told the panel and the audience.

The convention authority played a new video it had produced showing the history of Las Vegas and meetings since 1959 with the opening of a much smaller convention center and new hotels incorporating large meeting rooms. One reason for pushing the convention business was to fill hotel rooms during the middle of the week; most of the tourists came on the weekends. And with tourism accounting for 46 percent of employment in southern Nevada, the greater the occupancy rate, the greater the job security. Familiar footage of celebrities and ordinary Americans wearing fashions from decades ago chronicled the changes over the years until 2012, when the convention center looks dated and slightly down at the heel after the recession.

Global business, though, is where Las Vegas is looking for growth. A third, international terminal opened in June 2012 with new business from Europe and South America. The city's website offers translations in twelve languages. Chris Meyer, vice president of convention sales for the Las Vegas Convention and Visitors Authority, told me that Las Vegas has been pushing the Obama administration to make all of the changes to put the country back on the global stage.

"Everything they're doing is a page from what we have done. A visitor's fee to pay for promotion, marketing on the Internet," he said. "We pushed hard for the Travel and Tourism Act because we all need national-level promotion. In Las Vegas our international guests make up almost one-third of our business."

"The beautiful thing about the federal government realizing the value of travel and tourism is that it means a change throughout," added Meyer.

He hopes that the United States will have a single national presence at the big tourism trade shows instead of the current arrangement where each of the fifty states—whether Nevada, California, New York, Florida, Illinois or Maine—has to put up a booth for itself. The result is sometimes laughable. I attended the New York travel and tourism show, where Thailand, for instance, had a handsome display with a dozen thick magazine-size pamphlets showing how to have a golf vacation, or a beach vacation, a hiking vacation, or a spa vacation in that country. A Thai dance ensemble performed at regular intervals and Thai food was served.

In the American section, the booths were from the eastern states, with less polished pamphlets extolling river canoe trips in Delaware and the rocky coast of Maine. The only federal presence was the U.S. customs and border protection booth that handed out instructional booklets on how to prepare to go through borders, why the U.S. was building a fence dividing the country from Mexico, or the fears of "agro-terrorism."

As Meyer said, that is no way to get the message out about the rich diversity of travel in the United States. The biggest foreign competitor for international meetings is Germany and its cities: Munich, Stuttgart, Frankfurt, Hamburg and Berlin. They do not waste time with some amateur presentations. "Germany has the infrastructure—the modern highways, railroads and rail links, airports and the top-tier—the tier-one—hotels and convention halls," he said.

Those competitors have representatives throughout the United States trying to grab some of the $460 billion annual business from meetings and events. Joe Lustenberger, a Swiss hotelier, represents an association called Euromic that books smaller conventions and meetings of groups from the United States in various European countries. He lives in Chicago and travels throughout the country drumming up business. He laughed at the idea that European countries are in competition with Las Vegas or Chicago with their enormous convention centers and hotels.

"Europe doesn't have such large hotels with rooms for all of the delegates and conference space. That's not what we offer. I don't see myself taking away meetings from American cities," he said in a telephone interview. "By the time an organization calls us, they know they want to have a meeting in Europe and we help figure out where."

An annual meeting in Rome with a weekend jaunt to the Mediterranean coast might sound more appealing than another trip to New York. With 1.8 million conventions, meetings, trade shows and exhibitions held in the United States every year, Europeans and Asians are making bids for the business.

What is a business conference to one person is a junket to another. Besides concerns about spending during a recession, the MICE slice of travel is routinely hit by revelations of lavish spending by adults who seem to be having too much fun on a so-called business trip. In 2012 the General Services Administration offered a prime example.

The GSA hosted a four-day training conference in Las Vegas in 2010 at the four-star M Resort Spa Casino that cost $823,000, nearly three times its original budget, and included extravagances such as a $75,000 "team-building exercise" to build bicycles together. The organizers paid $44 a person for breakfast and $94 each for dinner—all taxpayer money at a time when the country was barely climbing out of recession. Congress was not amused when the trip was exposed two years later, and imposed new restrictions on government meetings.

Incentive travel—the *I* in MICE—also nearly disappeared in the wake of scandalous excess when the American International Group took its executives on a lavish trip in September 2008, just days after receiving an $85 billion bailout from the government. The practice returned in a subdued form with the economic recovery. Employees and executives are more likely to travel within the United States and stay at four-star, not five-star, hotels.

The most surprising facet of the appeal of Las Vegas is its insistence that good labor relations is part of its hospitality—what the mayor and nearly every other official told me during my stay in the city. Emanuel had blamed the unions for Chicago's decline in the convention business, but Las Vegas has stronger union labor than Chicago.

Meyer of the Convention Authority said that by signing a five-year union contract, Steve Wynn set the standard for solid management-labor relations. "Labor knows what's going on in the hotels. All of our major brands are based here—Caesar's, MGM, Wynn—it is still the case that labor unions work well in Las Vegas and that management values the training and engagement of union workers."

The labor movement agrees. John Wilhelm is a former union organizer in Las Vegas who is now president of the powerful Unite Here labor group, the parent union of workers in the hotel, airport, restaurant, gaming, food-service and textile industries. The backbone of the success of labor in Las Vegas is the Culinary Workers Union, which picketed for years until it won accreditation and helped raise wages in Las Vegas.

"Every major hotel on the strip is unionized except the Venetian," he said during an interview at his union office in Washington, D.C. In the last two decades all unions have lost momentum and membership. By contrast the service industries have shown growth. Since tourism is the biggest service industry, Mr. Wilhelm sees opportunity, city by city. The greater the union density, the better leverage for hotel workers, he said.

That leverage comes from union efforts, not from either political party or from the government, he said. Under the George W. Bush administration, labor laws lost most of their power. And with hotel chains now managing rather than owning hotels, there "is a huge problem of knowing who makes decisions and is responsible for wage and benefits."

He pointed to Nevada, with a history of anti-union measures, and Massachusetts, which is a pro-union state, as proof that no political party is guaranteed as an ally in the union movement. In Boston in 2009 the Hyatt hotel chain laid off 100 housekeepers who were paid an average of $15 an hour with health benefits and replaced them with contractor employees. The contractor paid the new housekeepers the minimum hourly wage of $8 and no benefits. The Hyatt hotels of Boston issued a statement saying the layoffs were "regrettably part of an ongoing drive to address challenging economic conditions." Governor Deval L. Patrick said no State of Massachusetts employee could stay in a Hyatt hotel.

By contrast, said Wilhelm, the Las Vegas hotels have shown they understand that tourism is a service industry that requires well-trained and well-paid employees. Las Vegas is the template, he said, for paying service employees the wages and benefits that allow them a decent living for a family and that, in turn, becomes the base for a successful tourism industry. Tourism is the ultimate service industry. In most American cities, service employees like waitresses and housekeepers live on or below the poverty line. In Las Vegas the employees have health care and paid vacations. The unions won these benefits with hard bargaining and concessions, reducing the number of job categories and making it easier for management to hold costs down while improving services.

"It's no exaggeration to say that the unions and management know that they are in this together in Las Vegas," said Wilhelm.

As tourism business becomes global, so do the unions. The United Nations' International Labour Organization in Geneva coordinates efforts to insure that workers' rights are respected in the vast industry. Wolfgang Weinz of the ILO said that, at a minimum, one out of ten workers in the world is employed by the tourism industry, a squishy figure that may be a serious underestimate.

"We do know that over sixty percent of the workers are young—under twenty-five years of age—and they are women," he said in a telephone interview from Geneva. "That is good—it means tourism opens the door for a career. The bad news is that the working conditions are not brilliant."

The wages are lower than in other sectors, he said, and the working conditions are "weak" at best. "Too many employers in the sector take advantage of these young women, many of whom are immigrants," he said. "Productivity and competitiveness depends most on technical training of the service employees as well as what we call soft skills—passion, friendliness, a relaxed comportment which will very much affect the atmosphere in a hotel."

The ILO only operates in countries where the government approves of its mission to improve relations between management and employees. They have no role in helping employees on cruise ships. India, he said, was a bright spot, as is South Africa, which has an entire program called Fair Trade in Tourism to insure that the lives of local employees are improved. "If you believe tourism is essential to alleviate poverty in the developing world, then you have to address the treatment of service employees," said Mr. Weinz. "Half of the developing world is using tourism to raise incomes—that is a tremendous mission, and its dimensions are incredible."

I was in Las Vegas to attend a conference on medical tourism, the newest big thing in the industry. I first heard about the notion of taking an overseas vacation in order to receive inexpensive medical treatment from my friend Dorothy McGhee. A real estate investor and solid member of the middle class, Dorothy is anything but poor. However, with American medical insurance and medical costs rising faster than the cost of living, she decided she could no longer pay for dental insurance.

"When you are self-employed like I am, dental insurance is a big expense and it isn't part of Medicare," she told me. And at sixty-five years of age Dorothy is very careful about medical expenses.

In 2010, during a routine dental checkup, she was told she would need two new caps on her teeth at a cost of $5,500. That was not in her budget. Instead, she took a five-day vacation to Puerto Vallarta, Mexico, for less than half that cost. "I emailed my friends, received several good recommendations and chose the dentist," she said.

Miguel Arden, the dentist, had done postgraduate studies in New York and would charge her $1,600 for the two caps. Her airfare was $500, and rental of a beachfront cabana in the fishing village of Sayulita was $60 a night with breakfast. She arrived Thursday, saw the dentist Friday, had her caps put on the following Monday and was home Tuesday night.

"It was as good a dental experience as I've ever had in the United States, and I got to spend a long weekend on the beach eating all the fish tacos I wanted," she said. "Dr. Arden said it was normal for him to have gringo patients from the United States—he called them medical tourists."

There are no comprehensive figures for medical tourists like my friend Dorothy. However, she is a typical medical tourist. She is an American fleeing rising U.S. costs who is wealthy enough to afford to travel but who cannot keep up with the rising costs of medical insurance. There are 5 million patients worldwide, the majority American like Dorothy, traveling the world looking for the best value for medical treatment and a nice vacation as well. The top ten destinations, in alphabetical order, are Brazil, Costa Rica, India, Korea, Malaysia, Mexico, Singapore, Taiwan, Thailand and Turkey.

What started with Americans crossing the Canadian and Mexican borders to buy inexpensive pharmaceutical drugs has mushroomed into a stream of Americans searching for medical care and a vacation. On the border with Mexico, American medical tourists became so numerous that a special highway lane was opened for them in April 2012. In the first three months over 1,500 passes to the lane were issued.

Early on, Costa Rica saw medical tourism as a good fit. The country has a solid reputation for medical care. The tourism sector was growing, and people traveling for health care fit well in the overall scheme of green tourism.

In most cases these countries have programs developed by their ministers of health and tourism to accommodate the growing number of foreigners seeking quality, inexpensive care as well as a pleasant trip overseas. In many cases the hospitals have international accreditation and some American health insurance plans cover the care and the cost of the trip. All of this raises serious questions about putting your life in the hands of a travel agent, questions that were answered at the MediTour Expo at the Flamingo Hotel in Las Vegas.

There were no more than two hundred in attendance: travel agents, doctors, foreign ministry officials and entrepreneurs. Every other speaker talked about the beginning of a sea change in medical care and then hedged that prophecy with caveats about responsibility and accountability of far-off doctors and hospitals.

"There are dysfunctional medical systems that are broke—God knows, the U.S. system has issues," said Dr. Arlen Meyers, a physician from Colorado who opened the conference. He talked about a global war for medical talent, of the need for a "seamless global referral system" and the construction of a city like "Las Vegas with health care at its base."

Then he asked a question uppermost in my mind: "Anyone can go on the Internet and sell medical tourism overseas—how can we measure its quality?"

Dr. Mary Wong Lai Lin, from the Healthcare Travel Council of the

Malaysian Ministry of Health tried to answer those questions when she discussed the astronomical growth of medical tourism to her country. The former British colony set up this medical tourism council in 2009 and designated thirty-five Malaysian hospitals throughout the country as participants in the program. In just two years, Malaysia attracted 400,000 medical tourists. "Many of them came with cash in their suitcases," Dr. Wong told me.

Following her detailed description of the top-flight medical care available, she showed us a video of the country's tropical beaches, its modern resorts, the capital city of Kuala Lumpur, with its sophisticated skyline and multiethnic enclaves. She even made a pitch for Malaysian cuisine: Malay, Indian, Chinese, Eurasian and Portuguese. "We are the ninth-most-visited country in the world," she said. "And we are ranked as the fifty-first most happy country."

Afterward we ate lunch together, and I asked her why Malaysia was so aggressive about promoting medical tourism, beach included. "It's the kind of overall economic development we want," she said. "We speak English, we have a high standard of medicine offering real value at prices less than half what you would pay in the United States. And we have five-star hotels at $150 a night. It is the perfect place to recover."

Dr. Wong has her Ph.D. in national health insurance and resource allocation. She said for Malaysia this "government initiative will accelerate our economic growth through tourism and investment in health care." If growth continues at this rapid pace, Malaysia believes it will attract 2 million medical tourists annually by 2020.

No one questioned why medical care should be incorporated into the tourism industry. It is one of the most presumptuous of the new fields that tourism has decided is part of its mandate. Although Dr. Meyers from Colorado did say he hated the term "medical tourism," it appears he has lost that battle. The conference was organized by the New York–based company Wallcott Holdings, which envisions creating medical villages or medical "zones" around the world to accommodate medical tourists with hospitals, hotels, shopping, activities and entertainment.

An estimated one in four working-age Americans do not have health insurance, while medical costs are rising. Dental insurance is even less common. The $2.6 trillion U.S. health care system is the best in the world, but it is becoming one of the most expensive and least accessible for the poor. The Centers for Disease Control said that 59 million Americans went without medical insurance in 2010 and failed to receive treatment they needed. With those figures, medical tourism is bound to rise even with the Obama reforms. While U.S. politicians argue over how best to reform the American health care system, Americans are voting with their feet, or airplane tickets, and going overseas for treatments they cannot afford in their own country. They are turning to their travel agent rather than their family doctor.

Dr. Sevil Kutay of the local Turkish-American Chamber of Commerce & Industry—Midwest lives in Chicago and sees Americans in need of health care. She attended the conference at the Flamingo in order to prod the Turkish government to do more to promote its website: www.medical tourisminturkey.org. "Why not promote medical tourism in Turkey?" she asked. "We are offering Americans a service, selling a service, as well as offering them a vacation in Turkey—it is an ideal package."

Associations like Patients Beyond Borders offer lists of doctors and destinations to help them decide where to look for care for a heart bypass, fertility treatments, face-lifts, dental implants, anywhere in the world. Some American health insurance companies now include coverage of both treatment and the cost of a trip overseas to certain preapproved countries and hospitals. It cuts their costs, even when a beach resort is included.

The marriage pages of the *New York Times* are a sociologist's playpen. Cultural shifts show up in the achievements of spouses and their parents, the photographs illustrating the couple and more recently the sexual orientation of the couples. One Sunday in May 2011, I spotted an announcement that described a groom as having earned a master's degree in tourism development from New York University in preparation for his employment as a director of tourism development for a New York City company.

Finally—a tourism degree made the marriage pages of the *New York Times* Style section. The study of tourism has been creeping into the curriculum at American universities and colleges for four decades, shadowing the growth of the industry. The degrees are in hospitality studies, tourism research, forestry, parks and recreation, national resources and recreation, the environment and tourism, hotel administration, hotel and restaurant administration, and tourism market development.

I searched the Internet with the help of an assistant and together we found tourism degree programs in over 450 colleges and universities. The Cornell School of Hotel Administration is the premier program in the United States and one of the oldest. The Ivy League program boasts 800 undergraduates from 30 countries, 70 graduate students and an astonishing 1,700 professionals who have enrolled for executive education courses.

Tourism has been transformed from a job to an occupation to a profession requiring a degree—explained in large part by the fact that tourism is creating jobs or professions for one out of every ten people in the world. Earning legitimacy as a field of study also lends tourism a seriousness that goes beyond the world of commerce.

Donald Hawkins, the Eisenhower Professor of Tourism Policy at George Washington University in Washington, D.C., has seen the growth firsthand. At GW the study began as a graduate program in 1970. In the 1990s it became a discipline in the business school; students can now earn bachelors and masters degrees and a Ph.D.

"For years tourism was studied mainly by anthropologists, who blamed tourism with exaggerated criticism for all the development curses," said Professor Hawkins in an interview in his campus office. "In business studies it is balanced. We look at environmental issues, at political issues, at sustainability and ecological questions. We look at good practices for management of the National Park System, for coastal areas."

His chair is endowed by Marriott International, headquartered in the Washington area, and named after President Dwight D. Eisenhower, who golfed with the Marriott founder. In the 1990s, Hawkins represented the United States at the U.N. World Tourism Organization before the U.S. government pulled out. "We should still be there. We need to be at the table.

"Tourism is the greatest modern voluntary transfer of wealth from rich countries to poor countries, and we need to belong to the UNWTO to help those developing economies. That is our future."

Hawkins received the first Ulysses Prize awarded by the UNWTO for creating and disseminating knowledge about tourism policy and management and has attracted students whom, he says, often have a touch of wanderlust. Studying tourism usually means travel in the future, moving from city to city or country to country for a career. In an earlier era, these students might have studied foreign affairs or business.

Anthony Mavrogiannis received his master's degree in tourism administration from George Washington, and he happily admits his primary purpose was to find a position in the business where he could travel frequently. After working as the in-house travel manager at the National Academy of Sciences, Mavrogiannis bought the Kentlands Travel Agency in suburban Washington and became his own boss. He is my travel agent.

In this age of the Internet and the ability to compare and buy airplane tickets, make hotel and restaurant reservations at one's own computer, many predicted the end of travel agents. Yet they have managed to retain approximately 30 percent of the travel business. The American Society of Travel Agents reports a steady if small increase in business since the digital revolution undercut so many agents. Now, rather than spending hours, if not days, looking for the right flight at the right time as well as an affordable hotel, people like me are turning to travel agents. Travel is expensive and making a mistake on the Internet is costly. During my years as a daily journalist my trips were arranged by the newspaper's travel agent. On my own I made a mess of my first attempt to arrange a complicated trip to Brazil; thereafter I have turned to Mavrogiannis. Besides having the security of a qualified agent making arrangements that actually work, I found I saved money with him.

During a morning spent at his office, the computer regularly pinged with notices, his printer spewed out airline tickets and hotel confirmations, and his telephone rang dozens of times. It was hard to imagine that travel agents once thought their profession would become extinct. It wasn't just consumers using the Web to plot their own trips that threatened his livelihood but airline companies and other parts of the industry that cut out or reduced commissions. His solution, shared by many other agents, was to diversify and specialize.

He keeps diversity by focusing 40 percent of his business on leisure travel and 60 percent on corporate. The leisure side still brings in the most money. "In the corporate world I'll write complicated, expensive tickets, but I receive the same flat commission per ticket no matter if it is a first-class eight-thousand-dollar ticket or a five-hundred-dollar economy class."

Specialties are loosely based on geography but also on the type of traveler. They are divided by lifestyle or age, with retirees a gold mine for the agency, especially since they travel in groups or buy packages that yield higher fees and commissions. "Americans like to travel in groups, to buy packages. They will buy a vacation where we plan their days, where they will eat, the sites they will see, where they will sleep."

Those of us who are old-fashioned and strike out on our own are becoming a minority and are known as FITs, or fully independent travelers. "For FITs we find the airline tickets and the hotels and that's about it."

His geographic specialty is Europe. One of his agents sells group tours to France and Italy for women. A Greek-American with a family home on a Greek island, Mavrogiannis is an expert on the Mediterranean. "We sell what we know," he said.

I asked him to demonstrate buying simple tickets for Bill and me to Minneapolis–St. Paul. For an earlier trip to the Twin Cities, Bill had spent half an hour on the computer and bought what he had considered a bargain even though it required changing airplanes in Milwaukee. In less than one minute, Mavrogiannis found a less expensive ticket and a direct route. "It's the software," he said. His commission was $42 per ticket.

Being a travel agent not only pays his bills but allows Mavrogiannis to travel frequently and spend long spells in Greece. He isn't getting rich, but he is leading the life he had imagined when he earned his master's degree at George Washington University.

America gave the world two great tourist concepts: the national park and the theme park: Yellowstone and Disneyland. Between the two, they define vacations in America and have gone some way to influencing how the rest of the world enjoys a holiday.

The U.S. National Park System of 394 parks has saved the wilderness and could help save the planet. They are public property, though, and not major profit centers. For the tourism industry, they are a lure to other venues in the United States. Despite the parks' offering of rare wilderness and phenomenal beauty, visits to them peaked at 287.2 million in 1987, just before the explosion in tourism around the world. The numbers are climbing back up. In 2009, the figure was 285 million visitors.

Compare that to Disney parks and resorts, which had 119.1 million paying visitors in the same year; the top ten theme park chains welcomed 326.5 million visitors in the United States. Those children and their families spent billions: Disney led the pack here, too, earning $2.41 billion. Disneyland and its offspring have become an integral part of childhood in the United States and, increasingly, around the world.

The trend is the opposite for national park vacations.

One reason for the disparity between wilderness and theme parks is the very nature of a visit. Theme parks are an extension of everyday life requiring no more than standing in line, going on rides, eating and repeating the process. At wilderness parks, visitors are removed from their comfort zones and hike, swim and often camp, making their own meals. Even when staying at park lodges or cabins the days are filled with exercise—and fresh air, wild animals and stunning scenery.

That has not changed in the last three decades, though. What has changed is the nonstop marketing and promotion of theme parks. What began with Walt Disney and his cartoon characters now encompasses a theme park chain built around Harry Potter and his young wizard friends in London and Orlando. The megabest-selling books and movies draw Potter fans to the theme parks just as the Disney franchise and its movies, books, videos and television have done for generations. Theme parks are part of the tourism industry; the national wilderness parks are not. The new federal tourism strategy could nudge attendance at the parks by highlighting them on the new national website and in promotions overseas.

I took my children to Disney World in Orlando, where my son celebrated his ninth birthday with stars in his eyes when Cinderella came over to help him blow out the candles. They loved the roller-coaster ride through a magic mountain; they hated the song "It's a Small World After All." One year later we stayed at a lodge near the Hoh Rain Forest in Olympic National Park in Washington State, climbing over fallen trees covered in slippery moss and prickly ferns, running up and down the red-dirt paths toward higher ground and a view of the Olympic Mountains on the mist-shrouded peninsula. I know which my favorite was and which was theirs. The next year we "compromised" and traveled to Schweitzer Mountain in the Idaho Rockies.

Globally both models have had their impact. Theme parks now stretch from Asia to Europe to the United States and are expected to gross $31.8 billion annually by 2017. Wilderness parks are even more ubiquitous, spread across all continents and created along the lines established by President Theodore Roosevelt at the turn of the twentieth century.

The social and environmental effect of those spreading theme parks has been questioned by some high-profile critics. The best-selling author Carl Hiaasen has made a mission to jab tourist developers in nearly every mystery novel he has written that climbed to the best-seller list. He writes children's books on similar themes featuring greedy tourist developers who destroy Florida. He read from his book *Scat* to a group of Washington, D.C., students one day, and I asked him afterward why he keeps pounding away at them.

He answered that that was the reason why he became a writer in the first place, to capture the dismay of watching Florida turned into a land of theme parks and tourists. "When I was a kid hanging out in the Everglades, going to the beaches, it was a cool way to grow up. When that is part of your childhood and you saw it paved over, you don't forget about it," he said. "The way it is in Florida, you can get away with anything until it starts upsetting tourism."

Mary, my youngest sister, turned sixty years old recently and we decided to celebrate with a sisters-only vacation. Our first stop was the Shenandoah National Park in the Blue Ridge Mountains. Its development was spurred by the Great Depression, when work crews from the Civilian Conservation Corps were employed to create the Skyline Drive, snaking through the park's crests overlooking the Shenandoah Valley. President Franklin Delano Roosevelt dedicated the park in July 1936, saving the mountains from development by entrepreneurs in nearby Washington, D.C., a two-hour drive to the east.

Mary is largely confined to a wheelchair today. In her youth she was an avid hiker and knew the parks around Seattle well. At the park's northern gate at Front Royal, a ranger told us Mary was eligible for a lifetime free pass. We drove off. Soon she was remembering hikes and sudden rainstorms in the Cascade Mountains. We stopped at the Dickey Ridge Overlook, then Elkwallow and the Skyland. Mary alternated between staying in the car and climbing out on crutches, taking in the views of the valley that were decidedly tame compared to the rugged Northwest. A deer with big ears and short legs bounded over a stone fence. At timbered Big Meadows Lodge we stopped for a break and told family camping stories about meals of potatoes, carrots and hamburger wrapped in foil and baked in the hot fire followed by roasted marshmallows on a stick. We drove all the way down the 105-mile park to Charlottesville and, after a long weekend, turned around and came back home via the Skyline Drive. Mary was quiet. "I'll have to come back," she said. "I miss parks."

Many young adults have a similar emotional attachment to theme parks. Tens of thousands of couples have been married at Disneyland and Disney World, making them two of the most popular "destination wedding sites" in the country. With fairy-tale castles, Cinderella coaches and an entire fairy-tale wedding department, brides can recreate a ceremony in which they resemble a princess with Prince Charming by their sides in the fairy-tale theme park that had been the scene of excitement and fun in their childhoods. The 2011 wedding at Westminster Abbey of the real British Prince William to Catherine Middleton, gowned in lace with a full-length veil framing her lithe figure, encapsulated all of the wedding fantasies played out for profit at the Disney theme parks.

The Kailua Beach and Dune Management Plan is a 70-page report describing how one of Hawaii's most spectacular beaches will disappear in the coming decades. Climate change is the culprit, raising the temperature of the planet, which in turn is raising the level of the Pacific Ocean, which in turn will erode the fashionable beach on Oahu. The report was prepared by the University of Hawaii and the Hawaii Department of Land and Natural Resources as the state began the painful process of imagining life when no amount of preservation efforts will hold back the sea.

Samuel J. Lemmo is the administrator of Hawaii's Office of Conservation and Coastal Lands which oversees 2 million acres of public and private land within the Hawaiian conservation district as well as the beach and marine lands out to the seaward extent of the state's jurisdiction. He is the man who watches the sand disappear.

"The thing is, in Hawaii we take access to beaches very, very seriously," he told me in his office in downtown Honolulu. "For us it is the highest tide of the year at the highest wash of the highest wave. Like access to Waikiki—this is a fascinating question especially now when we're staring sea rise in the face."

Tourism is Hawaii's number-one industry; tourist spending has risen to $1.01 billion a month following the slow recovery from the 2008 recession. The future of Hawaii depends on tourism and those seemingly endless beaches on multiple islands in the blue Pacific Ocean. Everything in Hawaii derives from planeloads and cruise ships of visitors—the hotels, restaurants, shops, and real estate firms. The only other game in town is the U.S. military, which owns prime territory, including Pearl Harbor (known to every schoolchild), Fort Shafter, Schofield Barracks, Marine Corps Base Hawaii, Wheeler and Hickam Air Force bases and the headquarters of the Pacific Command, which is the forward base with responsibilities for an area of roughly half the globe north to south from both poles and east to west from the western coast of the United States to the west coast of India.

"Sometimes it freaks people out when I talk about the erosion," said Lemmo, who speaks in the low-key style of the island and ends his emails with "Mahalo" a Hawaiian expression which literally means "in the presence of the divine" but is used as a familiar form of "thank you." He also wears aloha shirts and sandals to work.

"People want to know what this talk does to the value of their property, their inheritance, their business—it's a touchy subject. All I can tell them is if you're on the shorefront, you'll be the first to go."

What the state can do is inventory the beaches and plan for triage, he said. Waikiki will be saved. The state has spent millions of dollars, with contributions from the hotels, to restore the beach by pumping sand in from offshore. "It's a man-made beach to begin with. It was marshland until people came in and filled and heavily engineered the south beach. From the 1930s to the 1960s they brought in at least 400,000 cubic yards of sand from other parts of the island. Now it supports prime real estate.

Lemmo helped initiate an economic study of beaches with the tourism authority to calculate future costs, knowing some of the shoreline had to be saved. "It doesn't matter how much beach restoration costs—if we don't do it, we undermine our vitality," he said.

There is little the state can do for locals who own stunning modern mansions on the beach. "We would advocate strategic retreat. First, we tell them to stop building near the beach. We encourage people to move away from the beach or to get a reverse mortgage for the homes you know will disappear."

The study covers the Kailua Beach, which includes a park and a stretch of sand where home prices are in the millions of dollars. President Obama routinely spends Christmas holidays on Kailua. The dunes are lovingly protected with scratchy native plants meant to hold the sand in place and in season, the waves are brisk. I walked half the length of the pure white beach one early morning and met only six people running or walking their dogs in the exclusive enclave.

The charts are unambiguous. While Kailua Beach is used to "an extremely dynamic coast system; a result of the variable wind and wave forces," it will require more dune restoration efforts, fencing, more plantings, and pulling back from the shoreline. Even then, the first blocks by the sea will be wiped away at the turn of the next century if nothing dramatic has been done to stall climate change.

Mike McCartney, the CEO of the Hawaii Tourism Authority, said his role is to balance the need to promote tourism which brings in 18 percent of the gross state product, with the need to protect the state and the environment. Only the military is as important—Hawaii can safely count on $1 billion a month from tourism and $1 billion from the military.

McCartney is a native-born Hawaiian of Irish and Japanese parents who speaks about the "aloha spirit" without self-consciousness. "Hawaii and the Aloha spirit are the future of the United States and the world, integrating peoples from around the world; that is the future."

He has set his sights on increasing the number of Chinese tourists and was on hand when the first charter airplane landed in Honolulu. At the same time, he worries that the island may lose its identity with too much development. "You can't just have growth, growth, growth." The prospect of beach erosion, threats to the ocean, a catalogue of things that can and are going wrong, bother him, but he refuses to be deterred. When a study showed problems with marine life in Kaneohe Bay, he banned jet skis there. "There were protests outside my house." And he ordered the study of climate change because he needs information to plot how to navigate that impossibly large crisis.

"You have to get used to the notion of crises in tourism and learn to work around it. I think that is Hawaii, finding the balance," he said. With Barack Obama, son of Hawaii, as the president of the United States elevating the significance of tourism, McCartney said he is confident that somehow the state will muddle through.

On the other hand, the balance could disappear. He has a nightmare of hordes of tourists flying in and out of Hawaii while the waves rise, eating away the sand.

Epilogue

As we glided under a bridge on the Copenhagen canal tour, our guide announced that we had entered a quiet zone. "This is a residential area," she said, nodding toward balconies where Danes were enjoying coffee—or maybe wine. "I'll resume talking in five minutes."

Like so many other countries, Denmark is experiencing a huge boom in tourism. Those quiet zones are emblematic of the country's approach to the industry: ensure that tourists blend into Danish life rather than the other way around. The question, said Henrik Thierlein, a spokesman for the city's tourism office, was: "How do you take advantage of the growth in tourism and not be taken over by mass tourism?"

That sums up the joys and the headaches of tourism since the initial publication of *Overbooked*. Never before has tourism offered unlimited possibilities in every corner of the globe for every taste from mountain climbing in the Himalayas to cooking in Provence. At the same time, cities and regions have been forced to cope with their popularity as never before.

In ways large and small the trends in tourism have accelerated since the initial publication of *Overbooked*. At one end, the industry is ecstatic at the growth: tourism outpaced nearly all other major industries and was responsible for 10 percent of the global GDP. With such numbers, the industry is being flooded with newcomers. The Internet has spawned giants like Airbnb catering to tourists. And old institutions as different as the Nature Conservancy and the *New York Times* are offering travel packages.

That popularity has also meant an acceleration of tourism's destructive impact. The city of Barcelona elected Ada Colau as its new mayor in 2015 in part because she promised to stop tourists from ruining the city. She immediately ordered a moratorium on new tourist accommodations and is investigating how cruise ships are impacting the city's historic center. Her biggest worry, she said, is that Barcelona will become "another Venice," shorthand for a city losing itself to throngs of tourists.

Barcelona represents a new tipping point in the industry brought about through short-term rentals of rooms and houses to tourists. Known as part of the new "sharing economy," this phenomenon has been driven by Airbnb. Founded in 2008, this start up has become a billion-dollar enterprise using the efficiency of the Internet to list homeowners renting space to strangers, usually at low rates. Absent regulations, these short-term rentals usually ignore local zoning rules, tax issues, noise variances, and all the other laws and regulations that govern residential neighborhoods. While this makes for happy consumers who save money and happy homeowners who make money, it has made for very unhappy neighborhoods.

In Barcelona, these short-term rentals have wreaked havoc in the historic city and turned neighbor against neighbor. In New York City, an official investigation found that one third of the Airbnb listings in the city were by commercial owners—not home owners—renting out apartments by the day to make more money and circumvent city laws, thereby increasing the shortage of affordable housing in the city. In New Orleans, the short-term rentals have eaten into the residential areas of the French Quarter, leading activists to complain that the city was choosing tourists over residents by refusing to enforce the rules that protect homeowners. Cities and nations are trying to adjust with new laws or new lawsuits.

China cemented its place in the tourism hierarchy by becoming the biggest source of tourists around the globe. Today more Chinese are traveling than any other nationality, prompting mixed reviews. The United States doubled the number of tourist visas for Chinese to 1 million in 2014. European businesses are pleased to sell luxury goods to the wealthiest visiting Chinese. However, other countries, many in Asia, are asking the Chinese visitors to improve their manners.

The summer of 2015 brought other signs of a tourism revolt. Outraged by tourists' boorish and disrespectful behavior, and responding to the complaints of their constituents, local officials around the world began to crack down on tourism, even in the face of opposition from national governments, which want the revenue from tourists.

No one could doubt that more than 1 billion tourist trips were changing the world. Two of the world's greatest population movements collided in the Mediterranean when vacationing Europeans met fleeing Syrian refugees on the beaches of Turkey and Greece. Many tourists gave them food and help. In tragic turns, tourists were increasingly caught in natural and man-made upheavals, from the massive earthquakes in Nepal to the Egyptian desert where a busload of Mexican tourists were mistaken for terrorists and killed by government soldiers.

In a sign that the industry is accepting greater responsibility for its global role, tourism groups came to the aid of Nepal in record numbers, offering humanitarian aid alongside more traditional development organizations. And tourism officials continued to work with their development counterparts in government and international organizations.

For the first time, the United Nations World Tourism Organization twinned with UNESCO, its cultural counterpart, to use tourism to protect rather than endanger cultural heritage. At climate change forums, tourism and travel officials are becoming part of the dialogue, accepting that they are contributing to global warming as well as threatened by it.

In the face of tourism's greater popularity and higher profile, Taleb Rafai, the secretary-general of the UNWTO, told me that every country needs strong and clear tourism policies "to advance tourism's sustainable growth and development."

What is clear is that travel is neither good nor bad. The travel industry, however, is having good and bad impacts, and governments, as never before, are central to determining what that outcome is. Tourists aren't neutral either. Individually they make profound choices and when traveling in hordes can do tremendous damage. The flash points of travel are now the same around the world: local communities feeling powerless in the face of their governments and big industry; the industry feeling hamstrung by opaque regulations and corrupt government officials; civil societies feeling ignored when they try to protect their forests and beaches, neighborhoods, and children; scientists and environmentalists feeling silenced when they warn that travel is one of the human activities that is changing our climate.

Since the publication of *Overbooked*, these issues are becoming part of the public debate.

September 2015

Acknowledgments

This was a rare book project where I was required to work hard and at the same time experience the joys and travails of travel. Thanks to a long list of people, I was able to do just that—investigate the tourism industry and measure the delights of travel along the way. In this regard, I chose my subject well.

I'll say more about my family, but at the head of the list of everyone to whom I am indebted is my husband, Bill Nash. Bill was my traveling partner and my first reader without whom I could not have written this book. He was my logistician, my navigator and my nudge who reminded me after missed flights, week-long jet lags and cancelled appointments why this book was important. He also kept track of the best restaurants.

To begin at the beginning, I want to thank my former colleagues, the incomparable reporters and editors at the *New York Times*, especially Jill Abramson and Richard L. Berke who appointed me the newspaper's international economics correspondent, the beat that sparked my curiosity about tourism's role in the global economy, and Tom Redburn, my editor at the *Times* who schooled me on the intersection of business, economics and politics. At Harvard University's Kennedy School of Government, I was the lucky recipient of a generous fellowship at the Joan Shorenstein Center on the Press, Politics and Policy where I studied tourism with the center's resident scholars and professors: thank you Richard Parker and Thomas E. Patterson for sharpening my ideas and Edith Holway for taking care of me.

When I wasn't traveling, I was mining the resources of Washington, D.C., my home town, which is filled with stellar institutions. The Library of Congress was invaluable, and the library at the National Geographic's headquarters is a gem. The Council on Foreign Relations, the Carnegie Endowment for International Peace, the Brookings Institution, and Politics and Prose Bookstore hosted speakers and discussions that enriched my research. I interviewed officials in Congress, the State Department, the Commerce Department and the office of the U.S. Trade Representative. And as the capital, Washington is home to trade groups, special interest groups and businesses that all want to influence the government, and those people were also generous with their time.

Indeed I am grateful to all of the officials, members of the tourism industry and experts whom I interviewed and quote in the book. Thank you for your insights, for speaking on the record and for opening up your corner of the industry for this book. I hope that I was faithful to your ideas and what matters to you and the business. Any mistakes are my own.

And thank you to the tourists whom I met along the way and whom I quote by first name only since you met me as a fellow tourist, not as a writer. You were generous and thoughtful and gave life to this story.

Several people went out of their way to help me contact essential people in the broader network of tourism. Thank you to Jonathan Tourtellot at the National Geographic for invitations to his awards ceremonies and sharing studies of the industry; to Kathleen Matthews of Marriott International who gave me essential introductions to the higher reaches of the industry; to Roland Eng in Cambodia; to Marcelo Risi at the United Nations World Tourism Organization who organized my visit there; to Thomas Fiedler, formerly of the *Miami Herald*, for his knowledge of Florida; to Geoffrey Freeman of the U.S. Travel Association who briefed me on the ins and outs of 21st century U.S. tourism; to David Barboza of the *New York Times* in Shanghai for opening up some of those doors; and to Marion Fourestier of the New York office of ATOUT, the official French tourism agency, who helped me set up the complicated research trip to her country.

In researching this book I followed basic journalistic guidelines and paid for my travel expenses with one exception. Bill and I spent several nights as guests of Geoffrey Dobbs at his hotel in Sri Lanka and, in recompense, made a donation to his charity Adopt Sri Lanka. In three instances, some of my travel expenses were paid by sponsors of conferences where I made speeches or led workshops. Friends in other countries opened their homes to me as I traveled, and I want to thank Marianne Faure-Chaigneau in France, Mark Storella in Zambia, and Christophe Peschoux in Cambodia. And I am especially grateful to Ann and Walter Pincus for offering regular refuge and hospitality at their beach house in North Carolina.

I am also grateful to my friends in our exercise group who regularly kept up my spirits: Megan Rosenfeld and Bonny Wolf, two writers; and Gayle Krughoff and Elisabeth Wackman, both photographers.

For reading all or part of my manuscript with a critical eye, I am grateful to Elizabeth Newhouse, whose years of editing travel books kept me on the right track; to Harold Wackman for helping me avoid myriad mistakes on Africa; and Karen DeYoung for reading the U.S. chapter. Others I will leave anonymous except for my talented in-house editor; my daughter Lily, who convinced me to scrap an essential chapter and start over again; and Thomas Minc.

All of my family sustained me through the research and writing of *Overbooked* by believing in the book. My son Lee Hoagland gave me evocative photographs and critical advice; in our blended family, Bill's daughter Rebecca and her husband Matthew Engelke had lively opinions on the text. Bill's grandchildren—Charlotte and Julia, Harriet and Louis—kept me young. My sisters Susan Becker Donovan, Janice Becker and Mary Becker Nelson are a constant pillar in my life. And in a category of his own, our dog Lafayette Jones was my faithful walking partner.

For years David Halpern, my agent at the Robbins Office, has made my writing life a joy, taking care of business so I could get on with my work. Finally, I want to thank the expert team at Simon & Schuster who were responsible for this book, including Karyn Marcus, a senior editor, Jonathan Cox, editorial assistant, and above all my editor, the legendary Alice Mayhew. She deserves every word of praise that has been used to describe her extraordinary talents. She understood dimensions of this book before I did, shaping it from start to finish with her refinements to the text and her penetrating questions. My debt to her is large, for this book and my previous book on Cambodia. Working with her is a privilege.

Notes

One: Tourism Becomes an Industry

7 *"I get their emails"*: Author interview with Stuart Emmrich, February 22, 2008.

8 *"There were three finalists"*: Author interview with Patrice Tedjini, Madrid, May 28, 2009.

9 *The first time the world powers*: Patrice Tedjini, "UNWTO: An Organization Serving the World Tourism Community," Madrid, May 2009.

9 *Nine years later tourism was recalibrated*: A. K. Bhatia, *Tourism Development: Principles and Practices* (New Delhi: Sterling Publishers, 2002).

9 *French Office National*: James Buzard, "Culture for Export," in Shelley Baranowski and Ellen Furlough, eds., *Being Elsewhere: Tourism, Consumer Culture and Identity in Modern Europe and North America* (Ann Arbor: University of Michigan Press, 2001), p. 301.

9 *A decade later a TWA 707 flew*: Anthony Sampson, *Empires of the Sky* (London: Hodder & Stoughton, 1984), pp. 134–35.

10 *In 1950, shortly after World War II*: UNWTO, *Tourism 2020 Vision, Europe, Volume 4* (Madrid: UNWTO, 2001), p. 11.

11 *"Before, only the elite could afford"*: Author interview with Arthur Frommer, April 20, 2009.

13 *Ten years after its debut*: Nora Ephron, *Wallflower at the Orgy* (New York: Viking Press, 1970), p. 124.

14 *Before 1990, Western Europe*: Frederico Costa, "European Tourism Forum: Analysis of Trends and Changes in European Tourism Demand": http://www.e.c.europe.eu/enterprise/sectors/tourism/files/forum_2008/frederic_costa_en.pdf.

14 *Robinson did his homework*: James Robinson III, WTTC Conference, 2010, Shanghai, China, http://www.globaltraveltourism.com/previous-summits/2010/china-content930c.html?page.

16 *the United Nations tourism organization*: UNWTO, *Tourism Satellite*

Account: Recommended Methodological Framework (Madrid: UNWTO, 2001).

16 *"economic and employment impact"*: Pacific Asia Travel Association, "Coming Soon to an NTO Near You: Tourism Satellite Accounts," Hotels Online Special Report, http://www.hotelonline.com/News/PressReleases1999_3rd/July99_PATATSA.html.

16 *"A movement has been started"*: Francesco Frangialli, *International Tourism: The Great Turning Point, Texts and Documents, 2001.2003, Vol. III* (Madrid: UNWTO, 2004), pp. 33–39, a speech at Vancouver, Canada, May 2001.

17 *The graph line for this travel*: see UNWTO, *Tourism 2020 Vision*, for figures of annual tourist arrivals.

17 *At least one out of every ten*: Author interview with Wolfgang Weinz, September 5, 2011.

17 *If frequent-flyer miles were a currency*: "Frequent-Flyer Miles: Funny Money," *The Economist*, December 20, 2005.

18 *Entire Austrian, Swiss and German*: Rosa Golijan, "Online Service Lets You Rent an Entire Country," MSNBC, April 15, 2011, http://digitallife.today.msnbc.msn.com/_news/2011/04/15/6475973-online-service-lets-you-rent-an-entire-country?lite.

19 *Ireland turned to tourism*: "Irish Prime Minister Recognizes That Tourism Is Critical for Economic Recovery," World Travel and Tourism Council, October 7, 2011, excerpts of speech by Taoiseach Enda Kenny, Prime Minister of Ireland, http://www.wttc.org/news-media/news–archive/2011/irish-prime-minister-recognises-tourism-critical-economic-recove/.

19 *Egypt sent out a plea*: Dina Zayed, "Egypt Awaits Tourism Recovery," Reuters, October 20, 2011, http://www.reuters.com/article/2011/10/20/uk-egypt-tourism-idUSLNE79J02920111020.

23 *The German-based Baedeker*: Karl Baedeker, *Jerusalem and Its Surroundings: Handbook for Travelers* (London: Dulau & Co., reprint, 1973), p. 22.

23 *For the handbook for Egypt*: Karl Baedeker, *Egypt and the Sudan: Handbook for Travelers* (New York: Scribner, reprint, 1929).

24 *the author's overland trek surveying the jungle*: R. E. Peary, "Across Nicaragua with Transit and Machete," *National Geographic*, 1, no. 4 (1889).

24 *Traveling by camel caravan*: Thomas H. Kearney, "The Date Gardens of the Jerid," *National Geographic*, July 1910.

24 *a winter's "ramble" through Concord*: Herbert W. Gleason, "Winter Rambles in Thoreau's Country," *National Geographic*, February 1920.

25 *A master of the genre*: Rebecca West, *Black Lamb and Grey Falcon* (London: Canongate Books, new edition, 2011).

26 *Stuart Newman was in on the ground floor:* Author interviews with Stuart Newman, February 28 and March 18, 2008.

28 *Michael Leahy was the:* Author interview with Michael Leahy, February 29, 2008.

29 *Nancy Newhouse was in charge:* Author interview with Nancy Newhouse, May 8, 2009.

30 *"Our competition is everybody and everything":* Author interview with Catherine Hamm, March 5, 2008.

31 *"If you take ethics seriously":* Author interview with Kelly McBride, March 11, 2008.

31 *Daily defends the free trips:* Author interview with Laura Daily, March 4, 2008.

32 *"our relationship with the lifestyle":* Author interview with Virginia Sheridan, March 11, 2008.

32 *thanks in part to Tom Fiedler:* Author interview with Tom Fiedler, February 26, 2008.

32 *The publicist for one:* Author interview with Doug Hanks III, February 28, 2008.

33 *"It's a pile of crap":* Author interview with Jane Wooldridge, March 12, 2008.

35 *"The issue of numbers of tourists, what they do":* Author interview with Luigi Cabrini, May 27, 2009.

37 *5 billion euros to Italy alone:* Annia Ciezadlo, "Hunger Games," *New York Times Magazine,* August 3, 2011, p. 21.

39 *redesigned in 2005 to reduce:* Alan Riding, "In Louvre, New Room with View of Mona Lisa," *New York Times,* April 6, 2005.

Two: Les Vacances

PAGE

44 *France has become the most visited:* UNWTO *Tourism Highlights, 2011,* http://mkt.unwto.org/sites/all/files/docpdf/unwtohighlights11enhr.pd. It is the most visited country in the world, with 82 million foreign tourists visiting the country annually. GDP (PPP): $2.130 trillion. Population: 65,073,482

44 *"More Chinese visited Paris":* J. W. Marriott, Jr., speaking at "Regaining U.S. Economic Growth and Global Leadership," discussion at the Council on Foreign Relations, Washington, D.C., November 30, 2010, http://www.cfr.org/economics/ceo-speaker-series-regaining-us-economic-growth-global-leadership/p23523.

45 *Among the emblematic stories:* Dianne Stadhams, "Look to Learn a Role

for Visual Ethnography in the Elimination of Poverty," *Visual Anthropology Review* 20, no. 1 (Spring 2004).

46 *"At a minimum"*: Author interview with Philippe Maud'hui, September 9, 2010.

47 *"We can't explain any of that, really"*: Author interview with Marco Marchetti, September 14, 2010.

49 *The first tourists were the intrepid*: Graham Robb, *The Discovery of France: A Historical Geography from the Revolution to the First World War* (New York: W. W. Norton, 2007), p. 27.

49 *"At last, and beyond all question"*: Mark Twain, *Innocents Abroad* (New York: Modern Library, reprint, 2007), p. 95.

50 *Gustave Eiffel said with slight exaggeration*: Jill Jonnes, *Eiffel's Tower* (New York: Viking, 2009), p. 92.

51 *"Nothing of this magnitude had happened"*: Robb, *The Discovery of France*, p. 312.

52 *including a 1936 law*: Joel Colton, *Leon Blum: Humanist in Politics* (New York, Knopf, 1966), pp. 132–33.

52 *When the United States extended aid*: Brian Angus McKenzie, *Remaking France: Americanization, Public Diplomacy and the Marshall Plan* (Oxford: Berghahn Books, 2005).

55 *People from the north—English, French*: Tony Judt, *Postwar: A History of Europe Since 1945* (New York: Penguin, 2005), p. 343.

58 *"Juppé has given us a work of art"*: Author interview with Christian Delom, May 28, 2010.

60 *"When I go to Asia"*: Author interview with Véronique Sanders, September 16, 2010.

62 *"There we stood together"*: François Mauriac, *A Mauriac Reader* (New York: Farrar, Straus & Giroux, 1968).

62 *"huge, huge and very strong"*: Author interview with Olivier Cuvelier, September 15, 2010.

62 *"I wrote the story of the last cargo ship"*: Author interview with Yves Harté, September 17, 2010.

63 *"I knew the English market very well"*: Author interview with Charlie Matthews, September 17, 2010.

64 *Juppé's plan was to rejuvenate*: Author interview with Stéphane Delaux, September 17, 2010.

65 *"I was not surprised"*: Author interview with Alain Juppé following his discussion at the Carnegie Endowment for International Peace, Washington, D.C., February 8, 2011.

67 *"the cultural offering"*: Christian Fraser, "How the Arts Are Funded Outside

the U.K.-France," BBC, October 20, 2010, http://www.bbc.co.uk/news/ entertainment-arts-11569883.

68 *"Those beautiful landscapes"*: Author interview with Patrick Falcone, September 9, 2010.

69 *"They have a higher education"*: Author interview with Jean-Philippe Pérol, June 30, 2010.

70 *Her apartment in Montmartre*: Author interview with Nina Sutton, May 12, 2010.

71 *"There was never any discussion"*: Author interview with Alain Minc, September 13, 2010.

72 *France is consistently rated*: *Sunday Times* (London), June 20, 2008, http://www.timesonline.co.uk/tol/money/consumer_affairs/article3215247.ece.

72 *"sheets ahead of its European counterparts"*: Sean Poulter, "France Tops Survey as Best Place to Emigrate," *Daily Mail* (London), September 22, 2010.

73 *"I didn't want to buy into a dying town"*: Author interview with Ambassador Frances Cook, September 4, 2009.

73 *Sir Ridley complained*: "Ridley Scott Loses Provence Chicken War," *Var Village Voice*, January 2010, p. 6, http://www.varvillagevoice.com (subscription only).

74 *Recently a British government report*: Matthew Taylor, "Living Working Countryside: The Taylor Review of Rural Economy and Affordable Housing," U.K. Department for Communities and Local Government, London, July 2008.

74 *"made aware in advance"*: Author interview with Lord Taylor, December 16, 2010.

Three: Postcard from Venice

PAGE

76 *Matteo Gabbrielli was easy to spot*: Author interview with Matteo Gabbrielli, June 3, 2010.

77 *Zoning favors the hotel business*: Between 2002 and 2008 the number of properties offering tourist accommodation has risen by 450 percent. Rachel Spence, "Is Tourism Ruining Venice?" *Daily Telegraph* (London), April 14, 2008. Cathy Newman, "Vanishing Venice," *National Geographic*, August 2009, cites an increase of 600 percent since 1999.

77 *The population of the historic city has dropped*: Population is tallied every decade. It halved from 121,000 to 62,000 from 1966 to 2006. John Hooper, "Population Decline set to Turn Venice into Italy's Disneyland," *The Guardian*, August 25, 2006.

78 *"When our population reaches under 60,000"*: Author interview with Flavio Gregori, Claudio Paggiarin and Marco Malafante, Venice, June 5, 2010.

80 *The 40xVenezia group has remedies*: 40xVenezia: *Appunti e riflessioni sulla città* (Venice: 40xVenezia, February 2010).

81 *"could help send the vulnerable Venice"*: The UNESCO advertisement appeared in the *International Herald Tribune*, September 2, 2009, p. 5.

81 *"greatest surviving work of art"*: Garry Wills, *Venice: Lion City—The Religion of Empire* (New York: Simon & Schuster, 2001), p. 11.

82 *pollution from the diesel engines that are kept running*: Jake Mooney, "A Plan to Cut Cruise Ship Pollution," *New York Times*, March 6, 2009.

82 *The air pollution from just one*: "Protect Our Oceans: Stop Cruise Ship Pollution; Cruise Ship Waste: Laws and Regulations." (Each day, a ship with 3,000 passengers and crew generates air pollutants equivalent to 12,000 automobiles. http://oceana.org/sites/default/files/o/uploads/cruiseship waste_uslawsandregulations.pdf.

83 *While Venetians may abhor these ads*: Elisabetta Povoledo, "Walls of Ads Test Venice's Patience," *New York Times*, September 13, 2010.

83 *Some citizen groups believe a new tax*: Anna Somers Cocks, "Tourists to Contribute to Costs of Venice," *Art Newspaper*, November 18, 2010, http://www.theartnewspaper.com/articles/tourists-to-contribute-to-cost-of -Venice/21786.

84 *the wave of Chinese tourism*: UNWTO, "The Chinese Outbound Travel Market with Special Insight into the Image of Europe as a Destination," 2008.

85 *"I remember when, for a few thousand lire"*: Donna Leon discussion at Politics and Prose Bookstore, Washington, D.C., April 11, 2011.

Four: Getting It Wrong

90 *"one of the few development opportunities"*: UNWTO, *Tourism and Poverty Alleviation* (Madrid: UNWTO, 2002).

90 *"It was daring of them"*: Author interview with Roland Eng, April 26, 2010, and January 11, 2011.

91 *In two recent surveys*: World Heritage Sites in *National Geographic Traveler*, November 2006, pp. 114–23; and *National Geographic* coastal destinations, November 2010, http://travel.nationalgeographic.com/travel/ coastal-destinations-rated/.

92 *"Left to itself"*: Roland Eng, "Cambodia: The future Challenge for Tourism," http://www.intracem/prgwefef2005/tourism_mega_cluster_papers/ Cambodia.

93 *pushing tourism to Cambodia:* Tourism statistics: Cambodia Ministry of Tourism website, http://www.tourismcambodia.org/mot/index.php?view=statistic_report.

94 *"enclosed in immense walls":* Georges Coedes, *Angkor: An Introduction* (Hong Kong: Oxford University Press, 1963), p. 45.

94 *"It is not good":* Author interview with Yut, April 26, 2010.

95 *"For sure, these temples":* Author interview with Dominique Soutif, April 26, 2010.

95 *Groslier and his father George:* Bernard-Philippe Groslier, *Angkor: Hommes et Pierres* (Paris: Arthaud, 1965).

96 *These countries, along with the United Nations:* "I.C.C.-Angkor: 15 Years of International Cooperation and Sustainable Development," UNESCO, 2009, http://unesdoc.unesco.org/images/0018/001890/189010e.pdf.

98 *Other organizations are less inhibited:* "Saving Our Vanishing Heritage," Global Heritage Fund Report, 2010, http://globalheritagefund.org/images/uploads/docs/GHFVanishingGlobalHeritageSitesinPeril102010.pdf.

98 *Son Soubert, an archeologist:* Author interview with Son Soubert, January 8, 2011.

98 *The World Bank sounded a similar alarm:* "Sharing Growth: Equity and Development in Cambodia," The World Bank Equity Report, 2007, http://siteresources.worldbank.org/INTCAMBODIA/Resources/293755-1181597206916/E&D_Full-Report.pdf.

99 *South Korea is a major patron:* staff, "South Korea to Increase Aid, Investment for Cambodia," Xinhua, January 14, 2010, http://www.chinadaily.com.cn/world/2010-01/14/content_9323040.htm.

99 *The largest project:* "Korea Plans to Establish a New Airport in Siem Reap in Order to Expand Tourism Sector," Investment News in *Cambodia Mirror*, March 14, 2011, http://investmentnewsincambodia-mirror.blogspot.com/2011/03/korea-plans-to-establish-new-airport-in.html.

99 *building a $400 million casino:* Daniel Ten Kate, "South Korean Developer Courts Harrah's for Casino at Cambodia's Angkor Wat," Bloomberg.com, July 29, 2010, http://www.bloomberg.com/news/2010-07-29/south-korean-developer-courts-harrah-s-for-casino-at-cambodia-s-angkor-wat.htmlcom.

99 *A Cambodian whistle-blower:* Peter Olszewski, "Two-Night Concert Could Resurrect Reputation," *Phnom Penh Post*, December 31, 2010.

100 *The "leakage" of money:* Author interview with Douglas Broderick, February 10, 2012.

100 *Broderick pointed to:* "Cambodia Country Competitiveness: Driving Economic Growth and Poverty Reduction," United Nations Development Program, discussion paper no. 7, April 2009, p. 39.

100 *"The province of Siem Reap is now"*: Uk Someth, "La Ceinture Verte de Siem Reap," *Cambodge Nouveau*, Janvier 2011, p. 8.

101 *Prime Minister Hun Sen argues otherwise*: "Cambodia P.M. Message on World Tourism Day: Commitment to Fight Poverty," Agence Khmer Press, September 27, 2010, http://namnewsnetwork.org/v3/read.php?id=134552.

101 *A website called Scambodia*: http://www.scambodia.com. Posted by blogroll, a local business that wanted to remain anonymous, March 8, 2009.

102 *"I now know why Angelina Jolie"*: http://www.travelpod.com/travel-blog -entries/wendyworld/4/1261194608/tpod.html.

102 *In 2012 the United Nations published*: "With the Best Intentions: A Study of Attitudes Towards Residential Care in Cambodia," Cambodian Ministry of Social Affairs, Veterans and Youth Rehabilitation and UNICEF, 2011, http://www.un.org.kh/index.php?option=com_jdownloads&Itemid=65& view=finish&cid=93&catid=4.

103 *"Sometimes I think people leave their brains at home"*: Author interview with Daniela Ruby Papi, April 25, 2010.

104 *"We can sell Cambodia to the world"*: Author interview with Thong Khon, Minister of Tourism, April 26, 2010.

105 *Tuol Sleng was a high school*: Elizabeth Becker, *When the War Was Over* (New York: Simon & Schuster, 1986).

106 *Cambodia is now on the circuit*: Steve Silva, "Genocide Tourism: Tragedy Becomes a Destination," *Chicago Tribune*, August 5, 2007.

106 *Questions were raised when a Pennsylvania farmer*: Richard Sharpley and Philip R. Stone, eds., *The Darker Side of Travel: The Theory and Practice of Dark Tourism* (Bristol, U.K.: Channel View Publications, 2009).

107 *"Holocaust institutions do everything they can"*: Author interview with Michael Abramowitz, January 19, 2011.

107 *"How can we learn"*: Author interview with Youk Chhang, February 13, 2011.

108 *Then one morning in 2005*: Kay Kimsong and Karen Hawkins, "Gov't Tourism Office Traded for Villa, Cash," *Cambodia Daily*, April 14, 2005.

109 *The dispossessed were never given market value*: "Borei Keila: Cambodia's Social Housing Project Five Years On," report by LICADHO human rights organization, December 19, 2008, http://www.licadho-cambodia.org/articles/ 20081219/84/index.html.

110 *LICADHO is one of a handful*: Others include: Centre on Housing Rights and Eviction COHRE/Asia; the Cambodian Human Rights and Development Association (ADHOC); the Community Legal Education Center (CLEC).

110 *"This group had a very strong claim"*: Author interview with Mathieu Pellerin, April 24, 2010.

110 *There is nothing hidden about this epidemic*: Committee on Economic, Social and Cultural Rights, U.N. Commission on Human Rights, 42nd Session, Geneva, May 4–22, 2009, http://www2.ohchr.org/english/bodies/cescr/cescrs42.htm.

110 *Global witness, the nonprofit*: "Country for Sale," a Global Witness Report, February 2009, http://www.globalwitness.org/sites/default/files/library/country_for_sale_low_res_english. Also, Adrian Levy and Cathy Scott-Clark, "Country for Sale," *The Guardian*, April 26, 2008, www.guardian.co.uk/world/2008/apr/26/Cambodia.

110 *"I have to make a decision"*: Kay Kimsong and Lee Berthiaume, "P.M. Reverses Freeze on Land Deals," *Cambodia Daily*, March 15, 2005.

112 *More than 100 families fought eviction*: "S'ville Residents Clear Privately Built Roadblock," *Cambodia Daily*, March 10, 2005.

112 *An army of bulldozers*: "Country for Sale," *The Guardian*.

112 *This is not to say that all foreign*: Kay Kimsong, "Paradise in the Making," *Phnom Penh Post*, January 22, 2011.

113 *To build just one*: Prak Chan Thul and Lee Berthiaume, "Poipet Casino Orders 218 Families to Move," *Cambodia Daily*, April 12, 2005.

113 *contribute only $17 million*: "Cambodia's Gambling Industry Contributes 17 Million USD in Tax Revenues in 2006," Xinhau, January 16, 2007, http://www.english.peopledaily.com.cn/200701/16/eng20070116_341731.html.

113 *These loose rules are poorly enforced*: "The Asian Gaming 50," Asian Gaming, September 2011, http://www.asgam.com/cover-stories/item/1288.html.

113 *Singapore approved the construction*: Michael Lenz, "Singapore 'Casino Royale,'" *Southeast Asia Globe*, April 2010.

113 *The government gave Chen Lip Keong*: "The Asian Gaming 50," Asian Gaming, September 2011, http://www.asgam.com/cover-stories/item/1288.html.

114 *NagaWorld made $35 million in profits*: NagaWorld Company Report, February 2010, http://www.nagacorp.com/assets/files/eng/analyst/research/SunHungKaiFinancial.pdf.

114 *"is operating to extract"*: "The Order of Hun Sen to Prohibit Khmer Citizens from Gambling in Casinos Is Not Applied by the Owner of the Naga Casino," *Cambodia Mirror*, March 17, 2010.

114 *like this one from Roise Reisen*: Michael Hitchcock et al., eds., *Tourism in Southeast Asia* (Honolulu: University of Hawaii Press, 2009), pp. 198–99.

114 *Yoko Kusaka*: Ibid.

114 *Brothels returned to Cambodia*: Colum Lynch, "U.N. Faces More Accusations of Sexual Misconduct," *Washington Post*, March 13, 2005.

115 *"Highway of Shame"*: Misha Glenny, *McMafia: A Journey Through the Global Criminal Underworld* (New York: Knopf, 2008).

115 *according to the U.S. Department of Justice*: "Child Sex Tourism," U.S. Department of Justice, Child Exploitation and Obscenity Section, http://www.justice.gov/criminal/ceos/sextour.html.

116 *Brett Tollman*: Comments at the World Travel and Tourism Council Conference, Florianópolis, Brazil, May 16, 2009.

116 *the Czech hotel industry lobbied*: Dan Bilefsky, "Financial Crisis Tames Demand of World's Oldest Service," *New York Times*, December 9, 2008.

116 *But even though every minute*: Siddharth Kara, *Sex Trafficking: Inside the Business of Modern Slavery* (New York: Columbia University Press, 2009), p. 3.

116 *"Sometimes a normal tourist"*: Author interview with Marina Diotallevi, May 27, 2009.

117 *80,000 Italian men*: Muireann O'Briain, Milena Grillo and Helia Barbosa, "Sexual Exploitation of Children and Adolescents in Tourism," The World Congress Against Sexual Exploitation of Children and Adolescents, Brazil, 2008, http://www.ecpat.net/worldcongressIII/PDF/Publications/CST/ThematicPaperCSTENG.pdf.

117 *Male tourists traveling to Cambodia*: Frederic Thomas and Leigh Mathews, "Who Are the Child Sex Tourists in Cambodia," Child Wise Report, December 2006, South Melbourne, Australia.

117 *"Visitors taking a trip"*: Nuon Rithy Niron, Yit Viriya and Laurence Gray, "Children's Work, Adult's Play: Child Sex Tourism, the Problem in Cambodia," World Vision Report with the Cambodian Ministry of Tourism and the Cambodian National Council for Children, Phnom Penh, 2001.

117 *Somaly Mam, a Cambodian woman*: Somaly Mam, *The Road of Lost Innocence: The True Story of a Cambodian Heroine* (New York: Spiegel & Grau, 2008).

118 *In a survey, tour agents estimated*: Caroline Putnam-Cramer, *Child Sex Tourism: Study of the Scope of the Problem and Evaluation of Existing Anti-Child Sex Tourism Initiatives*, The Protection Project at Johns Hopkins University and COSECAM (Phnom Penh, COSECAM Publications, 2005).

119 *in response to growing pressure from Europe*: Christine Beddoe, C. Michael Hall and Chris Ryan, *The Incidence of Sexual Exploitation of Children in Tourism* (Madrid: UNWTO, 2001), pp. 37–44.

119 *"Most of the young children are sold by"*: Author interview with Ron Dunne, April 19, 2010.

Five: Cruising: Destination Nowhere

PAGE

125 *We had flown:* Our cruise was aboard the *Navigator of the Seas* of the Royal Caribbean cruise line from December 14 to 19, 2009.

128 *"a little like backpacking":* Author interview with Kathy Kaufmann, March 15, 2010.

130 *The penalty for disobeying this policy:* Royal Caribbean official website, "Corporate Governance," http://www.rclinvestor.com/phoenix.zhtml?c=103045&p=irol-faq.

133 *"a classic tale of the American dream":* Official history section of the Carnival Cruise Lines called "The Fun Begins," http://phx.corporate-ir.net/phoenix.zhtml?c=200767&p=irol-history.

133 *Arison was not born poor:* Biography of Ted Arison, from the Arison School of Business, Herzliya, Israel, http://portal.idc.ac.il/en/main/academics/business/Pages/TheArisonName.aspx.

134 *he died in 1999:* Amotz Asa-el and Dan Gersenfeld, "Ted Arison, World's Wealthiest Jew, Dies in Tel Aviv," jweekly.com, October 8, 1999.

135 *He volunteered in the Jewish brigade:* Arison biography, Arison School of Business.

137 *In his book* Selling the Sea: Bob Dickinson and Andy Vladimir, *Selling the Sea: An Inside Look at the Cruise Industry* (New York: John Wiley & Sons, Inc., 1997), a history of Arison and Carnival, p. 33.

138 *It is no anomaly:* "Iata Says Airlines Suffered 'Worst Year' in 2009," BBC News online, January 27, 2010, interview with Giovanni Bisignani, director general, International Air Transport Association: "In terms of demand, 2009 goes into the history books as the worst year the industry has ever seen. . . . We have permanently lost 2.5 years of growth in passenger markets and 3.5 years of growth in the freight business." http://news.bbc.co.uk/2/hi/8482654.stm.

139 *They pulled down their Union Jack flags:* Alexandra Madaraka-Sheppard, *Modern Maritime Law and Risk Management* (London: Cavendish Publishing, 2001), esp. p. 278.

139 *Former Secretary of State Edward Stettinius:* Liberian registry at GlobalSecurity.org, http://www.globalsecurity.org/military/world/liberia/registry.htm; Liberian International Ship and Corporate Registry, http://www.liscr.com/liscr/AboutUs/AboutLiberianRegistry/tabid/206/Default.aspx.

140 *"Many countries, including the United States":* Dickinson and Vladimir, p. 65.

140 *Cruise lines gain another enormous advantage:* Doug Frantz, "Sovereign Islands," *New York Times,* February 19, 1999.

140 *"the competitive nature"*: "Royal Caribbean to Reflag Six Ships to Baha-mian Registry," Cruise Critic, September 15, 2004, http://www.boards .cruisecritic.com/archive/index.php/t-81298.html.

141 *Today the two firms account*: U.S. cruises are two-thirds of the market. UNWTO, *Worldwide Cruise Ship Activity* (Madrid: UNWTO, 2003), p. 17.

141 *phenomenal growth rate of 1,000 percent*: UNWTO, *Turismo de cruceros: Situación actual y tendencias* (Madrid: UNWTO, 2008).

142 *They opposed the use of flags*: International Transport Workers' Federation, " 'Sweatship' Conditions on Many Cruise Ships," 2003, http://www.itfsea farers.org/sweatship.cfm.

142 *Representative William Clay, Sr.*: Ross A. Klein, *Cruise Ship Squeeze: The New Pirates of the Seven Seas* (Gabriola Island, B.C.: New Society Publish-ers, 2005), pp. 75–76.

143 *raising the issue of Dickensian wages*: "Sweatships: What It's Really Like to Work on Board Cruise Ships," by Celia Mather, published by War on Want and International Transport Workers Federation, 2002, p.19.

143 *Adam Goldstein is the president*: Author interview with Adam Goldstein, March 3, 2010.

145 *Mr. Goldstein, whose annual salary and compensation*: Compensa-tion of Adam Goldstein, Forbes online, http://people.forbes.com/profile/ adam-m-goldstein/69059.

146 *"Onboard spending is becoming"*: Author interview with Ross A. Klein, January 11, 2010.

146 *"the idea is that you should be able"*: Dickinson and Vladimir, *Selling the Sea*, p. 270.

147 *Theresa Franks, the owner*: Author interview with Theresa Franks, February 22, 2010.

147 *mainstream media including CBS*: "Cruise Art Auctions: Great Bargain or Lousy Deal?" *Inside Edition*, February 11, 2008.

147 *and the* New York Times: Jori Finkel, "Art Auctions on Cruise Ships Lead to Anger, Accusations and Lawsuits," *New York Times*, July 16, 2008.

148 *Ms. Franks also won her appeal*: WIPO document: *Global Fine Art Registry LLC v. Cartoon Heaven*, http://www.wipo.int/amc/en/domains/decisions/ html/2008/d20080-1203.html.

148 *Eventually, some of the customers banded together*: Park West lawsuit: "A Complaint and Demand for Jury Trial was filed on 23 December 2008 against Park West Galleries, Inc., Albert Scaglione and Morris Shapiro (owner and gallery director, respectively) and Royal Caribbean Cruises Ltd., by the Farmington Hills, MI, attorneys, Kaufmann, Payton and Chapa,

for Plaintiffs Albert and Vivian Best, Sharon Day, Julian Howard, Deborah Austin, Cheryl Crist, Heidi Rice, Michael and Maria Vallillo and Martha Szostak, all customers of Park West Galleries and all, except for Albert and Vivian Best, Fine Art Registry members."

148 *"We got standing"*: author interview with Donald L. Payton, October 5, 2012.

148 *Goldstein wrote in his company blog*: www.answeritroyally.com/blog/?p=1257.

148 *This is what they spend*: UNWTO, *Turismo de cruceros*, p. 17.

149 *Carnival Cruise Lines could report $13 billion*: Gene Sloan, "Downturn? What Downturn? Cruise Giant Carnival Posts a $1.8 Billion Profit," *USA Today*, December 18, 2009.

149 *Diamonds International was founded by David Gad*: "DIAMONDS IN-TERNATIONAL: David Gad, an Israeli immigrant, founded the company, his heirs have run it: Morris and Albert." Diamonds International history at http://www.royalresorts.com/diamonds-international.asp; and Diana Jarrett, "Dror Galili: Innovation in the Diamond Industry," Jewelry & Gem Artisans http://www.jewelrygemartisans.blogspot.com/2010/02/dror-galili-innovation-in-diamond-htm.

149 *more than 125 stores*: Kevin Shereves, "Diamonds International Expands," Cayman Net News online, March 2, 2010, http://www.caymannetnews.com/local.php?news_id=20364&start=0&category_id=1.

150 *Jane Semeleer, the president of Aruba's Central Bank*: Author interview with Jane Semeleer, February 3, 2011.

151 *More common is this description by Terry Dale*: Author interview with Terry Dale, April 2, 2010.

152 *"Cruise ships have changed the face of tourism"*: Author interview with Paul Bennett, February 8, 2010.

153 *In a study with the Center*: "Cruise Tourism in Belize: Perceptions of Economic, Social and Environmental Impact," Center on Ecotourism and Sustainable Development in Collaboration with the Belize Tourism Board. September 2006, http://www.summitfdn.org/foundation/pdfs/cruise-tourism-belize.pdf.

153 *In Europe, an impartial study*: Zrinka Marusic, Sinisa Horak and Renata Tomlienovic, "The Socio-Economic Impacts of Cruise Tourism: A Case Study of Croatian Destinations," *Proceedings of the 5th International Coastal and Marine Tourism Congress: Balancing Marine Tourism Development and Sustainability* (Auckland: AUT University, 2007).

153 *I spoke to Anna Dominguez-Hoare*: Author interview with Anna Dominguez-Hoare, March 1, 2010.

154 *When I put that question to James Sweeting:* Author interview with James Sweeting, March 2, 2010.

154 *"No Caribbean country has survived intact":* Author interview with Jonathan Tourtellot, January 11, 2010.

156 *Human activity has damaged the seas:* "Overview of Shipping and Navigation History by the International Maritime Organization," http://www.imo.org/incudes/blastDataOnly.asp/data_id%D21794/Overviewofshippingand navigationhistory.pdf.

156 *the average cruise ship produces:* "Draft Cruise Ship Discharge Assessment Report," Environmental Protection Agency, EPA842-R-07-005, Washington, D.C., December 2007.

156 *Cruise companies won an exemption:* Claudia Copeland, "Cruise Ship Pollution: Background, Laws and Regulations, and Key Issues," Congressional Research Service (RL32450) Washington, D.C.: February 6, 2008.

157 *Significantly, cruise lines are not required:* "Marine Pollution: Progress Made to Reduce Marine Pollution by Cruise Ships, but Important Issues Remain," General Accounting Office, GAO/RCED-00-48, Washington, D.C., February 2000.

158 *Royal Caribbean was convicted:* David Rosenzweig, "Cruise Line Fined $18 Million for Dumping Waste at Sea," *Los Angeles Times,* July 22, 1999.

160 *"That shocked the hell out of us":* Author interview with Gershon Cohen, May 11, 2010.

160 *The Alaskan legislature passed laws:* Seattle Times staff and news services, "New Alaska Tax Cracks Down on Cruise Lines," *Seattle Times,* August 24, 2006, http://www.seattletimes.newsource.com/html/travel/2003223150_webcruisetax24.html.

162 *Antarctica has banned:* "Coming Antarctic Season, the Last for Big Cruise Ships," South Atlantic News Agency, April 24, 2010, http://www.en.merco press.com/2010/04/24/coming-antarctic-season-2010-11-the-last-for-big-cruise-ships.

162 *"Without regulations, we are going":* Associated Press, "Nations Take Steps to Curb Tourism to Antarctica as Threat of Human, Environmental Disasters Rises," *New York Daily News,* December 10, 2009.

162 *The Atlantic Treaty members are reducing:* Richard Gray, "Plans to Limit Tourism in Antarctic," *The Telegraph* (London), April 11, 2009.

162 *The Norwegian environment minister:* Minister of the Environment Helen Bjørnøy: "The Norwegian Government Bans the Presence of Heavy Fuel Oil On Board Ships in Svalbard's Eastern Waters," press release, March 6, 2007.

163 *As previously mentioned:* Lee van de Voo, "Green Cruising or Cruise Ship

Pollution?" The Daily Green, http://www.thedailygreen.com/environmen tal-news/latest/cruise-ship-pollution-460810#ixzz0xByrNZqx; and "Cruise Ships to Plug In to Reduce Pollution: Using Dock Power Is Part of Regional Plan," *Seattle Post-Intelligencer*, http://www.seattlepi.com/local/ article/Cruise-ships-to-plug-in-to-reduce-pollution1155569.php#ixzzlwCm Ra2oa.

163 *The United Nations Environment Programme:* Author interview with Amy Fraenkel, March 10, 2010.

163 *Responding to the growing evidence:* Juliet Eilperin, "Cruise Ship Lines, Alaska Officials Question New Air Pollution Limits," *Washington Post*, July 23, 2012.

164 *initially adopted by the International Maritime Organization:* coast-guard.dodlive.mil/index.php/2010/03/imo-adopts-200-mile-north-american -emissions-control-area/.

164 *In a recent assessment, Lloyd's:* Lloyd's Cruise International Market Assessment 2008 Recommend by 2009 CLIA Report, http://www.lloydscruise international.com.

165 *The industry also has made friends:* For an example of fundraising rates, see http://www.cruisevacationcenter.com/fundraising_cruises.htm.

Six: Desert Fantasies

PAGE

167 *"one of the world's leading case examples":* World Travel and Tourism Council website, http://www.wttc.org/eng/Tourism_Initiatives/Regional_Initiatives/ Middle_East_Chapter/.

169 *Dubai's leader Sheikh Mohammed:* "The CEO Sheikh," *Newsweek*, August 5, 2007, http://www.newsweek.com/2007/08/05/the-ceo-sheik.html.

169 *Taliban commanders:* Carlotta Gall, "Losses in Pakistani Haven Strain Taliban," *New York Times*, April 1, 2011.

171 *The sheikh went ahead anyway and built an airfield:* Sayed Ali, *Dubai: Gilded Cage* (New Haven: Yale University Press, 2010), p. 109.

171 *the region's first duty-free shopping:* Ibid., p. 22.

172 *"To win landing rights in many countries":* Author interview with Ed Fuller, May 17, 2009.

173 *Thanks to that gift of geography:* "Rulers of the New Silk Road," *The Economist*, June 5, 2010.

173 *In a few years it could be* the hub: Jad Mouawad, "Will All Flight Paths Lead to Dubai?" *New York Times*, February 13, 2011.

174 *"We have more transfers from Dubai":* Author interview with Alain St. Onge, May 18, 2011.

174 *Other airlines have called foul:* "Rulers of the New Silk Road."

176 *This is one of the planet's "hottest shopping spots":* Rory Jones, "Dubai, the World's Hottest Shopping Spot," *The National* (Abu Dhabi), April 12, 2011.

179 *experts were predicting the demise of the emirate:* Joshua Hammer, "Good-Bye to Dubai," *New York Review of Books*, August 19, 2010.

179 *Dubai's public debt:* "Debt Forgetfulness," *The Economist*, January 1, 2011.

181 *In 2011, during the wave of revolutions:* "Dubai Tops Middle East and Africa's Destination Cities," eTN *Global Travel Industry News*, June 6, 2011.

182 *they paid the Bedouins to protect:* Steven Heydemann, *War, Institutions and Social Change in the Middle East* (Berkeley: University of California Press, 2000).

183 *The government of Indonesia:* Norimitsu Onishi, "As Indonesians Go to Mecca, Many Eyes Follow Their Money," *New York Times*, August 6, 2010.

183 *In Bangladesh, political groups successfully lobbied:* By a staff correspondent, *Daily Star* (Dhaka), October 1, 2009.

183 *In Afghanistan, the minister of Hajj:* Shakeela Abrahimkhil, "Afghan Hajj Minister Charged with Corruption," TOLOnews.com, April 20, 2011.

184 *In 2008 the demand proved so great:* "Emirates Airline Announces Additional Flights for Hajj," press release, November 9, 2008, The Emirates Group, www.theemiratesgroup.com.

184 *Rising in the center of Mecca:* Nicolai Ouroussoff, "Mecca Gets a New Look: Brash and Gaudy," *International Herald Tribune*, December 31, 2010.

184 *Sami Angawi, an expert:* Laith Abou-Ragheb, "Dr. Sami Angawi on Wahhabi Desecration of Makkah: Developers and Purists Erase Mecca's History," Reuters, July 12, 2005.

185 *The only way foreign Christians can make a pilgrimage:* Ana Carbajosa, "Dispatch Bethlehem," *London Observer*, December 26, 2010.

187 *"I have no idea, honestly, what goes on there":* Author interview with Wolfgang Weinz, June 3, 2011.

187 *In the seminal investigation:* "Building Towers, Cheating Workers: Exploitation of Migrant Construction Workers in the United Arab Emirates," Human Rights Watch, November 2006.

188 *A British report was even harsher:* Nick Meo, "How Dubai, the Playground of Businessmen and Warlords, Is Built by Asian Wage Slaves," *The Independent* (London), March 1, 2005.

188 *considering the UAE has a per capita income:* UAE per capita income was $48,821 in 2010, according to the International Monetary Fund, http://www.imf.org/external/pubs/ft/weo/2011/01/weodata/index.aspx.

189 *Bangladeshi maid who cut off:* Wafa Issa, "Maid Cuts Off Employer's Penis After Being Sexually Harassed," *The National,* April 13, 2011.

190 *Tourists have heard the stories:* The National staff, "Hotel Encounter Costs Unmarried Couple a Year in Prison," *The National,* June 16, 2011.

190 *and go to bars and clubs like the York:* Nick Tosches, "Dubai's the Limit," *Vanity Fair,* June 1, 2006.

190 *beautiful women prostitutes are plentiful:* William Ridgeway, "Dubai: The Scandal and the Vice," Social Affairs Unit 5, April 2005, www.socialaffairs unit.org.uk/blog/archives/000345.php.

191 *"destination for men and women":* U.S. Department of State, Trafficking in Persons Report, 2011, http://www.state.gov/g/tiprpt/2011.

192 *The financial rewards outweighed the cultural complaints:* Alan Riding, "The Louvre's Art: Priceless. The Louvre's Name: Expensive," *New York Times,* March 7, 2007.

192 *Organized by New York artists:* "130 Artists Call for Guggenheim Boycott over Migrant Worker Exploitation," WordPress.com, New York, March 17, 2011, http://www.gulflabor.wordpress.com.

193 *create an elite battalion of foreign mercenaries:* Mark Mazzetti and Emily B. Hager, "Secret Desert Force Set Up by Blackwater's Founder," *New York Times,* June 7, 2011.

193 *host its first Green Tourism conference:* World Green Tourism Conference, Abu Dhabi, November 27–29, 2010.

195 *Masdar is attempting to do just that:* Nicolai Ouroussoff, "In Arabian Desert, a Sustainable City Rises," *New York Times,* September 26, 2010.

195 *Eventually this refuge should show the way:* Ucilia Wang, "Abu Dhabi, Rise of a Renewable Energy Titan?" January 2011, http://www.renewableenergyworld .com/rea/news/article/2011/01/abu-dhabi-rise-of-a-renewable-energy-titan.

196 *the UAE has had the worst score:* Living Planet Report 2010, World Wildlife Fund, p. 14, http://www.worldwildlife.org.

196 *Dead fish in the rivers:* Vesela Todorova and Tim Brooks, "Tonnes of Dead Fish Wash Up in Creek," *The National,* October 7, 2009.

197 *Bali, the ultimate paradise:* Author interview with Olivier Pouillon, November 19, 2009.

198 *drawing on the native concept of hema:* M. A. Zahran and H. A. Younes, "Hema System: Traditional Conservation of Plant Life in Saudi Arabia," King Abdulaziz University, Jeddah, Saudi Arabia, http://www.kau.edu.sa/ Files/320/Researches/52341_22648.pdf.

198 *"perhaps more than any other region in the world":* Abdulaziz al Midfa, David Mallon, Kevin Budd, "Ten Years of Conservation Workshops for the Fauna of Arabia, 2000–2009," *Biodiversity Conservation in the Arabian*

Peninsula, Zoology in the Middle East (series), September 3, 2011, Heidelberg, http://www.kasparek-verlag.de/PDF%20Abstracts/PDF-SUPP3%20Weboptimiert/007-012%20AbdulazizMidfa.pdf.

199 *"We have seen what has been going on"*: Author interview with Graham Evans and Anthony Kirkham, August 23, 2011.

200 *Environmentalists say this is a disaster in the making*: Caroline Shearing, "Dubai Golf Drive Upsets Greens: Plans to Open 11 New Golf Courses in Dubai Have Hit Environmental Opposition," *The Telegraph*, April 25, 2008.

202 *Abu Dhabi Policy Agency: Dubai: Gilded Cage*, p. 181.

Seven: Safari

PAGE

208 *The Europeans conquered some 10 million square miles*: Thomas Pakenham, *The Scramble for Africa* (London: Abacus, 1993).

208 *Nearly 50 million visitors*: UNWTO, Tourism Highlights, 2011 Edition, Africa, http://mkt.unwto.org/sites/all/files/docpdf/unwtohighlights11enlr.pdf.

209 *the $76 billion in revenue*: WTTC: Travel and Tourism, Economic Impact, 2011, Africa, http://www.wttc.org/site_media/uploads/downloads/africa2.pdf.

210 *"It has a stable and functioning government"*: Author interview with Ambassador Mark Storella, May 21, 2011.

210 *Last year, tourism made a small leap*: WTTC, "Zambia Economic Impact Report 2011," http://www.wttc.org/bin/pdf/original_pdf_file/zambia.pdf.

210 *but copper is king*: Central Intelligence Agency, *The World Fact Book: Zambia*, https://www.cia.gov/library/publications/the-world-factbook/geos/za.html. Copper represents 65 percent of exports, and the 2011 GDP was $17.5 billion.

210 *compared to the $41 billion*: WTTC, "South Africa Economic Impact Report 2011," http://www.wttc.org/bin/pdf/original_pdf_file/south_africa.pdf.

210 *I discovered this at a mass*: St. Ignatius Parish, Lusaka, May 22, 2011.

217 *"That's a sable"*: Author interview with Andy Hogg, May 25, 2011.

217 *Born in East Africa in 1912*: Norman Carr, *The White Impala: The Story of a Game Ranger* (London: Collins, 1969); and Lynn ten Kate, "Obituary: Norman Carr," *The Independent* (London), May 1997.

219 *The rise in human population*: John Reader, *Africa: A Biography of the Continent* (London: Penguin, 1998), pp. 255–56.

220 *3 million elephants roamed the continent*: World Wildlife Fund, "Afri-

can Elephants," http://www.panda.org/what_we_do/endangered_species/elephants/african_elephant.

221 *Alarmed, officials banned the international trade in ivory*: WWF, "African Elephants."

221 *"The slaughter of our elephants is economic sabotage"*: Author interview with Richard Leakey, October 12, 2011.

221 *Then Leakey started grappling with the mundane*: Richard Leakey and Virginia Morell, *Wildlife Wars: My Fight to Save Africa's Natural Treasures* (New York: St. Martin's, 2001).

222 *"tourism may be the biggest industry"*: Author interview with Harold Wackman, May 12, 2011.

223 *an American couple made it their mission*: Jeffrey Goldberg, "A Reporter at Large: The Hunted," *New Yorker*, April 5, 2010.

224 *ZAWA, an underfunded organization*: Adam Pope, World Bank, "A Study of Nature-Based Tourism: Zambia," 2005, http://www.aec.msu.edu/fs2/zambia/resources/Progress%20Report%20Part%201_Adam_Pope.pdf.

224 *the Norwegian government has given*: Norwegian Agency for Development Cooperation, "Evaluation of Norwegian Development Support to Zambia (1991–2005)," April 2007.

225 *"Norway's continuous and long-term support"*: Author interviews with Trond Lovdal, July 11, 2011.

226 *but at the last minute she decided against*: Author interview with Megan Parker, assistant to Jody Allen, July 12–17, 2011.

229 *The Honorable Catherine Namugala*: The 5th IIPT Africa Conference, May 15–20, Lusaka, Zambia, hosted by the Zambian Ministry of Tourism and organized by the International Institute for Peace Through Tourism, a Vermont-based nonprofit organization.

233 *In dozens of studies*: Dan Brockington, Rosaleen Duffy and Jim Igoe, *Nature Unbound: Conservation, Capitalism and the Future of Protected Areas* (London and Sterling, Va.: Earthscan, 2008).

234 *sawing off the horns of stuffed rhinos*: Greg Neale and James Burton, "Elephant and Rhino Poaching Is Driven by China's Economic Boom," *The Observer* (London), August 13, 2011.

234 *Esmond Martin, one of the leading investigators*: Esmond Martin and Lucy Vigne, "The Ivory Dynasty: A Report on the Soaring Demand for Elephant and Mammoth Ivory in Southern China," Elephant Family and the Aspinall Foundation, and Columbus Zoo and Aquarium, http://www.elephantfamily.org/uploads/copy/EF_Ivory_Report_2011_web.pdf.

235 *Writing in* Vanity Fair *a few months*: Alex Shoumatoff, "Agony and Ivory," *Vanity Fair*, August 2011.

235 *a group of Vietnamese officials flew to Johannesburg*: Donna Bryon, "South Africans, Vietnamese Meet on Rhino Poaching," Huffington Post, September 28, 2011.

236 *China's wealth has helped fuel*: Lloyd Gedye, "China's Boom Swells the Coffers of African Economies," Mail & Guardian online (South Africa), May 6, 2011; "Trying to Pull Together: The Chinese in Africa," *The Economist*, April 23, 2011, p. 29.

236 *the ugly side of Chinese investments*: Mutuna Chanda, "China in Zambia— Jobs or Exploitation?" BBC online, December 12, 2010.

237 *there was an immediate outcry*: David Smith, "Robert Mugabe Asked to Be UN 'Leader for Tourism,' " *The Guardian*, May 29, 2012.

239 National Geographic *produced an inspiring film*: National Geographic DVD, *Africa's Lost Eden*, www.shop.nationalgeographic.com.

239 *The story of Gorongosa was told in lyrical detail*: Philip Gourevitch, "The Monkey and the Fish," *New Yorker*, December 21, 2009.

239 *I met Carr on one of his visits*: Author interview with Greg Carr, March 23, 2010.

240 *After a lecture in Washington*: Author interview with Nicky Oppenheimer, Council on Foreign Relations, Washington, D.C.: June 9, 2011.

241 *The millions of tourists have trampled*: "Galapagos: On the Extinction of Species—Tourism Is Imperiling a Wildlife Paradise," *The Economist*, June 5, 2010.

241 *Beginning in 2012, only four cruise ships*: Laura Mortkowitz, "Travel Restrictions to Galapagos Islands," *Physician's Money Digest*, November 14, 2011, http://www.physiciansmoneydigest.com/your-life/Travel-Restrictions-to-Galapagos-Islands.

241 *In his description of Maasai dancing*: Edward M. Bruner, "The Maasai and the Lion King: Authenticity, Nationalism and Globalization in African Tourism," *American Ethnologist* 28, no. 4 (2001).

243 *Paulla A. Ebron, a professor*: Paulla A. Ebron, "Competing Narratives of Memorialized History," paper presented at "Slavery and Public History: An International Symposium," Yale University, November 2–4, 2006, http://www.yale.edu/glc/publichistory/ebron.

244 *The most famous modern "Roots" trip*: Barack Obama, *Dreams from My Father: A Story of Race and Inheritance* (New York: Three Rivers Press, 2004), pp. 346–56.

Eight: Becoming Green

PAGE
245 *On our fifth day sailing:* Cruise from Panama to Costa Rica aboard the National Geographic's *Sea Lion*, March 12–19, 2011.
247 *Those guidelines were recently hammered out:* "The Global Sustainable Tourism Criteria of the Global Sustainable Tourism Council," http://new.gstcouncil.org.
250 *Costa Rica was the poorest of the Spanish colonies:* Sterling Evans, *The Green Republic: A Conservation History of Costa Rica* (Austin: University of Texas Press, 1999), pp. 5–20.
251 *One of his star pupils was Gerardo Budowski:* Encyclopedia of Forestry, "Gerardo Budowski," http://www.encyclopediaofforestry.org/index.php/Gerardo_Budowski.
251 *Costa Rica has more species of birds:* Martha Honey, *Ecotourism and Sustainable Development: Who Owns Paradise?* (Washington, D.C.: Island Press, 1999).
253 *Chain saws and bulldozers:* Evans, *Green Republic*, pp. 5–20.
253 *They named it Monteverde:* Honey, *Ecotourism and Sustainable Development.*
255 *The small country has averaged over 2 million:* The numbers of tourists released by the Costa Rican Tourism Board (ICT) showed a record-breaking figure. In 2010 an estimated 2,099,829 tourists came to Costa Rica, its highest recorded number.
256 *Tolls to go through the canal can be steep:* http://www.pancanal.com/eng/maritime/tolls.html.
256 *The* Disney Magic *cruise liner paid:* Prensa.com, June 24, 2008, Panama, http://mensual.prensa.com/mensual/contenido/2008/06/24/hoy/negocios/1416962.html.
256 *For the same amount of money:* Price of a deluxe suite aboard the *Allure of the Sea*, August 27, 2011, http://www.royalcaribbean.com/dealsandmore/hotdeals.do?cS=NAVBAR&pnav=3&snav=1&SID=P3005613882&247SEM.
258 *earning then-President Daniel Oduber:* http://www.corcovadofoundation.org.
259 *Costa Rica is a laboratory:* Mario Boza, Diane Jukofsky and Chris Wille, "Costa Rica Is a Laboratory, Not Ecotopia," *Conservation Biology* 9, no. 3 (June 1995).
259 *published a survey in 2011:* Laura Driscoll, Carter Hunt, Martha Honey and William Durham, "The Importance of Ecotourism as a Development

and Conservation Tool in the Osa Peninsula, Costa Rica," CREST, April 2011, www.responsibletravel.org.

260 *I was covering the negotiations:* Elizabeth Becker, "A Pact on Central America Trade Zone, Minus One," *New York Times*, December 18, 2003.

261 *From 1985 to 1991, visits to the park quadrupled:* www.travelcostaricaon line.com/costa-rica-history.html.

262 *I reviewed all the categories for sustainable tourism:* "The Global Sustainable Tourism Criteria," http://new.gstcouncil.org/resource-center.

264 *"Sustainability is just like the old business adage":* U.N. Foundation press release, October 6, 2008, http://www.unfoundation.org/press-center/press -releases/2008/ted-turner-global-sustainable-tourism-criteria.html.

264 *"We grew up seeing tourism":* Author interviews with Erika Harm, March 25, 2008, and July 14, 2009.

266 *"We are more like the police":* Author interview with Janice Lichtenwald, September 9, 2011.

267 *"The industry had become all about promoting":* Author interview with Jonathan Tourtellot, September 23, 2011.

267 *South Carolina's newspapers published the findings:* Jake Spring, "Grand Strand Rated One of Worst Beaches by National Geographic," *Myrtle Beach Sun News*, November 20, 2010, http://www.thesunnews.com/2010/ 11/20/1823436/strand-rated-one-of-worst-beaches.

268 *"The Thai tourism authority asked":* Author interview with Don Hawkins, March 9, 2009.

268 *Her ideas have gone mainstream:* See, for example, Hillary Rosner, "Have Heart, Will Travel: Leave Your Destination Better Than You Found It with These Five Types of Eco-Friendly Trips," *Town & Country*, April 2010.

268 *"The big worry today is the conglomerates":* Author interview with Martha Honey, May 5, 2009.

269 *"There is not an international market":* Author interview with Harold Goodwin, September 25, 2011.

269 *9th Annual Summit:* Florianópolis, Brazil, May 15–16, 2009.

270 *(Academics and economists dispute):* Alan A. Lew, "Tourism is NOT the World's Largest Industry," May 1, 2008, http://www.tourismplace.blogspot .com.

274 *"Watch your step, hold on to the railings":* Juma Sustainable Development Preserve, Amazonas, Brazil, May 18, 2009.

Nine: Postcard from Sri Lanka

PAGE

279 *Cooray thought Sri Lanka might:* Author interview with Hiran Cooray, October 11, 2009.

279 *"We'll need a czar here":* Author interview with Geoffrey Dobbs, October 13, 2009.

280 *She told me her phone started ringing:* Author interview with Libby Owen-Edmunds, October 12, 2009.

282 *"No hotel should be taller than a coconut palm":* Author interview with Bernard Goonetilleke, October 9, 2009.

282 *a theme of the novel* Anil's Ghost: Michael Ondaatje, *Anil's Ghost* (New York: Knopf, 2000).

282 *In the chilling prose:* "Sri Lanka: Time for Accountability," Human Rights Watch, January 2010, http://www.hrw.org/features/sri-lanka.

Ten: Golden Weeks

PAGE

292 *Whole cities were devoted to the manufacturing:* David Barboza, "In Roaring China, Sweaters Are West of Socks City," *New York Times*, December 24, 2004.

293 *"Tourism Should Become a Comprehensive Industry":* Honggen Xiao, "The Discourse of Power: Deng Xiaoping and Tourism Development in China," *Tourism Management* 27, Issue 5 (October 2006), pp. 803–14.

293 *The Chinese spent $40 billion on stadiums:* "Beijing Olympics by the Numbers," New York Times online, August 3, 2008, http://www.nytimes.com/2008/08/03/sports/playmagazine/803NUMBERS-t.html.

294 *For example, I met three couples:* Author interview with Herb and Ellen Herscowitz, Donald and Susan Poretz, and Arthur and Amy Kales, October 27, 2011.

295 *"I don't know what I was expecting":* Author interview with Rick and Jewell Dassance, January 10, 2012.

295 *China will replace France:* UNWTO, *The Chinese Outbound Travel Market with Special Insight into the Image of Europe as a Destination* (Madrid: UNWTO, 2008); see also Malcolm Moore, "China to Become Number One in Seven Years," *The Telegraph* (London), January 29, 2011, http://www.telegraph.co.uk/finance/china-business/8290378/China-to-become-No-1-for-seven-years.

295 *China climbed to number three:* UNWTO, "International Tourism: First Results of 2011 Confirm Consolidation of Growth," May 11, 2011.

297 *the city was encompassed by 25 miles*: Tiziano Terzani, *Behind the Hidden Door: Travels in an Unknown China* (New York: Henry Holt, 1984), p. 22.

298 *"it was as if my own flesh was being torn off"*: Ibid., p. 27.

298 *Every storybook about old China*: Patrick Wright, *Passport to Peking* (Oxford: Oxford University Press, 2010).

300 *Others were foreign students*: Stephen Fitzgerald, *China and the Overseas Chinese* (Cambridge: Cambridge University Press, 1972), pp. 133, 163.

300 *there were exactly 2,500 beds for foreigners*: "How Hotels Tell the Story of a Nation," *Beijing Youth Daily*, no. 71, October 1999.

300 *Deng took time*: Honggen Xiao, "The Discourse of Power," pp. 10–16.

301 *Deng's basic requirements for China's*: Bruce Gilley, *Tiger on the Brink: Jiang Zemin and China's New Elite* (Berkeley: University of California Press, 1998), p. 65.

301 *For one talk on tourism*: China National Tourism Administration, "Deng Xiaoping on Tourism," 1979, http://www.chinatourism.ch/eg/event_show.php?id=28.

302 *China's rule of Tibet*: "The Effect of Tourism on Tibet," Free Tibet, http://www.freetibet.org/about/tourism.

302 *"Water pollution in the Lijiang River"*: Honggen Xiao, "The Discourse of Power."

303 *China asked for help to make domestic*: Author interview with Patrice Tedjini, May 28, 2009.

303 *"We took a group from the Atmospheric Research Center"*: Author interview with Barbara Dawson, January 18, 2012.

304 *Deng scored his first impressive economic victory*: James Mann, *About Face: A History of America's Curious Relationship with China, from Nixon to Clinton* (New York: Knopf, 1999), p. 156.

304 *Great Wall Hotel*: Richard Baum, *Burying Mao: Chinese Politics in the Age of Deng Xiaoping* (Princeton: Princeton University Press, 1994), p. 169.

304 *"One hundred percent funded by American dollars"*: Author interview with Dean Ho, December 29, 2011.

305 *Equally important was the Chinese*: UNWTO, *The Chinese Outbound Travel Market with Special Insight into the Image of Europe as a Destination* (Madrid: UNWTO, 2008).

307 *"They brought in low-market tourism"*: Author interview with George Hickton, November 29, 2010.

308 *They were shuttled around in crowded buses*: Feng Sabrina Tian, "Is Auckland Ready for Chinese Travellers? An Analysis of Chinese Tourists' Urban Destination Requirements and Auckland's Capability to Provide Them," thesis, Auckland University of Technology, School of Business, 2008.

308 *New Zealand's only recourse:* New Zealand tourism website, http://www
.tourismnewzealand.com/developing-nz-tourism/ads-china-monitoring
-unit/the-ads-code-of-conduct.

309 *The profile that emerged confirmed the obvious:* UNWTO, *The Chinese
Outbound Travel Market.*

309 *besting even Great Britain:* "China Overtakes U.K. to Become Fifth-Largest
Wine-Consuming Nation," China Travel Trends online, January 12, 2012,
http://www.chinatraveltrends.com/category/type/statistics.

309 *One study found that while Chinese:* "Taking Off—Travel and Tourism in
China and Beyond," Boston Consulting Group press release, March 2011,
http://www.bcg.com.

310 *Today the Chinese version:* "A New Grand Tour," *The Economist,* December 18, 2010.

310 *Chinese translators are poised at cosmetics counters:* Steven Erlanger, "After
a Long March, Chinese Surrender to Capitalist Shrines," *New York Times,*
September 15, 2011.

311 *"I don't know what I'll do":* Author interview with Rashmi Sharma, May 27,
2011.

311 *The fee to attend was $900:* Roy Graff, Business Development, February 29,
2012, www.roygraff.com.

Eleven: The Chinese Market

PAGE

312 *China had 271 billionaires:* "The Hurun Wealth Report," http://www.hurun
.net/hurun/listreleaseen451.aspx.

312 *China is expected to need 5,000:* Randy Tinseth, Vice President of Marketing for Boeing, press release, September 12, 2011.

312 *Typical of the tourism professionals:* Author interviews with Javier Albar,
October 24–26, 2011.

313 *those connections came overnight:* "Marriott International to Acquire Renaissance Hotel Group," February 18, 1997, http://www.prnewswire.co.uk/
cgi/news/release?id=17424.

314 *Marriott announced plans:* "Marriott International Announces Its 100th
Hotel in China," Marriott press release, November 25, 2011, http://news
.marriott.com/2011/11/marriott-international-announces-its-100th-hotel-in
-china.html.

314 *the number of international-brand hotel rooms:* Nancy Trejos, "U.S. Hotels
Expand Their Reach into China," *USA Today,* November 16, 2011.

315 *"They are doing very well":* Author interview with David Barboza, November 1, 2011.

315 *the average monthly wage for Chinese:* http://www.worldsalaries.org/china .shtml, using official Chinese statistics given to ILO; and http://www.world salaries.org/hotelreceptionist.shtml.

316 *By the eighteenth century, China was crisscrossed:* Jonathan D. Spence, *Chinese Roundabout: Essays in History and Culture* (New York: W. W. Norton, 1992), pp. 165–204.

317 *One example is Zhang Mei:* Author interviews with Zhang Mei, October 18–20, 2011.

319 *"Every day was planned to the minute":* Author interview with Bonny Wolf, January 24, 2012.

320 *"We don't subscribe to that":* Author interview with David Fundingsland, Beijing, October 19, 2011.

321 *China banned foreigners:* Andrew Jacobs, "China Bars Foreigners from Making Visits to Tibet," *New York Times*, September 23, 2009.

321 *The government built a road to the village:* Andrew Jacobs, "In China, Bankrolling a Shrine to an Adversary," *International Herald Tribune*, February 20, 2012.

323 *"more and more tourists come to China":* "Shanghai Wins World Expo 2010 Bid," People's Daily online, December 3, 2002, http://english.peopledaily .com.cn/200212/03/eng20021203_107892.shtml.

323 *Like Beijing, Shanghai razed:* Carol Huang, "China's Shanghai Expo," *Christian Science Monitor*, April 29, 2010, http://www.csmonitor.com/ World/Global-News/2010/0429/China-s-Shanghai-Expo-2010-by-the -numbers.

323 *Those numbers set a record:* Shanghai expo official website, http://en.expo 2010.cn/news/indexjn.htm.

324 *The first phase of the resort:* Keith Bradsher, "The Mouse's Surprise—Hong Kong Rival," *New York Times*, November 4, 2009.

324 *300 million live within:* Ronald Grover, "Disney Gets a Second Chance in China," *Businessweek*, April 14, 2011.

325 *"The first visitors were often people":* Author interview with William Patrick Cranley and Tina Kanagaratnam, Shanghai, October 2011.

327 *All of this maneuvering:* Premier Wen Jiabao, "Statement on Accelerating the Tourism Industry Development," November 25, 2009, China Outbound Tourism Research Institute, http://www.slideshare.net/thraenhart/ china-outbound-tourismitb-berlincotr11marchi2010.

327 *Six billion Chinese have visited:* "China to Further Expand Red Tourism," People's Daily online, June 17, 2011, http://english.peopledaily.com.cn/ 90001/90776/90882/7413445.html.

328 *It was a huge leap:* Jonathan D. Spence, *The Search for Modern China* (New York: W. W. Norton, 1991), p. 328.

328 *Then in July 2011, a few months:* Sharon LaFraniere, "Five Days Later, Chinese Concede Design Flaw Had Role in Wreck," *New York Times*, July 29, 2010.

333 *while in private taking extraordinary precautions:* Adrienne Mong, "Beijing Residents Call Foul over the Air," MSNBC online, November 9, 2011.

333 *more than half of China's wealthiest people:* Shi Jing and Yu Ran, "Chinese Rich Are Keen to Emigrate," *China Daily*, November 3, 2011.

335 *A French Catholic missionary:* Henry Nicholls, *The Way of the Panda: The Curious History of China's Political Animal* (New York: Pegasus Books, 2011), p. 104.

335 *The power of the panda cult:* www.chinatours.us.com/TravelNews/sichuan -attractions-earthquake-09032702.

Twelve: America the Exceptional

PAGE

347 *It is also the only wealthy nation:* Rebecca Ray and John Schmitt, "No-Vacation Nation," Center for Economic and Policy Research, May 2007.

348 *She arrived in 2003 with high hopes:* Author interview with Connie Morella, March 10, 2008.

350 *he saw government's role in tourism:* Edwin McDowell, "Travel Industry Visits Washington, Where Support Is Waning," *New York Times*, October 29, 1995.

350 *President Clinton opened the event:* President Bill Clinton, "Remarks to the White House Conference on Travel and Tourism," White House Transcript, October 30, 1995; "Speech by President Bill Clinton," C-Span, October 30, 1995, http://www.c-spanvideo.org/program/68016-1.

351 *the second-largest employer:* "America's Wake-Up Call," *Tourism Management* 17, no. 2 (March 1996), pp. 139–41.

352 *He pushed through Congress a budget:* Alfred Borcover, "Collapsing Umbrella, Federal Tourism Office to Shut down in April," *Chicago Tribune*, February 25, 1996.

352 *"It's an absolute outrage":* Edwin McDowell, "Correspondents Report: Finis to Tourist Agency on Eve of the Olympics," *New York Times*, March 10, 1996.

353 *$94 billion in lost revenue:* U.S. Travel Association and Oxford Economics, "The Lost Decade—The High Costs of America's Failure to Compete for International Travel," February 2010.

354 *(It was a rare moment when the skies cleared):* David Travis, http://www
.pbs.org/wgbh/nova/transcripts/3310_sun.html; http://www.geotimes.org/
june04/geophen.html.

354 *has become a lightning rod for complaints:* Roger Roots, "Terrorized into
Absurdity," *Independent Review*, Spring 2003.

355 *plunged by 17 percent:* U.S. Travel Assoc. and Oxford Economics, "The
Lost Decade."

355 *"For sixty years what had determined":* Author interview with Geoff Freeman, March 27, 2008.

355 *the travel association conducted a survey:* Travel Industry Association, "A
Blueprint to Discover America," January 31, 2007, http://www.powerof
travel.org.

355 *"spirit-crushingly frosty reception":* Matt Rudd, "Travel to America, No
Thanks," *Sunday Times* (London), January 20, 2008.

356 *The writer, Ed Vulliamy, described:* Ed Vulliamy, "America—More Hassle
Than It's Worth?" *The Guardian*, February 12, 2008.

356 *The story of Rick Giles:* Joelle Dally, "Canterbury Man Gets out of Detroit
Jail," *The Star* (Canterbury, N.Z.), July 11, 2007, http://www.starcanterbury
.co.nz/localnews/storydisplay.

356 *Another visa victim:* Jennifer Gabler, "Women in Squash—Valeria Wiens,"
U.S. Squash online, http://www.ussquash.com/audiences/content.aspx?id
=4454.

357 *Most of the uproar:* U.S. Travel Assoc. and Oxford Economics, "The Lost
Decade."

357 *For the foreigners who needed a visa:* Edward Alden, "The Closing of
the American Border," *The Globalist*, September 24, 2008, http://www.the
globalist.com/storyid.aspx?StoryId=7254.

358 *This new policing of the American border:* Edward Alden, "The Price of
Security," *The Globalist*, September 25, 2008, http://www.theglobalist.com/
storyid.aspx?StoryId=7255.

358 *"We're not in the business of encouraging":* Author interview with Susan
Jacobs, April 11, 2008.

359 *"believes that tourism promotion activities":* Letter from John J. Sullivan,
General Counsel of the United States Department of Commerce, to Senator Daniel Inouye, June 26, 2007, files of the Senate Committee on Commerce, Science and Transportation.

360 *"I'm not against the idea":* Author interview with Isabel Hill, May 8,
2008.

360 *As part of its retrenching:* U.S. Travel Assoc. and Oxford Economics, "The
Lost Decade."

361 *"We had no idea he was coming"*: Author interview with Geoff Freeman, May 3, 2012.

362 *"a rather harrowing experience"*: Michelle Higgins, "Chicago's Loss: Is Passport Control to Blame?" *New York Times*, October 2, 2009.

362 *"When IOC members are commenting to our President"*: Roger Dow, "Olympic Decision Demonstrates the Need to Change Impressions for International Travelers, U.S. Travel Association Chief Says," press release, October 2, 2009, U.S. Travel Association.

362 *"working on this for a very long time"*: President Obama comments on White House video, http://www.youtube.com/watch?v=jJzbRctI8LI.

363 *"They couldn't get a visa"*: Freeman interview.

364 *Beatrice Camp marked the occasion*: Sudeep Reddy, "Lengthy Visa Waits Deter Travel to the U.S.," Wall Street Journal online, September 8, 2011, http://online.wsj.com/article/SB10001424053111904103404576557021589570928.html.

364 *Obama showed up at Disney World*: Jackie Calmes, "For Obama, a Day at Disney World and a Night of Fund-Raisers," *New York Times*, January 20, 2012.

365 *On average, every Brazilian visiting*: U.S. Travel Association, "Ready for Takeoff: A Plan to Create 1.3 Million U.S. Jobs by Welcoming Millions of International Travelers," May 12, 2011.

365 *President Obama tied together*: Nick Verrastro, "White House Launches National Tourism Strategy, An Historic First," travel market report, May 10, 2012, http://www.travelmarketreport.com/international?articleID=7221&LP=1.

365 *New Yorkers who have to navigate*: Liz Robbins, "Follow That Tourist," *New York Times*, July 22, 2012.

367 *received $21 million from the family of Sheldon Adelson*: Mike McIntire and Michael Luo, "The Man Behind Gingrich's Money: Casino Mogul Is Friend to Israel and Boon to Campaign," *New York Times*, January 29, 2012.

368 *The gangsters Meyer Lansky*: Sally Denton and Roger Morris, *The Money and the Power: The Making of Las Vegas and Its Hold on America* (New York: Random House, 2002).

368 *the opening up of China*: Evan Osnos, "The God of Gamblers: Why Las Vegas Is Moving to Macau," *New Yorker*, April 9, 2012.

369 *Kung Fu Mahjong*: Desmond Lam, "Chinese Gambling Superstitions and Taboos," http://www.urbino.net/articles.cfm?specificArticle=Chinese%20Gambling%20Superstitions%20and%20Taboos.

369 *soon followed and opened the Wynn Macau*: Donald Frazier, "Gam-

bling Titan Steve Wynn Fights for Top Prize: China," *Forbes*, March 28, 2012.

370 *When I attended:* Las Vegas Convention and Visitors Authority meeting, May 8, 2012.

370 *Rahm Emanuel:* Jonathan Alter, "Meet the New Boss," *The Atlantic*, April 2012.

371 *"Who is he kidding?":* Author interview with Mayor Carolyn Goodman, May 7, 2012.

371 *"Everything they're doing is a page from what we have done":* Author interview with Chris Meyer, May 8, 2012.

373 *"Europe doesn't have such large hotels":* Author interview with Joe Lustenberger, April 27, 2012.

373 *The GSA hosted a four-day training conference:* Sheryl Gay Stolberg and Michael S. Schmidt, "Agency Trip to Las Vegas Is the Talk of Washington," *New York Times*, April 3, 2012.

374 *"Every major hotel on the strip is unionized":* Author interview with John Wilhelm, April 26, 2011.

374 *the Hyatt hotel chain laid off:* Katie Johnston Chase, "A Hard Ending for Housekeepers: Uncommon Outsourcing Eliminates 100 Hyatt Jobs," *Boston Globe*, September 17, 2009.

375 *"We do know that over sixty percent":* Author interview with Wolfgang Weinz, June 3, 2011.

376 *"When you are self-employed like I am":* Author interview with Dorothy McGhee, March 6, 2012.

376 *she is a typical medical tourist:* James Surowiecki, "Club Med," *New Yorker*, April 16, 2012, for a description of who are medical tourists.

376 *There are 5 million patients worldwide:* Patients Beyond Borders, http://www.patientsbeyondborders.com/medical-tourism-statistics-facts.

377 *What started with Americans crossing:* Kate Pickert, "A Brief History of Medical Tourism," *Time*, November 25, 2008.

377 *questions that were answered:* The Third International MediTour Expo, Las Vegas, May 6–8, 2012.

379 *The Centers for Disease Control said:* Maggie Fox, "Nearly 59 Million Americans Went Without Health Insurance Coverage for at Least Part of 2010," Reuters, November 10, 2010.

379 *Americans are voting with their feet:* Corrie MacLaggan, "In Pain and Uninsured, a Texas Truck Driver Goes to India to Get His Hip Fixed," *Austin American-Statesman*, October 26, 2008.

379 *an announcement that described a groom:* "Tucker Woods, Reginald Charlot," *New York Times*, May 1, 2011.

380 *"For years tourism was studied mainly"*: Author interview with Donald Hawkins, March 9, 2009.

381 *Anthony Mavrogiannis received his master's degree*: Author interview with Anthony Mavrogiannis, May 2, 2012.

381 *Yet they managed to retain*: American Society of Travel Agents, http://www .asta.org.

383 *the figure was 285 million visitors*: "National Parks Failed to Break Attendance Record in 2009," Associated Press, published in *USA Today*, http://www.usatoday.com/travel/destinations/2010-03-01-national-parks -attendance_N.htm.

383 *the top ten theme park chains*: AECOM Economics, "Theme Index: The Global Attractions Attendance Report," http://www.aecom.com/deployed files/Internet/Capabilities/2009%20Theme%20Index%20Final%20 042710_for%20screen.pdf.

383 *Disney led the pack*: Brooks Barnes, "Media Decoder: Profit Grows 21% at Disney on Cable TV Gains and a Surge in Resorts Business," *New York Times*, May 9, 2012.

384 *Theme parks now stretch from Asia to Europe*: "Global Theme Park Market to Reach U.S. $31.8 Billion by 2017, According to New Report by Global Industry Analysts, Inc.," PRWeb, March 14, 2012, http://www.prweb.com/ releases/theme_parks_water_parks/amusement_parks/prweb9282694.htm.

384 *The best-selling author Carl Hiaasen*: Politics and Prose Bookstore, Washington, D.C., January 9, 2009.

385 *a 70-page report describing*: "Kailua Beach and Dune Management Plan," State of Hawai'i, Department of Land and Natural Resources and University of Hawai'i, Sea Grant College Program, December, 2010.

386 *"The thing is, in Hawaii we take access*: Author interview with Samuel J. Lemmo, June 28, 2011.

386 *tourist spending has risen to $1.01 billion*: http://www.hawaiitourismau thority.org/default/assets/File/2011%20State%20Factsheet%20updated%20 8-21-12.pdf.

386 *The only other game in town*: Sarah Vowell, *Unfamiliar Fishes* (New York: Riverhead Books, 2011).

387 *"Hawaii and the Aloha spirit are the future"*: Author interview with Mike McCartney, June 29, 2011.

Index

Quakers, in Costa Rica, 253–54
Quest, Richard, 173, 193

"race to the bottom," 145
Raffles Hotels, 90–91
Rainforest Alliance, 264
rainforests, 246, 258, 271
Rainier, Mount, 346
Rajapaksa, Mahinda, 278
Rashid Al-Maktoum, Sheikh, 171, 172
Razan Khalifa Al Mubarak, Princess,
    197–98
Reid, Harry, 362
Renaissance Hotel Group, 313
Reno, Janet, 159
Republican Party:
    government spending on tourism
        opposed by, 352–53, 365, 367
    in 2012 election, 366–67
Resorts World Sentosa, 113
retirees:
    in France, 72–73
    as tourists, 18, 37
rhinos, threatened extinction of, 221
Rialto Bridge, Venice, 78–79
Rice, Condoleezza, 273
Ridge, Tom, 359
Riklis, Meshulam, 136
Riley, Richard, 199
Rio de Janeiro, Brazil, 276
    as 2016 Olympics host, 273, 276, 362
Risi, Marcelo, 34, 35
Road of Lost Innocence, The (Mam), 117
Robb, Graham, 51
Robinson, James, III, 14–15, 270
Rome, pilgrimages to, 182
Romero, Oscar, 254
Romney, Mitt, 367
Roosevelt, Franklin D., 354, 384
Roosevelt, Theodore, 239, 384
Roots (Haley), 242–43
"Roots" tours, 242–44
Roth, Toby, 352
Rough Guide to the World (TV show), 271

Rousseff, Dilma, 365
Royal Caribbean International, 125, 128,
    130, 134, 136, 140–41, 143, 151, 247,
    256, 257
    art sales lawsuit against, 148
    Diamonds International and, 128,
        149–50
    illegal waste water dumping by, 158–59
    ship registry of, 140
    waste treatment systems of, 161
Rushmore, Mount, 345
Ruskin, John, 82

Saadiyat Island, 191
sable (African antelope), 215, 217
safaris, see Africa, national parks in,
    safaris in
St. George's Castle (Elmina), 242
St. Ignatius Church (Lusaka), 210–11
St. Onge, Alain, 174
Salas, Isabel, 247, 249, 251
Sanders, Daniel, 60
Sanders, Véronique, 60–61
Sands Macao, 369
San Giorgio Maggiore (Venice), 82
San Miguel, Mexico, 129
Santiago de Compostela, pilgrimages to,
    182, 185–86
Sarajevo, Bosnia, 106
Sarkozy, Nicolas, 48, 71
Sata, Michael, 238
Saudi Arabia, 167
    and commercial development in
        Mecca, 184–85
    Hajj pilgrimage controlled by, 182–83
Save the Rhino Trust, 218
Scat (Hiaasen), 384
Schweitzer Mountain, 384
Scott, Ridley, 73–74
"scramble for Africa," 208
Sea Lion (ship), 245, 246, 248, 255–57,
    262
Selling the Sea (Dickinson and Vladimir),
    137

About the Author

Elizabeth Becker is an award-winning author and former correspondent of the *New York Times*. As the *New York Times* International Economics correspondent, she reported from Europe, Asia and South America on trade, agriculture, international finance, and the effect that rapid change was having on people both in the U.S. and overseas. Born in a small town in Iowa, Ms. Becker graduated from the University of Washington in Asian studies and began her career as a war correspondent in Cambodia for the *Washington Post*; she is an expert on modern Cambodia and the Khmer Rouge. She was the Senior Foreign Editor at National Public Radio, overseeing all of the network's foreign bureaus and their reporting. She has won awards from the Robert Kennedy Book Awards, Overseas Press Club, and DuPont-Columbia. She was a Goldstein fellow at Harvard's Shorenstein Center where she began her research on the travel industry. She is the author of three books on Southeast Asia, has lived in Asia and Europe, and travels extensively. She lives in Washington with her husband and her dog "Lafayette Jones" and is the mother of two grown children.